WHERE TO GO WILD
IN BRITAIN

WHERE TO
GO WILD
IN BRITAIN

DK

LONDON, NEW YORK, MELBOURNE,
MUNICH AND DELHI

Senior editor Paula Regan
Project art editor Anna Hall

Managing editor Debra Wolter
Managing art editor Karen Self

Production editor Maria Elia
Production controller Linda Dare

Managing cartographer David Roberts
Cartographer Paul Eames
Regional Directory maps
Encompass Graphics Ltd

Art director Bryn Walls
Publisher Jonathan Metcalf
Associate Publisher Liz Wheeler

Produced for Dorling Kindersley by
cobaltid
The Stables, Wood Farm, Deopham Road,
Attleborough, Norfolk NR17 1AJ
www.cobaltid.co.uk

Editors Louise Abbott, Kati Dye, Maddy King,
Sarah Tomley, Marek Walisiewicz

Designers Darren Bland, Claire Dale,
Rebecca Johns, Paul Reid, Lloyd Tilbury

First published in Great Britain in 2009
by Dorling Kindersley Limited
80 Strand, London WC2R 0RL

A Penguin company
Copyright © 2009 Dorling Kindersley Limited

2 4 6 8 10 9 7 5 3 1

A CIP catalogue record for this book is available from the
British Library

ISBN 978-1-4053-3512-6

Printed and bound in Singapore by Star Standard

Every effort has been made to ensure that this book is as up-to-date as possible at
the time of going to press. Some details, however, such as telephone numbers,
opening hours, and travel information are liable to change. The publishers cannot
accept responsibility for any consequences arising from the use of this book, nor for
any material on the third-party websites, and cannot guarantee that any website
address in this book will be a suitable source of travel information.

Discover more at
www.dk.com

CONTENTS

Remember to always follow the Countryside Code, available at www.countrysideaccess.gov.uk

Featured site

HOW TO USE THE MAPS

The location of each featured site is marked on the maps by a red dot. The UK is divided into seven areas which correspond with the Regional Directory on pages 312–328, in which details of all the sites, including those listed in the "Where Else To See" panels, are given:

SC – Scotland
N – Northern England
NI – Northern Ireland
M – Midlands
W – Wales
SE – Southeast England
SW – Southwest England

Below: The towering peaks of Snowdon, in north Wales (see pp.172–173).

FOREWORD

LET'S START WITH SOME INCONTROVERTIBLE FACTS: a walk in the countryside to look for wildlife is cheap, healthy for the mind and body, and great fun. However, I am often surprised by how few people I bump into when admiring a blaze of orchids in a summer meadow, or flocks of wading birds over an estuary in winter. So why are many of our finest nature locations still woefully under-visited? Well, part of the reason may be down to the fact that the Great British public needs more of a guiding hand when deciding where to go and when to visit.

Irrespective of where you live, or when you take your holiday, every page of this book is brimming with ideas about where to go each month to see the very best of our wildlife. You'll discover where to find the most glorious bluebell woodlands in spring, the finest seabird colonies in summer, the most impressive red deer rut in autumn, and the greatest high-tide winter wader roosts. I am lucky enough to spend most of the year filming the best wildlife Britain has to offer, but I was astonished by the abundance of new ideas for future filming trips.

Britain may not have the awe-inspiring great game spectacles of the east African plains, or the immense biological diversity of the Amazon rainforest, but our islands do possess an astonishing mosaic of habitats, which, as the seasons shift, play host to a constantly changing cast of characters. In my adopted city of Bristol, for example, I am no more than an hour's drive (or train ride) away from ancient woodland, rolling grassland, vast estuaries, and primeval wetland; all of which reveal a multitude of differing wildlife treats depending on the month visited.

Only by making the most of Britain's unique wildlife heritage will our most precious sites be ultimately cherished, conserved, and protected for future generations. All you need to do now is pack your camera, your binoculars, and this book, put your walking boots on, and get out there and enjoy!

MIKE DILGER

WHEN WAS THE LAST TIME NATURE TAPPED YOU ON THE SHOULDER? You know, one of those moments where you have a connection with something wild that changes the course of your whole day?

Moments like those are the reason the RSPB exists. From the surprise and delight you feel when a robin, bold as you like, lands on the handle of your garden spade, to the sense of awe and humility that grips you when you're confronted with an ancient landscape, we're here to protect the things that have the greatest power to move us. We have a million members speaking out for birds and wildlife – people like you, who nature enchants, tickles, relaxes, inspires, and rewards.

So often these days, wildlife is an afterthought, and sometimes not thought of at all. At the RSPB, we believe that the environment should be at the top of the agenda when people plan where to build houses, put up wind farms, handle transport problems, put out fishing boats, or educate our children. We're there to be a voice for nature, never giving up, getting things done, changing things for the better – for wildlife and for you.

To be enchanted by nature, you really need to experience it firsthand, and that is what this book is all about. It picks a selection of the finest places and most extraordinary sights the British Isles have to offer, whether on RSPB land or elsewhere. Some, like roosting gulls, boxing hares, dancing grebes, or purple heather moorlands, are found in many places. Others are truly rare, but all are special.

Our nature reserves punctuate the landscape, but our campaigning voice speaks up for wildlife wherever it lives. The whole nature conservation movement wants you to share enjoyable moments with wildlife. Nature is amazing – please help us to keep it that way.

MARK BOYD
www.rspb.org.uk

JANUARY

Where to Go: **January**

January is a stepping-stone to the rest of the year – but what a start! The cold weather and bare landscapes present a unique opportunity to see the barren bones of the world around us, especially among the woods and hedgerows, and to appreciate what lies beneath the best wildlife places, before they are smothered in the green growth of spring. Birds are abundant in lowland areas, especially near the coast: flocks of ducks and geese feed on the mudflats of our estuaries, which provide such a vital refuge from bitter winter weather farther north and east. Inland, floods and reservoirs provide opportunities to see swans, ducks, and gulls, and you might, with luck, come across a water vole, or a couple of resting brown hares. Higher up, on the northern

INLETS AND ESTUARIES

DEE ESTUARY View across the Dee estuary from Hilbre Island.

DEE ESTUARY
CHESHIRE/NORTH WALES [N]

This wide, shallow estuary divides Wales from England, and is a great place to watch waders and ducks in the water, while short-eared owls hunt overhead.
See pp.14–15

FAL ESTUARY
FALMOUTH, CORNWALL [SW]

One of southwest England's most beautiful estuaries, with pale, gleaming mudflats, rockpools to explore, and "meadows" of eelgrass amongst which scuttle crabs and cuttlefish.
See pp.20–21

BURRY INLET
GOWER PENINSULA, SOUTH WALES [W]

Thousands of birds live on these mudflats and saltmarshes. Little egrets, great crested grebes, grey herons, and brent geese can all be seen in January.
See pp.14–15

CHICHESTER HARBOUR
WEST SUSSEX [SE]

Watch wading birds probe the mudflats for food at low tide, and then, as the tide comes in, move on to their roosting sites to huddle in their thousands.
See pp.14–15

> At low tide, the Dee estuary reveals swathes of golden sand interspersed with sinuous channels of water, lazily making their way to the sea.

EXE ESTUARY
EXETER, DEVON [SW]

Over 20,000 birds winter here, including avocets, glossy ibises, lapwings, redshanks, and ducks. Harvest mice, otters, and water shrews live around the shore.
See pp.14–15

WETLANDS

OUSE WASHES Bewick's swans at dawn over the Ouse Washes.

OUSE WASHES
CAMBRIDGESHIRE [SE]

Come here to see the largest concentration of Bewick and whooper swans in the country, swooping in groups of thousands across the water.
See pp.22–23

ATTENBOROUGH GRAVEL PITS
NOTTINGHAMSHIRE [SE]

Reclaimed land that has been imaginatively landscaped and managed to provide a range of wildlife habitats for birds, animals, and plants.
See pp.26–27

LEE VALLEY PARK
ESSEX/HERTFORDSHIRE [SE]

This huge country park, a "green lung" for Greater London, is the perfect, wildlife-rich getaway for city-dwellers.
See pp.26–27

> Up to one-tenth of the British wintering population of bitterns can be found in the Lee Valley Park

COTSWOLD WATER PARK
GLOUCESTERSHIRE [SE]

Thousands of birds spend the winter on the 140 man-made lakes that make up the site, while up to 25 hobbies hunt over their waters.
See pp.26–27

NEWPORT WETLANDS
GWENT, SOUTH WALES [W]

This is a great place to see otters and also fantastic starling roosts – huge "swarms" of birds that fill the sky as the day ends.
See pp.16–17

WILD IN THE CITY

LONDON WETLAND CENTRE Look for the endangered water vole.

> This wetland centre is a green oasis surrounded by urban sprawl – a true wildlife haven, just a stone's throw from central London.

LONDON WETLAND CENTRE
LONDON [SE]

This award-winning site is ideal for a tranquil walk in search of shy bitterns and water voles, but also organizes plenty of family activities, both indoors and out.
See pp.16–17

WINNALL MOORS
HAMPSHIRE [SW]

The River Itchen flows right through this reserve, just 1km (½ mile) from Winchester city centre, attracting all the wildlife associated with chalk streams.
See pp.16–17

BOUGH BEECH RESERVOIR
SEVENOAKS, KENT [SE]

A great location for ducks; there are also bird feeders that allow close-up views of shy species such as brambling and great spotted woodpecker.
See pp.16–17

STAINES RESERVOIR
MIDDLESEX [SE]

Nestling below the flight path of Heathrow this reserve attracts plenty of birds, including peregrine falcons, which like to scan for prey from the pylons.
See pp.16–17

Previous page: A winter greeting between two brown hares.

moors, mountain hares will be clad in their thick white winter coat. In mainland Scotland, and around the Hebridean islands, you can more easily see beautiful red deer.

Woodland birds gather into nomadic mixed flocks, roaming through the trees in search of food; you'll normally hear them first as they noisily give themselves away. Suddenly there are more birds than you can watch all at once – and then they all fly off, leaving the woods eerily quiet. On the coast, you might still see grey and common seals, and have fun poking about in the rockpools left by the outgoing tide. It is, however, the birds that dominate even here by the sea, with turnstones, oystercatchers, and purple sandpipers among the winter gems.

COAST

DRURIDGE BAY The long, wind-blown sand dunes fill with birds.

HEATH AND MOOR

GELTSDALE Both red and black grouse make their homes here.

ISLANDS

ISLAY Seals can be found in bays around the island.

DRURIDGE BAY
NORTHUMBERLAND [N]

Druridge Bay is the longest beach in Northumberland; thousands of wintering birds live on its sand dunes and lagoons in January, including geese, swans, and ducks.
See pp.20–21

PAGHAM HARBOUR
SIDLESHAM, WEST SUSSEX [SE]

The shingle spits that border this harbour are filled with dark-bellied brent geese, wigeons, black-tailed godwits, knots, and avocets.
See pp.20–21

THE NORTH YORK MOORS
YORKSHIRE [N]

Red grouse, golden plovers, and curlews brave the northern winter here, along with merlins – the UK's smallest birds of prey.
See pp.24–25

ISLAY
INNER HEBRIDES [SC]

The southernmost Hebridean island, with something for everyone: seals, deer, otters, wintering seabirds, and birds of prey including the magnificent golden eagle.
See pp.12–13

In winter, hen harriers hunt over the lower Islay moors, and you just might have a once-in-a-lifetime encounter with a golden eagle.

LINDISFARNE
NORTHUMBERLAND [N]

The extensive sand dunes and long sandy beaches of this tidal island sparkle in winter sunshine, while rock pools shelter all manner of sea creatures.
See pp.20–21

YNYS-HIR
POWYS, SOUTH WALES [W]

The bracken-covered slopes of this reserve are hunting grounds for birds of prey. Polecats and badgers also live here.
See pp.18–19

GELTSDALE
BRAMPTON, CUMBRIA [N]

This forbidding landscape is home to red and black grouse, and birds of prey, including hen harriers, buzzards, and short-eared owls.
See pp.24–25

ISLE OF SKYE
INNER HEBRIDES [SC]

A dramatic place to see eagles, red and roe deer, seals, otters, dolphins, whales, porpoises, and thousands of seabirds.
See pp.12–13

HOLKHAM
NORTH NORFOLK [SE]

The sight of some 150,000 birds that winter on the mudflats, nearly all pink-footed geese from the Arctic, is unmissable. The pinewoods and the beach are beautiful too.
See pp.18–19

The blanket bogs, heath, and woods stretch out before you in a glorious wilderness; the short, crisp days are perfect for walking.

ISLE OF MULL
INNER HEBRIDES [SC]

A mountainous isle lying just off the Scottish mainland, this is perhaps the most beautiful place to watch the white-tailed sea eagle and golden eagle commanding the skies.
See pp.12–13

ST CATHERINE'S POINT
ISLE OF WIGHT [SE]

Winters can be mild on this south coast island, with beautiful cliff downlands and headlands from which to watch for seabirds.
See pp.20–21

MINSMERE
SUFFOLK [SE]

This is a great time to look for birds of prey hunting over the heathland, and flocks of tits and finches among the trees, as well as enjoying the water birds.
See pp.26–27

ISLE OF ARRAN
NORTH AYRSHIRE [SC]

Three species of striking diving ducks winter here. The last berries on the unique Arran whitebeam provide welcome food for hungry perching birds.
See pp.12–13

NORTH UIST
OUTER HEBRIDES [SC]

This unspoilt Western Isle is home to the rare corncrake, along with wheeling Arctic terns and noisy gannets.
See pp.12–13

WHERE
Islay, Argyll and Bute, Scotland.

CONTACT
RSPB Loch Gruinart Reserve, Bushmills Cottage, Gruinart, Bridgend, Isle of Islay, Argyll and Bute PA44 7PR, Scotland;
tel: 01496 850505;
loch.gruinart@rspb.org.uk

GETTING THERE
Ferries leave from Kennacraig three or four times a day on weekdays and Saturdays, and twice on Sundays. The Loch Gruinart reserve is signed from the A847 Bridgend to Bruichladdich Road, 4.8km (3 miles) from the turn-off. The nearest bus stop to the reserve is at this turn-off.

ACCESS AND FACILITIES
The RSPB reserve has good access to viewing points and one hide is specially adapted for wheelchair users (access by car can be arranged). The centre has full-access toilets for all abilities, parking, and refreshments, and is pushchair friendly. The woodland trail is not suitable for wheelchairs.

OPENING TIMES
The reserve is open at all times. The visitor centre is open daily from 10am to 5pm.

CHARGES
None.

Legend of the goose

Barnacle geese are not named for a fondness for barnacles – their preferred food is leaves, stems, roots, and seeds – but gain their name from old English folklore. The belief was that they spent the summer developing underwater in the form of barnacles, only to emerge in winter in bird form (thus explaining the sudden arrival of the birds in winter). This convenient legend permitted Catholics to see these birds as sea life, and so eat their flesh during Lent, when believers were supposed to abstain from meat and poultry.

Above (left to right): A golden eagle; the Mull of Oa; the beach near Kidalton, on the south shore of the island.
Main: Cliffs overlooking the Mull of Oa, Islay.

HEBRIDEAN HIGHLIGHT

SLAY IS THE SOUTHERNMOST ISLAND OF THE INNER HEBRIDES, lying at the entrance to the Firth of Lorn. Its vast range of habitats supports a terrific variety of wildlife. In winter, hen harriers hunt over the lower moors and you just might have a once-in-a-lifetime encounter with a golden eagle, especially in the rugged south of the island towards the Oa peninsula. Look out, too, for red-billed choughs on the tidelines of the sandy bays, feeding on insects found in the seaweed.

Islay has 130 miles of indented coastline, with sand and shingle beach, mudflats, and cliffs. Loch Indaal and Loch Gruinart, both with mudflats and smooth green marsh at the head of enclosed bays, are marvellous places for wintering waders, divers, grebes, and sea ducks such as eiders and scaups. But it is the extraordinary population of geese that everyone comes to see in winter: around 37,000 barnacle geese and 13,000 white-fronted geese inhabit the island from autumn until April, creating a magnificent sight and sound. The barnacle geese from Greenland are indistinguishable from barnacle geese breeding in Spitsbergen (which spend the winter on the Solway Firth), while the orange-billed, white-fronted geese are darker than the much more numerous pink-billed ones from Siberia, and form a distinct race. You can see both species around the head of Loch Gruinart.

Look out too, for the shyer island inhabitants, like the red, fallow, and roe deer, and the secretive otters. Common and grey seals can be found around the coast, in places such as Killinallan Point, east of Loch Gruinart. The Rhinns in the north and the Oa in the south are good for birds of prey, including golden eagles, buzzards, hen harriers, peregrines, merlins, and kestrels; while common and black guillemots, razorbills, kittiwakes, fulmars, and shags fly around the cliffs. The blue-grey rock doves, truly wild and untainted by domestic stock, feed on cliff-top grasslands and nest around the seacliffs.

Islay's many offshore islets, particularly in the south, provide perfect places for grey and common seals to haul out of the water and bask in any winter sun.

Inset: Common seals with their thick, insulating layer of winter blubber.
Below (left to right): Barnacle geese in flight; white-fronted geese foraging.

WHERE ELSE TO SEE
ROCKY ISLANDS

There are hundreds of islands around the Scottish coast, many of which are uninhabited by people, but are home to thousands of birds. They can be reached by special boat trips, or by ferry, in some cases.

The **Isle of Skye** is the largest island of the Inner Hebrides. Its northern tip provides a dramatic backdrop for seabirds, including fulmars, kittiwakes, and shags, while Broadford Bay in the south is good for seeing rarer migrants. [SC]

The **Isle of Mull** (see pp.226–227), another Inner Hebridean island, is well known both for its seabirds and its birds of prey, which hunt over the moors and fish over the lochs and sea. [SC]

The **Isle of Arran** (see pp.42–43), has two distinct halves: a moutainous northern half, and moorlands in the south. Its large bird population lives alongside otters, red deer, and red squirrels. [SC]

North Uist (see pp.108–109) has rocky shores, freshwater lochans, sea lochs on the east of the island, and machair habitat along the west coast. There is an RSPB reserve at Balranald where you can see corncrakes. [SC]

THROUGH THE YEAR
ISLAY

In **spring** Islay comes alive with the songs of lapwings, redshanks, and curlews, and the drumming displays of snipe. All the birds can be easily seen at the RSPB reserve at Loch Gruinart.

A special **summer** bird is the corncrake, whose rasping notes can be heard in May and June, mostly at night. Common terns and ringed plovers nest on the beaches.

In **autumn** the geese return, and many wintering ducks including wigeons, teals, and scaups. Fieldfares and redwings pass through in autumn. Look for purple sandpipers and rock pipits along the shore.

Below: Corncrakes nest on undisturbed farmland.

JAN
FEB
MAR
APR
MAY
JUN
JUL
AUG
SEP
OCT
NOV
DEC

WHERE
The Dee Estuary lies between Thurstaston, Wirral CH61 0, England, and the Point of Ayr CH8 9, North Wales; www.deeestuary.co.uk

CONTACT
Wirral Country Park: 0151 6484371/3884;
Hilbre Island Nature Reserve: 0151 6324455;
Wirral Rangers: coastalpark@wirral.gov.uk
RSPB Dee Estuary: 0151 3367681.

GETTING THERE
There are several access points along the estuary. From Chester take the A55 towards Queensferry, then you can either take the A548 along the Welsh side, to reach places such as Talacre and Point of Ayr; or take the A540 to visit places on the English side such as Parkgate and West Kirby. There is a bus to the RSPB reserve at Gayton Sands, Parkgate, every hour from Neston, which is the nearest rail connection, at 3km (2 miles) away. To walk to the islands, start from the Dee Lane Slipway at West Kirby.

ACCESS AND FACILITIES
There are public toilets at the Dee Lane Slipway. The most easily accessible viewing points are the sea wall at the Point of Ayr, and Parkgate promenade or Parkgate Old Baths car park, near The Boathouse pub.

CHARGES
None.

Chinese mitten crab

In 2006, an Asian species of crab, the Chinese mitten crab, was found to have invaded the Dee Estuary. They had colonized other rivers in the south coast of England, where they caused both environmental problems – by burrowing into the riverbanks, causing them to collapse – and health problems, as they carry a parasitic flatworm called a lung fluke. The crab's identifying features are the dense patches of hairs on its white-tipped claws, from which it acquired its unusual name.

Above (top to bottom): Brent geese look out from an island on the Dee Estuary; a dunlin forages in the water.

Below: Weaver fish hide just under the sand, and their poisonous spines impart a vicious sting – if stung, apply hot flannels to the wound for at least 15 minutes.

Right panel (top and bottom): Bright-billed oystercatchers search for cockles, their favourite food; the Dee Estuary divides Wales from England.

Main: Oystercatchers and cormorants roosting on Little Eye after the high tide forces them inland – Hilbre Island is visible in the distance.

ACROSS THE SANDS OF DEE

I T'S NOT SURPRISING THAT SO MANY ARTISTS HAVE BEEN INSPIRED by the Dee Estuary. At low tide, the vast mouth of the estuary reveals swathes of golden sand interspersed with sinuous channels of water, lazily making their way to the sea. The wide, shallow estuary divides North Wales from northwest England, covering approximately 150sq km (58 sq miles). It is one of the best places to see large numbers of breeding, wintering, and migrating birds, and it is internationally recognized for its wealth of habitats, which support an amazing variety of wildlife. There are tidal rivers, mud and sand flats, lagoons, sand dunes, saltmarshes, and even cliffs.

The seemingly endless marshlands of Parkgate and Burton, lying fairly far inland on the English side, are good places to watch short-eared owls hunt, or seabirds and waders start to rise up in flocks as the tide pushes them inland. Travelling along the Welsh side you can really appreciate how the estuary moves from being a

Looking out from the dunes at the Point of Ayr, you begin to see why the estuary is home to 130,000 waders and wildfowl in winter.

Above: The main channel of the Dee Estuary at low tide.

THROUGH THE YEAR
DEE ESTUARY

The Dee Estuary is an important breeding site for little and common terns, which both start nesting in May. **Spring** is a busy breeding time for many other birds within the estuary, including oystercatchers, redshanks, and skylarks, and also for the scarce natterjack toad, which breeds in the dunes at Talacre.

There is a large colony of grey seals that haul up on West Hoyle bank, just south of Hilbre island in **summer**. During August you can see up to 500 seals; although many leave during the winter months, non-breeders stay, so you usually see seals all year round. The summering flock of non-breeding black-tailed godwits is one of the largest in the UK. Botanists will enjoy seeking out specialities like the rare petalwort and sea spleenwort; there is also a subspecies of rock sea-lavender here that is found in only a few other places in in Europe.

Thousands of waders fly in to the estuary in **autumn** to feed on the mudflats. Large flocks of ducks can be seen escaping the rough open seas. The berried bushes of Thurstaston Country Park provide welcome food for fieldfares and redwings, while Greenfield welcomes many elegant great crested grebes.

WHERE ELSE TO SEE
ESTUARY WILDLIFE

Britain is lucky to have many other estuary sites that are renowned for birds and other wildlife.

Visit **Chichester Harbour**, West Sussex, in autumn or winter to see many different waders and wildfowl, including curlews, whimbrels, godwits, oystercatchers, snipe, and grey plovers. [SE]

The **Exe Estuary** (see pp.286–287), in Devon, is one of the best places to see waders and wildfowl, including wintering avocets and brent geese. [SW]

Burry Inlet, Gower (see pp.122–123), supports thousands of birds on its mudflats and saltmarshes. Little egrets, great crested grebes, grey herons, and brent geese can all be seen in winter. [W]

Slimbridge (see pp.34–35), on the Severn estuary, is excellent for wild ducks, swans, and geese. [M]

freshwater river to a salty sea mouth. At Connah's Quay the ducks can still enjoy freshwater and salt-water habitats; about half way along the estuary, at Greenfield, the mudbanks are exposed at low tide, encouraging waders and shelducks. Walk out to the shingle spit at the Point of Ayr, protuding right out to sea, and you'll see wondrous numbers of roosting waders, including knots, oystercatchers, curlews, and bar-tailed and black-tailed godwits.

Rising out of the sands towards the mouth of the estuary lie three sandstone islands: Middle Eye, Little Eye, and Hilbre Island. At low tide you can walk to Hilbre: check the tides before you go, as you can easily become cut off. The shoreline here has fascinating inhabitants: red beadlet anenomes, dog whelks, and winkles hide among the rocks; sea spleenwort grows on the cliff faces; and sabellaria reef worms live in the sandy seabed. But watch out for weaver fish, which can hide just under the sand at low tide, exposing their venomous dorsal spines. There's also an unwelcome visitor to the Dee Estuary, the Chinese mitten crab, which probably arrived in ships' ballast water. While striking in looks, it is causing environmental problems (see box, left).

JAN
FEB
MAR
APR
MAY
JUN
JUL
AUG
SEP
OCT
NOV
DEC

Left: The three-storey Peacock Tower hide gives amazing views over the whole centre.

Right (left to right): A colony of water voles live at the centre; pochard ducks visit in winter; around 200 moorhens forage for food; the kingfisher is often seen around water within the reserve.

WHERE
London Wetland Centre, Barnes, London
SW13 9WT; www.wwt.org.uk

CONTACT
London Wetland Centre, tel: 020 8409 4400;
info.london@wwt.org.uk

GETTING THERE
By car, turn off the A306 (the South Circular) at Barnes and follow signs to the centre. By train, travel to Barnes or Barnes Bridge. The nearest London Underground station is Hammersmith. A bus runs from here directly to the centre: Duck bus no. 283 (stand K). Bus nos. 33, 72, and 209 all stop nearby. By cycle, follow the Sustrans Cycle Route.

ACCESS AND FACILITIES
There is a free car park, and extensive facilities including multi-storey hides, a viewing tower, and a discovery centre. There are mini-beast safaris and pond-dipping sessions for children. The site is wheelchair friendly, with good paths, access to heated hides, and lifts to the tower and restaurant.

OPENING TIMES
All year round; 9.30am–9pm in summer; 9.30am–6pm in winter.

CHARGES
Yes, for non-WWT members (all children under 4 go free).

Bats galore

The London Wetland Centre is one of the most popular sites in the UK for seeing bats – six different species have been recorded here, including the large noctule, the tiny pipistrelle, and Daubenton's bat (*shown below, catching fish*). The bats hibernate through the winter, but the centre lays on guided evening bat walks during the spring and summer, where special bat detectors are provided, to help visitors hear and see the bats more clearly.

Main: The vast expanse of the London Wetland Centre is a welcome sight to inflying migrant birds. **Far right:** Grey heron with water vole.

CITY WILDERNESS

THE LONDON WETLAND CENTRE IS A LARGE SPLASH OF GREEN surrounded by urban sprawl. The result of a huge project by the Wildfowl & Wetlands Trust to turn a Victorian reservoir complex by the Thames into a true wetland wildlife haven, just a stone's throw from central London, it has been a huge success since it opened to the public in May 2000. Today, lagoons, reedbeds, grazing marsh, and small wooded areas cover over 40 hectares (100 acres), and attract a wide range of birds. Visit in January and you'll see both wild ducks and those captive in the various enclosures at their best, having moulted into their breeding plumage. The World Wetlands Walk takes you through the natural habitat sets of various countries around the world, and features representative species of captive wildfowl. Out on the lagoons – which can be viewed from the comfort of various hides – wildfowl include gadwalls, teals, wigeons, shovelers, pintails, and the two commoner diving ducks: the tufted duck and pochard.

Above: An eye-catching female wasp spider – the males are simply brown.

JAN

FEB

MAR

APR

MAY

JUN

JUL

AUG

SEP

OCT

NOV

DEC

Like feathered commuters, globetrotting birds flock to this city sanctuary to join the resident wildlife.

THROUGH THE YEAR
LONDON WETLAND CENTRE

In **spring**, many migrant birds visit the centre. These often include hobbys, garganeys, yellow wagtails, and various species of wader.

Little ringed plovers, reed and sedge warblers, kingfishers, and sand martins are some of the avian highlights in **summer**. Look out for reptiles: grass snakes, common lizards, and slow-worms populate the wilder areas. Butterflies abound in specially planted areas, and dragonflies are numerous. If you like bugs, follow the sounds of grasshoppers and crickets, and you might see a wasp spider, which weaves intricate webs to catch its prey.

Migrant birds arrive in **autumn**, along with visiting winter birds. Visitors can help to harvest blueberries, cranberries, primroses, and nettles – and learn ways in which to use them. Autumn is often the best time to see owls flying over these wetlands, and occasionally a soaring peregrine or hovering kestrel.

WHERE ELSE TO SEE
URBAN WETLANDS

Some cities have nature reserves within a few kilometres of their centre, boosting the numbers of birds and butterflies within the area as a whole.

Staines Reservoir in Middlesex nestles below the flight path of Heathrow and attracts plenty of wintering wildfowl. In spring and autumn it has a large number of passage waders and terns. [SE]

Bough Beech Reservoir, in Kent, is a great location for ducks in winter. The surrounding woodland is rich in birdlife, and an orchard feeding station offers close-up views of shy species such as brambling and great spotted woodpecker. [SE]

Newport Wetlands, in Wales, has an excellent mix of habitats, including reedbeds, saline lagoons, wet grassland, and scrub. It's a great place for birds, orchids, butterflies, dragonflies, and otters. [W]

Winnall Moors nature reserve is 1km (½ mile) from Winchester city centre. The River Itchen flows right through it, attracting all the wildlife associated with chalk streams. [SE]

Numbers of wildfowl and waders on the reserve at any one time can depend on the state of the tide, as some species – such as teal – often leave the reserve to feed on the Thames at low tide. Bitterns sometimes overwinter here, and January is one of the best months in which to spot this normally shy species. Look along the edge of reedbeds and stay alert for movement, as they are superbly camouflaged. Peregrine falcons hunt over the reserve and can cause mayhem when on the attack. A typical winter visit will give you views of stonechats, Cetti's warblers, meadow pipits, and siskins feeding in the alders. Both fieldfares and redwings can often be seen along the trails. If you hear a call similar to a piglet squealing, it is probably a water rail; look for it quickly – it's so shy that you'll only get the fleetest of views before it darts for cover. There are more than 20 water rails here in winter, and they soon establish their winter feeding territories.

On a cold day it's sometimes hard to leave the warmth of the centre's cafe, but climb up the Peacock Tower hide – or take the lift – and you'll get a great view of the whole reserve. Then it's impossible to resist the network of paths beckoning you down to explore the wildlife.

WINTERING GEESE

THE SOUND OF A WILD GOOSE FLOCK IS ONE OF THE DELIGHTS of a short winter day on the coast. Variously barking, yelping, murmuring, or honking geese, according to species, migrate to Britain for the winter from a huge swathe of the Arctic, from Canada to Siberia. On the north Norfolk coast, most numerous is the pink-footed goose, where in recent years the total population has reached around 150,000. And it is still increasing, helped by the availability of their favoured foods: spilt grain among stubble and sugar-beet tops.

The pink-footed geese roost on the mudflats and shallow waters of The Wash and Scolt Head Island, and fly to and from these at dusk and dawn to their feeding grounds. As they move around to forage for food, it can be difficult to predict where they will be during the day, although at one site – the grazing marshes at Holkham – the availability of marshland grass is sufficiently constant to make this a reliable location. Park in Lady Ann's Drive,

WHERE
Holkham Nature Reserve, Holkham, Wells-next-the-Sea, Norfolk, NR23 1AD; www.naturalengland.org.uk

CONTACT
Natural England, tel: 01328 711183; enquiries.east@naturalengland.org.uk

GETTING THERE
The reserve is 4.8km (3 miles) west of Wells-next-the-Sea on the A149. By rail, travel to either King's Lynn (closest) or Sheringham. By bus, catch the hourly Norfolk Coasthopper, which stops at the entrance. By cycle, take the National Cycle Network Route no.1.

ACCESS AND FACILITIES
There are three access points, at Burnham Overy, Wells Beach Road, and Lady Ann's Drive. The Norfolk Coastal path links the car parks. At Lady Ann's Drive, opposite Holkham Hall, there are no facilities but there is a pub and café at the park entrance. Wells car park has public toilets. This site is not easy for wheelchair or pushchair users due to the soft sandy tracks.

OPENING TIMES
Open all year round.

CHARGES
None, except for car parking charges at Lady Ann's Drive and Wells Beach Road.

Almost half of the world's pink-footed geese spend their winter on the north Norfolk coast.

Introduced species

Distinction is drawn in goose populations between the wild and the not-so-wild. Most of our greylags (*pictured*) and Canada geese, and all our Egyptian geese, are derived from birds once kept for ornamental purposes that have escaped. Increases in the numbers of these birds are of concern because they stir up mud and produce producing copious droppings, which have a detrimental effect on water quality. This has led to attempts to control their numbers by egg-pricking and direct culling.

JAN

FEB

MAR

APR

MAY

JUN

JUL

AUG

SEP

OCT

NOV

DEC

scan the fields, and there they will be, often with up to 500 European white-fronted geese and a few thousand wigeons. Continue down to the beach, across the dunes, and you have a good chance of finding a flock of snow buntings and perhaps a few Lapland buntings and shore larks feeding along the strandline. The marshes also hold flocks of dark-bellied brent geese, a smaller and more compact visitor from Siberia that's often best seen from the nearby Wells Beach Road.

Careful examination of goose flocks can reveal much rarer vagrants within them. A Ross's goose or two, largely white and black, may be among the pink-feet, while the brents could be hiding a North-American black brant. Add to these the resident feral greylags, Canada geese, and Egyptian geese, and a few barnacle geese of uncertain origin, and you have the chance to see almost any goose on the British list. Whether feeding in a tight flock, or flying over in successive V-formations, the sight and sounds of wild geese in these huge skies adds drama to any winter day at Holkham.

WHERE ELSE TO SEE
WINTERING GEESE

Greenland and Icelandic geese winter in huge numbers in northwest Europe, and particularly in the UK. They are generally found around the coasts, but can be seen at a few sites further inland.

Slimbridge in Gloucestershire (*see pp.34–35*) is one of the most important wintering sites in the UK for white-fronted geese. You might also see taiga, bean, and pink-footed geese, or a rare lesser white-fronted goose. [M]

Look for Greenland white-fronted geese at **Ynys-hir** (*see pp.106–107*) near Machynlleth, Wales. There is a winter flock of pale-bellied brent geese on **Anglesey** in North Wales, which is sometimes joined by black brant, or the Pacific brent goose. [W]

The **Ken-Dee Marshes**, near the Solway Firth in Dumfries and Galloway, are home to migrant white-fronted geese. **Mersehead** and **Caerlaverock** on the north Solway shore have barnacle geese, which can also be seen on a number of Hebridean islands, such as **Tiree**. [SC]

THROUGH THE YEAR
HOLKHAM BAY

As **spring** approaches, the geese depart from Holkham, their calls replaced with the territorial piping of redshanks and oystercatchers. Marsh harriers settle into their reedbed breeding territories, alongside a few hen harriers lingering from the winter. In the pine plantations on the dunes there may be crossbills nesting as early as February.

In **summer**, the sand dunes burst into flower, with sea-holly, pyramidal orchid, and the vile-smelling hound's-tongue. Where pools have formed, look for marsh helleborines and southern marsh orchids, and breeding natterjack toads.

Attention turns to the pines in **autumn**, which are a magnet for migrant songbirds such as goldcrests, and even, after northeasterly winds, rarities like Pallas's warblers and olive-backed pipits. Fungi spring up in their many and varied forms: look out for earth-stars, fly agaric, and the sweet-smelling dune stinkhorn.

Above: Brent geese flying in formation.

Main: Thousands of geese winter at Holkham.

Left panel (top to bottom): Both pink-footed and greylag geese have pink legs, but pink-footed geese have short necks, and almost-black heads; Egyptian goose.

Below: The white-fronted goose is white on its bill, not – as you might expect – on its chest.

Below: Holkham Bay is perfect for tranquil walks in summer.

WHERE
Druridge Bay Country Park, Red Row,
Morpeth, Northumberland NE61 5BX;
www.northumberland.gov.uk

CONTACT
Druridge Bay Country Park Visitor Centre,
tel: 01670 760968;
druridgebay@northumberland.gov.uk
Northumberland Wildlife Trust,
tel: 0191 2846884; mail@northwt.org.uk

GETTING THERE
Druridge Bay Country Park is off the A1068,
near Amble. By rail, travel to Widdrington.
By bus, take the 518 bus between Morpeth
and Alnwick, which stops at Hadston, a
15-minute walk from the bay.

ACCESS AND FACILITIES
The nearest facilities are at the Druridge Bay
Country Park's wheelchair-friendly visitor
centre, which includes a café, shop, toilets,
play areas, parking, and access to one part
of the beach by wheelchair. Hauxley Nature
Reserve, at the other end of the bay from the
country park, also has ample car parking, an
information centre, and full-access toilets.

OPENING TIMES
Access to the bay all year round.

CHARGES
None.

Strutting sanderlings

Sanderlings are small, pale sandpipers known for
enjoying themselves on the beach: they are often
seen in flocks chasing the receding waves, and
then running up the beach again as the waves
come up behind them. In fact, this comical
behaviour has a purpose: the birds are rushing in
to pick up invertebrates stranded in the sand as
the waves recede, and probe around in the wet
sand for other food. Some non-breeding adults
stay in their winter home all year round.

Above (top and bottom): Flocks of sanderlings gather
at the shoreline to forage; Coquet Island, a bird
sanctuary, is just 1.6km (1 mile) off the coast at Amble.

Below: Grey herons are often seen feeding on the eels
of Druridge's freshwater pools.

Right (top and bottom): The pintail duck favours
intertidal habitats; snow buntings can be seen around
Druridge Bay through the winter, taking off for their high
Arctic breeding grounds in April.

Main: Druridge Bay is the longest uninterrupted stretch of beach and dune habitat in Northumberland.

A BRACING BEACH WALK

S TRETCHING FROM AMBLE IN THE NORTH TO CRESSWELL IN THE SOUTH, the 9.6km (6 mile) sweep of
Druridge Bay takes in some of the finest birdwatching locations in the northeast of England. Parts of the bay
are under ownership of the National Trust, while other sections are protected as nature reserves.

The bay can be a cold place in January, but the great birdwatching on offer will soon make you forget the
weather. The bay is defined by a long sandy beach behind which are sand dunes, scrub, hedgerows, and a series of
lagoons – formed through the landscaping of former open-cast coal-mining sites. At the southern end of the bay,
Cresswell Pond is a brackish lagoon fringed by reeds and marsh, where wintering waterfowl are the main
attraction in January, and at dusk the pond is sometimes used by roosting pink-footed geese and whooper swans.
The pink-footed geese feed in the large fields at the back of the bay and can often be seen on the larger lagoons, or

Above: Little stints are sometimes seen probing the sands for food.

THROUGH THE YEAR
DRURIDGE BAY

Large numbers of birds pass through the area on passage in **spring**, most notably little gulls, black terns, kittiwakes, and garganeys. Waders may include greenshanks, whimbrels, sandpipers, and little stints.

Breeding birds around the area in **summer** include various warblers, particularly the grasshopper warbler, which can be heard "reeling" (singing) in the scrub in the dunes and around the pools. On the beach, gulls and terns regularly sit in flocks and you may see some roseate terns, which breed on nearby Coquet Island.

In **autumn** you can see many returning waders, including the pectoral sandpiper, and passage seabirds including terns and skuas. Look out also for smaller birds such as wheatears, whinchats, redstarts, and pied flycatchers. You've also got a good chance of seeing some rare birds.

Viewed from below, the pretty snow bunting looks completely white, giving it the fond nickname of "snowflake".

WHERE ELSE TO SEE
SAND DUNES

Sand dunes are a nationally declining habitat, but many are actively managed to encourage wildlife.

Lindisfarne, Northumberland (*see pp.274–275*), offers extensive sand dunes, long, sandy beaches, and vast areas of tidal mudflats swarming with birds in winter. **Seal Sands**, on Teesmouth, East Yorkshire (*see pp.304–305*), offers great winter birdwatching, right in the middle of an industrial heartland. [N]

The red-breasted merganser can be seen on the **Fal Estuary**, Cornwall, which leads to the Carrick Roads – a deep waterway served by the River Truro. [SW]

Pagham Harbour in West Sussex is bordered by shingle spits, and is a great place to see passage waders in autumn. St Catherine's Point, on the **Isle of Wight** (*see pp.224–225*) is a good place to see many of the Druridge birds. [SE]

Kenfig Reserve in South Wales regularly sees bitterns, shovelers, ruddy ducks, smews, merlins, and peregrines. At ground level, look out for the endangered fen orchid in June and July. [W]

flying overhead. If you walk in a northerly direction away from Cresswell, you come to Druridge pools. These large lagoons are surrounded by scrub and reeds, and bordered by sand dunes to the east and farmland to the west. There's always a great variety of birds here, though those on the lagoons can be quite distant, so bring a telescope if you can. Red-breasted mergansers are regular visitors, and you might see smews in January. Walk through the dunes to the beach and scan for waders: both the bar-tailed godwit and the sanderling prefer sandy areas to mud. Offshore, divers, grebes, and sea ducks such as scoter and long-tailed duck are possibilities.

On the beach itself you may find snow buntings, easily identified by their twittering call and flash of under-wing white while flying. Venturing further north you reach East Chevington, where pools and reedbeds attract wildfowl and rare birds. At the northern end of the bay, Hauxley Nature Reserve has hides overlooking a freshwater pool, which attracts wintering ducks such as pintails, scaups, wigeons, and sometimes long-tailed ducks and smews. The berry-laden hedgerows and bushes at the reserve are popular with wintering thrushes, redwings, and fieldfares.

JAN FEB MAR APR MAY JUN JUL AUG SEP OCT NOV DEC

WINTERING SWANS

WILD SWANS MAKE ONE OF THE FINEST WILDLIFE SIGHTS IN THE UK, and the Ouse Washes are home to the largest concentration of Bewick and whooper swans in the country. The site forms a spectacular setting for the tens of thousands of swans, geese, gulls, and ducks that make their home here in winter, when the floodwater rises, forming temporary lakes that run in dead-straight lines for over 32km (20 miles) across the Cambridgeshire countryside. Don't wait for a clear, sunny day – these majestic birds are best seen on a misty day when all looks soft, grey, and mysterious, and the breathy whistle of the swans' wings takes on an ethereal charm.

Two or three decades ago the great majority of the swans were Bewick's swans from northern Siberia. These smaller swans, around two-thirds the size of the familiar all-year-round mute swan, are still big, dramatic birds, which are completely white except for their black and yellow bills. Now, whooper swans from Iceland have

WHERE
RSPB Ouse Washes, Welches Dam, Manea, March, Cambridgeshire PE15 0NF; www.rspb.org.uk

CONTACT
RSPB Ouse Washes, tel: 01354 680212; ouse.washes@rspb.org.uk

GETTING THERE
By car, leave the village of Manea and turn right at the T-junction, then left opposite the Rose and Crown pub. Turn left at the next T-junction towards Welches Dam, continuing to the signposted car park. The bus stops in Manea, which is 4km (2½ miles) from the reserve. Manea Station is 5km (3 miles) from the reserve.

ACCESS AND FACILITIES
The visitor centre is wheelchair friendly with car parking, toilets, refreshments, picnic tables, and accessible hides. There are 10 hides in total and one short nature trail.

OPENING TIMES
The birdwatching hides are open at all times. The visitor centre is open 9am–5pm every day except Christmas and Boxing Day.

CHARGES
None, but the RSPB welcomes donations.

Above (top to bottom): Black-tailed godwits from northern Europe take refuge from harsher winters on the Ouse Washes; a cormorant drying its wings.

Main: Bewick's swans at dawn on the Ouse Washes.

Below (left to right): The Ouse Washes attract many wintering birds of prey, such as this short-eared owl. Washland ditches were created in the 17th century to retain flood waters, so preventing farmland from flooding; mute swans live in the UK all year round; whoopers are winter visitors from Iceland.

Family affairs

Bewick's and whooper swans are much wilder than our regular mute swans. They can seem deceptively tame when seen in spectacular close-up from the Ouse Washes hides, especially when they are being fed. But find them away from here – grazing on nearby farmland, for instance, or on a small lake or a riverside meadow – and they will be quick to fly off. They are much more vocal too, and to hear their quiet, bubbling conversation softly through a thick mist is extra-special.

become almost as numerous at times, especially on the more northerly washes, where swans are fed daily with barrows of grain. The whoopers are as big as mute swans, but they look more like Bewick's, with black and yellow colouring on the face and beak. Bewick's have more irregular but essentially rounded yellow patches against the black, while whoopers have longer, more wedge-shaped bills with a narrow, triangular wedge of yellow on each side.

Adult swans can be identified individually by their face patterns, which remain fixed. Studies have shown that they mate for life, and at the Ouse Washes you can often see mother and father together with one, two, three, or more dull-grey youngsters, depending on the success of the breeding season in the far northern tundra. Families stick together and perform frequent greeting ceremonies, and interact with other groups, leaning forward with stretched necks and raised wings and calling in concert.

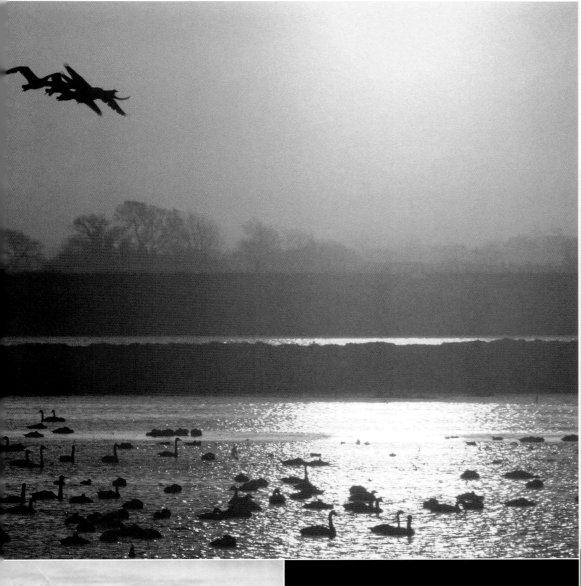

WHERE ELSE TO SEE
WINTERING SWANS

Mute swans live in the UK all year round, and they are joined from October to March by migratory colonies of Bewick's swans from Siberia and whoopers from Iceland.

A little further north on the Washes, the Wildfowl & Wetland Trust's **Welney** reserve is also a prime site for wintering swans. [SE] Visit the Trust's reserve at **Slimbridge** (see pp.34–35), Gloucestershire, to see Bewick's swans and flocks of wild ducks around the collections of captive ones. Around 250 Bewick's arrive at Slimbridge from Siberia every winter. [M]

Loch of Strathbeg, Scotland, is the UK's largest dune loch – a loch entirely surrounded by sands – which becomes home to thousands of wild geese, swans, and ducks in the winter. These migrating birds also gather in large numbers around **Mersehead** and **Caerlaverock**, both of which lie on the north shore of Scotland's Solway Firth. [SC]

Another great place to see large gatherings of swans is **Lindisfarne Island** (see pp.274–275), situated off the coast of Northumberland. [N]

THROUGH THE YEAR
OUSE WASHES

In **spring**, search drier areas for migrating flocks of ruffs, often showing off their spectacular breeding plumage, and black-tailed godwits. Watch out for dramatic snipe and lapwing displays.

Avocets and marsh harriers can often be seen in the **summer**, unless flash floods have forced them to leave. Foxes are often seen here and you may be lucky enough to catch a glimpse of an otter; more likely sightings are of stoats.

Autumn is a good time to see migrant wading birds, terns, and gulls. Look out for tree sparrows and finch flocks along the tideline of the floods, as they search for washed-up seeds. Cormorants like to roost on overhead wires and you can often find short-eared and barn owls, merlins, hen harriers, and sparrowhawks hunting over the embankments.

Below: Bewick's swans are a familiar sight on the Ouse Washes.

JAN

FEB

MAR

APR

MAY

JUN

JUL

AUG

SEP

OCT

NOV

DEC

Left: Geltsdale is famous for its black grouse.

Right (left to right): Geltsdale is part of the Pennine Area of Outstanding Natural Beauty; brown hares winter on the moor; red foxes prey on smaller animals in winter.

Right, below: Buzzards live in large numbers at Geltsdale – listen out for their distinctive, challenging "mew" call.

WHERE
RSPB Geltsdale, Stagsike Cottages, Hallbankgate, Brampton, Cumbria CA8 2PW; www.rspb.org.uk

CONTACT
Reserve Information Point, tel: 01697 746717; northernengland@rspb.org.uk

GETTING THERE
From the A69 near Brampton, take the A689 to Hallbankgate and Alston. At Hallbankgate, take the minor road that runs in front of the "Belted Will" pub. By train, Brampton Junction is around 3.2km (2 miles) away. The nearest bus stop is at Hallbankgate.

ACCESS AND FACILITIES
The small car park is in Hallbankgate. There are full-access toilets, a picnic area, and a live camera. There are several trails, of varying lengths. Wheelchair access over the moor is difficult due to the terrain, but it can be pre-arranged by contacting the Reserve Information Point (see above). The tarn viewpoint will soon be fully accessible.

OPENING TIMES
Trails are open all day, and the Reserve Information Point is open from 9am to 5pm.

CHARGES
None.

Stoat in ermine

In January, look out for the stoat. This sharp-eyed predator is red-brown on top and creamy-white beneath, with a bushy black-tipped tail. In the north in winter, some become white except for the tail tip. Known as ermines, these are familiar as the black-spotted white furs of ceremonial robes. Stoats keep to cover but are apt to run over open ground, even along drystone walls, and are incurably curious. If a stoat dives out of sight, keep still and quiet and it will often reappear.

Main: Geltsdale is a walker's paradise in winter, providing stunning views, such as this one from the summit of Talkin Fell.

NEW YEAR ON THE MOORS

THE NORTH PENNINES ARE AT THEIR MOST BLEAKLY DRAMATIC IN WINTER; on Geltsdale, the blanket bogs, heath, upland farmland, and woods stretch out before you in a glorious wilderness, and the short, crisp days are perfect for walking, with only the occasional bird of prey for company.

This is a harsh, challenging environment and few birds and mammals are equipped to cope with it. It is, however, one of the UK's few sites for nesting hen harriers, and they wheel above the forbidding landscape all year round, joined by hunting buzzards and short-eared owls. Smews occasionally visit the glistening tarns, making the most of their seclusion, which will disappear when the lapwings, redshanks, snipe, and curlews arrive early in spring. In hidden little gullies with thickets of thorns, fieldfares and redwings feed on the berries in late autumn, but even they have to move out on to open pastures below the moor in winter.

Above: Cattle grazing on the RSPB Geltsdale reserve in summer.

January's short, crisp days are perfect for walking, with only the moor's wild creatures for company.

THROUGH THE YEAR
GELTSDALE

Lapwings, redshanks, snipe, and curlews arrive early in **spring** and can be seen on the fields around the moor before dispersing to their territories. The hum of drumming snipe overhead and the rippling, bubbling songs of curlews are typical of the wetter parts of the moor. Take the woodland Bruthwaite Trail to look for warblers and redstarts.

In **summer**, meadow pipits, swallows, and stonechats are evident. Barn owls and short-eared owls hunt in the evenings. Breeding birds include golden plovers, curlews, ring ouzels, merlins, and short-eared owls. Stoats are raising their young, which will be fully independent and able to hunt their own prey by the end of the season.

Fieldfare and redwing flocks arrive in **autumn**, when black grouse become more visible around the reserve trails.

WHERE ELSE TO SEE
PENNINE WILDLIFE

Many of the animals and birds at Geltsdale can be found around the UK, in similar environments. However, some, such as the red grouse, are virtually restricted to heather moorland. Golden plovers, merlins, and hen harriers breed mainly on moorland.

The **North York Moors** (*see pp.232–233*) have many of the birds and flowers of Geltsdale. They are good for finding red grouse and have a few golden plovers and curlews. A colony of stoats lives in the ruins of **Mount Grace Priory**, North Yorkshire. [N]

Stoats are widespread in many habitats but are always rather unpredictable. They can be seen hunting along the estuary track at **Conwy** (*see pp.278–279*) in North Wales. [W]

Hen harriers can be seen in the summer in Scotland on **Islay** (*see pp.12–13*) and **Orkney** [SC]. In winter they can be found around the **Solway Firth**; for example at Campfield Marsh RSPB reserve, on the English side [N].

Red grouse also live on the moor all year round. These are tough birds, associated with the low, dense carpets of ling heather. In winter, you might see little groups, which fly off low and fast, hugging the hillside, before diving out of sight with a raucous, throaty cackle, "go-back go-back, back, back" – this is one of the great sounds of the hills.

Geltsdale is famous for its black grouse, too: bigger birds with a much greater difference between the sexes. Females are grey-brown, but the males are stunningly blue-black, with white wingbars, a white puffball under the tail, and red fleshy wattles over the eyes. When they wish to mate, these males will gather on open spaces to display, calling and mock-fighting in a spectacle known as the "lek", designed to impress the watching hens (*see pp. 102–103*).

The extensive blanket bogs of the moorland are characterized by multicoloured sphagnum mosses, which form a natural sponge, holding water in the hills and forming deep deposits of peat. These areas, often drained and eroded, are being restored through reducing grazing by sheep and heather-burning, and the blocking of artificial moorland drains.

JAN
FEB
MAR
APR
MAY
JUN
JUL
AUG
SEP
OCT
NOV
DEC

LEE VALLEY PARK

WHERE
Lee Valley Park, Essex and Herts;
www.leevalleypark.org.uk

CONTACT
Lee Valley Regional Park Visitor Centre, tel:
01992 702200; info@leevalleypark.org.uk

GETTING THERE
The park extends from Ware in Hertfordshire
to Leyton in London, stretching for 42km (26
miles) on both sides of the River Lee. The
Regional Park Visitor Centre at Fisher's Green
is signposted from the B195 just north of
Waltham Abbey (M25 junction 26). By train,
travel to Waltham Cross for the south of the
park; Cheshunt for the central park; and
Broxbourne for the north. By bus, nos. 211,
212, 213, 240, 250, 251, and 505 all serve
the park area.

ACCESS AND FACILITIES
The bittern watchpoint is at Fisher's Green,
Stubbins Hall Lane, EN9 2EF. Parking is free.
Access to disabled toilets is with key only.
There are various facilities across the valley;
contact the Lee Valley Regional Park Visitor
Centre or visit the park's website for details.

OPENING TIMES
Open all year round.

CHARGES
None.

East Anglian bitterns

While many of Britain's overwintering bitterns are
believed to be refugees from frozen wetlands on
the continent, ringing and radio-tracking studies
have demonstrated that at least some of the Lee
Valley birds move between the park and several
established breeding sites in East Anglia. Work is
under way to extend and improve the reedbed
habitat within the Lee Valley, both to safeguard
the bitterns' winter haunts and to encourage
them eventually to stay and breed.

FORMING THE BOUNDARY BETWEEN ESSEX AND HERTFORDSHIRE, the River Lee lies
within a broad valley that penetrates to the very heart of London. It has been hugely
modified by human activities, but our influence has been far from negative. Our need for
drinking water and construction aggregates has resulted in the creation of a complex series
of reservoirs and gravel pits that together form a wetland of international significance.

The best place to start is the Lee Valley Regional Park Authority's visitor centre at
Fisher's Green, near Waltham Abbey. From here it is a short walk to Seventy Acres Lake, one
of the flooded gravel pits, which is overlooked by a series of hides, including the renowned

Walthamstow Marsh nature
reserve is an important part of the
Lee Valley Park, together with
Coppermill Fields and Leyton
Marsh – remnants of London's once
widespread river valley grasslands.

bittern watchpoint. Up to one-tenth of the British wintering population of bitterns can be
found in the Lee Valley, and the small reedbed in front of the watchpoint often holds one or
more. Be patient and you may well be rewarded with close views as a reclusive bittern stalks
out of the reeds and starts to fish in the cleared channels.

While you are waiting, listen out for the squeals of water rails, and scan the waterfowl
on the lake. Among the mallards, coots, and Canada geese you should find gadwalls and
shovelers, tufted ducks and, if there has been hard weather on the continent, a few smews.
Most will be "redheads" – brownish females and young birds – but you might see an adult
male, stunningly white with a tracery of black, which makes for effective camouflage against
sunlit ripples. There may be a few goosanders, which are equally attractive but much larger.

A midwinter walk around Fisher's Green, or any of the other nature reserves in the
valley, including Amwell and Rye Meads, will be enlivened by flocks of small birds. Roving
bands of blue, great, and long-tailed tits often include an overwintering chiffchaff, and the
alder trees on the margins of the lakes could reveal a twittering group of redpolls and siskins.

Main: Lee Valley Park covers 405 hectares (1,000 acres) of land across Essex and Hertfordshire.
Below (left to right): An acrobatic siskin in an alder tree; a goosander lands on water; the striking adult male smew.
Inset: Walthamstow Marsh Nature Reserve provides a restful respite from the city on a winter's day.

Above: A mute swan cygnet on the River Lee in spring.

JAN

FEB

MAR

APR

MAY

JUN

JUL

AUG

SEP

OCT

NOV

DEC

WILDLIFE CALENDAR
LEE VALLEY PARK

Spring is a good time to try to find one of the small local otter population: try Rye Meads, in the early morning. Bird breeding is under way, including grey herons in the alders at Waltham Abbey (now called Gunpowder Mills). Herons, swans, cormorants, and nowadays a few little egrets also breed around Walthamstow Reservoirs.

During the **summer**, the wetlands come alive with insect life, especially dragonflies and damselflies. One part of the valley, Cornmill Meadows (*see pp.210–211*), is managed especially for this fascinating group of insects, but they can be seen anywhere. At least 17 species are known to breed here, including such scarce species as hairy dragonfly and ruddy darter. An evening visit will reveal several species of bats, including Daubenton's bat, typically skimming low over water in search of food.

Waterbird numbers build up rapidly from late summer into the **autumn**. Tufted ducks and pochards arrive to moult; and as they become flightless, they favour the middle of the larger lakes, well out of the way of ground predators.

WHERE ELSE TO SEE
MAN-MADE WETLANDS

There are many places where wildfowl and other waterbirds have moved onto wetlands created over the past century, which began their lives as reservoirs.

The **Cotswold Water Park**, Gloucestershire, consists of more than 140 lakes, where thousands of birds spend the winter. Look out for pochards, gadwalls, goosanders, smews, Caspian gulls, yellow-legged gulls, and little egrets. [M]

Also in the Midlands, **Attenborough Gravel Pits**, Nottingham, has a good selection of waterbirds, as does **Rutland Water** reservoir in Rutland. [M]

Pensthorpe wildlife reserve near Norwich, has many waterbirds, and **Abberton Reservoir**, Colchester, hosts 30,000 or more in the early winter. Look for bitterns along the coast, at **Minsmere** (*see pp.100–101*) and **Walberswick** in Suffolk. [SE]

FEBRUARY

Where to Go: **February**

Winter fades out gradually and rather uncertainly to spring: February is an in-between month, and global warming has made the weather quite unpredictable. There are few signs of the wildlife of warmer months, which remain hidden or abroad. Birds and seals bring life to our coasts and offshore islands, and in the north and west of the country, you might come across an otter.

Inland, the wetlands – lakes, reservoirs, and marshes – have ducks, coots, and swans, but there are many other birds, too, from great crested and little grebes, coots, and moorhens, to beautiful jewel-like kingfishers and delicate, dancing grey wagtails. If they all suddenly take off in panic, look around for a sparrowhawk, or, if you're really lucky, a peregrine falcon.

ISLANDS

ARRAN The Kilbrannan Sound and the Mull of Kintyre.

WETLANDS

SLAPTON LEY The rare Cetti's warbler hides in the reeds here.

WOODLANDS

SHERWOOD FOREST An historic royal hunting forest and ancient woodland.

FARNE ISLANDS
NORTHUMBERLAND [N]

Visit Farne to see 100,000 pairs of wintering seabirds, including puffins and guillemots, and to watch the antics of one of Europe's largest grey seal populations.
See pp.42–43

BROWNSEA ISLAND
POOLE HARBOUR, DORSET [SW]

Black-tailed godwits can be seen here, along with large numbers of native red squirrels.
See pp.38–39

SLAPTON LEY
KINGSBRIDGE, DEVON [SW]

The largest freshwater lake in southwest England supports around 75,000 birds in winter. The starling roost is spectacular.
See pp.40–41

KINGLEY VALE
WEST SUSSEX [SE]

The yews of the ancient forest here are among the oldest living things in Britain. Their dark majesty is highlighted by the bareness of the winter scene.
See pp.36–37

ISLE OF ARRAN
NORTH AYRSHIRE [SC]

Red squirrels live in the south of the island, while the resident ducks are joined by goldeneyes, teals, and wigeons in February.
See pp.42–43

The Isle of Arran is known as "Scotland in miniature" for its dramatic, rugged mountains, carved valleys, and aged woodlands.

SLIMBRIDGE
GLOUCESTERSHIRE [SE]

There's plenty to do and see at the original site for the Wildfowl & Wetlands Trust; in winter, it shelters hundreds of Bewick's swans and other water birds.
See pp.34–35

STODMARSH
STOUR VALLEY, KENT [SE]

A wonderful place too see birds, including hen harriers and ducks in winter, as well as rarities. Look for the insect-eating greater bladderwort plant in the dykes.
See pp.46–47

WINDSOR GREAT PARK
WINDSOR, BERKSHIRE [SE]

This royal park has several woodlands, and in winter you can see many of its roe deer. Little owls and tawny owls look for prey at night.
See pp.36–37

ISLE OF SKYE
INNER HEBRIDES [SC]

The largest island of the Inner Hebrides provides a dramatic backdrop for seabirds, including fulmars, kittiwakes, and shags.
See pp.42–43

HICKLING BROAD
NORFOLK [SE]

The largest of the Broads shelters thousands of birds, including reedbed specialities, such as bitterns and water rails.
See pp.46–47

It is clear from its 1790 description that the Major Oak – Sherwood's oldest tree – has been hollow for at least two centuries.

SHERWOOD FOREST
NOTTINGHAM [N]

One of Britain's oldest trees lives in the famous Sherwood Forest; it may be 1,000 years old.
See pp.36–37

ISLE OF MULL
INNER HEBRIDES [SC]

The island is well known both for its seabirds and for its birds of prey, which hunt over the moors and fish over the lochs and sea.
See pp.42–43

SOMERSET LEVELS
SOMERSET [SW]

This great network of ditches, grazing marshes, and peatland, has wading birds and otters among its varied wildlife.
See pp.46–47

WISTMAN'S WOOD
DEVON [SW]

This ancient wood grows at high altitude, and its dwarf oak trees grow tangled and twisted among moss-carpeted boulders, like a fairy-tale forest.
See pp.36–37

EPPING FOREST
ESSEX [SE]

Enjoy the largest public open space in the London area and the wildlife that makes its home here. The woods contain many venerable trees.
See pp.36–37

Flocks of birds come together at dusk to roost: tens of thousands of starlings take up perches in trees and reeds, and hundreds, sometimes thousands, of woodpigeons, stock doves, rooks, and jackdaws descend in noisy, tumbling flocks into the dark shelter of the woods. Bands of fieldfares and redwings roam the fields by day, but they too come together to roost in trees and thickets each night, seeking out warmth and safety in numbers in the still-short, cold winter days. By the end of the month, however, there are inklings of spring, and the landscape begins to show flecks of colour and life. Look out for cascades of yellow hazel catkins, golden early celandines, and the flat orange flowerheads of coltsfoot – all signs that the seasons are changing.

HEATH AND MOOR

EXMOOR Home to Britain's most famous wild ponies.

UPLANDS

GIGRIN FARM Hundreds of red kites feed here daily.

INLETS AND ESTUARIES

POOLE HARBOUR Witness huge flocks of birds on the Dorset coast.

EXMOOR
DEVON AND SOMERSET [SW]

Enjoy the dramatic beauty of the moor without the crowds, but look in the gentler, wooded valleys, too, for snowdrops and other harbingers of spring.
See pp.44–45

WESTHAY MOOR
SOMERSET LEVELS {SW}

The moor hosts a huge starling roost – in some years it can include up to 8 million birds.
See pp.40–41

Small, stocky goats survive on Exmoor in winter with the help of a layer of fine hair – cashmere – next to their skin, which keeps out the cold.

THE NEW FOREST
HAMPSHIRE [SW]

At this time of year, while the trees are still bare, seeing deer is easier: see if you can identify all three of our native species – red, roe, and fallow deer.
See pp.36–37

DARTMOOR
DEVON [SW]

The biggest, wildest area of open country in England offers shelter to deer, foxes, otters, badgers, grey squirrels, and hares in the winter.
See pp.44–45

GIGRIN FARM
RHAYADER, MID WALES [W]

This wildlife-friendly farm offers unparalleled views of red kites – at "feeding time", up to 400 of these spectacular raptors gather in one field.
See pp.32–33

LOCH KEN
SOUTHERN UPLAND WAY [SC]

In February you can see birds of prey, including red kites, peregrines, and barn owls here, together with the rare Greenland white-fronted geese.
See pp.32–33

BLACK MOUNTAIN
BRECON BEACONS [W]

Escape to the wide-open spaces of this National Park, where red grouse hide among the upland moorlands and birds of prey, such as red kites, fly overhead.
See pp.44–45

The Brecon Beacons landscape is extraordinary, with fantastic waterfalls, amazing caves, and the highest mountains in southern Britain.

SYMONDS YAT
WYE VALLEY [M]

This famous viewpoint is a superb vantage point for watching birds of prey – ospreys, honey buzzards, goshawks and, if you're lucky, red kites.
See pp.32–33

WIDEWATER LAGOON
SHOREHAM, WEST SUSSEX [SE]

The sea filters in during high tides, making this the perfect home for herons, mute swans, oystercatchers, and redshanks.
See pp.38–39

LANGSTONE HARBOUR
HAVANT, HANTS [SE]

Thousands of waders and brent geese migrate from the Arctic to feed and roost in safety here.
See pp.48–49

POOLE HARBOUR
DORSET [SW]

This vast natural harbour is full of wintering birds, including the elegant, black-tailed godwits, scarce grebes, curlews, grey plovers, knots, and dunlins.
See pp.48–49

PAGHAM HARBOUR
WEST SUSSEX [SE]

Shelter in one of the hides to watch waders, or take a walk out to Pagham Spit where, especially at high tide, you can see seaducks, divers, and grebes.
See pp.48–49

BELFAST LOUGH
ANTRIM [NI]

See black-tailed and sometimes bar-tailed godwits at incredibly close quarters from the RSPB's cosy observation room here.
See pp.38–39

WHERE
Gigrin Farm, South Street, Rhayader, Powys, LD6 5BL, Wales.

CONTACT
Gigrin Farm information, tel: 01597 810243; lena@gigrin.co.uk

GETTING THERE
Gigrin Farm is on the A470, 1km (½ mile) south of the town of Rhayader. Network trains are available to Llandrindod.

ACCESS AND FACILITIES
The farm is wheelchair friendly, and three of the hides have ramps. Facilities are good, with toilets, a shop, and refreshments. Feeding takes place at 3pm in summer and 2pm in winter.

OPENING TIMES
Open every day, except Christmas Day.

CHARGES
Yes, except for children 4 years and under.

Feasting on carrion

Red kites are opportunists, feeding mainly on carrion and scavenging any handouts they encounter. They take only small live prey, such as young pigeons, rabbits, and invertebrates. Sheep carrion is a favourite, but because of their relatively weak bills, they rely on ravens, buzzards, foxes, or cats to open carcases for them. Recent legislation has meant fallen animals have to be removed and incinerated, which has eliminated one of the kites' best potential food sources.

Above (top to bottom): Birdwatchers take in the spectacle at feeding time; the kites must defend their meal from opportunistic crows, ravens, and buzzards.

Right panel (top and bottom): The sky fills with birds just before feeding time; the pale grey head of the kite features pin-sharp, hooded amber eyes.

Below: Red kites often feed in mid-air, once safely away from other birds, who might steal the food.

Main: With its massive wingspan, the majestic red kite effortlessly soars and glides through the air.

RED KITES FEEDING

THE FIRST THING YOU NOTICE ABOUT A RED KITE is its extraordinary wingspan, stretching nearly 2m (5½ft); it is so wide in comparison to its light bodyweight that this bird can stay in the air for hours with hardly a beat of its wings. You might notice its distinctive forked tail, and the beautiful autumnal colours of its body, before realising, as you watch it in an aerobatic display, that this is also a bird of incredible agility.

Gigrin Farm in Wales offers unparalleled views of these spectacular raptors – at times more than 400 kites assemble for a daily offering, and in some weeks more than 250kg (around a quarter of a ton) of meat is thrown to the kites. Feeding takes place each day in the early afternoon, which makes the food effectively a "top up", as kites wake up hungry and hunt for food in the early morning. As an official feeding station for these birds since 1992, Gigrin Farm has helped draw people away from the nesting sites – which suffered badly from egg thefts – and

As feeding time draws near, tension starts to build, as both birds and spectators wait for the show to begin.

THROUGH THE YEAR
GIGRIN FARM

Red kites, common buzzards, and ravens all come to the farm to feed in **spring**. Other possibilities include peregrines, goshawks, merlins, and barn owls. Polecats live around the area, but are rarely seen. You might be luckier with the water voles, and there are a few badger setts within the surrounding woods.

Gigrin Farm is set in a landscape of open heather and grass moorland that's wonderful in **summer**. The ancient oakwoods are full of pied flycatchers, redstarts, and wood warblers, and there is also a 2km (1½ mile) nature trail around the farm that links it to the RSPB's Dyffyn Reserve, attracting gadwalls and herons.

The feeding station is still busy in the **autumn**, with hundreds of raptors visiting the farm. If you are accompanying children, you might enjoy visiting the farm animals, too, including ponies, donkeys, goats, ducks, chickens, and even a peacock.

WHERE ELSE TO SEE
RED KITES

Away from mid Wales there are a few locations in Britain where you can see reintroduced red kites.

Red kites fly around Symonds Yat in the **Wye Valley** (*see pp.80–81*), together with goshawks, hobbies, ospreys, and honey buzzards. Afternoon is the best time to visit. [M]

Loch Ken, on the Black Isle in the north of Scotland, is a collection of marshes centred around a loch. In winter you'll see a good collection of birds of prey, including red kites, peregrines, and barn owls, and also Greenland white-fronted geese. Red kites were reintroduced to the Black Isle in the late 1980s, and Scotland now has 122 breeding pairs. [SC]

More than 90 red kites were released into Gateshead's **Lower Derwent Valley** between 2004 and 2006, and they are most easily seen between Burnopfield and Rowlands Gill. [N]

Above: Red kites hatch in tree nests during April and May.

JAN FEB MAR APR MAY JUN JUL AUG SEP OCT NOV DEC

guaranteed food for the hungry young kites, many of whom were dying over the winter. Although, when times are hard, kites will take a range of live prey that even stretches to earthworms, at Gigrin Farm they are fed beef, fit for human consumption.

As you sit in the hides just before feeding time, the tension starts to build as kites start arriving; some alight in nearby trees, while others glide high above the hills. Crows and common buzzards join them, also waiting for the food to arrive. The deep "rronk, rronk" of ravens builds in the background. Once the meat has been thrown out, crows are quick to try to snatch a scrap but immediately the kites rush in, rarely if ever landing – they pluck the food in their talons from the ground, or – cheekily – from the crows' claws. They twist and turn, dive and climb, and there are so many of them it becomes a maelstrom of spectacular aerobatics.

Visit Gigrin Farm in February and you may be lucky enough to see kite pairs in a courtship flight, or rival males grappling each other by their talons, spinning and spiralling towards earth. By the end of the month these fearsome birds can be seen avidly nest-building.

WILDFOWL AT SLIMBRIDGE

FLOWING IN A GREAT ARC FROM MID WALES THROUGH SHROPSHIRE, the mighty Severn river reaches the sea in a huge estuary. Where the river broadens into the sand and mudflats, there are green, watery pastures on the east side, including the New Grounds at Slimbridge. Here the Wildfowl & Wetlands Trust was founded by Sir Peter Scott, a great conservationist, after he watched several thousand white-fronted geese spending the winter here. With warmer winters, geese no longer come in such numbers – 7,000 declining to just 550–750 in recent years. Most now need fly no farther than the Low Countries on their annual migrations from Russia.

The other famous winter birds at Slimbridge, Bewick's swans, have also declined in number, but you can still see around 200, and often they fly to the pools beside the visitor centre to give exceptional views. There, too, you can see pochards, wigeons, shovelers, and pintails, as the wild ducks mingle with the Trust's captive species.

WHERE
Wildfowl & Wetlands Trust, Slimbridge, Gloucestershire, GL2 7BT;
www.wwt.org.uk

CONTACT
Tel: 01453 891900;
enquiries@wwt.org.uk

GETTING THERE
By car, leave the M5 at either junctions 13 or 14 between Gloucester and Bristol, then follow the brown duck signs. The nearest train station is 6.4km (4 miles) away at Cam and Dursley Station. Cyclists should take the Sustrans route 41.

ACCESS AND FACILITIES
Of the 15 hides, 12 are accessible by wheelchair and buggy. There's also free electric scooter and manual wheelchair loan. The wheelchair-friendly centre has toilets, baby-changing facilities, restaurant, gallery, shop, and parking. The centre offers 4WD "safaris", visits to the crane school, and guided walks around the reserve.

OPENING TIMES
Winter (November–March) 9.30am to 5pm. Summer (April–October) 9.30am to 5.30pm.

CHARGES
Yes, for non-WWT members.

Long-distance traveller

Eels have long been a part of the River Severn's history, and elver fishers still trawl for them in the river at night. Mysteriously, no one has ever seen an eel spawn – because it takes place at 100–150 fathoms deep, in the Sargasso Sea 6,400km (4,000 miles) away from Britain. The elvers grow as they swim towards Europe, arriving when they are around three years old. They either stay in tidal lagoons or, like the elvers of the Severn, make their way up rivers to live in fresh water.

Main: One of the many bustling pools at Slimbridge that allow the public to see wildlife at close range.

Left: Bewick's swans enjoy a greeting ceremony between families.

Right (left to right): European eels live in the waters of the Severn; the spectacular view from Sloane Tower.

Right panel (top and bottom): Wigeon gather at Slimbridge; the Severn Bore, a large tidal wave that sweeps up the river, brings food for the waterfowl.

Bewick's swans are especially dramatic under the evening floodlights, but the geese attract most birdwatchers; it's fun to pick out bean, barnacle, and pink-footed geese mixed up with so many white-fronts from continental Europe. In some years there are even very rare lesser white-fronted geese. You can search for these strangers in comfort from Sloane Tower, which provides panoramic views across the entire reserve. On the pastures the scene is dominated by flocks of wigeons, which advance on foot across the fields, grazing sweet grasses and shoots. Rich-brown females set off the blue-grey-bodied, pink-breasted males, each with a blaze of palest primrose on the forehead. Few ducks match the wigeons for visual appeal, or for their wild chorus of whistles if they are disturbed into flight. Out on the estuary, thousands of gulls gather to roost. Those that feed inland fly out in the evening and, when this coincides with the high-tide roost of diners from the beaches, 10,000 black-headed gulls and 7,000 lesser black-backed gulls create an amazing spectacle.

WHERE ELSE TO SEE
BIRDS AT CLOSE QUARTERS

Slimbridge is the perfect wildlife reserve for accessibility: it has a large, educational visitor centre, walkways that bisect the habitat areas, and lots of hides. It's possible to see many of the animals at close range, and to feed the captive birds. Several other well-managed sites in the UK also aim to make the wildlife experience more accessible.

Welney is one of the UK's most popular wildlife sites, with around 30,000 visitors during the winter swan season. Its observatories, heated hides, and guided tours are among the easiest ways to see the Ouse Washes, and increase your knowledge. [SE]

The **London Wetland Centre** (see pp.16–17) may just be the best urban wetland centre in Europe. It has a unique "bird airport" observatory, six hides, and an adventure area where children can enjoy mini-beast safaris and pond-dipping sessions. [SE]

Llanelli is the national wetland centre for Wales, and it has some fun ways to see wildlife, including canoe safaris and bike trails (you can hire the bikes). On a wet day, the indoor interactive Millennium Discovery Centre brings you closer to the wildlife. [W]

Slimbridge occupies 365 hectares (900 acres) of water meadows, bordering the mud flats of the Severn.

THROUGH THE YEAR
SLIMBRIDGE

Spring sees the movement of wading birds such as lapwings, dunlins, redshanks, and curlews, as well as swallows and sand martins. Listen for the noisy call of sedge warblers, and for whitethroats in the hedgerows and thickets.

In **summer**, you might see shelducks on the marsh, and there is a chance of a kingfisher. Slimbridge is the only place in Europe where you can see, among the exotic captive birds, all six species of flamingo.

Autumn is good for returning wading birds of many kinds – look in the enclosures for water rails. Starling numbers increase and large flocks can be seen swirling overhead in dramatic shapes before settling to roost.

Below: Flamingo chicks are a popular sight in summer at Slimbridge.

JAN
FEB
MAR
APR
MAY
JUN
JUL
AUG
SEP
OCT
NOV
DEC

VETERAN TREES

WHERE
Sherwood Forest, Nottinghamshire;
www.forestry.gov.uk

CONTACT
Sherwood Pines Forest Park, Edwinstowe,
Nottinghamshire NG21 9JL
Recreation Rangers, tel: 01623 822447;
enquiries.sherwood@forestry.gsi.gov.uk

GETTING THERE
Sherwood Pines Forest Park is off the B6030
between the A6075 and the A616, 32km
(20 miles) from Nottingham, near to Kings
Clipstone, formerly known as Old Clipstone).
Follow the brown tourist signs for Sherwood
Pines Forest Park, between Old Clipstone and
Ollerton. To take a bus to the forest, call the
Buses Hotline on 0870 6082608.

ACCESS AND FACILITIES
All the forest walks and cycling trails start at
the visitor centre, which has a full range of
facilities, including toilets and refreshments.
The centre is fully wheelchair friendly and
there are surfaced paths to the Major Oak.

OPENING TIMES
The forest is open all year round; the visitor
centre is open every day from 8am to dusk.

CHARGES
Charge for car parking only.

FOREVER LINKED WITH THE NAME OF ROBIN HOOD, the legendary medieval outlaw, Sherwood Forest was one of the royal hunting forests created by King William I after his victory over the English in 1066. It was never a continuous tract of woodland, but a "wood pasture", with areas of grassland, sandy heath, and oakwood.

Astoundingly, some of its trees are almost as old. The Major Oak in Birklands Wood – the only surviving large area of woodland in Sherwood – was a huge, ancient tree when it was first described by Major Hayman Rooke in 1790, and the trunk's immense 10m (33ft) girth has barely increased since. Tree girth is one of the best indicators of age, and it suggests

> Surviving for 500 or even 1,000 years, some of the ancient trees of Sherwood are among the oldest living organisms on Earth. Their hollow trunks form refuges for all manner of of woodland animals, especially in winter.

that the tree is between 800 and 1,000 years old. Such a lifespan seems almost incredibly long, but trees can live longer. Some Californian bristlecone pines are known to be nearly 5,000 years old, and several British churchyard yew trees may be well over 2,000 years old.

The Major Oak certainly looks ancient, with its hollow trunk and lower branches supported by steel poles. These signs of decay might seem to threaten its imminent demise, but it is clear from the 1790 description that it has been in this state for at least two centuries. In fact, the fungi that eat out the dead wood at the heart of a hollow tree leave the outer wood and bark as a living shell, and since a broad, hollow trunk is stronger than slender, solid trunk of the same weight, such trees often survive storms that destroy much younger trees.

They may also save energy by dying back at the crown, creating the "stag-headed" effect that reduces the tree's vulnerability. Ancient forestry practice played a part, as many trees had their branches lopped to encourage new growth, in a technique called "pollarding". This prolonged the life of the tree by lowering its centre of gravity, making it less likely to blow over. These ancient pollards are best seen in winter, when there is no foliage to obscure their shape. Such veteran trees are among the national monuments of Britain.

Main: A gnarled ancient yew tree in the forest. Some yews in the UK are believed to be over 2,000 years old.
Below (left to right): At home in the trees: a noctule bat; a great spotted woodpecker; a tawny owl.
Inset: Sherwood Forest covers 180 hectares (450 acres), with its spectacular ancient oaks still guarding Birklands Wood.

Forest parasite

Forever associated with Christmas, mistletoe is seen on the branches of deciduous trees in the forest – especially ash, hawthorn, and lime. This evergreen is a semi-parasite, taking nutrients from its host tree, but photosynthesizing to make its own carbohydrates. Its seeds are eaten by birds, passing intact through their digestive systems, before being deposited on the branch of another tree; "mistletoe" is derived from the Anglo-Saxon words, *mistel* (dung) and *tan* (twig).

Above: "Chicken of the woods" fungus is mostly found on oak trees.

JAN

FEB

MAR

APR

MAY

JUN

JUL

AUG

SEP

OCT

NOV

DEC

THROUGH THE YEAR
SHERWOOD FOREST

In **spring**, the woodlands around the Major Oak are full of birdsong as woodland birds – including many returned migrants – claim their breeding territories. The abundant insect life provides plenty of food for their nestlings, but these conscientious parents must be wary of sparrowhawks, which also have young mouths to feed.

In **summer**, the forest is a good place to look for woodland butterflies such as the speckled wood, ringlet, and white admiral. At dusk, nightjars can often be heard giving their strange, mechanical "churring" call from patches of heathland within the reserve.

Autumn brings a flush of autumn colour and a host of fungi, including several that live on the veteran trees. Over 200 different species have been recorded growing on the trees and the woodland floor.

WHERE ELSE TO SEE
ANCIENT TREES

Veteran trees are a speciality of Britain, and especially England. In continental Europe it is rare to find a tree more than 200 years old, but in England trees twice this age are common, especially in churchyards, old parkland, and ancient woodlands. Many grow in hedgerows, where they mark medieval boundaries.

The oldest-known trees are yews. Those of **Kingley Vale** in West Sussex (*see pp.310–311*) are at least 500 years old, and many churchyard yews may be much older. [SE]

The yew in **Much Marcle** churchyard, Herefordshire, is at least 1,000 years old. [M]

There are many ancient oaks in **Windsor Great Park**, Berkshire (*see pp.258–259*), and **The New Forest** in Hampshire (*see pp.174–175*). **Epping Forest**, on the borders of London and Essex, contains many venerable trees, most of which were pollarded in the past. [SE]

Wistman's Wood in Devon (*see pp.160–161*) dates back to prehistoric times. [SW]

WHERE
Belfast Lough RSPB Reserve, Belvoir Park Forest, Belfast, Antrim, Northern Ireland BT8 7QT.

CONTACT
RSPB Belfast Lough, tel: 02891 479009; belfast.lough@rspb.org.uk

GETTING THERE
The reserve is in Belfast Harbour Estate (10 minutes from central Belfast). Two entrances are signposted along the A2 (Belfast to Holywood road). From the Dee Street entrance the reserve car park is a further 3.2km (2 miles) and from the Tillysburn entrance it is1.6km (1 mile).

ACCESS AND FACILITIES
The reserve has two hides and a cosy observation room. The observation room and one hide have good access for wheelchair users. Facilities include a car park, full-access toilets, and an information centre.

OPENING TIMES
The two outdoor hides are always open. The observation room is open Tuesday–Sunday, from 9am–5pm.

CHARGES
None.

The black-tailed godwit

The black-tailed godwits that spend the winter on the reserve come all the way from Iceland. They rarely breed in the UK, where there are fewer than 40 pairs. Many waders can be tricky to identify, but black-tailed godwits are easier than most: the black tail of their name is only really visible when they fly, but you can always spot their long straight bills, stilt-length legs, and – in February – pretty grey plumage. In spring and summer they sport beautiful deep-red underparts.

Left: A ring-billed gull makes its distinctive call: a shrill "oooww" followed by a series of short "a-a-as".

Right (left to right): The red-breasted merganser diving duck; a common tern stretches its wings; a teal on the waters of the Lough; a view of Belfast Lough RSPB reserve, which is a sheltered lagoon off the main lough.

Main: Seals on their way along the coast rest on the islets of Belfast Lough. **Far right:** Oblivious to passing ships, herons, gulls, and black-tailed godwits mingle at the reserve.

LIFE AT THE CITY LIMITS

BELFAST LOUGH IS AN OASIS OF CALM just outside Belfast city centre. In February, the first thing you notice might be a gentle group of light-bellied brent geese floating gracefully on the water, or the bobbing heads and somnolent silhouettes of harbour seals. At high tide, however, the deeper water teems with birds: great northern and red-throated divers, grebes, and large numbers of sea ducks – long-tailed ducks, scaups, goldeneyes, eiders, scoters, and the tufty-headed, red-breasted mergansers. Scaups seem to love the lough, and sometimes you can see more than 500 in February, the white stripes around their bodies looking like wide bandages.

On one side of the lough, the RSPB manages a reserve, the centrepiece of which is a large brackish lagoon. Wildfowls and waders gather on the lagoon at high tide, and the star species in February are the leggy black-tailed godwits, which poke about the mudflats with their long, fine bills, looking for worms and molluscs. They come

JAN

FEB

MAR

APR

MAY

JUN

JUL

AUG

SEP

OCT

NOV

DEC

Above: Swifts fly over the Lough constantly in spring.

THROUGH THE YEAR
BELFAST LOUGH

Passage waders in **spring** include greenshanks, common sandpipers, and whimbrels, as well as the much loved black-tailed godwits. You may be lucky and chance upon a garganey. Swallows and swifts hawk over the lagoon, while the common terns are busily courting. Look out for young foxes – there is a managed population of this predator at the Lough.

In **summer**, the common and Arctic terns breed on the reserve – head to one of the hides for close-up views of them raising their young. The observation room also brings wonderful views of reed buntings, linnets, and greenfinches.

Every **autumn** migrant flocks arrive to take advantage of the easy food-pickings at Belfast Lough. The black-tailed godwits are joined by overstcatchers, redshanks, dunlins, and, curlews with their elegant, long, curved bills.

Over 180 different species of birds can be found on the 13-hectare (32-acre) RSPB reserve beside Belfast Lough.

WHERE ELSE TO SEE
WETLAND LAGOONS

There are a number of wildlife areas in the UK that feature lagoons and their associated wildlife.

Widewater Lagoon, Shoreham, West Sussex, is an area of brackish water landlocked by a shingle bank and home to herons, swans, oystercatchers, and redshanks. **Titchfield Haven** in Hampshire, behind the Solent, also has a large population of black-tailed godwits and a few bitterns. [SE]

Black-tailed godwits can be seen along the **Exe Estuary**, Devon (see pp.286–287), and on **Brownsea Island**, Dorset (see pp.56–57). [SW]

Blithfield Reservoir, just outside Burton upon Trent, Staffordshire, has many of the same winter birds as Belfast Lough, and occasionally rarer grebes, scaups, and smews. You need to apply for permits to access the better, northern half of the reserve; otherwise take binoculars to the causeway. [M]

incredibly close to the heated observation room overlooking the reserve in winter, and there is no better site in Britain for seeing this otherwise rarely seen species. The wetland formed when the area was enclosed from the sea and used for dumping silt dredged from the lough. Birds soon spotted its potential and started to use it, until eventually the lagoon was actively developed into a natural habitat more attractive to a wide range of birds and animals. Today it is considered to be one of the richest bird reserves in Ireland.

Wigeons, teals, and shovelers may be joined by vagrants such as the North American green-winged teal, which sometimes overwinters here. This estuarine habitat attracts many species to feed, and the numbers of birds present on the reserve's lagoon tends to be tide-dependent. At high tide, large numbers of gulls come in to roost; look among them for the rarer "white-winged" gulls such as the glaucous and Iceland gull. The younger birds appear to be all-white – they have no black in their wings – which is why they are collectively referred to as "white-winged". Look even closer, and you may spot one or two rare ring-billed gulls from North America hiding among them.

WINTER STARLING ROOSTS

SOME WILDLIFE EXPERIENCES ARE SO EXTRAORDINARY that they defy comprehension. A broad swathe of wild flowers may dazzle the eye, or the leap of a migrating salmon make your heart skip a beat, but you can understand why or how these things arise. The aerial ballet of starlings going to roost is of a quite different order. It is both dazzling and even heart-stopping but, for most of us, it is above all a joyous, defiant mystery.

Some winter starling roosts are colossal, with more than a million birds gathering to spend the night together for warmth and safety in numbers. But small can be beautiful too, and all over Britain, local starlings put on performances that draw the crowds. One of the best is to be seen over Slapton Ley on the south Devon coast, where the reedbeds attract up to 75,000 birds each night outside the breeding season. In February the nights draw in early, so you need to arrive by about 4pm to catch the first flocks arriving, shortly before dusk.

WHERE
Slapton Ley National Nature Reserve, Slapton, Kingsbridge, Devon TQ7 2QP; www.slnnr.org.uk

CONTACT
Slapton Ley Field Centre, tel: 01548 580466; enquiries.sl@field-studies-council.org

GETTING THERE
By car, the reserve is accessed via minor roads from the A379, 30km (18 miles) east of Plymouth, 15km (9 miles) south of Totnes, and 10km (6¼ miles) east of Kingsbridge. The nearest train stations are in Totnes and Plymouth. A bus service runs from Plymouth.

ACCESS AND FACILITIES
The car park near Torcross has toilets and a hide adapted for disabled access. There are hides and a 2.5km (1½ mile) nature trail; guided walks are organized by the Field Centre. The starlings roost happens in the Ireland Bay reedbed. The nearest refreshments are at Slapton and Torcross, 0.5 km (⅓ mile) away. There are toilets and picnic sites at the A379 car parks.

OPENING TIMES
Open all year round.

CHARGES
None.

Vast flocks, several thousand strong, swirl through the night air in a breathtaking aerial dance.

Dwindling populations

The spectacle of starlings swirling overhead in what is poetically known as a "murmuration" was once common in towns and cities. Yet breeding populations have drastically declined, especially in urban areas, largely because starling nest sites in roof spaces are being eliminated by modern roofing techniques. However, most of the birds that roost in rural areas in winter are seasonal migrants from Europe, attracted by the mild winter climate, so their aerial displays should continue to amaze us well into the future.

Main: A roosting starling flock is a breathtaking sight.

Panel (above left): The view across Slapton Sands.

Left: The vast, open skies of Slapton Ley.

Right (left to right): A starling flock roosting in trees; the winter plumage of a male adult starling; a roosting flock can often look like a shoal of fish.

As the flock gathers over the reedbeds, other flocks arrive to join it, swelling its numbers until there are several thousand starlings flying in tight formation. And then it begins. From being a mass of birds, the flock is transformed into an immense super-organism in which each individual becomes subordinated to some instinctive choreography of the air. They swirl through the sky in looping, fluid shapes, like a vast shoal of fish in a tropical sea.

The flock can tighten to a knot, then expand in a split second to apparently fill the air, surging overhead with a crackling hiss of massed wings. Sometimes a sparrowhawk or peregrine appears, but often seems mesmerized by the spectacle and unable to latch onto a target. Then suddenly it all ends. As if sucked down a drain, part of the flock pours out of air into the reedbed, disappearing in an instant. The rest billow up and drop down again to allow more to cascade into the roost. Bit by bit the airborne flock dwindles until the last group dives for cover. They are gone.

WHERE ELSE TO SEE
STARLING ROOSTS

Despite recent serious population declines, starlings are still common throughout the British Isles, and their aerial performances are a regular feature of the winter scene. They usually occur over woodlands, shelter belts, and reedbeds, but the birds may also roost on pylons and in derelict buildings.

The largest starling roost is the reedbed at **Westhay Moor** on the Somerset Levels, which in some years attracts up to eight million birds. The area is a nature reserve, but its popularity with visitors at roosting time means that the site can get overcrowded. [SW]

One of best-known roosting sites is the ruined West Pier at **Brighton** in East Sussex. Here the birds often swirl against the backdrop of the sun setting over the sea, creating an unforgettable spectacle. [SE]

There is a large reedbed starling roost near the Wildfowl & Wetland Trust site at **Slimbridge** (*see pp.34–35*) in Gloucestershire. The reserve at **Marazion Marsh** in Cornwall also includes a large reedbed that attracts thousands of starlings on winter evenings. [SW]

THROUGH THE YEAR
SLAPTON LEY

In **spring** Slapton Ley reserve welcomes thousands of migrant birds from further south. They may include rare vagrants such as golden orioles as well as passage migrants that drop in to feed before continuing their journey. April also sees the mass spawning of fish in the channel of Slapton Ley itself.

An evening walk through the reserve in **summer** is likely to be rewarded by the sight of glow worms in the grassy banks. By day the insect life includes a wide variety of butterflies, some attracted by the maritime plants that bloom on the shingle ridge.

On dark **autumn** nights thousands of eels leave the Ley via the weir at Torcross on their way to the tropical Atlantic to breed. The water also provides a hunting ground for ospreys, while the reedbeds shelter big flocks of pied wagtails.

Below: Peregrine falcons are often found around starling roosts.

JAN

FEB

MAR

APR

MAY

JUN

JUL

AUG

SEP

OCT

NOV

DEC

SCOTLAND IN MINIATURE

OF ALL THE BRITISH ISLANDS, ARRAN MUST BE THE MOST SPECTACULAR destination for nature lovers. Whether you're an animal, plant, or geology enthusiast, Arran will never fail to disappoint. It is one of the many islands in the Firth of Clyde between Ayrshire and Kintyre, which are Scotland's most southerly isles, but still retain many aspects of Scotland's highlands and lowlands. You can understand why this stunning island is known as "Scotland in Miniature". It has a vast wealth of habitats, from dramatic, rugged mountains in the north to gently rolling hills, carved valleys, and woodlands in the south. A trip here at any time of the year is wonderful, but winter is especially rewarding.

WHERE
Isle of Arran, Scotland;
www.ayrshire-arran.com

CONTACT
Countryside Ranger Service, Brodick Castle and Country Park, Isle of Arran, tel: 01770 302462. Ayrshire and Arran Tourist Board, tel: 0845 2255121; info@ayrshire-arran.com

GETTING THERE
There's a daily ferry service from Ardrossan (North Ayrshire) to Brodick, which takes 55 minutes, and another service from Claonaig to Lochranza. For details of all ferry services contact www.calmac.co.uk Regular buses connect from the ferries around the island, contact Stagecoach on Arran, tel: 0141 3326811.

ACCESS AND FACILITIES
Contact individual sites for access details, and the Arran Tourist board for specific information (details above). Brodick Castle (www.nts.org.uk) has facilities and some access for wheelchair users (notably Wilma's Walk).

OPENING TIMES
Contact individual sites for details.

CHARGES
Admission fee to Brodick Castle (free to NTS members).

Scanning the wide skies above may reward you with spectacular views of soaring golden eagles, which practise their impressive display flights in February.

The Gulf Stream ensures that winters are usually mild, making the north's wild, mountainous glens surprisingly busy in February. You may catch fleeting views of white ptarmigan and red grouse across the moors, while the awesome golden eagles soar overhead. Red deer roam in large herds and you've got a good chance of spotting them just north of the String Road, which cuts across the island from Brodick on the east coast. In extremely bad weather deer sometimes wander through villages.

The many lochs and tarns are a welcome home for birds. Mallard, shelduck, goosander, and eider are a few of the resident species, and these are joined in winter by many others, including goldeneye, teal, and wigeon. The larger areas of moorland support a large population of hen harriers; Machrie Moor is a good place to see them with other moorland birds. In the leafy woodlands on the south of the island, you may spot a red squirrel. Grey squirrels have never been brought to the island, so the rare red species thrives on Arran. One of the best places to look is in the grounds of Brodick Castle. Otters can sometimes be seen down on the shoreline, especially in February, when the young are born. Although they readily hunt in salt water, they are not sea otters, as commonly misidentified.

Main: The calm, western bays of Arran are sheltered by the Kilbrannan Sound and the Mull of Kintyre.
Below (left to right): Rock ptarmigans are white in winter and brown in summer; otters feed on fish around the west coast; the mountain Cir Mhor, meaning "big comb", in reference to its likeness to a cockscomb. **Inset:** A golden eagle.

Island divers

Arran has become one of the best places in the UK to see three different species of divers, or loons as they are sometimes called, because of their yodelling breeding calls. In winter you can see red-throated (*shown below*), black-throated, and great northern divers as they come and shelter on inland and coastal lochs. Although these elegant birds may not be in their smart breeding plumages at this time of year, they are still a delight to watch.

Above: *Allium ursinum* – wild garlic – carpets the woodland in spring.

JAN
FEB
MAR
APR
MAY
JUN
JUL
AUG
SEP
OCT
NOV
DEC

THROUGH THE YEAR
ISLE OF ARRAN

Some of the first flowers in **spring** to appear are wood anemone and golden saxifrage; later, many woodland floors are covered in ramsons, bluebells, and bugle.

In **summer** Arran's damp meadows are alive with stands of purple loosestrife, meadowsweet, valerian, and hemp agrimony. The unusual Arran whitebeam is a tree species unique to the island.

The **autumn** brings chances of sighting migrating ospreys, and it is worth visiting the Cock of Arran, just north of Lochranza, where basking sharks can sometimes be seen offshore.

WHERE ELSE TO SEE
ISLAND WILDLIFE

All of the islands off the British coasts have much to offer – they are often dramatic landscapes with unusual and changing wildlife.

The **Farne Islands** (*see pp.126–127*) have around 100,000 pairs of wintering seabirds, including puffins and guillemots, and one of Europe's largest grey seal populations. [N]

The **Isle of Skye** is the largest island of the Inner Hebrides. Its northern tip provides a dramatic backdrop for seabirds, including fulmars, kittiwakes, and shags, and its waters are home to Britain's largest jellyfish, the moon jellyfish. [SC]

The **Isle of Mull** (*see pp.226–227*), another Inner Hebridean island, is well known both for its seabirds and its birds of prey, which hunt over the moors and fish over the lochs and sea. A particular attraction are the breeding pairs of reintroduced white-tailed sea eagles. [SC]

WHERE
Exmoor National Park, Devon/Somerset;
www.exmoor-nationalpark.gov.uk

CONTACT
National Park Authority, Exmoor House,
Dulverton, TA22 9HL, tel: 01398 323665;
info@exmoor-nationalpark.gov.uk; Dulverton
Visitor Centre, tel: 01398 323841;

GETTING THERE
Exmoor is easily accessible by road from the
M5, junction 27. There is also a bus network
through the park (www.travelinesw.com or
tel: 0871 2002233). The nearest train
stations are at Barnstaple, Taunton, and
Tiverton Parkway.

ACCESS AND FACILITIES
There are visitor centres with facilities at
Cross Street, Combe Martin, EX34 0DH;
Dunster Steep, Dunster, TA24 6SG; Fore
Street, Dulverton, TA22 9EX; Blackmoor Gate,
Lynmouth, EX35 6EQ; and the Old School,
High Street, Porlock, TA24 8QD. For
information on opening times, events, and
on wheelchair access throughout the park,
visit www.exmoor-nationalpark.gov.uk

OPENING TIMES
Open all year round.

CHARGES
None.

The Dartmoor pony

Dartmoor (*see also pp.244–245*) has its own
native breed of ponies, which have lived there
for many centuries. They are around the same
size as Exmoors, and are equally tough, but they
are good-tempered and approachable. They
can be almost any colour and many have white
"blazes" on their foreheads giving them a less
distinctive look, although their stocky build,
deep bodies, thick neck, long manes, and
short legs make them instantly recognizable.

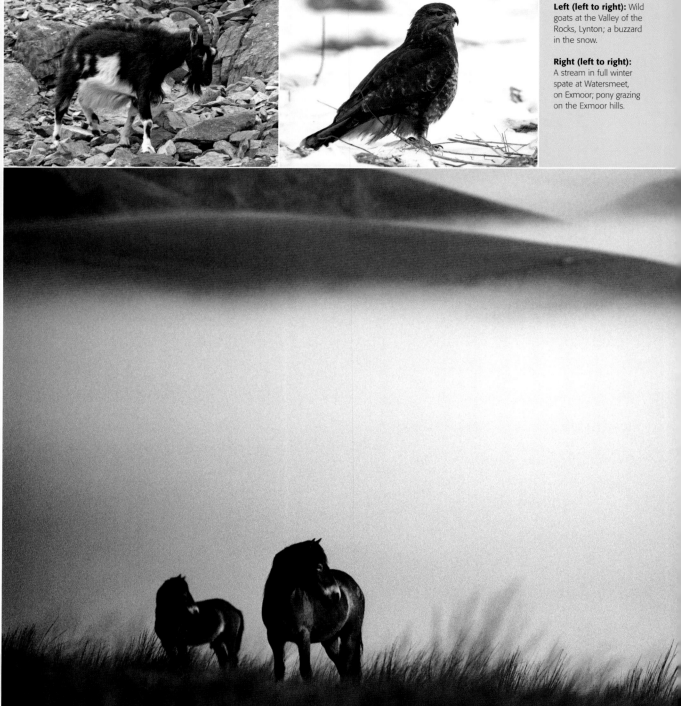

Left (left to right): Wild
goats at the Valley of the
Rocks, Lynton; a buzzard
in the snow.

Right (left to right):
A stream in full winter
spate at Watersmeet,
on Exmoor; pony grazing
on the Exmoor hills.

Main and far right: A pair of Exmoor ponies on a fog-shrouded moor.

WILD EXMOOR

PONIES LIVE WILD IN SEVERAL AREAS OF BRITAIN, but the rolling heather moorlands and stark coastal
cliffs of Exmoor provide their most dramatic habitat. Here they are essential parts of the moorland landscape,
where their grazing and browsing have played an important part in the ecosystem for thousands of years.

The Exmoor pony is the most primitive of the UK's native ponies, and its oldest breed – predating the
arrival of the Romans in Britain. It is an extremely hardy little pony, resistant to disease and with great powers
of endurance, and its long survival on the cold, wet – but beautiful – moor with little food or shelter is testimony
to its strength. In February you can really see how the pony has evolved to survive: it grows a soft, woolly
undercoat, topped by a longer, oily, water-repellent outer coat. Look for the broad fan of hair at the base of
the tail – known as the "ice tail" or "snow chute" – that helps channel cold rain away from the body.

Above: Looking from the heather-clad moor over the Devon countryside.

> There are still areas
> where climate and
> soil have resisted all
> attempts to plough,
> where the deer and
> the ponies hold sway.

THROUGH THE YEAR
EXMOOR

Exmoor was designated a National Park in 1954, and covers a 692 sq km (267 sq mile) area that falls within Devon and Somerset. Its mixture of woodland, scrub, bracken, grassland, bog, and upland heath makes it home to many rare plants and animals.

In **spring** the moor's seven rare species of whitebeam – none found outside Britain – are covered with clusters of white flowers. Look for them in old coastal oakwoods such as Watersmeet, Woody Bay, and Culbone. Look out for stonechats, whinchats, wheatears, and rare birds of prey such as the merlin.

Exmoor's native red deer are most easily found on higher ground, among the heather, during the **summer**. The smaller roe deer and fallow deer usually hide in darker woodland areas. Look out for some of Britain's rarest butterflies: the heath, marsh, and high brown fritillary butterflies.

The majestic red deer start mating in **autumn**, and the sound of clashing antlers fills the woodlands. The woodlands burst into glorious colour, and their floors are peppered with rare fungi, such as the sandy stilt puffball and ballerina waxcap fungus.

WHERE ELSE TO SEE
WILD PONIES

The national parks of the **New Forest** (*see pp.174–175*), Hampshire [SE], and **Dartmoor**, Devon [SW], are home to thousands of wild ponies.

You can see wild ponies at several sites in Wales: **Black Mountain**, in the Brecon Beacons National Park; the great raised bog of **Cors Caron** at Tregaron (*see pp.190–191*); and on the saltmarshes of the **Burry Inlet**, on the north shore of the **Gower Peninsula** (*see pp.122–123*). The rare Carneddau ponies can be found on the hills of **Snowdonia** (*see pp.172–173*). [W]

The hills of the **Lake District** have provided habitat for rare fell herds for around 2,000 years. These stocky ponies are predominantly black, with full manes and tails, and "feathering" on the legs. [N]

Always some shade of brown or bay, the pony's distinctive appearance comes from its wide forehead with large, pale-ringed eyes, its mealy nose, strong, thick neck, broad back, and sturdy, short legs. The pale rings around the eyes ("hooded" or "toad" eyes) are actually thick fleshy surrounds to protect the eyes against the frequent rain that lashes the moor in winter. Their teeth are also unusually suited to the environment – an extra molar ensures they can easily chew coarse, thorny plants. Even the nose and ears have evolved efficiently: small ears keep heat loss to a minimum, while large nasal passages help to warm the freezing air before it reaches the lungs.

Exmoor was used as a training ground during World War II, and great numbers of ponies were killed: only some 50 survived. Local people rescued the remaining herds but numbers remained low until the early 1980s. The total now stands at between 1,000 and 2,000; these are caught once a year and branded for conservation reasons. However gently they nuzzle their young, the ponies you see today are direct descendants of those that once pulled mighty chariots for the fearsome Celts. The ponies are approachable, but can kick, so stand well clear of their hind legs.

JAN

FEB

MAR

APR

MAY

JUN

JUL

AUG

SEP

OCT

NOV

DEC

THE HEART OF BROADLAND

THE NORFOLK BROADS ARE JUSTLY FAMOUS both for the beauty of their landscape, with their intricate system of waterways graced by sailing boats, motor cruisers, and windmills, and their abundant wildlife. Hickling is the largest of the broads, stretching over 200 hectares (500 acres); like the other broads, it is thought to have been formed by peat and clay-digging and is only around 1.5m (5ft) deep with a gravel bottom. It includes one of the largest areas of open water in the whole of East Anglia, fringing marshes, reedbeds, sedge beds, and patches of scrub, sprinkled with tracts of wet alder, willow, and birch "carr" woodland. Hickling offers the best birdwatching in the whole of the Broads, including reedbed specialities such as bearded tits, bitterns, and water rails – all resident breeders – and a very wide range of spring and autumn migrants. The winter landscape may seem empty by comparison, but you just need to look more carefully: the quality is wonderful.

WHERE
Hickling Broad National Nature Reserve, Stubb Road, Hickling, Norwich NR12 0BW; www.norfolkwildlifetrust.org.uk

CONTACT
Norfolk Wildlife Trust, tel: 01603 625540; wild@norfolkwildlifetrust.org.uk

GETTING THERE
Hickling Broad is 6.5km (4 miles) south of Stalham, off the A149 Stalham to Caister-on-Sea road, Norfolk. From Hickling village follow the "brown badger" tourist signs. Buses from both Norwich and Cromer stop in Hickling village; the reserve is a 20-minute walk away.

ACCESS AND FACILITIES
There are hides overlooking pools and a boardwalk trail suitable for pushchairs and wheelchairs. At this time of year, the nearest public toilets are in Hickling village. The reserve's visitor centre has full-access toilets and refreshments.

OPENING TIMES
The nature reserve is open all year round, 10am–5pm. The visitor centre opens 10am–5pm, April–September.

CHARGES
Small charge for entry, except for children and NWT members.

Hickling Broad is the largest of the Norfolk Broads, with over 200 hectares (500 acres) of open water, and 485 hectares (1,200 acres) of wildlife-friendly land.

Return of the cranes

Much of the UK breeding population of the common crane (*Grus grus*) can be seen wintering around Hickling Broad. Cranes recolonized the Norfolk Broads in the 1980s after an absence of around 400 years. Today, reintroduction programmes are in progress, aimed at boosting their population in East Anglia by rearing eggs imported from wild birds in Germany. The elevated watchpoint at Stubb Mill provides excellent views of the birds.

Wildfowl include whooper and Bewick's swans, pink-footed geese, goldeneyes, smews, and goosanders, and if you head over to the special viewing area by Stubb Mill around mid-afternoon, you'll get some superb views of birds of prey as they fly in to their roost sites. Marsh harriers are guaranteed, with over 40 birds often recorded, while hen harriers, sparrowhawks, and merlins are likely. An even greater thrill comes from seeing the huge common cranes: despite their name, they are very rare in Britain, and this is the best place to see them. Standing 1m (3ft) tall, with broad wings spanning as much as 2.2m (over 7ft), they are even bigger than the grey herons.

The grazing of hardy eastern European ponies, cattle, and sheep at Hickling Broad is a key tool in managing the site and keeping the restored areas of the reserve clear of invasive vegetation. Reed and sedge beds are regularly mown and water levels maintained at optimum for the wading and breeding birds.

Main: Hickling Broad is a medieval man-made lake.

Above (top and bottom): A marsh harrier in flight; a golden plover in winter plumage forages for food.

Left panel (top and bottom): Lapwings can be seen year-round, but are most abundant in winter; the barn owl has a distinctive heart-shaped face.

Below: Large pike are to be found in Hickling's waters.

WHERE ELSE TO SEE
FENS AND REEDBEDS

Fens and large areas of reeds are a scarce and threatened habitat throughout Europe. Britain does have a significant proportion of the total, but there are few very large reedbeds.

Strumpshaw Fen RSPB Reserve, in the Broads nearer Norwich (*see pp.152–153*), and **Wicken Fen** Reserve in Cambridgeshire (*see pp.204–205*) both contain rich collections of wetland plants and animals, many of them rare. [SE]

Stodmarsh National Nature Reserve in the Stour Valley, Kent, is a wonderful place for seeing birds, including hen harriers and ducks in winter, as well as rarities. Look for the insect-eating greater bladderwort plant in the dykes. [SE]

The **Somerset Levels**, extending from Bridgwater Bay into the heart of Somerset, include many wildlife reserves protecting the great network of ditches, grazing marshes, and peatland, where you can see masses of wildflowers, dragonflies, wading birds, and otters, among much other wildlife. [SW]

THROUGH THE YEAR
HICKLING BROAD

Spring bird migrants range from Temminck's stints and other rare waders to scarce black terns, little gulls, spoonbills, and ospreys. From March onwards, the golden yellow flowers of marsh marigolds appear on the site, with early marsh orchids and water violets joining them in May.

In **summer**, you can enjoy the yellow iris flowers lighting up the banks of the broad and look for swallowtail butterflies between mid-May and June (with smaller numbers in August) along the Weaver's Way path. You may also find the equally striking green-and-black caterpillars feeding on the forked leaves of milk parsley plants.

Summer visitors that stay to nest include handsome little garganey ducks, common and little terns, and reed, sedge, and grasshopper warblers. As well as being a good time for checking out migrant birds, **autumn** sees the gradual build-up of birds of prey and cranes at the roost site, from October onwards.

Below: The southern hawker dragonfly lays its eggs in pond vegetation.

JAN
FEB
MAR
APR
MAY
JUN
JUL
AUG
SEP
OCT
NOV
DEC

WHERE
Poole Harbour, Dorset;
www.pooletourism.com

CONTACT
Poole Welcome Centre, Poole Quay, Poole,
Dorset, BH15 1HJ; tel: 01202 253253;
info@pooletourism.com
Dorset Wildlife Trust, tel: 01305 264620;
mail@dorsetwildlife.co.uk

GETTING THERE
By car, take the A31 or A352 to Poole
Harbour. Travel to Wareham by train or coach.

ACCESS AND FACILITIES
The best way to see the wintering birds in
the Harbour is by boat: the RSPB run cruises
from Poole Quay about every six weeks in
winter; book early via Brownsea Ferries
(01929 462383). There are many places to
enjoy general facilities around the harbour.
Visit www.pooletourism.com for information
on parking, including blue-badgeholder-
reserved spaces. For Brownsea Island and
Arne, see pages 56–57 and138–139.

OPENING TIMES
The many wildlife sites have varying opening
times. No vehicular access to Poole Park
6am–10am Monday to Saturday.

CHARGES
Charges may be levied at some reserves.

Home to egret chicks

The thriving colony of little egrets on Brownsea
Island is a recent arrival. These beautiful white
herons were once only very rare visitors to Britain,
with a mere nine birds recorded up to 1950. After
a gradual increase, there was a dramatic influx
starting in 1989. By 1996 the first pair bred in
England, at Brownsea Island, and subsequently
spread to other parts of southern England, East
Anglia, and the south coast of Ireland. They feed
along muddy creeks and river channels, and roost
in trees or along the saltmarsh.

Above (left to right): The shingle beach of Poole Harbour; oystercatchers feed in the intertidal zone; avocets winter around the harbour.
Main: The wildlife has the whole of Poole Harbour virtually to itself at dawn.

SAFE HARBOUR FOR BIRDS

O NE OF THE WORLD'S LARGEST NATURAL HARBOURS, Poole Harbour's great sweep encloses 96km (60 miles) of coastline and contains several islands. The wealth of habitats includes huge areas of intertidal sand flats and mud flats, saltmarsh, reedbeds, and woodlands. Many thousands of birds from the far north seek the shelter of the harbour in winter, including waders such as the elegant black-tailed godwits – in internationally important numbers – curlews, grey plovers, knots, and dunlins; wildfowl, such as brent geese and red-breasted mergansers; and scarce grebes. By the shipping entrance to the harbour, the seaward side of the peninsula at Sandbanks can be a good place to see sea-ducks, particularly eiders and common scoters, divers, grebes, and auks. On the western and southern shores of the peninsula known as the Isle of Purbeck, two reserves protect outstanding lowland heath: RSPB Arne (see pp.138–139) and the National Nature Reserve of Studland and Godlingston Heath. Their birdlife is particularly rich.

You can't help noticing the beautiful little egrets: the black of their legs contrasts so sharply with the bright yellow of their feet, as if they had been dipped in paint.

Poole Park, just behind the quay, is a major winter site for Canada geese, tufted ducks, and pochards, and, especially in cold weather, other scarcer ducks such as scaups, goosanders, red-breasted mergansers, smews, and goldeneyes. Look on the boating lake for these scarcer species, and for occasional grebes and divers. The many common species of gulls sometimes include much scarcer species, such as yellow-legged, glaucous, or Iceland gulls. It's worth visiting some of the harbour's eight islands: three of them, including Brownsea (see pp.56–57), are home to the beleaguered red squirrel. Head for the four hides on Brownsea that overlook the brackish mud and water of the lagoon, where you can see one of the largest groupings of avocets in Britain: over 1,000 of these graceful black-and-white birds roost here. In the trees nearby, grey herons nest colonially, along with increasing numbers of pristine white little egrets.

Inset: Little egrets grace the harbour in winter.
Below (left to right): A preening red-breasted merganser; dunlins take flight.

WHERE ELSE TO SEE
ESTUARY WILDLIFE

Britain contains many other estuary sites that are renowned for birds and other wildlife, including several near to Poole that you might like to visit on a journey along England's south coast.

Langstone and **Chichester** harbours, farther east on the Hampshire/West Sussex border, also have a huge area of mudflats and saltmarshes. A winter visit will guarantee sightings of many different waders and wildfowl, as well as little egrets. [SE]

Pagham Harbour, a little farther east along the West Sussex coast, has shingle spits, wet grassland, mud, and pools, and is a notable site for migrant birds in spring and autumn. [SE]

Travelling west from Poole, the **Exe Estuary** (see pp.286–287) in Devon is one of the best places to see waders and wildfowl, including flocks of wintering avocets and brent geese. [SW]

THROUGH THE YEAR
POOLE HARBOUR

Spring is a good time to visit the reserves at Arne and Studland, where sprightly little Dartford warblers sing from the tops of gorse bushes before modestly diving out of sight. At Brownsea, the little egrets are at their most splendid from May to June, sporting long, delicate plumes hanging down from the nape.

During **summer** you can enjoy watching the sandwich and common terns that breed on artificial nesting rafts in the lagoon on Brownsea Island. Just after dusk on the heaths, nightjars sing their strange churring song, and snap up beetles in their huge gapes. Take a wildlife-watching boat trip that ventures beyond the harbour, and you may see a few puffins among the breeding seabirds on the Purbeck cliffs.

In **autumn**, the wintering birds begin to return to the shelter of the harbour. It's also a good time to look for red squirrels among Brownsea's pinewoods, less shy as they search out extra food for the winter.

Below: Dorset supports 80 per cent of the south coast's puffins.

JAN

FEB

MAR

APR

MAY

JUN

JUL

AUG

SEP

OCT

NOV

DEC

MARCH

Where to Go: **March**

The onset of spring cannot be denied now, though there may be many false dawns before the days of frost and grey fog are behind us. Frogs and toads gather in shallow ponds in a frenzy of mating and spawning. On the open fields, brown hares box each other's ears as males and females get to know each other more intimately. A sudden rash of molehills reveals unseen activity below ground.

In undisturbed woods, grey herons are nesting. They build great platforms of thick sticks and lay eggs very early in spring: by late March, many have noisy youngsters and the heronries become busy, lively places. Down on the woodland floor, lesser celandines, primroses, and wood anemones add colour to the well-rotted leafmould, in which hungry woodcocks probe deeply for worms.

WETLANDS

RADIPOLE LAKE The rich reedbeds of Radipole reawaken in spring.

PARKS AND GRASSLANDS

LYME PARK Boxing hares perform courtship rituals in March.

WOODLANDS

RANNOCH Woodland, lochs, and moor can be seen at the Black Wood.

RADIPOLE LAKE
WEYMOUTH, DORSET [SW]

This classic urban nature reserve is the place to hear the explosive song of the Cetti's warbler.
See pp.60–61

LYME PARK
STOCKPORT, CHESHIRE [N]

Watch "mad March hares" boxing in the grounds of a magnificent Tudor house.
See pp.62–63

The estate's real charm lies in the rough grassland of the surrounding medieval deer park, where brown hares court in the spring.

KIELDER FOREST
NORTHUMBERLAND [N]

The huge reservoir of Kielder Water lies at the heart of this forest, where you can see sparrowhawks and red squirrels.
See pp.66–67

SOMERSET LEVELS
LANGPORT, SOMERSET

Head for Swell Wood in the West Sedgemoor RSPB reserve to see not only nesting herons but also dainty little egrets; look down to see primroses and other early flowers.
See pp.54–55

REGENT'S PARK
LONDON [SE]

Reed warblers, mistle thrushes, and pied wagtails chatter in the trees in spring, while around 20 herons can be seen nesting by the boating lake.
See pp.54–55

BLACK WOOD OF RANNOCH
PERTH AND KINROSS [SC]

The open woodlands of aspen, holly, and juniper are home to many rare animals and flowers, including capercaillies and the carnivorous Scottish wood ant.
See pp.66–67

Glossy black capercaillies perform dramatic displays, strutting about and leaping in the air while uttering bizarre sounds.

BLACKTOFT SANDS
HUMBERSIDE [N]

Set off early – not only are there water birds to be seen, but the dawn chorus here is rightly famous: reed and sedge warblers, reed buntings, and bearded tits all greet the new day.
See pp.60–61

NORTHWARD HILL
HOO, KENT [SE]

Kent's Hoo peninsula is alive with the noisy calls of herons, as spring dawns in the UK's largest heronry at Northward Hill.
See pp.54–55

SALFORD FOREST PARK
GREATER MANCHESTER [N]

The lakes and riversides here provide a breath of fresh air for city-dwellers.
See pp.54–55

BRECKLAND
NORFOLK/SUFFOLK [SE]

Forest birds here include rare and elusive golden pheasant, goshawks, hobbies, woodcocks, and woodlarks.
See pp.66–67

BLEASDALE
PRESTON, LANCASHIRE [N]

There is a thriving brown hare population in Bleasdale, which benefits from the protection of local farmers.
See pp.62–63

KINGLEY VALE
WEST SUSSEX [SE]

This ancient woodland is one of the finest yew forests in Europe, and has trees that are more than 2,000 years old.
See pp.66–67

LESNES ABBEY WOODS
LONDON [SE]

The 12th-century ruins of Lesnes Abbey are surrounded by an ancient forest filled with daffodils and bluebells in spring.
See pp.58–59

Previous page: A red squirrel foraging for food – perhaps an overlooked cache of nuts from the autumn.

Even though snow may still fall thick and soft in the northern hills, golden eagles, peregrines, and ravens are nesting, and often squabbling above their respective cliffs, being uneasy neighbours; all are spectacular to watch, especially during their electric courtship display flights. Look, too, for red deer moving up to the hills, and the roe deer, still in their dark winter brown coats, but beginning to show a hint of the rusty-red coat that comes with summer. In lowland Britain the sudden appearance, on a mild sunny day, of a bright, pale yellow spot dancing through the garden or along a hedgerow marks the brimstone butterfly, generally the earliest butterfly to emerge from hibernation. The land is warming, and the animals are awakening.

COAST

BRAUNTON BURROWS Britain's first UNESCO biosphere reserve.

UPLANDS

FARNDALE MOOR A daffodil delight in early spring.

ISLANDS

JERSEY The seas around Jersey hide wonders like the cuckoo wrasse.

HAVERGATE ISLAND
ORFORD, SUFFOLK [SE]

Famous for its breeding avocets and terns, this reserve also has a flourishing brown hare population, which is most evident – and entertaining – during their March courtships.
See pp.62–63

THE GOLDEN TRIANGLE
GLOUCESTERSHIRE [SE]

The area around Newent and Dymock used to be served by a "daffodil train" from London, and is still famous for these and other spring flowers.
See pp.58–59

JERSEY
CHANNEL ISLANDS [SW]

Spring is an ideal time to enjoy Jersey's mild climate. This island offers a huge number of wildlife habitats in a small area – or, suit up to explore the fascinating waters around its shores.
See pp.64–65

BRAUNTON BURROWS
DEVON [SW]

Shelter in the dunes of Braunton Burrows, which are studded with miniature flowers in spring, including sand mouse-ear, spring sandwort, and dune pansies.
See pp.68–69

GRASMERE
CUMBRIA [N]

The Lake District has so many beautiful landscapes, but at this time of year, the one that inspired the poet William Wordsworth is a must.
See pp.58–59

SCILLY ISLES
OFF LAND'S END [SW]

Colourful and unusual plants are matched by the birdlife: golden orioles, hoopoes, and woodchat shrikes are among the many spring migrants here. Seals and dolphins swim offshore.
See pp.64–65

THE LIZARD
CORNWALL [SW]

This frost-free habitat has many rare plants that cannot survive elsewhere, including the Cornish heath, and breeding choughs have made a welcome return.
See pp.65–66

FARNDALE MOOR
HUTTON-LE-HOLE, YORKSHIRE [N]

Here on the southern flanks of the North York Moors, a walk alongside the pretty River Dove will reveal that spring is slowly vanishing winter.
See pp.58–59

The heather-clad hills of the North York Moors hide red grouse, meadow pipits, wheatears, and adders, basking in the warm spring sunlight.

BROWNSEA ISLAND
POOLE HARBOUR, DORSET [SW]

One of the last strongholds of the red squirrel in southern Britain; courting pairs leap from branch to branch among the pine woods in March.
See pp.56–57

One of the largest shingle and sand dune bars in Britain, Culbin Sands sees huge flocks of knots, bar-tailed godwits, and oystercatchers.

CULBIN SANDS
MORAY FIRTH [SC]

The sand dunes here line the Moray Firth, and in spring they host migrating birds such as sandwich terns. Dolphins play in the waters of the Firth.
See pp.68–69

QUEEN ELIZABETH FOREST PARK
STIRLING, SCOTLAND [SC]

Ospreys, kestrels, peregrines, and golden eagles quarter the skies here, while badgers come out to forage at night.
See pp.56–57

SCOLT HEAD ISLAND
NORTH NORFOLK [SE]

Resident birds are joined by many migrants in spring, including flycatchers, warblers, and chats. The saltmarshes are considered to be the UK's finest.
See pp.68–69

LINDISFARNE
NORTHUMBERLAND [N]

Stunning beaches, lots of birds, and rockpools filled with delights such as anemones, starfish, and sponges.
See pp.68–69

WHERE
Northward Hill RSPB Reserve, High Halstow, Kent ME3 8DS.

CONTACT
RSPB North Kent Marshes, tel: 01634 222480; northkentmarshes@rspb.org.uk

GETTING THERE
By car, leave the M2 at junction 1 and take the A228 towards Grain, then turn left to High Halstow. Two RSPB car parks are signposted at the T-junction in the village. By train, travel to Strood; trains run every hour from London. Buses run from Strood to High Halstow village (every 30 minutes), from where it is a short walk to the Woodland car park.

ACCESS AND FACILITIES
There are full-access toilets at the Bromhey Farm car park. There are four trails varying in length from 0.8–6.5km ($\frac{1}{2}$–4 miles). The site is not easily accessible for wheelchair users as the tracks are unimproved paths.

OPENING TIMES
Open at all times.

CHARGES
None.

Striking a pose

Grey herons nest colonially, usually in trees, but in more exposed areas of the UK they sometimes nest in bush tops or, rarely, on the ground. Breeding pairs greet each other and respond to others close by using very deliberate postures, such as a "stretch" display (above), where the wings are outstretched, and the head and bill point skywards. Aggression is indicated by an arched neck, raised crest, and erect body plumes. Look out for these postures at Northward Hill in March, as the herons begin the breeding season.

Above (left to right): A little egret tests the water; a sparrowhawk searches for prey; the Northward Hill reserve.
Main: A breeding pair of grey herons.

HERONS AT HOME

JUST NORTH OF HIGH HALSTOW, ON KENT'S HOO PENINSULA, there is a ridge with the most wonderful view across the Thames Estuary marshes. This is the home of a splendid RSPB nature reserve – Northward Hill – a huge area of grazing marsh, woodland, and farmland. If you can follow one of the two circular routes through the wood, you'll hear some particularly weird and wonderful noises in March: the sharp, barking calls and rattling bills of courting and nesting grey herons.

This is the UK's largest heronry, with 100–150 pairs. In recent years the herons have been joined by one of the largest colonies of little egrets in the UK, which first nested here in 2000, but now number more than 100 pairs. Watch over the sanctuary area and you'll see herons flying in and performing their ritual greeting and courtship displays at their big treetop nests. These large birds can look surprisingly pale against the dark woodland canopy at this time of year, while the smaller egrets are almost startlingly white. In March, the shrubs and trees are still largely leafless,

giving you a better chance to see Northward's songbirds, although the migrant warblers will not yet have arrived. The dawn chorus here is an unforgettable experience, with blackbirds, song thrushes, robins, wrens, dunnocks, great tits, and woodpigeons. Nightingales sing from the denser undergrowth later in spring, when the open parts of the wood are carpeted in bluebells.

The longest trail leads out to three new marshes, recently recreated from arable farmland by raising water levels. They have made an immediate impact, with avocets nesting on islands in the newly created lagoons, while lapwings and redshanks breed close by. Marsh harriers hunt over the open countryside, and in March you could see a merlin or peregrine, too, or even a sparrowhawk displaying over its nesting woods. Look out for its unusually slow, rhythmic wingbeats, which precede a series of steep switchbacks and a sudden dive.

Herons fly with remarkable grace for such large, long-legged birds, as their 1.5m (5ft) wingspan takes them swooping through the air.

Inset: The huge grey heron in flight.
Below (left to right): A heron fishing; these heavy birds need large nests.

WHERE ELSE TO SEE
HERONS

Herons love water – you may see them in wetland marshes, reservoirs, estuaries, lakes, or rivers. If you have an ornamental fish pond, you might even be lucky enough to attract one into your garden!

Grey herons nest in a few easily seen places, including **Regent's Park** in London. [SE]

Herons are often seen beside urban lakes and riversides, including **Salford Forest Park**, in Greater Manchester. In the spring you can see them nesting at **Muncaster Castle**, in the Lake District, Cumbria, and the **Waterton Countryside Discovery Centre**, Wakefield, Yorkshire. [N]

West Sedgemoor RSPB Reserve in the Somerset Levels has one of the largest heronries in the UK in Swell Wood. In spring they can be seen building large nests from sticks in the woodland trees. [SW]

The Quoile Pondage nature reserve at **Strangford Lough** (see pp.288–289) in Northern Ireland has a freshwater lagoon overlooked by hides where you can see herons, cormorants, and grebes all year. [NI]

THROUGH THE YEAR
NORTHWARD HILL

In **summer,** hobbies hunt dragonflies over the marsh. You could see the rare white-letter hairstreak butterfly in the woodland, where its caterpillars rely on elms, and perhaps turtle doves on overhead wires.

In **autumn,** swallows gather around farm buildings and on wires before migration and you should see jays flying over the woods with their stores of acorns.

The marshes are full of wildfowl in **winter,** including teals, shovelers, wigeons, and pintails. Hen harriers, kestrels, merlins, and peregrines hunt over the estuary. Wintering thrushes, finches, and buntings – especially redwings and fieldfares – are often seen in the orchards below the wood. One spectacular feature at Northward Hill is the gathering of up to 4,000 rooks as they come to roost in the woodland.

JAN

FEB

MAR

APR

MAY

JUN

JUL

AUG

SEP

OCT

NOV

DEC

Below: Grey heron chicks hatch in late spring.

Left (left to right): Poole Harbour; maritime pine trees on Brownsea Island.

Right (left to right): A carpet of pine cones gnawed by squirrels; a red squirrel feeding on hoarded nuts.

Panel (below right): Squirrels can not only climb but descend trees at speed.

WHERE
Brownsea Island, Poole Harbour, Dorset BH13 7EE; www.nationaltrust.org.uk

CONTACT
National Trust, tel: 01202 707744; brownseaisland@nationaltrust.org.uk

GETTING THERE
Ferries operate from Poole Quay, Sandbanks Jetty, Bournemouth Pier, and Swanage. Contact Brownsea Island Ferries (tel: 01929 462383, www.brownseaislandferries.com), Dorset Cruises (tel: 01202 558550; www.dorsetcruises.co.uk), or Greenslade Pleasure Boats (tel: 01202 631828, www.greensladepleasureboats.co.uk).

ACCESS AND FACILITIES
The island has full-access toilets at the visitor reception, visitor centre, and the Baden-Powell Outdoor Centre. There is a shop and café, both accessible by wheelchair. Tracks on the island can be rough in places, but tractor trailer trails are available for the less mobile.

OPENING TIMES
The island is open from March to November. Booked groups only during the winter.

CHARGES
Yes.

Grey invader

Red squirrels favour conifer woodland, where they enjoy a mixed diet. However, oaks are the predominant tree in lowland Britain, and this suits grey squirrels, because they can live on a diet of acorns alone. This has enabled the greys to build up their numbers to the point where they eat most of the available nut crop in autumn, leaving little for the reds, who then starve. Further north there are more pines and fewer oaks, giving red squirrels the edge they need to survive.

Main: Squirrels are active for most of the day, and have few natural predators, so are easy to spot.

RED SQUIRREL STRONGHOLD

N THE WAKE OF THE LAST ICE AGE, SOME 8,000 YEARS AGO, the rising sea levels that created the North Sea and English Channel also flooded a network of low-lying river valleys in southern England to form the broad expanse of Poole Harbour. In the process, a sandstone hill rising above the valleys was cut off, to become Brownsea Island, and among the animals that found themselves isolated on the island was a recent arrival from Europe, the red squirrel. A few thousand years later this was to prove a blessing, because when the American grey squirrel was introduced to the UK at the turn of the 20th century – with disastrous consequences for its smaller, less aggressive relative – the island was one of the few places in England that it could not colonize. As a result, Brownsea is now one of the last strongholds of the red squirrel in southern Britain. But as you approach Brownsea on the ferry on a bright March morning, the narrow strip of glittering water that separates it from the mainland

Above: A red squirrel shelters under its tail.

JAN
FEB
MAR
APR
MAY
JUN
JUL
AUG
SEP
OCT
NOV
DEC

WHERE ELSE TO SEE
RED SQUIRRELS

Competition from the grey squirrel has driven the red squirrel out of most of England and Wales, and on the British mainland it now lives mainly in Scotland, where it is still fairly common. However, there are a few scattered colonies further south, and it is also widespread in Ireland.

There is a red squirrel colony in **Parkhurst Forest** on the Isle of Wight (see pp.224–225), where – as on Brownsea – the island location prevented a grey squirrel invasion. The forest welcomes visitors, and has a red squirrel viewing hide and safari trail. [SE]

Red squirrels also survive in good numbers on the island of **Anglesey**, off North Wales. [W]

Red squirrels are still doing well in parts of northern England, such as the **Lake District** and the **Formby Pinewoods** Red Squirrel Sanctuary, near Ainsdale Dunes (see pp.88–89), Merseyside. [N]

A good place to see red squirrels in Scotland is the **Queen Elizabeth Forest Park**, Stirling. [SC]

THROUGH THE YEAR
BROWNSEA ISLAND

In **summer** the open heaths of Brownsea are bright with flowers that attract butterflies such as the small copper, the common blue, the silver-studded blue, and the green hairstreak. Big-jawed green tiger beetles can also be seen hunting other insects.

In **autumn** the red squirrels are very active gathering nuts and other food to fatten up for the winter. Treecreepers and nuthatches forage over the tree trunks while goldcrests and coal tits feed higher up in the pines.

Winter is the time to come to see avocets, black-tailed godwits, and other waders that feed in the lagoon to the northeast of the island. There is a birdwatching hide close to the landing stage. There is also a large heronry to the north, which attracts breeding herons in February and March.

> Brownsea provides a refuge for 200 to 250 red squirrels – just enough to form a self-sufficient population.

seems a flimsy defence against invasion, and at first you may get little sense of the uniqueness of the place. Head west, away from the landing area, and you will soon find yourself surrounded by pine woodland. Before long you may come across signs of squirrel activity, such as the gnawed cores of pine cones, surrounded by the woody scales that the squirrels bite off to get at the seeds, or the shattered shell fragments of hastily eaten hazelnuts.

In the hot summer months such clues may be all you see, but in March the squirrels are much more active, and a commotion in a Scots pine may well herald the appearance of a courting pair chasing through the treetops. The squirrels prefer a "closed canopy" where they can leap from tree to tree without coming to ground, and they display amazing agility and speed as they jump and scramble through the branches, using their long bushy tails for balance. Their sharp claws enable them to cling to the bark with just one foot, and they frequently run headfirst down trees. With their chestnut fur and long ear tufts they are irresistibly attractive, the more so when they pick up food with their forepaws so they can gnaw at it in comfort.

GOLDEN DAFFODILS

EVERYBODY LOVES A DAFFODIL, AND BETTER STILL A MASS OF THEM, brightening up a dull March day with the promise of spring. There can be barely a garden in the country that doesn't have daffodils, but these are often large, vivid, blowsy flowers, very different to our genuine native form, with its dainty flowers and long, narrow trumpets.

In areas where wild daffodils are a feature in the landscape, they are valued and celebrated by local people and visitors alike. In the beautiful, deep valley of Farndale, on the southern flanks of the North York Moors, you are greeted in March by the astonishing sight of daffodils everywhere – broadly lining the 5km-long (3 mile) daffodil walk.

WHERE
Farndale Moor, Hutton le Hole, North Yorkshire, England; www.naturalengland.org.uk

CONTACT
Natural England, tel: 01904 435500; York@naturalengland.org.uk

GETTING THERE
Farndale is the area surrounding the village of Hutton le Hole, which is 3.2km (2 miles) north of Kirbymoorside. Take the A170 west of Pickering, and park in the Hutton le Hole car park. Then take the special Daffodil Shuttle Bus, which leaves from the car park and goes straight to the daffodils. The buses run on Sundays, from 23 March to 20 April, and Friday to Monday over the Easter weekend, except Easter Sunday itself.

ACCESS AND FACILITIES
There are no facilities here, and as the terrain is variable, wheelchair access is difficult. The nearest public toilets are at Low Mill.

OPENING TIMES
Open all year round.

CHARGES
No charge applies to the daffodil walk, but there is a small charge for the Daffodil Bus.

Until the mid-19th century, wild daffodils – *Narcissus pseudonarcissus* – bloomed prolifically all around Britain, carpeting the riverbanks, woodlands, and meadows of every county in spring.

The walk starts from the tiny post office at Farndale's Low Mill, from which you follow the well-trodden footpath down to the tranquil River Dove. It is here that you realize what a phenomenon this is – the wide banks of the river, the meadows, and the open woodland are awash with thousands of yellow, swaying flowerheads. The walk remains interesting throughout the season: as spring progresses, so a range of other spring plants appear, including yellow primrose, lesser celandine, and patches of the starry white flowerheads of wild garlic. As the trees and bushes burst into leaf, the flowers of bird cherry, blackthorn, and goat willow start to attract insects on sunny days – bumblebees, peacock butterflies, and others, looking for food after their long hibernation. The first chiffchaffs are likely to be singing in the alders, while grey wagtails and dippers feed along the river bank. In April, listen out for male redstarts delivering their short, melancholy song from the tree tops.

If you want a more challenging walk, look for waymarked paths from the daffodil walk onto the open moorland above. The heather-clad hills may look rather weatherbeaten at this time of year, but red grouse, meadow pipits, and the first wheatears can be found, while adders bask alongside the paths, especially early in the morning on a sunny day.

Daffodils under threat

The true wild daffodil is a plant of delicate beauty, but it is at risk, mainly from genetic pollution. Well-meaning but misguided attempts to brighten the countryside sometimes result in people planting daffodils – very often garden varieties (*as below*) – which look out of place in the wild. The rule for wild daffodils is: don't pick them, don't dig them up, and don't try to add to them. Simply enjoy nature at its purest and best.

Main: The banks of the River Dove, Farndale, are lined with wild daffodils.
Below (left to right): Primroses follow the daffodil season; the goat willow ("pussy willow") has catkins in March; lesser celandine.
Inset: Wild daffodils have paler petals than garden varieties, and a narrower trumpet.

Above: The view acxross the moor in winter.

JAN

FEB

MAR

APR

MAY

JUN

JUL

AUG

SEP

OCT

NOV

DEC

THROUGH THE YEAR
FARNDALE MOOR

As spring gives way to **summer**, Farndale fills up with summer birds – spotted flycatchers, willow warblers, wood warblers, and redstarts in the riverside woods. Tree pipits deliver their beautiful song in flights from isolated trees. At the same time, the damp grassland bursts into flower, with marsh marigold giving way to meadowsweet, common valerian, and wild angelica as the season progresses.

By **autumn**, the surrounding moorland comes into its own, the purple haze of common heather, or ling, becoming home to noisy groups of red grouse before the winter chill descends. In **midwinter**, look at the alders by the river – with a little patience, you should find parties of lesser redpolls and siskins feeding on the seeds in the treetops, alongside roving parties of tits and other small birds.

WHERE ELSE TO SEE
WILD DAFFODILS

Wild daffodils are found over much of England and Wales, but especially in the west and around the valleys of the uplands.

The Lake District village of **Grasmere** is famous for its daffodils, descendants of those that inspired William Wordsworth's famous poem. [N]

The "golden triangle" around the villages of **Newent** and **Dymock** in Gloucestershire, and **Ross-on-Wye** in Herefordshire, is so well known for its daffodils that it was once served by a "daffodil train" from London. [M]

The valleys of **Dartmoor** and **Exmoor** (*see pp.44–45*) provide many opportunities to see daffodils at their best, often extending out of the valley bottoms onto the bracken-clad hillsides. [SW]

Even the London area has its share of wild daffodils – try **Lesnes Abbey Woods** in Bexley. [SE]

WHERE
RSPB Radipole Lake, Weymouth, Dorset
DT4 7TZ; www.rspb.org.uk

CONTACT
Radipole Lake Visitor Centre,
tel: 01305 778313;
weymouth.reserves@rspb.org.uk

GETTING THERE
By road, head for the Swannery car park, off
the A354 in Weymouth; the reserve is next
door. By train, Weymouth Station is less than
400m (350 yards) from the reserve.

ACCESS AND FACILITIES
Parking is available in the council-run Swannery
pay-and-display car park. The nearest parking
to the centre is 10m (30ft) from the entrance.
The centre is wheelchair friendly, and so are
some of the trails and hides. Refreshments
include snacks and drinks; there's also an
RSPB shop. There are two trails, of 1.5km
(¾ mile) and 2km (1¼ miles).

OPENING TIMES
The visitor centre is open daily 9am–5pm
(closes 4pm in winter); the hide is open
8.30am–4.30pm.

CHARGES
There is a charge for parking and for
non-RSPB members to use the hide.

Reed management

Radipole has over 200 plant species, and the
largest reedbed in southwest England. Sections
of the reedbed are cut back between autumn
and spring to promote new growth, which will
give rise to better quality seed heads the
following autumn. This process ensures a food
supply for wintering birds, especially the bearded
tits, while the new reedbed growth provides a
home for insects that the birds eat in spring, and
then plenty of seeds for the birds to eat in winter.

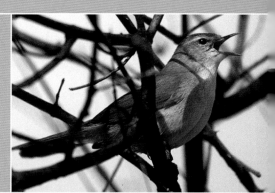

Left: Cattle graze on the
urban marshland.

Right (left to right): The
timid Cetti's warbler is a rare
resident; a bird's-eye view of
the RSPB Radipole reserve.

**Below right (top and
bottom):** The snipe is a
regular winter visitor to the
reserve; a grey heron keeps
watch among the reeds.

Main: Extensive reedbeds at Radipole are the largest in the southwest of England.

GO WILD IN WEYMOUTH

RADIPOLE LAKE IS A CLASSIC URBAN NATURE RESERVE, where a river has backed up behind a coastal
sandbar to create a wet marsh. It is served by excellent footpaths and hides, but turn away from the housing
to the west and look instead along the reedbeds and pools – you might be on a much wilder stretch of coast.

　　The first thing to remember when you arrive at the reserve, which is close to the middle of Weymouth,
is not to neglect the car park. In March, there are often gulls scattered across the tarmac, some of which may
be quite rare, such as the Mediterranean gull. Check in the visitor centre to find out what's about.

　　Then take the path across the bridge to the Buddleia Walk. The buddleias are not out in March, but the
bushes alongside the path have one special bird, one of a handful of warblers that stay over winter in the UK:
Cetti's warbler. It is small, rather dark, reddish-brown above and pale below, with a noticeable grey tinge, and has

Radipole Lake is an urban oasis for people and wildlife – providing peace and security within wide open spaces.

Above: A small tortoiseshell on the reserve's Buddleia Walk.

THROUGH THE YEAR
RADIPOLE LAKE

In the **summer**, Radipole is alive with birds over the water and reeds, including swallows and house martins; even secretive water rails feed in the reeds. Reed, sedge, and willow warblers create a wonderful early morning chorus. Butterflies are busy on the flowering shrubs along the Buddleia Walk and in the reserve's flower-rich meadows, including migrants such as painted ladies and clouded yellows, whose numbers vary greatly from year to year.

In **autumn** (as in spring), the unpredictable nature of bird migration is likely to throw in unexpected species. Go early in the morning, before the trails are too disturbed, and you may see some rarities. Bearded tits are easiest to find in autumn, as are hobbies (swift-flying falcons) – which are out hunting dragonflies and martins.

Radipole Lake is at its best for wildfowl in **winter.** Pochards, shovelers, and teals spend the winter on the lake, and shy water rails come out of hiding. Patience may be rewarded by a rare sighting of the elusive bittern among the reedbeds.

WHERE ELSE TO SEE
URBAN WILDFOWL

Urban reedbeds are few and far between, but they are worth seeking out for a locally based day out.

Cardiff in Wales boasts a great town centre park with good lakes, but **Conwy** (see pp.278–279) on the North Wales coast is a reserve that combines accessibility with even more wildlife interest. [W]

London has a number of large parks, but not that many feature the rarer forms of wildfowl. The **London Wetlands Centre** in Barnes, south west London (see pp.16–17), is an exception. [SE]

Southport on Merseyside is a good wildlife town, but the best place for viewing birds also seen at Radipole is probably **Blacktoft Sands** in East Yorkshire (see pp.158–159), on the Humber estuary. [N]

JAN
FEB
MAR
APR
MAY
JUN
JUL
AUG
SEP
OCT
NOV
DEC

a pale line over the eye. A broad, rounded tail helps distinguish it from other possibilities, but in early spring before the reed and sedge warblers arrive, there is little to confuse it with. Listen for its sharp, sudden "quilp" calls. Much more distinctive, once it gets going in spring, is its song: a sudden, loud outburst of rich, fast, musical notes. March is a good time to enjoy this bird and its sweet song, as there is little aural competition, and the vegetation is still relatively sparse; later in the year this secretive warbler can be particularly hard to spot.

Radipole's birds are not all so difficult. From the bridge you can often see a wide variety of cormorants – developing quite handsome spring colours in March – with gulls, moorhens, and ducks of several kinds, including tufted ducks and pochards. Walk on until you reach the shelter and the farthest hide, where you can often see grey herons and wading birds, including snipe and perhaps a kingfisher if you are lucky. Look out for little egrets, especially in the evening when they come to roost. Even bearded tits have been known to put in an appearance in this remarkable sanctuary, compressed between Weymouth's suburbs, railway, roads, and the town centre.

WHERE
Lyme Park, Disley, Stockport, Cheshire,
SK12 2NR;
www.nationaltrust.org.uk/main/w-lymepark

CONTACT
Lyme Park, tel: 01663 762023. National
Trust infoline, tel: 01663 766492;
lymepark@nationaltrust.org.uk

GETTING THERE
By road, the entrance is on the A6, 10.5km
(7 miles) southeast of Stockport, 9.3km
(12 miles) northwest of Buxton. The house
and car park is 1.6km (1 mile) from the
entrance. By train, Disley is 0.8km
(0.5 miles) from the park entrance. The
TrentBarton no. 199 Buxton–Manchester
Airport bus stops at the park entrance.

ACCESS AND FACILITIES
There's a licensed restaurant and café in The
Timber Yard and a refreshment kiosk in the
main car park. There are full-access toilets
throughout the site and wheelchair access
to the buildings and parts of the grounds, but
there are steep slopes and uneven ground.

OPENING TIMES
The park is open all year round; the house
is open March–November.

CHARGES
Yes, for non-National Trust members.

High-speed hares
Unlike rabbits, which bolt for their burrows at
the first hint of danger, long-legged hares rely
on their speed to escape attack. A brown hare
can accelerate to 45mph (72kph) on level
ground, and is so light that it can easily turn
in its tracks and dart off in a different direction
to outwit a heavier pursuer. For centuries, pitting
greyhounds against each other in pursuit of hares
was a popular sport. Since 2004, "hare coursing"
has been banned in Britain, but illegal coursing
is still a problem in some regions.

Above (top and bottom): The Cage observation
tower overlooking Lyme Park, an ideal place to spot
hares; some of the park's red deer hinds.

Below: A tree clings to a rocky outcrop at Lyme Park's
West Park gate.

Far right (top and bottom): An alert hare checks
for danger; another keeps a low profile in a hollow,
or "form", in an arable field.

Main: Boxing hares are not – as was once thought – two competitive males, but a female fending off a potential suitor.

BOXING HARES

SET IN OPEN COUNTRYSIDE A FEW MILES SOUTHEAST OF STOCKPORT, and overlooked by the brooding
mass of Derbyshire's High Peak, Lyme Park is one of the most magnificent buildings in Cheshire. Originally
a Tudor country house, its exterior was remodelled in the 18th century to create a grand Palladian facade,
complete with a huge neo-classical portico and superb formal gardens. For many, however, the estate's real
charm lies in the rough grassland of the surrounding medieval deer park, because in spring this is an ideal place
to watch one of the most bizarre of all natural spectacles: the stand-up boxing matches of the wild brown hares.

     Immortalized by Lewis Carroll in *Alice's Adventures in Wonderland*, the "mad March hare" has mystified
wildlife watchers for centuries. Unlike smaller, less agile rabbits, brown hares spend their lives above ground in
open country, and in spring when the grass is short their extraordinary courtship rituals are conducted in full

Above: Red deer in winter at Lyme Park.

JAN

FEB

MAR

APR

MAY

JUN

JUL

AUG

SEP

OCT

NOV

DEC

THROUGH THE YEAR
LYME PARK

In **summer** the moors and woodlands of Lyme Park are good places to look for insects, and especially butterflies and moths. The hares are still active, but harder to see in the long grass.

Autumn sees the annual rut of Lyme Park's resident herds of fallow and red deer. Watch and marvel at the dramatic spectacle, but don't venture too close because the rutting stags can turn on intruders. The park is a great place to go fungi-spotting; it often has a great show of the almost-fluorescent red *Hygrocybe splendidissima* – the splendid waxcap.

Lyme Park tends to get a dusting of snow in **winter**, providing excellent conditions for tracking animals that come out mainly at night. Look for the trails of foxes, with their characteristic single lines of prints. Sometimes a fox trail shadows that of a rabbit, with its pattern of short fore-prints and long hind-prints. Following a trail may lead you to the site of a kill.

Bounding, leaping, sparring, dancing – the hares' mad display signals the dawn of spring.

WHERE ELSE TO SEE
BROWN HARES

Although introduced to Ireland, the brown hare is native to mainland Britain – or has been since Roman times. It is most numerous on open fields and pasture, but it may use nearby woodlands as refuges, especially in cold weather. Since it is largely nocturnal it is rarely seen in broad daylight. It is also easiest to see in spring before crops and grasses grow too tall.

Hares are particularly common on the broad fields and fenlands of East Anglia, but are so wide-ranging that spotting them is a matter of luck. **Havergate Island** in Suffolk – an RSPB reserve more famous for its breeding avocets and terns – has a flourishing hare population. [SE]

There is a thriving brown hare population at **Bleasdale** near Preston, Lancashire, where the animals are encouraged by local farmers. [N]

view. If you want to witness these extravagant rituals at Lyme Park, one of the best places is The Cage, an ornate 18th-century hunting lodge that offers a vast panorama of the Cheshire Plain and even the foothills of Snowdonia, and provides a fine vantage point for hare-watching.

Arrive as early as possible: brown hares are most active at dawn and dusk, but you will need the morning light. If hares are about, you will see groups out in the open, clearly visible through binoculars. Males and females look alike, but if one dashes off, chased by several others, she will be a female in breeding condition. Her pursuers are males, each intent on mating with as many females as possible. One may shadow her more closely than the others, even driving them away, but the common belief that boxing hares are rival males is wrong. A female frequently becomes so irritated by an ardent suitor that she turns and delivers a swift punch. He retaliates, and the two may rear up on their long hind legs to exchange a flurry of blows. No damage is done, and quite often the wild chase resumes almost immediately. Eventually his persistence may pay off, and she will allow him to mate – after which he immediately starts looking for another female.

SPRINGTIME ON JERSEY

THE LARGEST OF THE CHANNEL ISLANDS, JERSEY IS THE SOUTHERNMOST outpost of the British Isles, lying some 160km (100 miles) off the south coast of England. Spring arrives early this far south, so a March visit is guaranteed to provide wildlife, and there's a good chance of fine weather. Apart from the specialities not found elsewhere in Britain, or only sparingly, the beauty of Jersey is that it offers a wide range of habitats within a compact area; it is easy to travel around, and its clear, rich seas add a further dimension to the natural scenes.

Broadly speaking, the coastline is cliffed in the north and southwest, with sandy bays, dunes, and wetlands on the west and south coast. The extensive clifftops are a good place to start, as the heaths, gorse, and heather combine to provide an ideal home for Dartford warblers, which are more obvious in March because of their towering song-flights. Stonechats are ever-present, together with rock pipits foraging from the cliffs below.

WHERE
Jersey, Channel Islands;
www.nationaltrustjersey.org.je

CONTACT
National Trust for Jersey, The Elms, La Chève Rue, St Mary, JE3 3EN, Jersey;
tel: 01534 483193;
enquiries@nationaltrustjersey.org.je

GETTING THERE
You can sail from Poole or Weymouth by ferry and be in Jersey in less than four hours. There are regular flights from London – about 12 a day – and around 25 other airports in the UK fly to the island.

ACCESS AND FACILITIES
Jersey welcomes all disabled visitors and has a website with helpful information:
www.jersey.com/English/aboutjersey/disabledinformation

CHARGES
There are charges for non-members for some National Trust reserves on the island.

Above: Offshore islets.

Main: The view over Plemont Bay from the clifftop.

Below: Two of Jersey's more unusual sea creatures, the beautiful cuckoo wrasse fish (*above*), and the short snouted seahorse (*below*).

Far right (top to bottom): The dunes are home to many interesting miniature plants; Jersey is the only natural home of the western green lizard; the lesser white-toothed shrew; the short-toed treecreeper is unique to Jersey within the British Isles.

Moving house

One of Jersey's more unusual mammals is the lesser white-toothed shrew. Within the British Isles, this species is found only on Jersey, Sark, and the Scilly Isles. The shrews produce 4–5 litters each year, each of which consist of 1–6 young. If the nest is disturbed, the mother leads her young to a new nest site by "caravanning": the little shrews follow her in a long line, each shrew holding on to the tail of the shrew in front of it. Adult shrews scent their new territory by dragging their bellies along the ground.

Prostrate broom may be just beginning to flower, though it will be a couple of months before the mosaic of sea campion, thrift, and ox-eye daisy completes the picture. A careful search could reveal some of the most sought-after flowers, such as sand crocus and spotted rock-rose, though the crocus closes in dull weather and the rock-rose drops its petals by about noon on the day it opens. Look out for green lizards on the heaths and dunes of the southwest. This is the largest lizard species in Britain, at up to 40cm (16in) long, and the male tranforms in the breeding season: his green body becomes stippled with black, and his throat turns a beautiful shade of blue.

The dunes, best seen at Les Blanches Banques, are also well worth a spring visit. Small plants are at the peak of their flowering, including the early sand-grass and the dwarf pansy, only seen on the Channel and Scilly islands. Wander further inland, and you'll find woodlands that are home to red squirrels, and a few stony banks with populations of the delicate Jersey fern.

WHERE ELSE TO SEE
MARITIME HEATHS

Some of the unusual features of Jersey's maritime heath can be found on other British islands, and even on the mainland.

The Lizard in Cornwall (*see pp.116–117*) and other parts of the southwest peninsula have similar ranges of habitats, including maritime heathland, but the unique geology of the Lizard ensures that it has a good range of additional rare plants that can't survive the frosts elsewhere. [SW]

The **Scilly Isles** are less dramatic scenically than Jersey, but they share some of its special species and a similarly rich marine environment. [SW]

Extensive maritime heaths, interspersed with dunes and sandy bays, can be found along the Welsh coast. There are some magnificent stretches in **Gower** (*see pp.122–123*) and the Pembrokeshire Coast (from Tenby to Cardigan), and some on the **Lleyn Peninsula** and **Anglesey** in the north. [W]

THROUGH THE YEAR
JERSEY

Summer on Jersey is the best time to seek out its special reptiles: the green lizard and the wall lizard, basking on rocks and walls. Although now rather scarce on the island, the Jersey (or "lax-flowered") orchid grows nowhere else naturally, and it flowers in early summer. In **August**, look along the large dune systems for the impressive and rare lizard orchid.

The sea is warmest in early **autumn**, and its meadows of eel-grass hide short-snouted sea-horses; boulders and seaweeds provide niches for ormers and spider-crabs. There's a wide range of fish, including the dragonet, tub gurnard, and the beautifully coloured cuckoo wrasse. Look too for bottlenose dolphins, basking sharks, and grey seals.

Winter is generally short and mild. Visit the eel-grass beds to see feeding brent geese of two distinct races: most are dark-bellied Siberian birds, but a fair proportion are pale-bellied birds from the east Canadian high Arctic population.

Below: The Jersey tiger moth has a wingspan of 42–52mm (1½–2in).

JAN

FEB

MAR

APR

MAY

JUN

JUL

AUG

SEP

OCT

NOV

DEC

WHERE
Black Wood of Rannoch, Kinloch Rannoch, Perth and Kinross, Scotland; www.perthshire.co.uk

CONTACT
Rannoch Moor Visitor Centre, Rannoch Station, Perth and Kinross PH17 2QA; tel: 01796 472215.

GETTING THERE
The Black Wood lies on the southern shores of Loch Rannoch. It is part of the Caledonian Forest Reserve, which is part of the Tay Forest Park, west of Dall. Kinloch Rannoch, off the B846, is the nearest town or village. Black Wood is 3.2km (2 miles) west of Kinloch Rannoch, on South Loch Rannoch road. Rannoch Station lies on the West Highland Line, between Glasgow and Fort William.

ACCESS AND FACILITIES
There are no facilities in the wood; access is from an unclassified road running south of Loch Rannoch. The nearest facilities (and tearoom) are at the Rannoch Moor Visitor Centre in Rannoch railway station.

OPENING TIMES
Trails open all year round. The visitor centre is open March–October, 10am–5pm.

CHARGES
None.

Rare insect life

In the Black Wood of Rannoch there are many ancient moss- and lichen-festooned birches intermixed with the pines. The living trees and the deadwood combine to make a rare habitat uniquely supportive of insects: two rare species of moths take their common names from the place: the Rannoch looper, and the Rannoch sprawler (*shown above*). The wood is also one of the few places to see the UK's timberman beetle, the larvae of which bore into the rotting wood of fallen pine trunks and stumps.

Above: The Scottish crossbill (*far right*) is very similar to the common crossbill (*centre*) and parrot crossbill (*left*).
Main: Red deer roam free in the wood.

IN THE BLACK WOOD

A WALK THROUGH A CALEDONIAN FOREST is a very different experience to visiting to an old-style, mature pine plantation, where the gloom cast by the serried ranks of conifers and the carpet of tough dead needles on the ground make for relatively little wildlife. It is far more open, with the pines interspersed with birch, rowan, alder, bird cherry, and willow. This allows the development of an understorey of shrubs such as aspen, holly, hazel, and juniper; while the acidic soil gives rise to a rich ground layer of plants, such as bell heather, crowberry, and bilberry (called "blaeberry" in Scotland). Rare wildflowers such as the lesser twayblade and creeping lady's-tresses orchids grow here, along with one-flowered wintergreen and twinflower, as well as many fungi.

This special habitat supports many uncommon or rare species of animals, from hoverflies and beetles, to red squirrels, rare wildcats, and pine martens, and several birds that live only or mainly here. The crested tit is a Caledonian forest bird, along with the Scottish crossbill, whose name refers to the crossed tip of the bill, an adaptation for extracting seeds from conifer cones. Recent estimates suggest there may be fewer than 2,000 of these remarkable birds left. Another Black Wood inhabitant lies at the other end of the size scale from these two songbirds: the capercaillie. The glossy black males are the size of a turkey, and perform dramatic displays to attract females at communal "leks" or displays, strutting about and leaping in the air while uttering bizarre sounds.

One of the most special birds of the Black Wood is the lively crested tit, named for its jaunty black-and-white crest. It excavates its nests in old, rotten pine stumps.

The wood is home to many rare moths and insects, including the Scottish wood ant, which makes large conical nests from the pine needles. These carnivorous ants tend and protect the greenfly aphids, which are prevalent in pine forests, in return for the honeydew they produce. But the ants themselves often fall prey to the green woodpecker, which digs its long beak into their nests, and scoops up the ants with its long sticky tongue.

Inset: Crested tits are found only in the Scottish Highlands.
Below: Rannoch Moor is dotted with lakes, including Loch Tulla.

WHERE ELSE TO SEE
CONIFER FORESTS

Although they lack the special features of the Caledonian forests, some mature conifer plantations in Scotland and other parts of Britain are also rich in wildlife. Apart from the lofty, red-barked Scots pine, Britain's only two other native conifers are the yew and the juniper.

Kielder Forest in Northumberland is one of the largest areas of planted forest in Europe. You can look for a wide range of birds among the conifers, including crossbills and that powerful and elusive relative of the sparrowhawk, the goshawk. [N]

Breckland, on the border between Norfolk and Suffolk, contains plantations of mature Scots pine and other trees, where forest birds include rare and elusive golden pheasants, goshawks, hobbies, woodcocks, and woodlarks. [SE]

Large areas of ancient yew woodland are rare, but in **Kingley Vale** in West Sussex (*see pp.310–311*), some of the trees may be over 2,000 years old. Their twisted and gnarled, glowing, deep-red trunks contrast with the almost blackish-green foliage. [SE]

THROUGH THE YEAR
BLACK WOOD OF RANNOCH

Early **summer** is a good time to see – and hear – breeding songbirds such as crested tits, tree pipits, and siskins. Wildflowers are in bloom, and insects are active. Do not try to watch capercaillies at their display grounds; a better site for this is the Osprey Centre at the RSPB's Loch Garten reserve (*see pp.86–87*), where it is possible to watch the birds without disturbing them.

Autumn can be a good time to see capercaillies, as more birds are about after breeding. They are less disturbed by vehicles than an approach on foot, but the best chance of an encounter is to book a trip with a reputable wildlife-watching company.

From autumn and through **winter**, crested tits start to group together in small roving flocks, often with other songbirds such as coal tits and goldcrests. Listen for the Crested tit's distinctive call: a purring trill.

Below: The capercaillie's song includes a sound like wine being uncorked.

JAN

FEB

MAR

APR

MAY

JUN

JUL

AUG

SEP

OCT

NOV

DEC

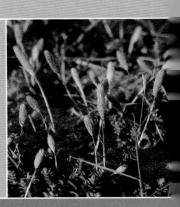

Left: Looking south along Saunton Sands beach, backed by Braunton Burrows.

Right (left to right): Sand cat's-tail; the dune-carpeting moss *Tortula ruraliformis*; sea mouse-ear.

Right, below: The diminutive dune pansy, instantly recognizable by its resemblance to showier garden pansies and violas.

WHERE
Braunton Burrows, Heddon Mill, Braunton, Devon EX33 2NQ.

CONTACT
Braunton Tourist Information Centre, The Bakehouse Centre, Caen Street, Braunton, Devon EX33 1AA; tel: 01271 816400.

GETTING THERE
From Braunton take the B3231 for 1.6km (1 mile), and turn left at Sandy Lane. Access is via the Coast Path/Tarka Trail. From Barnstaple, take A361 towards Braunton, and just before you reach the village take the left turn signposted to Crow Point. Follow this lane straight to Sandy Lane car park in the centre of the dunes, or turn left down the toll road to Broad Sands car park, near Crow point.

ACCESS AND FACILITIES
There are no facilities. The nearest are in Braunton. Caution: the Ministry of Defence still use a part of the dunes as a training area and if there is to be any live firing it will be indicated with red flags.

OPENING TIMES
Open all year round.

CHARGES
None.

The Burrows biosphere

Braunton Burrows is a UNESCO Biosphere Reserve. This means it is considered a "living laboratory" for testing integrated management of land, water, and biodiversity. Biosphere Reserves must demonstrate the conservation of biodiversity together with sustainable use. The unique collection of wildlife habitats at Braunton Burrows is recognized as owing much to the long-standing use of traditional farming and fishing practices within the area.

Main: The dunes at Braunton Burrows are dominated by marram grass, the roots of which form a three-dimensional anchoring mesh in the sand.

JEWELS IN THE DUNES

LIFE ON SAND IS STRESSFUL FOR PLANTS. Blown into dunes, sand is inhospitable, mobile, and very prone to drought in the summer. But the plants that can tolerate the dry conditions are immensely useful – they help to stabilize the sand, helping it to grow into dunes, sometimes forming extensive systems. This is the situation at Braunton Burrows, where dunes up to 30m (100ft) high dominate the mouth of the Taw-Torridge estuary.

At the start of spring, it might seem surprising to find botanists exploring the windswept dunes. They are there because some plants are already flowering, miniature delights that really repay a closer look. The turf is studded with the tiny bright-blue flowers of early forget-me-not; white stars of sand mouse-ear, whitlow-grass, and spring sandwort; the yellow or purple (or both) faces of dune pansy; and grasses like the diminutive sand cat's-tail and dune fescue. This kaleidoscope of colour forms a turf rarely more than a few centimetres tall.

JAN
FEB
MAR
APR
MAY
JUN
JUL
AUG
SEP
OCT
NOV
DEC

Braunton Burrows is the largest sand-dune system in England; it is significant at an international level.

Above: The vivid spikes of viper's bugloss.

THROUGH THE YEAR
BRAUNTON BURROWS

In **summer**, Braunton Burrows features many interesting plants, from the attractive blue viper's bugloss and pink sea bindweed, to scarce species such as sea stock and some very rare flora: the round-headed club-rush is found at only a handful of British sites. There are nesting birds too – wheatears and shelducks breed in rabbit holes on the dunes.

Autumn brings migrating songbirds, attracted especially by the berries and shelter provided by sea buckthorn. The low turf landward of the main dunes supports a number of brightly coloured waxcap fungi.

The windswept dunes have few birds in **winter**, with skylarks and meadow pipits making up the majority. But viewing from the southern tip, Crow Point, at low tide should reveal large numbers of wading birds, including curlews, golden plovers, and lapwings, and perhaps also seals at high water.

WHERE ELSE TO SEE
SAND DUNES

Sand dunes may form wherever there is a supply of wind-blown sand, and where the angle of the coast means that winds are predominantly onshore.

South Wales used to have an almost unbroken dune system from the river Ogmore to the Gower peninsula; much has now been lost, but a magnificent remnant can be found at **Kenfig**, near Port Talbot. On Anglesey, there are two large systems, **Newborough Warren** (see pp.142–143) and **Aberffraw**. [W]

On the east coast, **Scolt Head Island** in Norfolk is accessible by boat trips from the quay at Burnham Overy Staithe, off the A149 coast road. [SE]

Much of **Lindisfarne**, (see pp.274–275) in Northumberland, is made up of dunes. [N]

In Scotland, **Culbin Sands** on the Moray Firth still has areas of open sand dune, although much of the area has now been planted with conifer trees. [SC]

The factor that links these plants is timing – they flower early in the season to survive the high summer stress as relatively drought-tolerant seeds. In fact many are winter annuals: plants that germinate in the autumn, grow slowly through the winter, flower, set seed, and die before the drought bites. Their whole life-cycle is adapted to avoiding the heat of summer.

Search carefully at ground level among the low-lying dune slacks and you might just find one of Braunton's rarest inhabitants, the internationally protected liverwort *Petalophyllum ralfsii*. Take a look, too, at the incredibly diverse mosses and lichens that grow here. Cushions of sandhill screw-moss are bright green, the silvery hair points on their leaves spreading like tiny stars – unless, that is, the last few weeks have been dry, in which case the moss is blackened and screwed up, waiting for the next rains, when it will rehydrate and carry on unperturbed. The carpets of grey lichens towards the back of the dunes, mostly of *Cladonia* species, have such an intriguing array of forms – from flat plates to branched bushlets to tiny cups – to be fascinating to novice and specialist alike.

APRIL

Where to Go: **April**

Showers and storms notwithstanding, April brings real, warm, delicious spring at last, and with it the great migrations of summer-visiting birds from southern Europe and Africa. As fieldfares, redwings, and tens of thousands of ducks and wading birds leave for the north and east, so we see warblers, chats, swallows, and martins arriving everywhere. Willow warblers have the most delicate spring song, but nightingales, perhaps, have the most mesmerizing and varied. Blackcaps and garden warblers compete to be the most musical, but even the lisping, slurred twitter of a newly arrived swallow is welcome to our ears. Woodlands become awash with bluebells, one of the great glories of Britain, and flowers are suddenly everywhere, multi-coloured

WOODLANDS

NORSEY WOOD Oaks, sweet chestnuts, hornbeams, birches, and alders.

WETLANDS

LEIGHTON MOSS The elusive bittern takes to the skies.

PARKS AND GRASSLANDS

CRICKLADE MEADOW The nodding heads of snakeshead fritillaries.

NORSEY WOOD
BILLERICAY, ESSEX [SE]

This 400-year-old deer park is utterly magical in late April, when it is full of bluebells, wood anemones, lily-of-the-valley, dog violets, and stitchwort.
See pp.84–85

WOOLSTON EYES
WARRINGTON, CHESHIRE [N]

A young reserve, created in 1980, this has over 220 bird species, including the elegant black-necked grebe. Watch out for the sharp features of inquisitive stoats.
See pp.76–77

CRICKLADE MEADOW
CRICKLADE, WILTSHIRE [SE]

This damp meadow has one of the few significant fritillary colonies left in Britain – several million fritillaries burst into flower here in April.
See pp.74–75

PERIVALE WOOD
LONDON [SE]

Don't miss a visit to this London woodland, which is only open to the public this month so that visitors may admire its glorious bluebells.
See pp.84–85

LEIGHTON MOSS
CARNFORTH, LANCASHIRE [N]

If you want to hear bitterns booming, visit the secret world of Leighton Moss in April. Courting pairs of marsh harriers fly overhead.
See pp.78–79

Few wild flowers can match the delicate beauty and poise of the snakeshead fritillary; its chequered blooms nod over slender, arched stems.

SALISBURY PLAIN
WILTSHIRE [SW]

Stone curlews, quails, whinchats, stonechats, and grasshopper warblers all live around this vast area of chalk grassland.
See pp.92–93

RYTON WOOD
WARWICKSHIRE [M]

The spring bluebells within this ancient oak woodland sit beneath chattering spring birds: six species of warblers live here, and woodpeckers and nightingales breed among its trees.
See pp.84–85

LOCHWINNOCH
PAISLEY, RENFREWSHIRE [SC]

Watch the entrancing dance of the great crested grebes, as they fan out their feathers, dive, and perform the "ghostly penguin" and "weed ceremony".
See pp.82–83

GRAFHAM WATER
CAMBRIDGESHIRE [SE]

Great grested grebes dance in courtship rituals around the lagoons. Flocks of waders fly overhead, and hobbies look for easy prey.
See pp.82–83

LEE VALLEY PARK
ESSEX/HERTFORDSHIRE [M]

This huge park is a great place to see spring migrating birds, such as terns and warblers, as well as foxes, and even otters, at Fisher's Green.
See pp.78–79

The ancient Caledonian forests still guard their red squirrels, roe deer, and rare crossbills within a rich ecosystem dating back to the Ice Age.

LOCH AN EILEIN
ROTHIEMURCHUS [SC]

This beautiful loch is surrounded by the magnificent pines of Rothiemurchus Forest, which provides shelter for red squirrels, capercaillies, and rare Scottish crossbills.
See pp.86–87

RUTLAND WATER
RUTLAND [M]

Ospreys and grebes breed here in April. A hide overlooking a badger sett is open to small guided groups from mid-April.
See pp.82–83

MAGDALEN COLLEGE MEADOW
OXFORD [M]

Beautiful fritillaries cover half the meadow here in April, uninterrupted by other flowers. The college grove is also home to fallow and muntjac deer.
See pp.74–75

Previous page: Fresh green foliage and a carpet of bluebells make woodlands vibrant with colour.

and hugely varied in form, demanding more of our time to inspect, identify, and enjoy them. Exciting rarities, such as fritillaries and pasque flower, can be found in a few treasured places, but in mild areas, even a quiet roadside verge can suddenly offer a long list, from early purple orchids to stitchworts and violets, creating a glorious swathe of colour.

Butterflies are beginning to appear, and fish such as chub and bream are spawning in our rivers, often rolling in the shallows in the ecstasy of their mysterious rituals. Everything seems to be seized with the urgency of spring. Riversides are great places in April, with kingfishers, dippers, common sandpipers, and sand martins all making the most of the warmer weather.

COAST

PORTLAND BILL Pulpit Rock welcomes migrating birds.

HEATH AND MOOR

WEETING HEATH A grassy heathland reserve with pine plantations.

LAKES AND WATERWAYS

WYE VALLEY A famous fishing ground for the brown trout.

PORTLAND BILL
DORSET [SW]

One of the UK's hotspots for the spring migration: thousands of birds pass through in April and May, sometimes including rarities such as the dark-eyed junco.
See pp.90–91

AINSDALE DUNES
SEFTON COAST, MERSEYSIDE [N]

These coastal dunes host sand lizards, great crested newts, and natterjack toads, which breed in the shallow dune pools in April.
See pp.88–89

By April the natterjack breeding season is in full swing, as the males gather around the pools to enchant the females with their ratcheting calls.

WINTERTON DUNES
NORFOLK [SE]

These dunes near Great Yarmouth have a flourishing colony of natterjack toads, as well as a large population of birds, and several adders. You can often see seals swimming just offshore.
See pp.88–89

DUNGENESS
LYDD, KENT [SE]

Pools behind the expanse of shingle attract interesting birds, including black-necked grebes, little egrets, marsh harriers, and avocets. Listen, too, for the call of marsh frogs.
See pp.90–91

CORRIMONY
HIGHLAND [SC]

Set in stunning moorland and Caledonian forest, this beautiful reserve is a real discovery for anyone who loves birds. Black grouse may be displaying; take care not to disturb them.
See pp.86–87

MAIDSCROSS HILL
LAKENHEATH, SUFFOLK [SE]

This dry Breck grassland provides the perfect habitat for Breckland birds and specialist plants, such as Breckland wild thyme.
See pp.92–93

WEETING HEATH
NORFOLK [SE]

Weeting Heath is recognized as the best place in the UK to see stone curlew, and hear its banshee-like call. Look out for wheatears and tree pipits among the pine trees.
See pp.92–93

The Breckland heath provides the perfect breeding ground for the yellow-eyed stone curlew, whose eerie call haunts the Brecks at night.

THE LODGE
SANDY, BEDFORDSHIRE [SE]

The reserve that surrounds the RSPB's headquarters will, when fully restored, form the largest stretch of heathland in this county.
See pp.82–83

THE WYE VALLEY
HEREFORDSHIRE [M]

The River Wye, rich in salmon, chub, and brown trout, lies below Symonds Yat – where peregrines can be seen diving from tremendous heights.
See pp.80–81

LOCH GARTEN
HIGHLANDS [SC]

The Abernethy native pine forest sits around this vast loch, and is home to ospreys, capercaillies, black grouse, buzzards, red and roe deer, and red squirrels.
See pp.86–87

CROMFORD CANAL NATURE RESERVE
PEAK DISTRICT, DERBYSHIRE [N]

This rich, freshwater habitat provides a home for kingfishers, herons, and little grebes, alongside water voles.
See pp.94–95

LLANGOLLEN CANAL
NORTH WALES [W]

Witness the electric-blue flash of a hunting kingfisher over these restored waterways. The birds are feeding their young in April.
See pp.94–95

WHERE
North Meadow, Cricklade NNR, Cricklade,
Wiltshire, SN6 6HA;
www.naturalengland.org.uk

CONTACT
Natural England Wiltshire, tel: 01380
726344; wiltshire@naturalengland.org.uk

GETTING THERE
Cricklade is off the A419 linking junction
15 of the M4 and Cirencester, with Cricklade
roughly halfway between the two. The
nearest railway station is Swindon, with a
bus link to Cricklade. There is some roadside
parking within 300m (330 yards) of the
reserve. A bus service that runs through
Cricklade stops at the meadow.

ACCESS AND FACILITIES
There is a small car park at the top end of
Cricklade High Street. From the bottom end,
a 20-minute walk along the Thames Path
leads to the meadow. You must keep to the
public footpaths as these delicate flowers are
easily damaged. There is a disabled access
gate at the site, although access is not
advised in very wet conditions.

OPENING TIMES
Open all year round.

CHARGES
None.

FIELDS OF GLORY

FEW WILD FLOWERS CAN MATCH THE DELICATE BEAUTY AND POISE of the snakeshead fritillary. For most of the year it is invisible, but for a few short weeks in April and May whole meadows are flushed with a garnet glow of delicate reddish purple as hundreds of thousands of fritillaries flower at once, their extraordinary chequered blooms nodding in the breeze on slender, arched stems.

Yet this abundance is an illusion, for nationally the plant is extremely rare. It now grows wild on just a few damp meadows – so few that there are only about 30 significant fritillary colonies left in Britain. To see one in its full glory is a rare privilege, and in late April one of the best places to go for just this sight is North Meadow, Cricklade, on the banks of the upper Thames. A century ago the floral richness of North Meadow would have been less remarkable, for it was one of thousands of riverside flood meadows set aside for a hay crop that was cut and dried in the sun in July, after most of its wild flowers had bloomed and set seed. This was not deliberate

Rare white fritillaries

The flowers of the snakeshead fritillary are typically dusky purple, but on many sites, including North Meadow, the drifts of purple are dotted with white, thanks to a white form of the flower that grows alongside the typical form. Delicately veined with green, this is a natural variation of the same species, caused by "recessive" genes that produce white flowers only if both parent plants are white too.

Main and far right: The bell-like flowers have curiously angled petals that are mottled like snakeskin.

Left (left to right): The cuckoo flower grows on the river banks; the early marsh orchid also enjoys the damp conditions in North Meadow.

Right (left to right): A brimstone butterfly; a tiny field vole forages in the short sward.

conservation, but a timetable dictated by the relatively short period when the meadows were dry after winter flooding. On most farms flooding is now prevented and the grass is harvested much earlier, but on the ancient common land of North Meadow the old regime is still followed, as it has been for at least eight centuries. The annual timetable of haymaking and winter grazing has allowed the grassland flowers to flourish and multiply, creating one of the best examples of a lowland hay meadow in Europe.

In particular it has provided ideal conditions for the fritillaries, which need damp, undisturbed ground where river silt deposited by floodwater provides nutrients essential to plant growth, but not so many that more vigorous plants outgrow and overwhelm them. The result is the breathtaking sight that greets any visitor to the site in spring, when in a good year there may be several million fritillaries in flower, dusky and mysterious on an overcast day, but gleaming like stained glass when the sun shines through their petals.

> This single meadow contains an astonishing 80 per cent of Britain's wild snakeshead fritillaries.

WHERE ELSE TO SEE
FRITILLARY MEADOWS

There were many fritillary meadows at the beginning of the 20th century, but they have gradually disappeared as the land has been drained or treated with fertilizers, which encourages other plants to grow at the fritillaries' expense. All those that remain are in the lowlands of southern and central England, where the plant originally grew in damp woodland clearings.

The most celebrated fritillary site after North Meadow is **Magdalen College Meadow** in Oxford. Here fritillaries cover roughly half the meadow in April, and they grow more or less alone, without other showy flowers such as dandelions to distract the eye. There is another site just outside Oxford in **Iffley**. [SE]

Another colony survives in flood meadows by the River Windrush in **Ducklington**, Oxfordshire, and is only open once a year on "Fritillary Sunday". [SE]

A colony at **Fox Meadow** in Suffolk was almost destroyed in the late 1960s, but survived by a fluke. As with the Ducklington meadow, this is open to visitors on just one day of the year. [SE]

THROUGH THE YEAR
NORTH MEADOW

As the fritillaries on North Meadow go to seed and die back in **summer**, their place is taken by a kaleidoscope of meadow flowers: meadow buttercup, ragged robin, ox-eye daisy, red clover, meadowsweet, and devil's-bit scabious. The flowers attract a host of butterflies, and skylarks sing overhead while swallows, house martins, and sand martins dart through the air.

By **autumn** the hay crop has been cut and the meadow is used for grazing animals such as cattle and horses. Many of the birds leave for the tropics, while others retreat to nearby hedgerows to feast on berries and seeds.

Though the Thames flows across the southwest corner of North Meadow, it is usually the River Churn, on the northwest side, that floods the meadow in **winter**, as it has done for centuries, attracting waterfowl and waders such as snipe.

Below: A skylark soars above the meadow in June.

JAN

FEB

MAR

APR

MAY

JUN

JUL

AUG

SEP

OCT

NOV

DEC

WHERE
Woolston Eyes, Weir Lane, Woolston, Warrington, Cheshire WA1 4QQ; www.woolstoneyes.co.uk

CONTACT
Apply via the Woolston Eyes Conservation Group at www.woolstoneyes.co.uk

GETTING THERE
There are several possible entrances, but the best route by car is to leave the M6 at junction 21 and take the A57 signposted to Warrington. After about 200m (220 yards), turn left down Weir Lane and park by Woolston Weir. The bus to Weir Lane (to access the reserve from the north side) along the A57 is the no. 3 from Warrington.

ACCESS AND FACILITIES
There is a public footpath from the end of Weir Lane along the west side of no. 2 bed and the north side of the canal to Thelwall Lane. You need a permit to access the rest of the reserve. There is parking at the top of Weir Lane, or in the dedicated car park at the end of Thelwall Lane. There are no facilities.

OPENING TIMES
Open all year round.

CHARGES
Parts of the reserve are free, but there's a fee for the areas requiring permit access.

A haven for newts
Woolston Eyes is home to quite a collection of reptiles and amphibians, including snakes, frogs, toads, and newts. Both the great crested newt and the smooth newt (*shown below*) can be found on the site – look for them around the water edges. On land, they eat insects and worms, catching them with their minute teeth; in the water they flick out their long tongues to capture insects, worms, and water snails. They emerge from hibernation in March.

Left: An alert weasel uses a well-decayed log as a lookout point.

Right (left to right): a pair of black-necked grebes mating; unhatched chicks make "peeping" noises to tell their parents that the eggs need turning or incubating more; for the first week after hatching, the grebe chicks are carried through the water on their mother's back.

Main: The Woolston Eyes reserve. **Far right:** Black-necked grebe sitting on nest.

WATERFOWL AT WOOLSTON

AN AMAZING ONE-THIRD OF THE TOTAL UK POPULATION of the stunning black-necked grebe can be found at Woolston Eyes. This young wetland reserve was only created in 1980 as a by-product of the Manchester Ship Canal, which lies right beside it, and which made use of the site as a dumping ground for its dredgings. The word "Eyes" comes from the Saxon "Ees", meaning "land near a looping river", which describes the area well. Over time the land has been used for grazing meadows, factories (during the Industrial Revolution), and then extensive canal building. Now it is a wonderful mosaic of man-made wetland habitats, with reedbeds and a network of islands.

This diverse habitat is an important breeding site for one of the UK's most attractive birds; some might argue, *the* most attractive of our birds. The black-necked grebe in breeding plumage is truly magnificent. It has a fiery red eye and bright golden tufts sweeping off either side of its face, which contrast dramatically against the

Above: Look for the black darter dragonfly in summer.

Grebes are almost entirely aquatic, spending around 15 per cent of their time under the water, in search of prey.

THROUGH THE YEAR
WOOLSTON EYES

Grasshopper warblers, common warblers, chiffchaffs, willow warblers, blackcaps, and common whitethroats breed around Woolston Eyes in **summer**. You can usually see nesting gulls from bed no. 3, and grebes from the centre. Plant life includes lots of orchids, including the southern marsh, common spotted, and bee orchid, and also the rare broad-leaved helleborine.

By the beginning of **October,** incoming wintering birds include fieldfares and redwings. There are often large numbers of skylarks and meadow pipits. Long-eared owls can sometimes be seen in the trees around the south bank in **autumn**.

Wintering wildfowl numbers build to a peak in January and February, and this is the best time to catch sight of the water rail. Try the feeders to the east of the Frank Linley hide for a sighting of the uncommon willow tit. Scaups and smews can be seen in the weir pool in **winter**.

WHERE ELSE TO SEE
BLACK-NECKED GREBES

Black-necked grebes like reservoirs, gravel pits, and estuaries. There are around 60 breeding pairs scattered around England and Scotland, with occasional birds spotted in Anglesey, Wales.

On the Kent coast, **Dungeness** (*see pp.162–163*) is teeming with interesting birds, including black-necked grebes, little egrets, marsh harriers, and avocets. [SE]

The Fal Estuary, Cornwall, and **Poole Harbour**, Dorset (*see pp.48–49*) are good places to look for grebes in April. There is a great selection of wild ducks and geese, including brent geese, on the **River Exe**, especially around the estuary in winter (*see pp.286–287*). [SW]

Slimbridge (*see pp.34–35*) in Gloucestershire, on the Severn estuary, is excellent for wild ducks, swans, and geese. [M]

black of its neck and back. The birds spend the winter at sea or on larger lakes, but in the spring they start to return to their favourite breeding sites, such as Woolston Eyes. Here they find the all-important undisturbed, invertebrate-rich habitat they need for successful breeding – sometimes even producing two broods in one season.

There are four main wetland areas at the reserve, referred to as beds; each one is numbered. If you haven't seen the elusive water rail for some time, head to bed no. 3 (ensuring that you have first secured a permit). When the water levels are low, in periods of drought, you can get some really good views. This bed is also a reliable place to see large numbers of grebes: black-necked, little, and great crested grebes can all be seen in the water here, and the great crested grebes put on elaborate courtships displays in spring.

This lush reserve has over 220 bird species, as well as many other animals that you notice as you wander around its quiet paths in April, including the very rare great crested newt, the much-loved dormouse, and the adder – freshly emerged from hibernation and feeling peckish.

JAN
FEB
MAR
APR
MAY
JUN
JUL
AUG
SEP
OCT
NOV
DEC

WHERE
RSPB Leighton Moss Reserve, Storrs Lane,
Silverdale, Carnforth, Lancashire LA5 0SW.

CONTACT
Tel: 01524 701601;
leighton.moss@rspb.org.uk

GETTING THERE
The reserve lies on the outskirts of Silverdale,
6km (4 miles) north of Carnforth. From the
M6, take the A6 north from junction 35.
Brown signs direct you off the A6 to the
reserve. Silverdale station is 150m
(165 yards) from the reserve; the Silverdale
shuttle bus stops just opposite its entrance.

ACCESS AND FACILITIES
The car park has bicycle racks. The
wheelchair-friendly visitor centre has a café,
shop, full-access toilets, and baby changing
facilities. There are 8km (5 miles) of trails,
some suitable for wheel-chairs and pushchairs.
One wheelchair available for loan.

OPENING TIMES
Open all year round (except 25 December),
9am–dusk. Visitor centre open 9.30am–5pm
(9.30am–4.30pm in winter).

CHARGES
Charges for admission to hides and nature
trails, except for RSPB members and those
who come by public transport or bike.

Masters of camouflage

Bitterns are relatively sluggish and slow in flight,
so rely heavily on camouflage to avoid predators.
If a bittern detects a threat, it will raise its bill to
the sky, showing a vertically streaked brown
breast that is virtually indistinguishable from the
surrounding reeds. It may even sway slowly to
match the movement of the vegetation in the
wind. The bird is not defenceless – its sharp bill
and claws are a strong deterrent and it will puff
out its feathers to make its body appear bigger
to a potential attacker.

Above (left to right): The reedbed wetland at Leighton Moss; bittern chicks in a nest made from reed stems close to the water-level.
Main: Bitterns remain motionless as part of their camouflage, but occasionally need to stretch their wings.

Above: A bittern drinks and washes its bill, knee-deep in water.

BOOMING BITTERNS

TURN LEFT FROM THE RAILWAY STATION AND LEFT AGAIN, to the visitor centre, and you hardly know you are near water: Leighton Moss is a wonderful, secret world in a quiet valley close to the Lancashire coast. Running through it is a series of clean, sparkling lagoons, thickly surrounded by reed. Bitterns need this intricate mix of water and reed: they must catch fish, so open water is vital, but they won't come into the open, so they have to find areas where water penetrates the reedbed. A series of narrow ditches through reeds standing in quite deep water make ideal bittern habitat. Unfortunately, this means that they are exceptionally difficult to see, especially as their streaked tawny-brown plumage matches the dead, upright stems of reeds to perfection.

Instead, you must listen for them – and luckily, this is not a difficult thing to do: when a bittern booms, it is hard not to notice. To see one, you'll need to sit quietly in one of Leighton Moss's hides overlooking the lagoons with your fingers crossed; but to hear one, just stop and listen: the sound of a bittern's boom carries right across the valley. Only the male booms; the sound is his territorial song, saying "Here I am, this is my patch. If you are male, keep away. If you're a female, I'm over here."

Bittern numbers are measured according to "booming males". Each "boom" is as individual as a fingerprint, making it possible to count the bitterns on a site. But all you need do is listen for the boom: an eerie sound, especially at dawn or dusk, or in the hours of darkness. If you are close, you might hear a short note, almost like an intake of breath, before a deep, booming, almost (but not quite) musical "whooomp!" It has been likened to the bellow of a bull, or the boom of a distant foghorn, or even the sound you can make by blowing across the top of a large, empty bottle. However you hear it, you are unlikely to mistake this amazing "boom" from the reedbeds of Leighton Moss for anything else.

It's easy to see that a bittern is a member of the heron family when you see one in flight; its feet trail beyond the tail, and its head is hunched into the shoulders.

Inset: A bittern in flight shows its broad wingspan.
Below (left to right): Lucky visitors to the reserve may see an otter; a bearded tit.

WHERE ELSE TO SEE
BITTERNS

Bitterns can be seen all year round, but they are more visible in winter, and their numbers are higher. However, their booming mating call is most often heard in spring, so head for a place where they are known to breed, and listen out for their distinctive call.

East Anglia provides a home for around two-thirds of the UK's bittern population. **Minsmere** in Suffolk is a favourite place for watching bitterns, but the **Norfolk Broads** also have a scattering of bittern pairs. You might see one in the reedbeds along the north Norfolk coast. **Ely Pits and Meadows** in Cambridgeshire is an important inland site. [SE]

Male bitterns have recently been heard again around the **Humber** estuary in Lincolnshire, within the **Far Ings** reserve near Barton on Humber. [N]

The **Lee Valley** regional park's Bittern Watchpoint at Fishers Green, Hertfordshire, is a popular place to see bitterns near London. It supports approximately 10 per cent of the UK winter population. [SE]

THROUGH THE YEAR
LEIGHTON MOSS

In spring and **summer**, the lakes, marshes, and trees of Leighton Moss are especially good for reed warblers and sedge warblers, as well as common woodland birds. Bearded tits breed and may be seen or heard, especially on calmer days; look for them at a "birdtable" set up on the central causeway public footpath. Watch out, too, for the spectacular aerial courtship of the marsh harriers.

In summer and **autumn**, listen for water rails in the reeds and watch for them on sheltered muddy patches beside the reedbeds. Autumn is often good for seeing roosting swallows.

Through the **winter**, Leighton Moss is excellent for ducks, including many gadwalls, teals, and pochards, and a few shovelers and pintails. You should also see a good-sized starling roost, with flocks performing fantastic aerobatics over the reeds at dusk.

JAN
FEB
MAR
APR
MAY
JUN
JUL
AUG
SEP
OCT
NOV
DEC

WHERE
The Wye Valley, Herefordshire;
www.visitwyevalley.com

CONTACT
Forestry Commission, tel: 0845 3673787;
Symonds Yat information assistant,
tel: 07736 792511

GETTING THERE
To reach Symonds Yat Rock, follow the brown
tourist signs on the B4432 to Symonds Yat
from Coleford, Forest of Dean. The viewpoint
is approximately 250m (270 yards) from the
car park; just follow the "peregrine viewing"
signs. There are also buses that run from
Coleford Bus Station.

ACCESS AND FACILITIES
There is an information point at Symonds Yat
Rock run by the RSPB and Forest Enterprise
who fund telescopes to help visitors see the
peregrines. There are toilets and a café on
site, and both are wheelchair friendly. A
refreshment kiosk is open daily during the
summer, from 10am to 4pm.

OPENING TIMES
Open all year round. Car park and toilets are
open 10 am to 8.30 pm, or dusk if sooner.

CHARGES
Free access, but car-parking charges apply.

Wild boars in the forest

Wild boars disappeared from the UK around 300
years ago, largely due to being over-hunted. The
Forest of Dean, in the Wye Valley, was one of the
boars' last homes, and it seems they are staging
a comeback. A large group of boars – the perfect
mixture of males, sows, and juveniles – escaped
from local farms in 2004 and started breeding in
the forest. There are now around 50 or so living
wild. Look out for exposed plant roots and turned
earth, which are signs of boar rooting – but if
you spot the boars themselves, keep well away.

Above (left to right): Jackdaws roost in the forest, and in the crevices of Symonds Yat; the woodlands cover 10,900 hectares (27,000 acres).

VIBRANT VALLEY LIFE

THE WYE VALLEY IS JUSTLY DESIGNATED an area of outstanding natural beauty. It is divided into two areas: the Lower Wye Gorge – between Chepstow and Symonds Yat, with dramatic limestone cliffs and a narrow floodplain far below; and the gentler Herefordshire lowlands – lying north of Ross on Wye, where the river meanders across red sandstone. Both offer some of the most beautiful views in Britain, and have been attracting visitors since the 18th century.

In the Wye Gorge, the river runs between small earth cliffs – in which kingfishers and sand martins nest – and mud banks, over which the river flows to flood the plain each year. Woods line the length of the gorge, and the area buzzes with wildlife. Dragonflies and damselflies fill the air in spring, and six different types of mussel live in the river among the extraordinary number of fish: more than 30 species have been recorded here. In the right conditions, you stand a chance of seeing brown trout, chub, perch, roach, and eels as you walk along the river banks. In spring, the many migratory species include salmon, sea and river lampreys, and Wye specialities such as the allis and twaite shad, all coming upstream from the sea to spawn.

For a really dramatic viewpoint on to the valley and a close-up of its most famous inhabitants – the peregrine falcons – visit the limestone cliffs of Yat Rock, a scenic viewpoint towering 120m (400ft) above the Wye on the Gloucestershire side. From April onwards you can witness the aerial displays of these fascinating birds of prey, demonstrating their incredible speed and control.

Down on the ground, the night draws out a few wary foxes and badgers, and there have been sightings of polecats, recently returned to the valley after an absence of more than a century. Otters have also returned to play along the tributary streams, while 15 different species of bats swoop through the air above them.

Kingfishers, peregrines, grey herons, and sand martins are among the many birds hunting in and over the wildlife-rich River Wye.

Main: The Wye river in its lush valley, as seen from Yat Rock.
Inset: Kingfishers are a common sight over the river.
Below (left to right): The Wye rapids at Symonds Yat; a brown trout.

WHERE ELSE TO SEE
VALLEY WILDLIFE

The Wye Valley is home to a unique collection of wildlife, but many of its inhabitants can be found at other sites around Britain.

Peregrines are found on rocky sea cliffs in the breeding season, and on marshes along the east coast – particularly Suffolk and Norfolk – in winter. They are also found nesting in cities, including **Chichester** (*see pp.134–135*). [SE]

The **River Avon** in Hampshire has a large fish population, which can be viewed from the bank at several popular beauty spots and small wildlife reserves. Visit Hampshire County Council's website – www3.hants.gov.uk – or livingriver.co.uk for details of the Avon Valley Path. [SE]

The Dove river, in **Dovedale** on the Staffordshire/ Derbyshire border, moves through valleys and gorges, and woods and meadows, and is home to a rich mix of wildlife. [M]

THROUGH THE YEAR
THE WYE VALLEY

There are grass snakes around the valley in **summer**, together with a number of dragonflies and butterflies, including holly blue butterflies. Hummingbird hawkmoths can sometimes be seen darting between flowers around the Symonds Yat Rock viewpoint during the summer. Look for chub, brown trout, and salmon in the River Wye, kingfishers along its banks, and otters in the tributary streams.

In **autumn** watch for buzzards, and keep an eye out at any time for peregrines. You should also see swallows and martins moving south through the valley and the appearance of a great variety of fungi in the woods.

The mild valley is good for seeing migrating **winter** birds such as redwings, fieldfares, and finches. Keep an eye out for foxes and fallow deer early in the morning and at dusk.

JAN
FEB
MAR
APR
MAY
JUN
JUL
AUG
SEP
OCT
NOV
DEC

Below: Peregrines have nested at Symonds Yat every year since 1982.

WHERE
RSPB Lochwinnoch, near Paisley, Renfrewshire, Scotland PA12 4JF; www.rspb.org.uk

CONTACT
RSPB Lochwinnoch, tel: 01505 842663; lochwinnoch@rspb.org.uk

GETTING THERE
The reserve is 29km (18 miles) southwest of Glasgow, beside the A760 Largs Road, which is off the A737 Irvine Road (easily reached from the M8 at Junction 28A). Lochwinnoch railway station is 400m (440yds) from the visitor centre. National Cycle Route 7 runs through the reserve, adjacent to the A737.

ACCESS AND FACILITIES
Parking is free at the visitor centre, which has toilets, snack- and drinks- vending machines, and a picnic area. Both nature trails are suitable for wheelchairs and pushchairs; the two hides have adapted viewing positions for wheelchair users. One wheelchair is available for loan. Dogs are allowed on all footpaths, but must be kept on a lead.

OPENING TIMES
Open daily, 10am to 5pm (except 25–26 December and 1–2 January).

CHARGES
Yes, for non-RSPB members.

Nesting time
Once a clutch of eggs is laid, both parents take turns to sit on the nest. While they are superb swimmers and divers, grebes are awkward birds out of water: their legs are set right back by the tiny tail and they have broadly lobed toes, useless for walking. As soon as the eggs hatch the birds gladly return to the water, carrying the striped chicks on their backs. Grebes feed their own downy breast feathers to their chicks, to prevent fish bones penetrating their stomachs.

Main: To the observer, male and female grebes look identical, heightening the symmetry of the courtship performance. **Far right:** the "weed ceremony".

THE DANCE OF THE GREBES

ONE OF THE LAST AND BEST WETLANDS IN SOUTHWESTERN SCOTLAND, Lochwinnoch is a perfect place to see water birds on the open loch. This watery haven is home to all manner of ducks, geese, and swans, but it is the great crested grebes that catch the eye with their intriguing performances in spring. Take the nature trail to the Aird Meadow Loch on a sparkling April day, keep quiet and still, and you should get good views.

In spring, the grebe's head is adorned with a short, black, two-horned crest, and a broad fan of very fine chestnut and black feathers, normally lying flat, on each cheek. In their courtship displays, the grebes raise these fans and horns to create a broad, saucer-like facial disc. You never can tell which is the female and which is the male; even when mating they take turns to be on top. Their courtship displays are instinctive and strictly ritualized, following an almost automatic, regimented sequence. Loud, growling calls initiate the ceremony.

Left (left to right): Aird Meadow Loch; coots fight over their prospective mates; Bar Loch, on the Lochwinnoch reserve.

Right (left to right): A grebe makes a streamlined approach to its partner, low in the water; bold eye markings combined with erect horns and ruff give the grebe an exotic, almost tribal look.

Watch until the pair come together, almost beak-to-beak, in a perfect, mirrored sequence of movements.

WHERE ELSE TO SEE
GREAT CRESTED GREBES

Great crested grebes can be seen on rivers, pools, and reservoirs throughout England and Wales but only locally in southern Scotland: from autumn to late winter, look for them on sheltered coastal bays.

Grafham Water (*see pp.302–303*) and the flooded gravel workings at **Little Paxton**, both in Cambridgeshire, have great crested grebes. [SE]

Grebes can be seen at both **Blithfield Reservoir** in Staffordshire and **Rutland Water** in Rutland. **Cotswold Water Park** in Gloucestershire has an important breeding population, together with other star wetland wildlife including otters and bitterns. [M]

Llangorse Lake in the Brecon Beacons National Park is a good place for seeing grebes (try the Llangasty hide). [W]

THROUGH THE YEAR
LOCHWINNOCH

A rich diversity of wetland wildlife can be seen at Lochwinnoch year-round. Watch for other wetland birds and an excellent range of warblers, from grasshopper warblers in rough grassy areas to sedge warblers in the bushy swamps and chiffchaffs, willow warblers, blackcaps, and whitethroats in trees, scrub and hedgerows. Listen for the shrill whistle and "plop" of a diving kingfisher or the pig-like squealing of a water rail in the reeds.

Lochwinnoch is great in winter, with whooper swans from **October** to **March**, a good variety of ducks including rather grebe-like goosanders, and greylag geese. If you are lucky, you might see a smew, a rare relative of the goosander.

Summer is the time to watch baby ducklings and cygnets, as well as many kinds of butterflies and damselflies: but try a visit at dusk, keep quiet and still, and you might see an otter.

Autumn is the time to watch roosting flocks: first of swallows and house martins, and later, of fieldfares, newly arrived from the continent.

One bird dives underwater, then resurfaces with just its head visible, swimming towards its mate, leaving a V-shaped wake (the "ripple approach"). The other raises itself from the water, with part-open wings, in the "cat display". The diving bird emerges with its back to its partner, rising up vertically but with its head bowed stiffly down, in the "ghostly-penguin" performance. It then rotates to face its mate, and the two begin the most easily seen part of the display, the ritual "head-shaking". In spring, this part of the ritual continues over a far longer period than any of the other actions. Both birds spread their crests, raise their heads, open their bills, and waggle their heads from side to side, making quiet "ticking" calls. This subsides into a silent, side-to-side waggle with closed beaks, and then they pretend to preen their wing and back feathers with an exaggerated sweep of the beak.

You might, if you are particularly lucky, witness the remarkable "weed ceremony", in which one or both birds carry weed in the beak and the two rise breast to breast in the weed dance: a beautiful performance to celebrate the pair's "engagement".

Below: A water rail forages in the shallows.

JAN
FEB
MAR
APR
MAY
JUN
JUL
AUG
SEP
OCT
NOV
DEC

A HAZE OF BLUEBELLS

IF THERE IS ONE FLOWER THAT SYMBOLIZES THE GLORY OF SPRINGTIME IN BRITAIN, it is the bluebell. Insignificant in itself, this slender wild hyacinth flowers by the million to create one of the most dazzling, yet ephemeral of all floral displays – a shimmering, fragrant haze of purest blue. This is a uniquely British spectacle, for only in Britain's mild, moist climate do bluebells flourish in such profusion. In the wetter regions of the west and north they may grow in the open, but over most of Britain the massed flowers appear in open broad-leaved woodlands like Norsey Wood, Essex – a 400-year-old deer park that becomes utterly magical in late April.

Bluebells thrive here because their life-cycle is adapted to fit in with that of deciduous woodland. They sprout in January when the trees are bare, and as spring sunlight floods the woodland floor they put on a spurt of growth that climaxes with a mass flowering just as the leaves begin to unfurl on the trees. Within a few days the

WHERE
Norsey Wood Nature Reserve, Outwood Common Road, Billericay, Essex CM11 1HA; www.norseywood.org.uk

CONTACT
Norsey Wood Information Centre, tel: 01277 624553; or Basildon Council Countryside services, tel: 01268 550088; nws@stones.com

GETTING THERE
Norsey Wood lies just northeast of Billericay. From the A127, take the A176; take the right fork at the far end of Billericay High Street (Norsey Road), then turn right on to Outwood Common Road. From the B1007, turn left at the roundabout after entering Billericay. At the end of the road, turn left, then right into Outwood Common Rd. By public transport: from Billericay Rail Station, take the 102NB bus.

ACCESS AND FACILITIES
Visitor centre with toilets and picnic area opens Saturdays and Sundays but closes if the ranger is needed at other sites. Access for wheelchairs is limited, but there is an easy-access trail and a mobility vehicle on site.

OPENING TIMES
The woods can be accessed all day.

CHARGES
None.

A native bluebell – *Hyacinthoides non-scripta* – takes seven years to grow from seed, and extends its range by only a modest 50m (165ft) in 35 years.

Spanish invaders

The native bluebell has a close relative, the Spanish bluebell, introduced to Britain long ago and discovered growing in the wild in 1909. Bigger, tougher, and with a spire of broader flowers, it interbreeds with the native species to produce vigorous fertile hybrids. These are now found in around one in six of the UK's woodlands. They threaten the survival of the more delicate native bluebell, as do milder winters: when trees spread their leaves earlier, they shade out the woodland flowers before they have set seed.

flowers fade to swollen seedheads, disappearing as the spreading tree canopy favours other plants that are able to cope with deep shade. For the rest of the year they stockpile food in their bulbs. This cycle evolved in natural oakwoods, and in the drier south and east of England bluebells are an indicator of ancient woodland. Norsey Wood is certainly ancient, but while it does have tall oaks, most of its hornbeam and sweet chestnut trees have been coppiced to make new shoots. This yields a renewable harvest of "underwood", traditionally used for making products such as woven hurdles. At Norsey the process is repeated in different areas of the wood each year, letting in light to encourage bluebells along with other spring flowers – wood anemones, lily-of-the-valley, dog violets, and stitchwort. These attract nectar-feeding butterflies such as brimstones, orange-tips, and speckled woods, while the spring flush of leaf-eating caterpillars is exploited by breeding wrens, blackcaps, and other birds, whose jubilant songs celebrate one of the finest wildlife shows of the year.

Main: Norsey Wood is an ancient mix of oak, sweet chestnut, hornbeam, birch, and alder.

Left panel (top to bottom): Norsey Wood's bluebells are the true native species; a badger snuffles along.

Above: Razor-strop fungus, also known as polypore fungus, lives on the bark of the birch trees.

Below: Tawny owls hunt in the woods after dusk.

WHERE ELSE TO SEE
BLUEBELLS

Bluebells – often known as wild hyacinths in Scotland – grow throughout most of the British Isles except Orkney and Shetland. They need moist soil, so in most regions they grow in damp, broad-leaved woodland, with tall oaks and ashes and shorter, often coppiced hazel or chestnut. They also grow along hedgerows – often a sign of vanished ancient woodland – and on open grasslands and coastal cliffs in the north and west.

Bluebell woods are still numerous throughout Britain, and some even survive in city parks and suburbs. These include **Perivale Wood**, London, normally closed but open to visitors at bluebell time, and the woods around Queen Charlotte's Cottage in **Kew Gardens** in Surrey. There are wonderful bluebells in the ancient woodland of the RSPB reserve at **Northward Hill**, Kent (see pp.54–55). [SE]

Ryton Wood, Warwickshire, is famous for bluebells, as is **Dole Wood** in Lincolnshire. [M]

In Scotland, head for **Carstramon Wood** near Gatehouse of Fleet, Dumfries and Galloway. [SC]

THROUGH THE YEAR
NORSEY WOOD

Most of the woodland flowers vanish in **summer**, shaded out by the trees, but the verges of the main ride and the well-named Butterfly Ride are bright with flowers and nectar-feeding insects. Visit the ponds in the northeastern corner of the wood to see a colourful variety of dragonflies and damselflies.

In **autumn** the wood glows with the russets and yellows of autumn colour while a wide variety of fungi push up through the gathering carpet of fallen leaves. Nocturnal dormice feed on nuts, seeds, and berries to fatten up for their winter sleep.

The bare branches can often provide good views of resident birds like the great spotted woodpecker in **winter**, while a dusting of snow illuminates the wood and may reveal the occasional prowling fox.

Below: The spiny casings of sweet chestnut.

JAN
FEB
MAR
APR
MAY
JUN
JUL
AUG
SEP
OCT
NOV
DEC

HIGHLAND ESCAPE

NOWHERE IN BRITAIN HAS SUCH A MARVELLOUS STRETCH of native pine forest as the western edge of the Cairngorms, including Abernethy and Rothiemurchus. These pinewoods are a world away from the more familiar uniform plantations found across the UK. They are light and airy, richly green, and bright with the orange of Scots pine bark. Situated around the vast and peaceful waters of Loch Garten, the Abernethy forest also has its own blue pools with grassy islands and busy wildlife. For centuries this has been a famous region for naturalists, "collectors", shooting parties, and stalkers, and some birds all but disappeared. But the capercaillie, gone by the 18th century, was reintroduced in 1837 and in spring you

WHERE
RSPB Loch Garten, Tulloch, Nethy Bridge, Highland PH25 3EF, Scotland; www.rspb.org.uk

CONTACT
Tel: 01479 831476; abernethy@rspb.org.uk

GETTING THERE
The reserve lies off the A95. By rail, go to Aviemore: 16km (10 miles) from the reserve. By bus, take the no. 34 from Aviemore to Grantown on Spey (ask for Raebreck junction). From here a footpath leads to the Osprey Centre (2km/1.6 miles). The reserve is on Route 7 of the National Cycle Network.

ACCESS AND FACILITIES
The site is wheelchair friendly with access to viewing hides. The visitor centre is pushchair friendly with full-access toilets, baby-changing facilities, and a live camera on the osprey nest. Cold drinks and snacks are available.

OPENING TIMES
Open daily 10am–6pm from April–August, with last entry at 5pm. The centre is also open earlier in April and May to watch for capercaillies (check times before visiting).

CHARGES
Yes, for non-RSPB members.

The capercaillies are a joy to watch in April, during their mating display. Holding their wings down, they fan out their tail feathers, then emit an extraordinary sequence of noises, including gurgles, wheezes, and intermittent popping sounds.

can see these highly active and feisty birds – occasionally a "rogue" male will even attack people or vehicles. The RSPB's Osprey Centre lies in the heart of the forest, and CCTV cameras around the site mean that you can catch every second of their nesting habits, thrilling flying displays, and prodigious hunting skills. As you walk the trails, you're also likely to see buzzards, black grouse, crested tits, crossbills, and siskins, and perhaps the shyer red and roe deer. Red squirrels are busy in the forest, their tails fading to pale cream in late spring. Pine martens are much more difficult to see, but keep your eyes open – even the very rare wildcats, Britain's most threatened wild mammals, live among these pines.

Abernethy is extraordinarily rich in insects and rare spiders, including 400 kinds of beetle. The forest is full of possibility: one recently discovered fly was new to science. You may see Scotch argus and dark green fritillary butterflies, and rare dragonflies such as the northern damselfly, which breed in the forest bogs and lochans. Rare wild flowers include intermediate and serrated wintergreen, and the lovely little twinflower. Abernethy is the only place in Britain to see nine species of microfungi, and there are many others that only grow in this habitat. These old Scots pines and juniper trees hide a multitude of plants, mammals, and insects.

Main: The hides of the RSPB Osprey Centre lie close to the shores of beautiful Loch Garten.
Below (left to right): Red squirrels climb in the Scots pines; ospreys catch trout from the freshwater loch.
Inset: In April, capercaillies move into more open woodland to "lek" – display – for prospective female partners.

Curious nests

Here and there in the forest you'll notice big, grey mounds of pine needles. If you look closely, you'll see that these mounds are alive with wood ants – Britain's largest ants – who collect the pine needles to make their dome-shaped nests. The needles are carefully placed to shed water very efficiently, keeping the nest dry. The ants' activity is crucial to the forest's ecosystem as they clear large areas of dropped pine needles that would otherwise smother the ground.

Above: Osprey in nest with young.

JAN

FEB

MAR

APR

MAY

JUN

JUL

AUG

SEP

OCT

NOV

DEC

THROUGH THE YEAR
LOCH GARTEN

In **summer**, watch the ospreys, tree pipits, redstarts, and crested tits. The woods are enlivened by lilac-pink heather, and the shiny greens of bilberry and cowberry.

Autumn sees most birds moving away but crested tits remain, as do the red squirrels, and there is a chance of a scarce migrant from the north such as a great grey shrike. Red kites wander widely at this time.

Pink-footed and greylag geese come to roost on Loch Garten in **winter**, and you should also see whooper swans, goldeneyes, and goosanders. Keep a look out for both red and roe deer.

WHERE ELSE TO SEE
PINE FOREST WILDLIFE

The UK's large native pine forests are all in Scotland. Pinewoods do not support a large diversity of plants and animals, but those that can survive in this habitat are generally rare, and well worth a visit.

Trails around **Loch an Eilean** in Rothiemurchus are good for crossbills, crested tits, and red squirrels, but please avoid searching for capercaillies, especially in spring and summer. They are rare birds, and it is illegal to disturb them when they are nesting. [SC]

Corrimony, west of Loch Ness, has black grouse, but not capercaillies. **Glen Affric** is a wonderful area with splendid patches of "Caledonian" forest and you can also see some of these native pinewoods around **Loch Maree** and **Beinn Eighe** (see pp.202–203) in Wester Ross. [SC]

Naturally there are no Scottish pinewoods in southern Britain, but you can see crossbills in the established Scots pines of **Breckland** in Norfolk. [SE]

Elsewhere in southern England, red squirrels can be found among the pine trees on **Brownsea Island**, Dorset (see pp.56–57). [SW]

Left (left to right): The dunes at Ainsdale on the Sefton Coast; a sand lizard.

Right (left to right): Toads breed in pools within the dune slacks; the male toad clasps the female as she lays her eggs; the female spawns a double-strand string of eggs.

Panel (below right): A natterjack's mottled brown skin provides camouflage.

WHERE
Ainsdale Dunes, Sefton Sands, Formby, Liverpool L37 1LJ; www.seftoncoast.org.uk

CONTACT
Natural England, site manager, tel: 01704 578774; northwest@naturalengland.org.uk

GETTING THERE
The reserve is between Ainsdale, 2km (1¼ miles) to the north, and Freshfield, near Formby, 2km (1¼ miles) to the south. All three towns are on the A565. By car, access to the reserve is via minor roads from the A565. The nearest train station is Ainsdale, a 20-minute walk from the site. The reserve is on the National Cycle Network, Route no. 62.

ACCESS AND FACILITIES
Access to the site is by permit only, which visitors need to apply for. Contact the site manager (tel: 01704 578774) for details. Three major trails pass through or near the reserve while public footpaths follow the perimeter of the reserve. The main path through the reserve is suitable for cycling and wheelchairs. The nearest toilets and refreshments are in local towns.

OPENING TIMES
Open all year round.

CHARGES
None.

New breeding pools
The natterjacks of the Sefton Coast owe their success to a dune conservation strategy developed in 1996 as part of the Sefton Coast Life Project. Scrub was cleared from the dunes, and grazing animals were introduced to prevent its return. Meanwhile more breeding pools were created, and within two years there were greater numbers of spawning natterjacks. Today they are flourishing all along the Sefton Coast, as are similar species such as the sand lizard.

Main: Natterjack toads are stocky and short-legged, with a body length of around 20cm (8in).

NATTERJACK CHORUS

COASTAL SAND DUNES ARE AMONG THE MOST EPHEMERAL of wildlife habitats. They can be literally here today and gone tomorrow, if there is a big storm overnight. If they escape this fate they tend to stabilize, sprout dune grasses, and evolve into scrubland. But as fast as this happens, new dunes tend to form, providing a mosaic of habitats for the often rare plants and animals that live among them.

The most extensive coastal dunes in Britain lie along the Sefton Coast near Merseyside. There are several good sites, but one of the best is Ainsdale Dunes. The whole "succession" of dune habitats exists here, including mobile dunes, fixed dunes, damp dune slacks, and scrub. Rare species such as sand lizards and great crested newts live in the dunes, and the extensive pinewoods support a thriving population of red squirrels. But in April the prime attraction for any wildlife watcher is the ringing chorus of the natterjack toads that breed in the shallow dune pools.

The massed chorus of up to 1,000 male natterjacks is so loud that it can be heard from well over 2km (1.2 miles) away.

WHERE ELSE TO SEE
NATTERJACK TOADS

In Britain the natterjack is restricted to warm, sandy habitats, usually within 100m (330ft) of sea level. It was once numerous on the sandy heaths and coasts of southern and eastern England, but its main strongholds are now in the northwest, from Merseyside to the Solway Firth.

Apart from the Sefton Coast, the main area for natterjacks in England is Cumbria. Try the vast sand-dune systems of the **Ravenglass Estuary**. [N]

A flourishing East Anglian natterjack colony breeds among the coastal dunes at **Winterton**, Norfolk, north of Great Yarmouth. The nature reserve also supports adders, many birds, and, later in the year, orchids and dragonflies. **Holme Dunes** National Nature Reserve near Hunstanton is another Norfolk natterjack refuge. **The Lodge**, in Bedfordshire – the RSPB's UK headquarters – also has a population. [SE]

Natterjacks also flourish on coastal dunes on the Scottish shores of the Solway Firth. They are most abundant on the saltmarsh margins of **Caerlaverock** National Nature Reserve, south of Dumfries. [SC]

THROUGH THE YEAR
AINSDALE DUNES

In **summer** the dune slacks are bright with flowers, including a number of rare species such as the dune helleborine, a type of orchid. Rare sand lizards also hunt among the dunes, and both adults and young lizards can be seen basking in the sun to warm up on August mornings.

The cooler weather in **autumn** makes lizards and natterjacks slip into hibernation, but it also sees the arrival of masses of migrant waders that feed along the tidal shores of the estuaries.

Winter can be a good time to look for the red squirrels that live in the pinewoods backing the dune systems. The area supports one of the main surviving red squirrel populations in England.

JAN FEB MAR APR MAY JUN JUL AUG SEP OCT NOV DEC

The natterjack is among the rarest of British amphibians, partly because it is on the edge of its habitable range in Britain – it thrives only in lowland heaths and dunes where it can find plenty of insect prey and burrow easily to escape the summer sun. Smaller and more agile than the common toad, with a distinctive yellow stripe down its back, it spawns in warm, shallow pools that are too brackish and short-lived to attract predators such as newts and diving beetles.

By April the breeding season at Ainsdale is in full swing, with hundreds of male natterjacks gathering around the pools and singing to attract females. You need to arrive near dusk to catch their post-sunset performance. The call is a racheting "rrrrRRP" that lasts for about a second but, multiplied many times over, creates a continuous trilling that can be astonishingly loud. Flick on a torch and you may see a male in mid-call, the vocal sac beneath his throat inflated to amplify the sound. Males and females pair up at random, each female slipping into a pool to lay long strings of eggs that the male fertilizes while clinging to her back. By dawn the whole process is over, and the natterjacks retreat to their burrows to prepare for a repeat performance the following night.

Below: A common lizard on the dunes along the Sefton Coast.

PASSAGE THROUGH PORTLAND

MAGINE YOU'RE A BIRD RETURNING NORTH to breed from your warm wintering home in southern Europe or Africa. You're exhausted, dropping closer and closer to the sea, when you chance upon Portland, jutting 10km (6 miles) out from the Dorset coast into the English Channel. Here you can rest and prepare yourself for the next stage of your journey. It's no wonder Portland Bill is such a birding hotspot for watching the spring migration. The "Bill" refers to Portland's most southerly point, so it tends to be the first stretch of land birds see. Migrants start returning in early March but the peak months are April and May, when thousands of birds pass through.

Certain factors can increase your chances of seeing more birds: ideally, you want strong southerly winds, bringing cloud and light rain overnight; and fog, which will naturally force birds to ground, and prevent the morning sun from moving them on too early. The earlier you can arrive, the more migrants you're likely to see.

WHERE
Portland Bill, Portland, Dorset DT5 2JT;
www.portlandbirdobs.org.uk

CONTACT
Portland Bird Observatory and Field Centre,
tel: 01305 820553; obs@btinternet.com;
Tourist Information Centre,
tel: 01305 861233;
portlandtic@weymouth.gov.uk

GETTING THERE
Portland Bill is joined to the mainland of Weymouth by Chesil Beach and a road bridge. By car from Weymouth, follow the signposts to Portland (along the A354) and then to Portland Bill. The nearest train station is in Weymouth, 14.4km (9 miles) away. There is also a regular bus service to Portland from Weymouth.

ACCESS AND FACILITIES
There is free parking at the Portland Bird Observatory and lighthouse. The Portland Tourist Information Centre is based at the lighthouse and there is a visitor centre there too. The area is not suitable for wheelchairs.

OPENING TIMES
The observatory is open all year round, the lighthouse from July to September.

CHARGES
Small entry charge for the lighthouse.

Portland spurge

Portland spurge is a low-growing, sprawling plant, restricted to coastal regions in southwest Britain, the Channel Islands, and of course, Portland. You may come across it either on sandy dunes or rocky ledges; its red-tinted flowers and red stems distinguish it from its close relative, sea spurge. As with all spurges, it has fleshy leaves, excellent for storing water, with a waxy coating that reduces evaporation by drying winds, The leaves and stems contain a white latex, which rabbits and other herbivores find unpalatable.

Left: Common whitethroat.

Right (left to right): The serin is a rare visitor to our shores; rock samphire on the cliff-top; a blue-headed wagtail.

Right panel (top and bottom): A hoopoe is an exotic sight; signs of quarrying are everywhere at the Bill – Portland stone was used in the building of both St Paul's Cathedral, London, and the Cobb at Lyme Regis.

Some of the regular migrants you can expect to see (sometimes in their hundreds) are chiffchaffs, willow warblers, pipits, wheatears, pied and spotted flycatchers, common redstarts, ring ouzels, and hirundines. If you're lucky you might see hoopoes, golden orioles, and honey buzzards; but, as every birdwatcher knows, migrations can produce spectacular rarities. Some of the Bill's very rare species include dark-eyed junco, northern water thrush, and Allen's gallinule.

Take extra care on the Bill if it's stormy. Wet conditions make the sea-level ledges very slippery, and large waves can easily wash you away if you are too close to the sea. Visit the Portland Bird Observatory at the Old Lower Lighthouse if you have time, as the logbook will tell you what's around, and bushes in the gardens provide good cover for birds. You might also enjoy visiting Portland's famous limestone quarries. Take care not to lose your footing when clambering through disused quarries. They can be fantastically atmospheric, and sometimes downright eerie.

The wheatear is the harbinger of spring at Portland – it's the first bird to return from wintering in Africa.

WHERE ELSE TO SEE
SPRING MIGRATION

As spring approaches, birdwatchers start licking their index fingers to "test" the all important wind direction. As birds return northwards from Europe and Africa, any winds that push birds towards the UK are welcomed. Most of the spring migration hotspots tend to be on promontories or islands.

Lizard Point (*see pp.116–117*), in Cornwall, is a long peninsula that exhausted birds home in on. Visitors include swallows, swifts, warblers, and flycatchers. From early March, firecrests and redstarts start arriving, followed by chiffchaffs, short-eared owls, wheatears, and swallows, swifts, and warblers. [SW]

Much of the east coast welcomes migrating birds, including **Dungeness** (*see pp.162–163*), Kent, and **Blakeney Point** (*see pp.214–215*), Norfolk. [SE]

Flamborough Head (*see pp.252–253*), Yorkshire, is another east-coast destination for migrants. [N]

The **Isles of Scilly**, off Land's End, Cornwall, are good for unusual birds, with regular sightings of golden orioles, hoopoes, and woodchat shrikes. [SW]

THROUGH THE YEAR
PORTLAND BILL

If you visit Portland in May and June, you're likely to see seabirds, such as fulmars, kittiwakes, and even a few puffins, breeding on the West Cliffs. Dolphins, basking sharks, and seals can be seen swimming around the Bill. Portland also has some impressive plant species: during the **summer** months, bee orchids and pyramidal orchids grow in the disused quarries. In early summer, you can see one of Portland's rarest plants – the beautiful early gentian. Look out for rare wall lizards basking in the sunshine on the rocks.

The birds that arrived in spring start to leave again as early as July, carrying on until the end of October. But even as the skylarks and pipits leave, there are new **autumn** arrivals, such as the continental warblers.

During **winter**, the harbour is a great place to look for divers, grebes, mergansers, and even eider ducks.

Below: Migrant butterflies like this painted lady also stop off here.

JAN

FEB

MAR

APR

MAY

JUN

JUL

AUG

SEP

OCT

NOV

DEC

WHERE
Weeting Heath Reserve, Hockwold Road, Weeting, nr Brandon, Norfolk IP26 4NQ.

CONTACT
Norfolk Wildlife Trust, tel: 01842 827615; www.norfolkwildlifetrust.org.uk

GETTING THERE
Weeting Heath Reserve is just west of Brandon; take the A1065 to Mundford; turn left to Weeting village and once there, turn left to Hockwold cum Wilton. The car park and visitor centre are signed 2.5km (1½ miles) west of Weeting. The nearest train station is Brandon. Buses from Brandon stop a short walk from the nature reserve.

ACCESS AND FACILITIES
The visitor centre has interpretive displays, information boards, and car parking. There are several hides on the reserve. The reserve is wheelchair friendly, with full-access toilets.

OPENING TIMES
The visitor centre and nature reserve are open April–September, 7am to dusk.

CHARGES
A small entry charge for adult non-members of Norfolk Wildlife Trust; children go free.

Stone curlew protection
Through concerted action under the Biodiversity Action Plan, stone curlew numbers in Britain have grown from around 170 pairs to more than 300 in the past decade. Nest site protection and targeted agri-environment schemes have played a major role, as has a better understanding of its habitat management needs. At Weeting Heath, a healthy rabbit population is crucial in maintaining the short grassy sward that supports high densities of the curlews' favoured insect prey – including this localized stripe-winged grasshopper.

Above (top to bottom): Weeting Heath visitor centre; the grazing of rabbits, seen in their dozens in the early morning, keeps the grasslands short and rich.

Below: Several rare speedwells grow at Weeting, including the Breckland speedwell, shown here.

Right panel (top and bottom): A woodlark finds the perfect perch for a song; a breeding pair of stone curlews, with their distinctive yellow eyes.

Main: The stone curlew uses a distraction display to lure an intruder away from its nest site.

GUARDIAN OF THE HEATH

THE BRECKLAND OF NORFOLK AND SUFFOLK IS A VAST AREA of wind-blown glacial sand, overlying chalk at variable depths. Infertile, freely-draining, and in the driest part of the country, it was colonized by Neolithic man, cleared of its sparse forest cover, and grazing stock were brought in. This is how the Breckland heaths were created, and they are more akin to the steppes of eastern Europe than anywhere else in Britain.

Unfortunately, the once-continuous heathlands have now been highly fragmented by the planting of conifers and the onset of intensive agriculture, causing the loss of some of its iconic birds, including the great bustard. However, some species have weathered the changes, such as the stone curlew, whose eerie nocturnal calls remain an integral part of the Breckland soundscape. This rare, strange-looking bird visits the UK in summer to breed, in very vulnerable nests on the ground. It is hard to see during the day, when it remains

JAN

FEB

MAR

APR

MAY

JUN

JUL

AUG

SEP

OCT

NOV

DEC

Above: Lapwings wintering in the Brecks.

The stone curlew is a secretive bird, but quick to defend its breeding territory on the close-cropped heathland of the Brecks.

THROUGH THE YEAR
WEETING HEATH

During the **summer**, the Breckland heaths continue to reveal their botanical delights, such as spiked speedwell and maiden pink. Ground-dwelling insects proliferate, especially grasshoppers, including the stripe-winged grasshopper, a speciality of this area. At dusk, listen to nightjars churring and watch the woodcocks' dusk "roding" flights (*see p.119*).

In **autumn**, deer become more obvious, as the red and fallow deer move out from the forestry plantations to embark upon the rutting season. Roe deer and muntjac deer, however, generally remain in dense cover – as secretive as ever.

Winter sometimes sees the arrival of a great grey shrike or two, and in some years there can be quite large numbers of crossbills in the conifers, breeding as early as February. Groups of bramblings or a few hawfinches may be found in favoured places, such as among beech or hornbeam trees.

WHERE ELSE TO SEE
BRECKLAND HEATH WILDLIFE

Breckland's climate is almost continental: high summer temperatures, low rainfall, and frequent frosts. Its chalk substrata, thinly covered by sand, makes it a unique habitat.

Breckland specialities can be found in many of the heathland reserves of East Anglia, including **East Wretham**, **Brettenham**, and **Cavenham Heaths**, but access may be restricted during the breeding season. **Maidscross Hill**, Lakenheath, and **Barnham Cross Common**, Thetford, are two sites where access is possible at all times. The **Suffolk Sandlings** (heathland between Lowestoft and Ipswich) has a small population of stone curlews. [SE]

Stone curlews are otherwise found mainly on **Salisbury Plain** [SW] and **Porton Down** in Wiltshire [SE], although much of these areas are out of bounds for military reasons.

largely inactive; your best chance is to visit the hides at the Norfolk Wildlife Trust's Weeting Heath reserve at dawn or dusk. You'll need to scan the ground very carefully to see these well-camouflaged birds, with their staring yellow eyes and stocky yellow legs, but wardens are on hand throughout the season to help you.

Other spring visitors to look out for are the wheatear – usually associated with the uplands, but here breeding in lowland rabbit burrows – and the tree pipit, which you usually hear before you see it, delivering its fluty song in flight or from the top of an isolated tree. The descending "lu–lu–lu" of the woodlarks can be heard too, adding to the uplifting spring melody.

One field on the reserve is managed as an arable field for rare plants. Here you can find three rare annual speedwells – spring, fingered, and Breckland – which grow only at a few sites in East Anglia, and are recognizable by their small, bright-blue flowers. As spring turns to summer, the delicate flowers of Spanish catchfly appears, along with field wormwood. All are specialities of the region, together helping to make the Brecks a unique botanical delight.

WHERE
Llangollen Canal, Llangollen, Wales LL20.

CONTACT
British Waterways, tel: 01606 723800; enquiries.wbc@britishwaterways.co.uk

GETTING THERE
The nearest towns are Llangollen in the south and Nantwich in the north, and the aqueduct is located near Cefn-Mawr. For Llangollen, take Junction 10A of the M6 for the M54 and Shrewsbury and continue along the M54 until it meets the A5, which takes you to Llangollen. For the Nantwich end, where the Llangollen Canal leaves the Shropshire Union Canal at Hurleston Junction, leave the M6 at junction 16.

ACCESS AND FACILITIES
There are no facilities on the canal towpaths, but there are plenty in nearby towns along the canal. Wheelchair access is variable, depending on which trail you take, but some towpaths are paved. You can take circular walks along Colemere and the Ellesmere Canal towpath.

OPENING TIMES
Open all year round.

CHARGES
None.

Ice-fishing

Kingfishers prefer to hunt in still or slow-flowing waters, making canals good habitats. However, canals freeze over more readily than do fast-flowing streams and rivers, which can make winter feeding a challenge – especially given that a kingfisher must eat at least its own bodyweight of fish every day. Birds may feed through holes in the ice or move away from their breeding habitats in winter. Some settle by nearby open water but others migrate to tidal estuaries or even sheltered coasts.

Above (left to right): Llangollen Canal; a kingfisher brings food to its young at a nesthole in a sandbank.
Main: A kingfisher leaving the water with its catch.

KINGFISHERS ON THE CANAL

ONCE VITAL ARTERIES OF COMMERCE, PULSING WITH TRAFFIC delivering the raw materials and products of heavy industry, the canals of Britain have undergone a dramatic transformation into refuges for wetland wildlife. Even restored canals carry so little traffic now that they remain tranquil havens for shyer animals. Waterways such as the Llangollen Canal on the North Wales border offer many opportunities for watching these more elusive animals, both from the towpath and from the slow-moving narrowboats that can be hired along the route. April is perfect, as there are few other boats on the water. If you sit quietly on a moving boat, animals will often allow you to get surprisingly close, providing memorably intimate views.

One of the most dazzling sights on the canal – almost literally – is the electric-blue flash of a hunting kingfisher. Often this flash is all you see, as the bird zips low over the water with a shrill whistle and disappears around a bend. But if you check the overhanging vegetation carefully you may spot one on its fishing perch, watching the water intently for prey. It can be surprisingly hard to pick out, despite its bright blue and orange plumage, because the brilliant streak down its back is often obscured until it flies. With luck, it will spot a likely target, and plunge into the calm, clear water with a splash, before reappearing with a small fish in its bill. Returning to its perch, it often beats its luckless victim against something hard before juggling it around in its long, stout bill to swallow it head-first.

Spring is the busiest time for kingfishers because they have extra mouths to feed. Each pair may have up to seven chicks, and each chick needs 12–18 fish a day. The birds nest in burrows in the bank, which are often identifiable by the white streak of droppings below the tunnel entrance. There is a regular nesting site on Blake Mere, one of several quiet lakes or "meres" flanking the canal near Ellesmere in Shropshire, which were formed by melting ice at the end of the last Ice Age. This is one of the best places to explore the canal on foot, providing access not only to the canal and wildlife-rich meres but also to the nearby Wood Lane Reserve: a quarry with a flourishing colony of sand martins. These smaller, browner relatives of house martins are among the earliest migrant birds to return to their nesting sites in spring, and by April the colony is bustling with birds bringing food to their young – a truly wonderful place to watch and marvel at the sheer exuberance of nature.

Below (left to right): The electric blue of a kingfisher's back; during courtship, a male, with his entirely black beak, offers fish to the female.

WHERE ELSE TO SEE
KINGFISHERS

Kingfishers are widespread throughout the British Isles, but favour lowland habitats where there are more slow-flowing rivers and canals. They generally remain near their breeding sites throughout the year unless forced to move by winter ice. They like water that has a lot of overhanging vegetation, so disused or quiet canals are ideal.

The **Basingstoke Canal** in Surrey and Hampshire is partly disused, making it an excellent place to search for kingfishers, who enjoy its tranquility. The **Lee Valley** country park (see pp.26–27), near Waltham Abbey on the northern outskirts of London, has a number of wetlands as well as the River Lee itself, offering plenty of potential fishing sites for hungry kingfishers. [SE]

The **Cromford Canal** Nature Reserve in the Peak District of Derbyshire is a rich freshwater habitat, with kingfishers as well as other water birds such as herons and little grebes. The canal is also one of the last strongholds of the declining water vole. [M]

THROUGH THE YEAR
LLANGOLLEN CANAL

In **summer** the canal develops luxuriant marginal vegetation, which is bright with the glinting wings of insects. By day these attract insect-eating birds, such as warblers, while at dusk you may see low-flying Daubenton's bats hunting over the water.

Many of the plants start to die down in **autumn**, and the water becomes dotted with autumn leaves that have fallen from overhanging trees. But many larger insects will still be flying, such as the brown hawker dragonfly, which has distinctive amber wings.

Many birds, such as herons and kingfishers, are easier to spot in **winter** – although they can see you more easily too. Watch especially for the elusive water rail, a colourful relative of the moorhen, which has a strange pig-like, squealing call.

Below: The Llangollen Canal aqueduct in winter.

JAN

FEB

MAR

APR

MAY

JUN

JUL

AUG

SEP

OCT

NOV

DEC

MAY

Where to Go: May

On the finest, sunniest days and long, lingering evenings, May is a match for any month in the countryside: it is a joyous time, when the trees, hedgerows, and meadows are at their glorious best. The intense purple-black of the rooks at their treetop nests contrasts most beautifully with the brilliance of the fresh, green spring leaves; the great spotted woodpecker in the wood is wonderfully contrasted against the fresh foliage. Bird song is evident everywhere and challenges us to test our powers of discrimination and identification. On the coast, seabirds collect in huge colonies at places such as Bempton Cliffs, where numbers need to be seen to be believed. Heathlands welcome back their rare reptiles and more widespread but elusive ones,

ISLANDS

NORTH UIST Wildflowers flourish on the dunes of North Uist.

NORTH UIST
OUTER HEBRIDES [SC]

The unique habitat of the machair, a shell-sand soil, gives rise to a vibrant coastal grassland in spring and a multitude of unusual flowers.
See pp.108–109

PAPA WESTRAY
ORKNEY ISLANDS [SC]

The meadows at the green southern end of the island are alive with corncrakes and twite, while the rocky cliffs of the north act as a summer home for puffins, razorbills, and kittiwakes.
See pp.112–113

COQUET ISLAND
NORTHUMBERLAND [N]

More than 18,000 pairs of puffins breed on this tiny island, which is most important for its tern colony, which includes the rare and endangered roseate tern.
See pp.126–127

THE FARNE ISLANDS
NORTHUMBERLAND [N]

These uninhabited islands provide a dramatic backdrop for watching thousands of seabirds.
See pp.126–127

HEATH AND MOOR

RUABON MOOR One of the UK's great wildernesses.

RUABON MOOR
WREXHAM, NORTH WALES [W]

Visit The World's End, below the limestone ride of Maesyrychen Mountain, to watch the amazing "lek" display of the black grouse. Birds of prey keep watch.
See pp.102–103

> Our native reptiles come to life in the increasing warmth of the sun; watch out for them basking on paths on the heath.

THURSLEY COMMON
SURREY [SE]

Lying just outside Guildford, the sandy heaths of Thursley Common are alive with reptiles: common and sand lizards, adders, grass snakes, and smooth snakes all bask and slither.
See pp.128–129

WESTHAY MOOR
SOMERSET LEVELS [SW]

Otters live along the riverbanks of the moorland, which are rich in sundew plants – a red, moss-like plant that digests unsuspecting insects.
See pp.120–121

STUDLAND HEATH
DORSET [SW]

This heathland is one of the last refuges of the rare, threatened sand lizard and the smooth snake, which live alongside healthy populations of common lizards and adders.
See pp.128–129

COAST

BEMPTON CLIFFS Nesting gannets cover the cliff tops.

BEMPTON CLIFFS
BRIDLINGTON, YORKSHIRE [N]

The cliffs are famous for their seabirds: more than 200,000 make their home here between May and August.
See pp.104–105

GOWER PENINSULA
SOUTH WALES [W]

A mix of estuary, saltmarshes, sand dunes, woods, reedbeds, and beaches, Gower is home to all manner of creatures, and rich in coastal wildflowers.
See pp.122–123

RATHLIN ISLAND
COUNTY ANTRIM [NI]

A favourite spot for seabird enthusiasts in Northern Ireland; you can also see many birds of prey here. Grey and common seals bask on the rocks; dolphins swim offshore.
See pp.104–105

LIZARD POINT
LIZARD, CORNWALL [SW]

The frost-free environment of The Lizard means that many rare plants can survive here that would die anywhere else in the UK. Stars include the pygmy rush.
See pp.116–117

BASS ROCK
FIRTH OF FORTH [SC]

So many gannets live on the rock that it looks as though it has been covered in icing. These, and other seabirds, breed here in spring.
See pp.104–105

Previous page: Puffins on the Farne Islands.

such as adders, which start to venture back into the sun. The heathland birds are suddenly everywhere, including one of the most mysterious and remarkable of all – the strange nightjar – which appears at dusk to sing and snatch moths in mid-flight. Butterflies, dragonflies, bumblebees, and hornets make this a good month for insects, and the nectar-feeders among them have an abundance of spring flowers to exploit. You can discover strange and colourful orchids in our chalk grasslands and dunes, and a veritable rock garden blooming on the cropped grassland of western clifftops. Islands offshore are sometimes swamped in bluebells and red campion, making a stunning backdrop to colonies of nesting gulls.

PARKS AND GRASSLANDS

HAMPSTEAD HEATH Home of London's finest dawn chorus.

HAMPSTEAD HEATH
HAMPSTEAD, LONDON [SE]

The woodlands, scrub, and grasslands of the heath fill with songbirds in May, and the dawn chorus is tremendous.
See pp.110–111

The longer, warmer evenings provide opportunities to observe a whole new cast of creatures that become active at night.

BERRY HEAD
TORBAY, DEVON [SW]

Stride out on this lovely headland, but pause, too, to admire its beautiful wild flowers, including the rare white rock rose. Bats throng the air in the evenings.
See pp.116–117

CLUMBER PARK
NOTTINGHAMSHIRE [M]

Interesting by day, but fascinating at dusk, when the large populations of nightjars and woodcocks mark out their territories.
See pp.118–119

KILLYKEEGHAN
COUNTY FERMANAGH [NI]

The cuckoo sings loudly here in May, above the largest limestone grassland in Northern Ireland. Peacock butterflies enjoy insects lured by its rare pink thyme.
See pp.114–115

WETLANDS

SHAPWICK HEATH Otters play on wetland once covered by the sea.

SHAPWICK HEATH
SOMERSET [SW]

The otters are the biggest draw here, but you can also see birds of prey, including more than 30 hobbies, and the rare garganey duck.
See pp.120–121

FINGRINGHOE WICK
ESSEX [SE]

The wetlands here overlook the tidal estuary, but the star attraction in spring is the liquid song of nightingales among the trees.
See pp.124–125

CLEY-NEXT-THE-SEA
NORTH NORFOLK [SE]

The large reedbeds and scrapes at this reserve are served by well-placed hides, bringing birds in their hundreds into easy view.
See pp.100–101

MINSMERE
SUFFOLK [SE]

The RSPB's flagship reserve, on the beautiful Suffolk coast. It lays on an extensive programme of guided walks and family-based activities.
See pp.100–101

UPLANDS

YNIS-HIR This colourful reserve lies at the head of the Dyfi estuary.

YNIS-HIR
POWYS [W]

One of the country's most stunning reserves in spring, the woodlands here feature a special trio of birds: the redstart, wood warbler, and pied flycatcher.
See pp.106–107

There is life at last in the huge flat fields where the lapwings breed, while the superb old oakwoods wake up to the calls of a myriad birds.

ORTON FELLS
CUMBRIA [N]

The rolling upland farmlands of this site are rich in limestone, with specialized plants such as rigid-buckler fern, limestone fern, and Solomon's seal.
See pp.114–115

UPPER TEESDALE
COUNTY DURHAM [N]

This unique fragment of the Ice Age contains three large waterfalls, attracting wagtails, dippers, and sandpipers. Botanical delights in May include the mountain pansy.
See pp.114–115

CORRIMONY
HIGHLAND [SC]

Take part in an RSPB minibus safari to watch black grouse in their extraordinary mating displays close to the track at this reserve in May.
See pp.102–103

WHERE
RSPB Minsmere, Westleton, Saxmundham,
Suffolk IP17 3BY; www.rspb.org.uk

CONTACT
Tel: 01728 648281;
minsmere@rspb.org.uk

GETTING THERE
By car, follow the brown tourist signs from
the A12. By rail, go to Darsham station; by
bus, travel to Leiston. Demand-responsive
Coastlink buses will meet buses and trains if
booked in advance (01728 833526). By
cycle, national cycle route 1 links with regional
route 42 (Suffolk Coast Cycle route).

ACCESS AND FACILITIES
The large car park has bike racks. There's an
information centre, toilets with baby-changing
facilities, RSPB shop, restaurant, and tearoom.
There is good wheelchair access throughout
the reserve, including the visitor centre.

OPENING TIMES
Reserve open daily from 9am to dusk.
Visitor centre open daily 9am to 5pm
(closes 4pm 1 November–31 January).

CHARGES
Yes, for non-RSPB members.

Viewing at the Scrape

Of Minsmere's seven birdwatching hides, four
– plus a viewing platform – overlook the Scrape.
This is the home of the waders, including the
avocets, spotted redshanks, spoonbills, black
terns, and even the scarce Temminck's stint. The
Scrape also has 416 species of invertebrates, or
"mini-beasts", many of which live on the margins
of the saline lagoons. The abundance of these
creatures is what draws in the hungry birds,
making viewing at the Scrape a must.

Left: In 1971, the only pair of
surviving marsh harriers in the
UK lived at Minsmere.

Right (left to right): A view
over the marshes of Minsmere;
the man-made islands of the
Scrape; in 1947 only 4 pairs
of bearded tits survived in the
UK – all at Minsmere.

Right, below: There are
around 100 breeding pairs of
avocets at the reserve today.

Main: A dunlin flock flies over the shallow lagoons that dominate the Minsmere reserve.

SUFFOLK SANCTUARY

DURING WORLD WAR II, COASTAL AREAS OF SUFFOLK were flooded as a defence against invasion. Luckily
the military invasion never occurred, but a wildlife invasion was almost instant – even the avocet, absent
from England as a breeding bird for decades, returned to the Suffolk shores. One of the RSPB's flagship reserves,
Minsmere's importance was quickly recognized, and today its breeding-bird list approaches 100. Many of these
birds can be seen on what is fondly known as "the Scrape", an extensive area close to the coast that has been
scraped clear of vegetation and is subject to controlled flooding around a number of small artificial islands.

One hundred pairs of avocets nest on these islands, feeding in the surrounding shallows that are just salty
enough for their favourite shrimps. They share the islands with black-headed gulls, lapwings, and common terns,
as well as non-breeding migrant waders. Black-tailed godwits and spotted redshanks linger all summer long.

Above: Red deer stags are at their most majestic during the October rut.

Minsmere has saved many birds from extinction, including the bittern, the avocet, and the marsh harrier.

THROUGH THE YEAR
MINSMERE

In **summer**, watch for butterflies and dragonflies, which attract hobbies. Yellow horned poppies flower on the beach-side shingle, where there is also sea kale, and you can find marsh mallow along the trails. Little terns nest on the beach.

The woods have a fine population of red deer, best seen, and especially heard, during the **autumn** rut in October, when the great stags are "roaring" and fighting over the hinds.

Winter wildfowl include wigeons and Bewick's swans and usually a few wild geese; shelducks, gadwalls, and shovelers are seen all year. Look for red-throated divers on the sea.

WHERE ELSE TO SEE
REEDBED BIRDS

Minsmere has a large diversity of habitats, attracting hundreds of different kinds of birds – many of which can be found at other sites along the east coast.

You can find large reedbeds and "scrapes" at **Cley-next-the-sea**, North Norfolk, and avocets now breed in a string of English east-coast nature reserves including **Elmley Marshes** in Kent (see pp.306–307). Marsh harriers are best seen in coastal reserves along the east coast, but can also be spotted above the **Norfolk Broads**. [SE]

Minsmere's migrant waders can be seen at other coastal lagoons, including **Saltholme** on Teesside. Avocets breed as far afield as **RSPB Marshside**, near Southport, Lancashire. [N]

After the harsh winter of 1947, bearded tits could only be found at Minsmere. But today you can see them at many places around the east and south coasts; there are breeding pairs at **Blacktoft Sands** (see pp.158–159) on the Humber estuary, between Lincolnshire and East Yorkshire. [N]

Minsmere has much more than the Scrape, though: it is surrounded by a fine reedbed, where you can hear bitterns and stand a good chance of seeing one flying overhead in May. Marsh harriers are guaranteed, and on a calm day when the reeds are still, you would be unlucky not to see a bearded tit. These are the three reedbed specials: but the lagoons also have great crested grebes, a good selection of ducks, and water voles – with a chance of an otter as well.

Minsmere's balance of salty lagoon and freshwater reed swamp is vulnerable to rising sea levels due to global warming, and there are fears for this very special mix of wildlife habitats. The wet meadows nearer the beach are full of wild flowers, including colourful southern marsh orchids, while the surrounding woodlands are excellent for butterflies and birds, including singing nightingales, and they are awash with nodding bluebells in May. There is heathland, too, and a chance to see an adder if you are sharp-eyed and stealthy enough; at dusk, watch out for glow-worms and nightjars. A few Dartford warblers and scolding stonechats live around the heaths, and in May show their concern for young chicks by calling at you from bush-tops if you get too close.

JAN
FEB
NOV
MAR
APR
MAY
JUN
JUL
AUG
SEP
OCT
NOV
DEC

THE BLACK GROUSE "LEK"

ALTHOUGH FEMALE BLACK GROUSE (OR GREYHENS) ARE QUITE SIMILAR to female red grouse, the males – blackcocks – are very distinctive. They are spectacularly plumaged birds: glossy black with white wingbars, and white beneath the lyre-shaped tail. They prefer the areas close to the edge of coniferous forests, where they can find a greater range of food, including buds, catkins, and the fruits of bilberries and crowberries. But their main appeal is their remarkable ritualized mating display, at communal display grounds, called "leks".

Ruabon Moors in North Wales, with its good access by road, is one of the best sites to watch these extraordinary performances. The World's End area below the great limestone ridge of Maesyrychen Mountain is a prime site, while another is on the moorland at Coed Llandegla. A dawn visit in spring is essential, since much of the activity occurs in the half-light, and April and May see the peak of activity.

WHERE
The best starting point for Ruabon Moors is the Coed Llandegla Forest Visitor Centre, Ruthin Road, Llandegla, Wrexham LL11 3AA.

CONTACT
Coed Llandegla Forest Visitor Centre, tel: 01978 751656; info@coedllandegla.com

GETTING THERE
Coed Llandegla Forest is located on the A525, 11km (7 miles) west of Wrexham; from Wrexham, follow the signs from the road. By train, travel to Wrexham; buses run from Wrexham to within 1.5km (1 mile) of the forest – catch the X50 service to Denby.

ACCESS AND FACILITIES
There is a café in the Coed Llandegla visitor centre, with full-access toilet facilities. From here you can take various walks or mountain bike routes. The well-marked Black Grouse Walking Route takes you to the RSPB bird hide overlooking Ruabon Moors. It takes around 2.5 hours and is 11km (7 miles) long. The walkers' trails are uneven, and may prove difficult for wheelchairs and pushchairs.

OPENING TIMES
The centre is open every day except Mondays, 10am–5.30pm.

CHARGES
Free access to moors walks.

Do not disturb

Approach a black grouse lek only in a vehicle and not on foot; human presence usually causes serious disturbance, whereas the birds take little notice of stationary vehicles. Make sure you arrive and switch off the engine before it is light, and park no nearer than 100m (330ft) away. Don't start the car engine again until activity has wound down, typically about two hours after dawn. Make sure you keep to footpaths to avoid disturbing nesting females and young and leave your dog at home if going to watch the grouse.

Left: Ruabon Moors are bounded by mountains to the north and south: Minera and Esclusham in the north; and Ruabon and Eglwyseg to the south.

Right: Lekking males jump vertically during their elaborate display.

Right panel (top and bottom): A female black grouse; a lekking male lets out a characteristic, wide-beaked "rookooing" call.

Wait patiently and safely (*see box, below left*), and you will be rewarded by one of the world's most unforgettable wildlife experiences. The dapper males, looking like gentlemen in evening dress with a glowing-red, fleshy comb above each eye, advance on one another in the twilight, spreading and raising their tails to reveal the fluffed-out white undersides, drooping their wings, and inflating their neck feathers. This is accompanied by a rhythmic dove-like cooing, known as "rookooing", rising and falling in pitch, interspersed with harsh explosive hissing sounds and the barking calls of the watching females. Males are promiscuous, but the females make just one choice.

In the early 1900s, Ruabon Moors was a popular shooting venue, but today a recovery project is underway to save the black grouse, including improvement of the habitat and control of the grouse's major predators: crows, foxes, and stoats. Fortunately, this seems already to be bearing fruit, as numbers of grouse have begun to flourish within the forest.

Half the black grouse population of Wales lives and breeds on this wild heather moorland.

WHERE ELSE TO SEE
BLACK GROUSE

Black grouse are far less common in Britain than the more familiar red grouse, for which large areas of heather moorland in northern England and Scotland are set aside for shooting. Black grouse are most numerous and widespread in Scotland but also breed in northern England and parts of Wales.

The population of black grouse in England is concentrated largely in the North Pennines. Good places to see them include the RSPB reserve at **Geltsdale** (*see pp.24–25*) in the Lake District; **Upper Teesdale** in County Durham (*see pp.114–115*); and **Durham**, where there is a large national nature reserve. [N]

Corrimony RSPB reserve, near Glen Affric, to the southwest of Inverness in Scotland, is one of the most beautiful, remote, and easy sites to see black grouse. Take part in an RSPB minibus "safari" to watch the birds display close to the track at their lek in April and May. [SC]

THROUGH THE YEAR
RUABON MOORS

The moorland is at its most beautiful between June and August when the heather is in bloom. **Summer** is also a good time to look for breeding birds, including peregrines, merlins, hen harriers, and goshawks. There's plenty of other wildlife – look for the common lizards and adders (take care!), which like to bask in the sun, especially around the old grouse-shooting butts or on the paths. Scarce wildflowers growing on limestone outcrops include dark red helleborine orchids and rigid buckler-fern.

Young black grouse become independent of their parents at about three months old, so you may be lucky enough to see some of them in **autumn**.

Winter can be bleak up on the moors, and at an altitude of up to about 500m (over 1,500ft) the roads can be treacherous or even impassable due to snow and ice. Blackcocks spend much of their time in groups together. Avoid looking for grouse after heavy snowfall, when the birds may be stressed.

Below: Ring ouzels are scarce spring passage migrants.

JAN

FEB

MAR

APR

MAY

JUN

JUL

AUG

SEP

OCT

NOV

DEC

WHERE
RSPB Bempton Cliffs, Cliff Lane, Bempton,
Bridlington, East Yorkshire YO15 1JD;
www.rspb.org.uk

CONTACT
RSPB Bempton, tel: 01262 851179;
bempton.cliffs@rspb.org.uk

GETTING THERE
By road, the reserve is on the cliff road from
the village of Bempton, on the B1229
Flamborough to Filey road. The nearest bus
stop is in Bempton village,1.5km (1 mile)
from the reserve. It's about 15 minutes on
foot from the White Horse Pub. Bempton
train station is south of the village about
20 minutes on foot from the reserve.

ACCESS AND FACILITIES
The RSPB visitor centre is wheelchair friendly,
with specially created cliff-top viewpoints.
There's also a café, information centre, toilets,
car park, picnic areas, and pushchair-friendly
trails. A bird feeding station is easily accessed,
as it is only 50m (54 yards) from the car park.

OPENING TIMES
The reserve is open all year; the visitor centre
is open daily March–October 10am–5pm,
November–February 9.30am–4pm.

CHARGES
Yes, for non-RSPB members.

Cormorant or shag?

The cormorant and shag are very similar birds –
their long necks and bodies give them a
primitive, almost reptilian look. The birds will
often stand with wings outstretched, in a very
imposing stance; they have a similar outline,
though the shag is smaller and slimmer, and its
plumage – which can at times look black – is
actually a deep, glossy green. They are most
easily differentiated by the narrow crest that
pops up on the top of the shag's head during
the breeding season.

Above (left to right): Bempton Cliffs; a gannet plunge-diving; a puffin perches on the cliff face.
Main: Tiers of gannets nesting on the cliff face at Bempton.

HIGH-RISE SEABIRD CITY

BEMPTON CLIFFS RISE SHEER FROM THE WAVES of the North Sea. At 120m (400ft), the cliff-top is no place for anyone scared of heights, but for those brave enough to venture near the edge, the site provides an awe-inspiring view onto one of the UK's largest seabird colonies. In fact, there are perfectly safe footpaths that run along the cliffs, and specially constructed viewpoints, so you can enjoy incredible sights without any danger.

Bempton has always been famous for its seabirds: kittiwakes and guillemots have long been abundant here, and they form the majority of the 200,000 or so seabirds that you might see around the cliffs between mid-March and early August. As you walk from the car park through the small visitor centre, nothing can prepare you for the sight, sound, and smell awaiting you at the edge of the cliff. Tiny guillemots and smart razorbills buzz around the cliff face, while the more graceful kittiwakes screech for attention like children in a playground, their black wing-tips looking as thought they've been dipped in ink. As your eyes travel up and down the cliff face you'll notice herring gulls and fulmars; look away from the rock, and you'll see shags and cormorants flying close by, over the sea. There are hundreds of seabirds everywhere you look.

In recent decades the cliffs have become famous for gannets: for years there was a small colony to the north, until numbers reached a certain critical point and the colony took off – now the path south of the entry point gives the best views. But there is one bird that everyone looks for: the puffin. Small numbers nest here, and, with patience and the use of binoculars, you should not be disappointed. They typically stand beside holes in the cliff, under boulders, or in steep cliff-top turf, and are much smaller than most people expect, but real gems nevertheless.

Nothing really beats the noise and action of a great seabird colony. These birds spend the winter far out at sea and it is almost miraculous that, from a cold, windswept wave-top, way out of sight of land, they can unerringly return to a favourite nesting ledge each spring. They have to come to land to breed, but they are ill-equipped to do much more than stand on their ledges, being so superbly adapted to live over, on, and – when they are feeding – under the sea. Whether you stay on the cliffs, or take a boat trip from nearby Bridlington, there is no denying the immense pleasure to be had from watching the guillemots and razorbills duck under the surface and swim down deep, using their short, slender wings to "fly" underwater.

Below (left to right): Similar to the cormorant, the razorbill is more heavily built with white underparts; a cormorant in flight.

WHERE ELSE TO SEE
SEABIRD COLONIES

Large colonies of seabirds tend to be found further north in the UK, though there are interesting smaller colonies to the west and south.

In Scotland, there are thriving seabird colonies on the **Mull of Galloway**, Dumfries and Galloway; at **Fowlsheugh**, south of Aberdeen; **Noss Head**, near Wick; and on several islands in **Orkney** and **Shetland**. The **Bass Rock** (*see pp.168–169*) near North Berwick, in the Firth of Forth, is by far the largest accessible gannet colony, but there is another on the mainland at **Troup Head** near Banff. [SC]

Rathlin Island, County Antrim, is a favourite spot for seabird enthusiasts in Northern Ireland. [NI]

Large numbers of seabirds can be seen on **Skomer** (*see pp.150–151*) and **Ramsey** (*see pp.182–183*), two Pembrokeshire islands. A smaller colony is found on **South Stack**, near Holyhead on Anglesey. [W]

In the south of England, the largest seabird colony can be seen at the **Berry Head** nature reserve in Devon, either from the cliffs or from kayaks. [SW]

THROUGH THE YEAR
BEMPTON CLIFFS

At any time, look out for tree sparrows near the visitor centre, and rock pipits along the cliffs. The pigeons here are feral pigeons – domestic birds turned wild – not, sadly, true rock doves.

The sea beneath the colony is dotted with resting and bathing birds all **summer**, although they feed much farther out. This is the time to watch baby birds taking their first tentative flights.

By August many of the birds have moved on, except the gannets, which stay until September, but you can see interesting seabirds, including skuas and shearwaters, offshore in **autumn**, as well as the chance of many migrant birds along the cliff-top path.

Bempton Cliffs are rather bleak in **winter**, but adjacent farmland is good for finding various birds from flocks of finches to hunting short-eared owls, as well as occasional roe deer and brown hares.

JAN FEB MAR APR MAY JUN JUL AUG SEP OCT NOV DEC

Below: A guillemot, a bird that winters out at sea, with its chick.

WHERE
Ynys-hir RSPB reserve, Eglwys-fach,
Machynlleth, Powys, Wales SY20 8TA;
www.rspb.org.uk

CONTACT
RSPB Ynys-hir, tel: 01654 700222;
ynys-hir@rspb.org.uk

GETTING THERE
By road, the reserve is between Machynlleth
and Aberystwyth. Turn off the A487 in the
village of Eglwys-fach and proceed for 1.6km
(1 mile) to the car park. The nearest train
station is Machynlleth. There is a regular bus
service between Machynlleth and Aberystwyth
that stops in Eglwys-fach. By bike, the reserve
is on National Cycle Network Route no. 8.

ACCESS AND FACILITIES
This is a rugged reserve unsuitable for
wheelchairs. Access to the visitor centre
and toilets is via steps or a steep slope. There
are seven hides, two viewpoints, and a 1.2m
(4ft) birdfeeder outside the visitor centre.

OPENING TIMES
The reserve is open daily 9am–9pm, or dusk
if earlier. The visitor centre is open 9am–5pm,
April to October, and 10am–4pm, November
to March (closed Mondays and Tuesdays).

CHARGES
None.

Range recovery

Ynys-hir is in a good area for polecats, but this
ferret-like creature is remarkably elusive. They
were once widespread across Britain, but heavy
persecution by gamekeepers and farmers took
its toll, and by 1915 the polecat's range was
restricted to just mid Wales. Today the species is
staging a recovery, but its range is still restricted
to Wales, the Midlands, Cumbria, parts of the
south coast, and a few other isolated areas.

Left: A wood warbler tends
to its young in the nest.

Right (left to right): An
oak tree at Ynys-hir; a male
redstart; the view over
grassland to the woods
at Ynys-hir.

Below right: A male great
spotted woodpecker.

Main: The view towards Foel Fawr Dyfi Estuary, on the RSPB reserve at Ynys-hir.

VIEWS ACROSS THE VALLEY

I N THE WEST OF WALES, LYING DEEP BETWEEN BEAUTIFUL WOODED HILLS and exposed moor and pasture
on the Cardiganshire coast, Ynys-hir is a real gem. It is a big reserve, and one of the RSPB's most beautiful, with
a varied habitat that allows it to support a huge variety of wildlife all through the year.

In spring, attention focuses on the lagoons to the east, where wading birds, including snipe and redshanks,
breed. In the west, the huge flat fields managed especially for breeding lapwings are showing signs of life; while
the superb old oakwoods wake up to the calls of a wide variety of birds. Set yourself an identification challenge:
the trees house both marsh tits and the slightly scruffier willow tits – with the minutest of differences between
them. This is when the wheatears, chiffchaffs, cuckoos, and blackcaps begin to arrive, and the meadow pipits
return to the moors. Grey wagtails and common sandpipers take to the streams, where dippers can be found all

Above: The saltmarsh and River Dovey at Ynys-hir.

In the spring, green-veined white and speckled wood butterflies fly over woodland carpets of bluebells.

THROUGH THE YEAR
YNYS-HIR

In **summer** the woods are quiet but lapwings flock and redshanks gather around the reserve pools. Keep an eye on the horizon for peregrines, red kites, and buzzards practising their aerial displays.

By early **autumn** there are flocks of meadow pipits and other signs of migration getting under way, and by late autumn the reserve sees the arrival of redwings and fieldfares.

In **winter** the lagoons and flat areas of closely cropped grass have dense flocks of teals and wigeons. A special visitor is the white-fronted goose: Ynys-hir is one of the very few British overwintering homes for the Greenland race. Look out also for lapwings, golden plovers, and birds of prey.

WHERE ELSE TO SEE
OAKWOOD BIRDS

British oak woodlands are considered internationally important because of the extensive diversity of their plant and animal communities. These complete ecosystems are worth seeing in several forms.

Oakwood birds can be found in many parts of Wales, including secluded valleys of **Snowdonia** (see pp.172–173), and the woodlands around the **Elan Valley** and the **Llangollen Canal** (see pp.94–95), which runs from Shropshire into North Wales. [W]

Visit Nagshead in the **Forest of Dean**, Gloucestershire, for the oakwood songbirds and birds of prey. [M]

Redstarts and wood warblers breed in the **New Forest** (see pp.174–175), Hampshire. [SE]

In **Coombes Valley**, North Staffordshire, you are almost guaranteed to see pied flycatchers, redstarts, and wood warblers. [M]

year round. Several trails cut through the woods, and a spacious hide lets you look through the canopy of the trees to watch birds at eye level. These western-UK oakwoods have a trio of special birds, which are harder to see in the east: redstarts, wood warblers, and pied flycatchers.

Redstarts and flycatchers nest in holes, or nestboxes, while the wood warbler nests among the dead leaves on the ground. All sing in the canopy, or from open branches just beneath, and this trio are well worth seeking out for their elegance of colour and design: the male redstart, especially, is a jewel. You are also likely to hear the sharp calls of great spotted woodpeckers, the boyish whistles of nuthatches, and the peevish calls of treecreepers before you see them, but they are all there for the patient watcher to find. The dawn chorus in these woods is a real delight.

Beyond the woods the reserve fades into grassland, saltmarsh, and muddy estuary. Look back at the woods and you might see buzzards and even a red kite or a goshawk. Look again at the estuary and you could find little egrets, shelducks, and oystercatchers. If you spot a spiky-headed duck, it's likely to be one of the red-breasted mergansers that nest here and feed on the river.

JAN
FEB
MAR
APR
MAY
JUN
JUL
AUG
SEP
OCT
NOV
DEC

WHERE
North Uist, Outer Hebrides, Scotland.

CONTACT
RSPB Balranald, tel: 01463 715000;
nsro@rspb.org.uk

GETTING THERE
North Uist is an island in the Outer Hebrides,
so you can reach it by boat or plane. It is also
linked by causeways to Benbecula and South
Uist. By boat, catch a car/people ferry from
Uig on Skye to Lochmaddy, or from Oban to
Lochboisdale on South Uist. Fly to Benbecula
from Glasgow. To reach Balranald RSPB
reserve, turn west off the A865 towards
Hougharry, 5km (3 miles) north of Bayhead.

ACCESS AND FACILITIES
The visitor centre at the RSPB reserve has
an information centre and toilets with
baby-changing facilities. Guided walks are
offered, but note that the nature trails are
unsuitable for wheelchairs. The circular
nature trail through the croft land of the
reserve is 4.5km (3 miles) long.

OPENING TIMES
The reserve and visitor centre are both open
at all times.

CHARGES
None, but donations help the RSPB to
continue their invaluable work here.

Shelly sands

Machair is a distinctive sand-dune formation that
is found only on the north and west coasts of
Scotland, and in western Ireland. It incorporates
siliceous sand from glacial sediments, and
calcareous sand from the shells of sea animals,
making it unusually rich for a sand-dune system.
Even more unusually, it has long been an
important agricultural resource. Ancient
cultivation practices, such as shallow ploughing,
have allowed harvesting without destruction of
the machair plants.

Above and below: Listen out for the rasping call of the
corncrake; North Uist has some of the highest densities
of nesting waders to be found anywhere in Britain,
including the dunlin, shown here nesting.

Right panel: Ragged robin (*top*) and yellow iris
(*bottom*) are among the moisture-loving plants that
grow in the wet, marshy areas (*centre*) that lie behind
the well-drained sandy shoreline and are threaded by
small channels.

Main: Classic machair flora on the shore of North Uist, which measures around 29km (18 miles) from east to west, and 19km (12 miles) from north to south.

MACHAIR IN BLOOM

PERCHED ON THE WESTERN EDGE OF EUROPE, North Uist lies within the Outer Hebrides, a chain of islands
running from north to south off the west coast of Scotland. Essentially treeless, the island is exposed to the
full force of Atlantic storms in winter, while in summer it can bask in more sunshine than most of the mainland.
Long, white, sandy beaches on the west coast contrast with a rugged, rocky coast on the eastern side. From May
through to July the island's west coast becomes bathed in colour, courtesy of one of Europe's rarest habitats:
machair. Wind-blown sand and broken shells from the beach give the soil of this habitat a calcium-rich start,
which is enhanced by the addition of the underlying peat to create a vibrant coastal grassland, with a multitude
of flowers. Vetches, clovers, corn marigolds, crane's bills, and orchids all thrive here. Ragged robin and yellow iris
beds run riot in the wetter areas, whose hollows are ablaze with the yellow of marsh marigolds.

Above: The stone circle of Pobull Fhinn ("Finn's People"), North Uist.

THROUGH THE YEAR
NORTH UIST

Flowers are in bloom on the machair through to August. In **summer**, breeding birds include oystercatchers, golden and ringed plovers, lapwings, dunlins, snipe, curlews, and redshanks. Red grouse and Arctic skuas breed on the moors, while some lochs have nesting mute and whooper swans. Ducks and terns breed on the dunes and beaches.

In the **autumn**, a few Manx shearwaters may be passing offshore, and there's a chance of seeing the rarer sooty shearwater. Look out for raptors – hen harriers, buzzards, kestrels, merlins, peregrine falcons, and even golden eagles hunt from North Uist's skies.

The island has spectacular **winter** storms. It is an important winter haven for both passage and overwintering birds, including pink-footed and white-fronted geese, pintails, scaups, and waders such as whimbrels and ruffs.

WHERE ELSE TO SEE
MACHAIR FLORA AND BIRDS

"Machair" is used to describe coastal grassy plains that are formed of wind-blown, shell-derived sands. These habitats develop in places with a damp and windy climate, as found on the northwest coasts of Scotland and Ireland.

Machair is a rare habitat, but can be found extensively on **South Uist** and **Benbecula**, and on smaller stretches of the island of **Harris**. It can also be found on some parts of the Inner Hebrides. On **Tiree**, for example, it covers almost half the island. [SC]

The corncrake likes hay meadows and damp pasture, and it is occasionally seen around the southwest, including **Portland** (see pp.90–91), **Land's End**, Cornwall and **Hengistbury Head** in Dorset. [SW]

Corn buntings are becoming increasingly rare, and their brown colouring makes them hard to see. Sites such as **East Fleetham** in Northumberland and **Swinefleet** in East Yorkshire are good places to look for them. [N]

Some of the best examples of uncultivated machair and its associated wildlife can be found on the Balranald RSPB reserve. This is one of the best places in Britain to see a corncrake, and May is ideal, as the flora is low enough to expose this notoriously secretive bird. The corn bunting, so rare on the mainland, is still found here, where it sits on fence posts singing its distinctive jingly song. The machair supports high densities of breeding waders, including snipe, lapwings, redshanks, and oystercatchers. Important populations of dunlins and ringed plovers nest here, but they have been badly hit by the introduction of hedgehogs in 1974; these animals roam across the machair at night, eating eggs and chicks.

Otters inhabit North Uist's coasts but are rarely seen. You may be luckier with red-throated divers, which are often seen just offshore in May – listen out for their distinctive quacking notes as they fly back to breeding lochs on the moorland. Roadside fence posts are favourite perching places for cuckoos and short-eared owls in May, and twites are commonly seen along the roadside. This northern bird, confined to Scotland and the north Pennines, is a relative of the linnet.

JAN
FEB
MAR
APR
MAY
JUN
JUL
AUG
SEP
OCT
NOV
DEC

DAWN CHORUS IN THE CITY

HAMPSTEAD HEATH IS ONE OF THE UK'S BEST CITY LOCATIONS to see and hear birds. Despite the fact that this big park – one of the capital's largest – is surrounded by main roads and houses, it is an oasis of green with a variety of habitats, including woodland, grassland, scrub, and over 30 ponds and lakes. It hosts a wide range of breeding birds and acts as a magnet to migrant birds, too. Evidence for this is provided every morning, especially in spring and early summer, as the dawn chorus strikes up.

You'll have to be up early, but one bonus of being out on the heath around dawn is that there are few people around to disturb the birds, and you can spot both the resident and passing migrant birds more easily. Some of the passage birds take part in the "avian orchestra", and you can test your skill by listening for their songs among the more familiar sounds of resident song thrushes, robins, blackbirds, and great tits.

WHERE
Hampstead Heath, North London;
www.cityoflondon.gov.uk/hampstead

CONTACT
London Borough of Camden:
tel: 020 7332 3322;
hampstead.heath@cityoflondon.gov.uk

GETTING THERE
The nearest London Underground stations are Hampstead Heath, Golders Green, and Kentish Town (all Northern Line); nearest overland train stations are Gospel Oak and Hampstead. The following buses stop at the park: 268, 46, 168, 24, C11, 210. By car, from central London take the A502, heading northwest via Chalk Farm and Belsize Park.

ACCESS AND FACILITIES
The park has many paths and rides, which are accessible to cycles, pushchairs, and wheelchairs. There are several car parks, and full-access public toilets in most areas.

OPENING TIMES
Open all year round. Dawn chorus meetings and walks are held in May, between 4 and 5am. Access-controlled areas open at various times around 8.30am and tend to shut at dusk.

CHARGES
None.

Urban foxes

It is estimated that up to 30,000 foxes now live in Britain's urban areas, with London being home to around 10,000 of these elusive creatures. They colonized cities in the 1930s, when houses in city suburbs were given larger gardens, making them attractive places to find food and shelter. If you're in a city park at dawn, you may see one of these beautiful animals – or even hear it barking along with the dawn chorus. Fox litters are born in March, and by May they are ready to leave the den, so watch out for playful cubs, too.

Left: Hampstead Heath offers birds a valuable mix of habitats.

Right (left to right): The female robin has her own feeding territory, so sings the dawn chorus as well as the male; in early May, wrens start singing especially vigorously.

Right panel (top and bottom): The blackbird sings like a flute, and then breaks into a babble, before pausing to begin again; look for spring migrants around the heath's lakes and ponds.

Singing is most intense around dawn because sound travels more easily then. On the whole, it is only male birds that sing the dawn chorus, although there are some exceptions: both male and female robins sing. The main purpose of the males' performance is to convey two messages – to rival males it says, "Go away, this is my territory", and to receptive females, "Come here, I want to mate". Gaps between bursts of song allow males to listen for replies from other males and gauge the strength of the opposition. They can pinpoint the direction from which the sound is coming and direct their vocal efforts accordingly, concentrating on males on the edge of their territory, or within it, that are attempting to take over. The mate-attracting versions of songs are often longer and more intricate than the territorial bouts. Singing uses up a good deal of energy and after a night with no food, a male capable of producing a loud, complex song is likely to be a strong and healthy one; it has been shown that females prefer such males and judge them on the quality of their songs.

WHERE ELSE TO HEAR
THE DAWN CHORUS

Woodlands are generally the best places to hear the dawn chorus, but city parks throughout Britain also resound with the calls of birds as the sun rises. If you can't make it at dawn, try listening to the dusk chorus; it's less spectacular, but still heart-lifting.

London is one of the world's greenest cities, and as such has many other parks that are great for wildlife, including **South Norwood Country Park** in the southeast, and **Kew Gardens** and **Richmond Park** to the southwest of the city. [SE]

Many of the RSPB's nature reserves around the UK have superb areas of woodland where the dawn chorus is particularly good. Organized walks are arranged where you can learn to identify birds and their songs with the help of experts. Visit www.rspb.org.uk for details.

Forestry Commission sites, National Nature Reserves (NNRs), and local nature reserves run by Wildlife Trusts are all worth investigating for local possibilities.

Birdsong is the perfect medium for communicating over long distances, in every direction at once.

THROUGH THE YEAR
HAMPSTEAD HEATH

The dawn chorus is at its most intense in spring and early **summer**, when male birds are establishing or defending a breeding territory or trying to attract a mate. In high summer, you can also enjoy watching breeding kingfishers at the special artificial sandbank built for them by the reserve pond, and look out for equally brilliant dragonflies.

Autumn is the time to look for a wide variety of fungi. Mammals that can be seen include foxes, weasels, badgers, and little muntjac deer.

There is still much of interest to be seen on the heath in **winter**, although few birds are singing apart from robins, which sing almost all year round. As well as grey herons, cormorants, and tufted ducks at the ponds, you can watch great spotted woodpeckers on the trees. Look out, too, for winter visitors such as redwings, siskins, and redpolls.

Below: Autumnal colour on Hampstead Heath.

JAN

FEB

MAR

APR

MAY

JUN

JUL

AUG

SEP

OCT

NOV

DEC

WHERE
Papa Westray, Orkney Islands, Scotland;
www.papawestray.co.uk

CONTACT
RSPB North Hill, tel: 01856 850176;
orkney@rspb.org.uk

GETTING THERE
Transport is by boat from Kirkwall, Orkney
mainland. Contact Orkney Ferries (tel:
01856 872004; www.orkneyferries.co.uk),
Pentland Ferries (tel: 01856 831226;
www.pentlandferries.co.uk), or
Northlink Ferries (tel: 0845 6000449;
www.northlinkferries.co.uk). You can also
fly from Kirkwall (contact Loganair, tel:
01856 872494; www.loganair.co.uk).

ACCESS AND FACILITIES
There's a visitor centre and observation point
in the former coastguard hut, with guided
walks in summer. The facilities are basic
and trails are not suitable for wheelchairs.
However, much of the accommodation on
the island is wheelchair friendly.

OPENING TIMES
Open all year round, depending on the
weather and ferries.

CHARGES
None, but the RSPB welcomes donations.

Scottish primrose

The Scottish primrose, *Primula scotica*, is on
the edge of extinction, and lives wild in only
two places in the world: Caithness and Orkney.
It grows on Papa Westray within the North Hill
Reserve, which provides the plant's ideal habitat:
moist, well-drained grassland near the coast. The
primrose has two flowering periods: a few plants
flower in late April–May, but the main season is
July–August, when they all burst into flower.

ALL AT SEA

KNOWN LOCALLY AS PAPAY, Papa Westray is one of the most northerly of the Orkney
islands. It's home to only around 65 people, but a fabulous population of birds. Its
southern end is green and cultivated, with sandy bays and islets, and flowery meadows,
where corncrakes and twites sing. The northern half of the island widens into a broad
heathery moor, fringed with quite low, rusty-brown cliffs and dramatic offshore rocks.

    The throng of seabirds here, with their chorus of calls and constant movements
to and from the sea, are a sight to behold. The low cliffs afford superb close views; the
combination of the thriving colony, surging sea, and rough cliff scenery is incomparable.

> This is one of Orkney's smallest
> islands, with a human
> population of less than 100,
> yet it easily accommodates
> thousands upon thousands of
> summer visitors – in the shape
> of breeding seabirds.

It was here, at Fowl Craig, that the last great auk was shot in 1813, ensuring the extinction
of the species. Today the seabirds are protected, and the cliffs provide a summer home for
guillemots, razorbills, puffins, and kittiwakes, while the moorland is filled with exciting
Arctic and great skuas, and Arctic terns. What you see depends on the food supply for these
seabirds: in recent years the terns and kittiwakes have all but given up, leaving early in the
season because sand eels have become so scarce as a consequence of rising sea temperatures.

    Many of the seabirds arrive at the cliffs in mid-March, with the terns being the last
to arrive in mid May. Terns and kittiwakes can be seen flying towards the cliffs to feed their
chicks, carrying fish in their beaks– only to have the hard-earned food stolen by the skuas.
Great skuas are big and bold enough to actually dip a gannet into the sea to steal its fish, but
the hundred or more pairs of smaller Arctic skuas depend on their supreme acrobatics and
persistence, chasing gulls and terns until they are forced to drop their catch – only to see the
skua snatching it up before it hits the ground. Skuas are said to be halfway between a gull and
a bird of prey – they will eat whatever is available, whether this is fish, carrion, or even the
chicks of other birds. In the air they are among the UK's most beautifully streamlined birds.

Main: Papa Westray is one of Orkney's smallest isles, at just 6km (4 miles) long by 1.6km (1 mile) wide.
Below (left to right): A razorbill rests on a nesting ledge with its chick; kittiwakes nesting on the cliffs; a great skua.
Inset: The wide sandy bays of Papa Westray.

Above: Orcas have been spotted just off the coast of Papa Westray.

THROUGH THE YEAR
PAPA WESTRAY

In **summer** the seabird colonies are in full swing and you can see oystercatchers, ringed plovers, curlews, purple sandpipers, and turnstones.

In **autumn**, watch for whales offshore on calm days, with orcas – killer whales – a possibility. You may also be lucky enough to see seals and seal pups. Watch the skies at night: the spectacular natural light show known as the aurora borealis, or "northern lights", occurs in September and October.

Winter days are short, with the sun barely leaving the horizon, but fulmars return to the cliffs and you can see grey and common seals hauled up on the rocky shore or surfing in the waves.

WHERE ELSE TO SEE
SEABIRD COLONIES

Many Orkney and Shetland islands have seabird colonies and skuas, but the birds are also seen on the east coast of England during spring.

Fair Isle, **Fetlar**, **and Hoy** are all wonderful places for seabird colonies. You can see skuas, too, on **Handa Island** off the Sutherland coast. Whales are often spotted from **Sumburgh Head** at the southern tip of Shetland's mainland. On mainland Scotland, visit **Duncansby Head**, just east of John O'Groats, for cliff-nesting seabirds and spectacular costal scenery. [SC]

Breeding terns can be seen on the **Farne Islands** in Northumberland (*see pp.126–127*). [N]

The coastlines of Norfolk, Suffolk, and Essex often plays host to migrating skuas and terns. **Blakeney Point**, on the north Norfolk coast (*see pp.214–215*), has a large breeding tern population that can be seen up close from seal-watching boat trips. [SE]

JAN

FEB

MAR

APR

MAY

JUN

JUL

AUG

SEP

OCT

NOV

DEC

A JOURNEY UP RIVER

UPPER TEESDALE IS A UNIQUE FRAGMENT OF OUR POST-GLACIAL LANDSCAPE, situated in the north Pennines. As a result of the extreme upland climate, its wildlife and landscape hark back to times just after the retreat of the last Ice Age. Start at Middleton, and follow the course of the River Tees upstream: the tumbling river descends over rocky rapids and waterfalls: Low Force, High Force (a magnificent 21m/70ft cascade over the Whin Sill), and Cauldron Snout. Grey wagtails, dippers, and common sandpipers flitter around the river fringes, using a bobbing action for camouflage. The yellow-flowered shrubby cinquefoil – native only here and in Cumbria – grow along the banks. Around High Force, take a wander through the juniper forest; this head-high woodland teems with willow warblers. The valley meadows are full of botanical delights, especially in May, when great burnet, globe-flower, northern bedstraw, wood crane's-bill, and melancholy thistle are bursting into flower.

WHERE
Moor House Upper Teesdale National Nature Reserve, Widdybank Farm, Langdon Beck, Forest in Teesdale, Barnard Castle, Co Durham; www.naturalengland.org.uk

CONTACT
Natural England: 0845 6003078; enquiries@naturalengland.org.uk

GETTING THERE
The Upper Teesdale side of the nature reserve can be reached by car from the B6277 Middleton-in-Teesdale to Alston road. By bus, there's a limited service from Middleton-in-Teesdale to Langdon Beck (and Cow Green on request). However, there's no bus service to the Moor House side of the reserve. By cycle, follow National Cycle Network Route no. 68. The Pennine Cycleway, the Eden Valley Cycleway, and the C2C all run close to the Moor House side of the reserve.

ACCESS AND FACILITIES
Car parking is available at Cow Green Reservoir, High Force, Hanging Shaw, and Bowlees. The reserve's tracks are unsuitable for wheelchair access.

OPENING TIMES
Open all year round.

Spring gentian

The spring gentian is a true Arctic-alpine plant, found in the higher mountain ranges of Europe and at lower altitudes in cold northerly regions. Elsewhere in the British Isles it is known only from the extensive limestone region of the Burren in western Ireland, near Galway Bay, where it can be seen right down to sea level. Along with other mountain plants it is at risk, mainly from climate change and overgrazing – it bloomed magnificently after livestock reductions following foot-and-mouth disease.

Main: Low Force falls, Upper Teesdale.

Left: Shrubby cinquefoil.

Right (left to right): Mountain pansy; yellow saxifrage; Cronkley Fell, home to many delicate botanical gems; lapwing bathing in a moorland stream.

Right, above: Upper Teesdale's attractive landscape can be an easy walk in summer.

Further upstream, around Cow Green Reservoir, you'll reach Cronkley Fell and Widdybank Fell. Their crumbly, crystalline sugar limestone provides a refuge for Arctic-alpine plants of extraordinary and fragile beauty: the mountain pansy, yellow or purple, shot through with fine inky-black veins; the slender alpine bistort; the fluffy pink cat's-foot; and the spring sandwort. All of these are dotted among the flowers of the area's iconic species – the indigo-blue spring gentian. There's yet more on the slopes: the subtle alpine bartsia, the delicate flower-globes of bird's-eye primrose, and twinkling yellow saxifrage. And everywhere, the sounds of breeding birds: golden plovers and dunlins on the high tops; redshanks, oystercatchers, lapwings, curlews, and snipe in the damp fields; ring ouzels and wheatears around the stone walls. Black grouse are numerous, and a large lek (*see pp.102–103*) is often visible from the road that crosses to St John's Chapel in Weardale to the north. Upper Teesdale is rightly considered a place of pilgrimage for wildlife enthusiasts.

WHERE ELSE TO SEE
LIMESTONE FLORA

The sugar limestone habitat of Upper Teesdale is extremely rare, but there are many interesting limestone pavements and grasslands to explore within northern England and Wales.

On **Orton Fells**, Cumbria, you can find the very rare rigid-buckler fern, limestone fern, and angular Solomon's seal. The grassland around the pavement gives rise to blue moor grass, bird's-foot trefoil, fairy flax, limestone bedstraw, and autumn gentian. [N]

The best-known limestone pavement in the UK is above **Malham Cove** in the Yorkshire Dales. [N]

Craig-y-Cilau nature reserve in Crickhowell, Wales, is part of a massive limestone escarpment with some very rare plants, including several species of whitebeam – one unique to this site. [W]

Killykeeghan and Crossmurrin Nature Reserve is the most extensive area of limestone grassland in Northern Ireland, and its grey limestone supports thyme, harebell, and yellow bird's-foot trefoil, as food for its common blue and peacock butterflies. [NI]

THROUGH THE YEAR
UPPER TEESDALE

As **summer** progresses, the Teesdale meadows provide an ever-changing mosaic of colour, and the chicks of the breeding waders hatch and grow. At least nine species of lady's mantle grow here, many not found anywhere else in the UK.

In late summer and **autumn**, a purple haze of heather blankets the hills, and the fruits of rowan trees ripen red and attract feeding thrushes. Look for giant bellflowers on river banks and woodland edges, harebells in short grassland turf, and the ivory-white flowers of grass-of-Parnassus in damp places.

By **winter** most birds have departed from the higher tops: only meadow pipits are numerous, forming the main prey of a few roving merlins. The upland reservoirs attract a few ducks; mainly mallards, teals, and wigeons. Don't let the lack of wildlife put you off – a frosty morning offers atmospheric landscapes.

The flowers of Upper Teesdale are not only Ice-Age survivors – they are lustrous botanical jewels.

Below: The graceful spires of the greater bellflower.

JAN FEB MAR APR **MAY** JUN JUL AUG SEP OCT NOV DEC

WHERE
Lizard Point, Lizard, Cornwall, TR12 7NT;
www.lizard-peninsula.co.uk

CONTACT
Lizard Countryside Office,
tel: 01326 561407;
lizard@nationaltrust.org.uk

GETTING THERE
By car, from the M5 at Exeter, take the A38
via Plymouth, or the A30 over Bodmin Moor.

ACCESS AND FACILITIES
Parking is very limited at the Point; it's best
to park in Lizard town or at the Lizard
Lighthouse. The paths to viewpoints
overlooking Lizard Point are wheelchair-
friendly but other areas are unsuitable due to
steep slopes. There are full-access toilets next
to the car park at the Lizard. There's ground-
level access for wheelchairs at the lighthouse
and also a café at the Point.

OPENING TIMES
There is year-round access to countryside
paths and to external views of the lighthouse.

CHARGES
Only to look round the lighthouse.

Above (top and botton): Grey seals and dolphins can
be seen in the sea around the Lizard; low-growing thrift.

Right: Early purple orchids grow on the Lizard's
heathland. **Inset:** The chough – Cornwall's symbol,
and according to legend, home to King Arthur's spirit
when he died.

Below: The rare long-headed clover, which until
recently was only found on the Lizard.

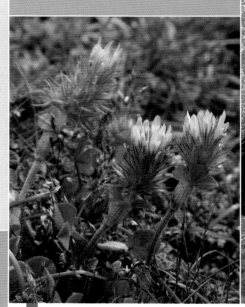

The Hottentot fig

The Lizard's unique nature may be due to its
frost-free climate, but this could also be its
undoing. Many invasive frost-sensitive plants
have become established here, and some are
encroaching very significantly into the wild.
Perhaps worst of all is the Hottentot fig, a South
African succulent with prostrate stems and large
yellow or pink flowers. Without frosts to keep it in
check, physical removal is the only real option to
give native plants the space they need to survive.

Main: The unusual rock formations of the Lizard are altered peridotite – part of the Earth's mantle, normally 30–200km (18–125 miles) below ground.

LIFE ON THE LIZARD

FORMING THE SOUTHERNMOST EXTREMITY OF MAINLAND BRITAIN, Lizard Point is a unique location for
wildlife. Its highly oceanic climate – wet and warm, with rarely any frost – coupled with its complex and
varied geology, based mainly on serpentine rocks, make this the premier site for rare plants in Britain.

If you start in the heart of the village, on Lizard Green, you are already among the rarities. Even around the
parked cars, the low turf has patches of fringed rupturewort, a mat-forming plant that grows nowhere else in the
country. A short walk brings you to the coastal path and its swathes of thrift, with added splashes of yellow from
bird's-foot trefoil and kidney vetch, and white sea campion just starting to flower. Around here you can start
looking for more of the Lizard's specialities: the south-facing slopes above Caerthilian Cove have an amazing
collection of rare clovers, including twin-headed, upright, long-headed, and western varieties. And if you're

Choughs returned to the Lizard in 2001, breeding the following year for the first time in England in 50 years.

Above: Look for convolvulus hawk-moths in autumn.

THROUGH THE YEAR
THE LIZARD

The dramatic, pink-spiked Cornish heath is abundant across the serpentine heaths that form the heart of the Lizard; at its best in July, it has been described as the commonest rare plant in Britain, on account of its local abundance. The wet heaths in **summer** have bog asphodel, cotton-grass, black bog-rush, and sundew in flower.

Into the **autumn**, the cliff-top grasslands are still blooming, with wild carrot, sea aster, rock samphire, harebell, and sheep's-bit scabious. Increasingly large areas are becoming orange, under the invasive, albeit attractive, monbretia. The Lizard is good for migrant songbirds in autumn, while seabirds and dolphins linger offshore. It is especially renowned for its moths and butterflies: hummingbird hawk-moths by day, convolvulus hawk-moths by night, and many, many more when the winds are from the south.

Winter never really arrives on the Lizard. Frost and snow are so infrequent that there are always plants in flower. The first cultivated daffodils, for instance, are usually ready to be cut in January.

WHERE ELSE TO SEE
COASTAL HEATH PLANTS

Many of the Lizard's plants are unique to this one area, so while there are similar habitats, none are a precise match.

Some heaths, such as those at **Arne**, Dorset (*see pp.138–139*), lack the species that dominates the Lizard – the Cornish heath – but do have plenty of interesting plants, and are especially dramatic in autumn. **Prawle Point** in Devon is an interesting area of cliff-top grassland. [SW]

The **Gower Peninsula** (*see pp.122–123*) and **St David's Head** in Wales have maritime and cliff-top grassland that echo the Lizard in plantlife. [W]

For a different kind of maritime grassland, try the limestone of **Berry Head** in Torbay, Devon, which is home to several very rare plants, including white rock rose – found at only two places in the UK. [SW]

interested in miniature plants, search out the shallow, damp depressions: they will reveal an array of diminutive stars, including pygmy rush and yellow centaury. The exposure to wind and salt spray on the cliff slopes is so severe that several plants have adopted prostrate growth forms to cope with it. The wild asparagus is a trailing plant closely related to the upright garden asparagus; but others are simply horizontal forms of a common species, such as the prostrate broom – here low and arching, but extremely dramatic in flower.

Such are the botanical riches that you might find yourself looking down and ignoring the rest of the landscape and wildlife. So it is perhaps lucky that the "star" bird, the chough, so noisily cries out its name. Having settled here as a breeding bird as recently as 2002, these cheeky black birds can be seen anywhere in the area, but the vicinity of Lizard Point is a good place to try, especially as there is a manned watchpoint here during the nesting season. With luck, their numbers will increase, and they will become a familiar sight on the Lizard, probing their slender red bills into the turf for food, and sky-dancing like wind-blown sprites on the air currents.

JAN
FEB
MAR
APR
MAY
JUN
JUL
AUG
SEP
OCT
NOV
DEC

BIRDS IN THE DUSK

OUR LONG, LINGERING TWILIGHT IS A WONDERFUL, MYSTERIOUS TIME. You might notice Venus, brilliant above the western horizon, or the silver light of a full moon gaining power as dusk falls. As it gets really shady, on bushy heaths or around the edges of old, wild woods, you sometimes hear one of the strangest wildlife sounds of all: the churring of a nightjar. Now and then it changes pitch abruptly, but this low, drill-like call is otherwise unchanging, perhaps for minutes on end, never seemingly pausing for breath.

Clumber Park is full of wildlife action at night, but it's huge – 1,500 hectares (3,800 acres) – and to hear nightjars, it's a good idea to do a bit of reconnaissance in daylight. Look for the heathy spots, with scattered pines and high, dead branches, which make ideal nightjar perches. At night, listen for the churring; as it stops, the bird launches itself with a few wing-claps, then sets off in pursuit of moths, or a rival. Like moths, it flies silently,

WHERE
Clumber Park, Worksop, Nottinghamshire
S80 3AZ.

CONTACT
The Estate Office, tel: 01909 544917;
Infoline, tel: 01909 476592;
clumberpark@nationaltrust.org.uk

GETTING THERE
The park lies between Worksop and Retford,
1.6km (1 mile) from the A1/A57 and 18km
(11 miles) from the M1. By rail, travel to
Worksop or Retford; by bus, travel to
Carburton which is 1km (½ mile) away.

ACCESS AND FACILITIES
Parking is available throughout the park, with
the main car park only 180m (200 yards)
from wheelchair-friendly visitor facilities with
full-access toilets, baby-changing facilities,
kiosk, restaurant, and child carriers/buggies
for hire. Dogs are allowed on the lead.

OPENING TIMES
Open all year round (except 16 August and
25 December). The shop and restaurant is
open all year round but the times do vary
throughout the year, so check before visiting.

CHARGES
Vehicle entry charge, and to visit Clumber
Park's traditional walled kitchen garden.

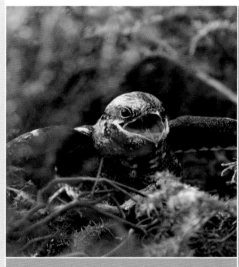

Above: The nightjar "gapes" with its extraordinarily wide mouth to scare off intruders.

Main: Look for the nightjar's striking silhouette at dusk.

Right (top to bottom): Woodcock "roding"; it is almost impossible to spot this woodcock nesting among dead leaves; the woodcock's eyes are unusually close to the top of its head, giving excellent peripheral vision.

Below: A nightjar in flight.

Finding a nightjar

You will probably hear a nightjar before you
see it, because its mottled grey-brown colouring
camouflages it well against the forest floor
(where it nests) or the brown bark of branches.
Scan the trees with binoculars (the bigger the
lenses, the more light they gather) and you
should see its low, big-headed, blackbird-sized
form on a branch. Unusually, the nightjar tends
to perch lengthwise along branches, and this
distinctive "gravy-boat" silhouette (*see above
and main picture*) is a useful identifier.

guided by large eyes that enable it to see in very low light-levels. In the air, it is a fantastic bird, a wraith; wonderfully acrobatic, twisting and spinning, its long wings equalled by a long, broad tail. It makes a new call in flight: a deep, vibrant "goo-ik" that floats eerily through the darkness.

Another call note may draw your attention to a quite different night bird: a woodcock in its circuitous, territorial flight, called "roding". Alternately it calls a sharp, thin "tswick" and a deep, guttural, repeated "croak"; sometimes the croak is heard first, sometimes the whistle. The woodcock lives by day on the woodland floor, but its colours camouflage it so effectively against the fallen leaves that you're unlikely to see it unless you accidentally disturb it, at which it will dash away, swerving from side to side. It feeds at night in soft, muddy ditches and drains, and your only real hope of catching a glimpse is when it flies over the treetops at dusk – a sharp-winged, fat-bodied, long-billed silhouette, zigzagging through the air.

WHERE ELSE TO SEE
BIRDS ACTIVE AT NIGHT

Nightjars breed mainly in southern England, but scatterings of these birds are found further north as far as central Scotland.

Heathland with nightjars, woodlarks, stonechats, linnets, and meadow pipits can be found on the **Surrey Heaths**, in and around the **New Forest** (see pp.174–175) in Hampshire, which has Dartford warblers, too. [SE]

The **Suffolk Sandlings**, a string of heathlands close to the coast, has nightjars, woodlarks, and linnets, and they can also be heard on **Chobham Common** and other heathland in Surrey. In the **Breckland** on the Norfolk–Suffolk border (see also **Weeting Heath**, pp.92–93), nightjars are often in areas of recently clear-felled plantation. Woodcocks can be seen in similar areas, but more often over denser woodland. [SE]

Cannock Chase in Staffordshire has scattered heathlands with nightjars, and woodcocks over its conifer plantations. [M]

THROUGH THE YEAR
CLUMBER PARK

Clumber Park has rich broadleaved woodland, farmland, and open, grassy parks as well as heaths, so birds are varied all year.

Watch for buzzards and sparrowhawks displaying over the woods in **summer**, and listen for drumming great spotted woodpeckers. Nuthatches are noisy, with loud trills and whistles.

In **autumn**, fieldfares arrive in nomadic flocks, feeding in hedges until the berries are finished and then moving on to open pastures. Fallow deer are frequent and you might come across a fox or, with real luck, a badger.

In **winter**, you might find flocks of siskins, redpolls, and goldfinches feeding in alders, taking seeds from the dark cones. Treecreepers, long-tailed tits, and goldcrests are easier to see with no leaves on the deciduous trees.

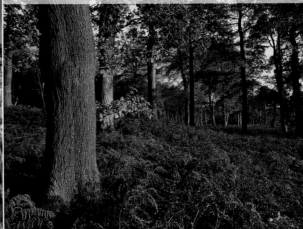

Below: Clumber Park is a feast of colour in autumn.

JAN FEB MAR APR MAY JUN JUL AUG SEP OCT NOV DEC

WHERE
Shapwick Heath, Shapwick, near Glastonbury, Somerset BA6 9TT; www.naturalengland.org.uk

CONTACT
Natural England, tel: 01458 860120; somerset@naturalengland.org.uk

GETTING THERE
The heath is 1km (¾ mile) north of Shapwick village and 7km (4¼ miles) west of Glastonbury. By car, access is from the A39 and B3151. The nearest train station is Castle Cary, 25km (15½ miles) away. Buses run between Castle Cary, Glastonbury, and Shapwick village. The reserve is near Route 3 of the National Cycle Network.

ACCESS AND FACILITIES
There is a car park at the Peat Moors Centre, not far from the reserve's main entrance, as well as a second car park at the other end of the reserve. There are also cycle racks at the site's entrance. There are no toilets or refreshments on site, however wheelchair access to hides is good, especially to the Mere Heath Hide, and there is also an easy-access boardwalk.

OPENING TIMES
Open all year round.

CHARGES
None.

A rarely seen dabbler

One of the rarer birds that you may be lucky to spot at Shapwick Heath, the garganey breeds in the UK during the spring and winters in Africa. It is a dabbling duck, like the shovelers, meaning that it feeds by filtering small particles from water passing through its bill, rather than by diving into the water. Garganeys take off from water swiftly and easily, using a fast twisting motion. Despite their secretive nature, if you do see one it is easily identified by the white stripe over the eyes.

Left: Surface water drains, or "rhyns", act as wet fences.

Right (left to right): Roe deer are born in May and June; look out for the marbled white butterfly in the rough grassland; hobbies can be spotted in the air from April to October; the UK's largest grasshopper, the large marsh grasshopper, can be seen in Shapwick's meadows.

Main and far right: Shapwick Heath was once completely covered by the sea; today, otters play in the river shallows.

THRIVING WETLANDS

SCAN THE SKY ABOVE SHAPWICK HEATH ON A SUNNY DAY IN MAY and you have a strong chance of spotting a hobby. In fact, you may see a flock of 30 or more of these small falcons hawking for dragonflies, as the locally breeding birds are joined this month by their migrant cousins at this large, historic nature reserve.

Lying in the heart of the Somerset Levels, Shapwick Heath was a bare peat-working just a few years ago, but it is now one of the finest examples of wetland flora and fauna in the UK. The star attractions are the river otters, which have around four territories within the reserve. The best time to see them is at dawn or dusk, from one of the Shapwick hides; but be patient and quiet – if alarmed, otters dive into water and swim off, and you'll just catch a glimpse of their sleek, glossy fur shimmering away under the surface. The real rarities here are the lesser silver diving beetles – an endangered species that is particularly fond of the still, peat-rich waters of this reserve. Large

Above: Visit at dusk in winter to witness the huge starling roost.

Shapwick Heath's many habitats – from reedbed and fen to meadow and woodland – make it a wildlife wonderland.

THROUGH THE YEAR
SHAPWICK HEATH

Dragonflies, butterflies, and breeding birds are the main attractions in **summer**. Look for the beautiful white admiral butterfly in a woodland glade off the pathway to the Mere Heath Hide.

Passage waders and an autumn roost of little egrets are among the best sights in **autumn**.

Visit in **winter** for one of the greatest avian spectacles in Europe. At dusk each day starlings in their hundreds of thousands and sometimes millions (six million have been counted) descend on the reserve to roost. A wide variety of wildfowl can also be seen during winter.

WHERE ELSE TO SEE
PEAT-WORKINGS

Old peat-workings make excellent nature reserves, once the peat extraction has stopped, because peat only forms in wetlands – so under conservational management, the wetlands revert to a perfect habitat for many different kinds of animals and flora.

Westhay Moor nature reserve, near Shapwick, is an old peat-working with remnants of a raised bog that is now managed for wildlife. Its resident plants and animals are similar to those at Shapwick, but it also features carnivorous sundew plants, which are unusual and fun. [SW]

Catcott Lows, Somerset, is grassland in summer, but flooded during the winter, making it a great place to see wintering wildfowl between November and April. [SW]

The **Humberhead Peatlands**, South Yorkshire, is a peatland remnant of moor, bog, and fen that once surrounded the head of the Humber estuary. [N]

marsh grasshoppers live in the sphagnum moss bogs, and the reed- and carr-fringed pools play host to a bird that can only be found in the UK during the summer: the small garganey duck, which lives in the northern tropics of Africa for the rest of the year. Other summer migrants include various common warblers, which come to the woodland and fen of the reserve to join the resident Cetti's warblers, water rails, and reed buntings. If you're walking the tracks in the early morning or around dusk, you may catch sight of a roe deer as it slips quietly across a path or hovers on a woodland edge, or see barn owls hunting over the grassland.

The wide range of habitats here allows for a rich flora and wide diversity of insects. The hay meadows are traditionally managed by rare breeds of cattle and sheep, and are covered in wild flowers, including the southern marsh orchids. The flowers draw in butterflies and dragonflies, such as the hairy dragonfly and marbled white butterfly. Even the drains that act as "wet fences" support life, harbouring greater water dock, yellow flag iris, purple loosestrife, and the beautiful frogbit – a tiny waterlily that floats on the surface, protecting the tadpoles and fish hiding beneath.

JAN
FEB
MAR
APR
MAY
JUN
JUL
AUG
SEP
OCT
NOV
DEC

THE WILD PENINSULA

A RECTANGULAR SLAB OF PALE LIMESTONE TOPPED by sandstone hills, all but detached from the south coast of Wales, the Gower Peninsula is a wonderful destination for the geologist, geographer, archaeologist, and wildlife enthusiast, with its big estuary, extensive saltmarshes, sand dunes, beaches, woods, moors, and reedbeds. Not least among its charms are the limestone cliffs and clifftop grasslands that run along its southern coast, from Mumbles Head to the magnificent Worm's Head, reaching far out into Carmarthen Bay. Beautiful panoramas extend across the Bristol Channel to Exmoor, Ilfracombe, Hartland Point, and Lundy.

The mild climate and south-facing prospect ensure a long, early growing season. In May, look out for the yellow whitlow-grass that grows on cliffs such as Pwll Du Head, and at Pennard Castle – it grows nowhere else in the UK. The open grassland above the cliff is at its finest at this time of year: ungrazed areas with deeper soils,

WHERE
Gower Peninsula, Swansea, South Wales;
www.welshwildlife.org
www.the-gower.com

CONTACT
Wildlife Trust of South and West Wales,
tel: 01656 724100;
info@welshwildlife.org

GETTING THERE
By car, follow the M4. You can access Gower from a number of different junctions. For South Gower and Mumbles, take junction 42, which will take you on the Swansea Bay road. For North Gower, take junction 47. By bus, National Express coaches run from London Victoria, Gatwick, and Heathrow airports, and stops around Yorkshire and the Midlands to Swansea bus station.

ACCESS AND FACILITIES
The peninsula covers 181 sq km (70 square miles) and is home to 19 nature reserves, most well served by rural businesses. At Rhossili and Llanmadoc there are pubs and cafés with full access for wheelchairs and pushchairs, plus car parking.

CHARGES
You are free to roam on much of the peninsula, while respecting private property; there may be charges for some reserves.

Wild ponies

Llanrhidian, a small, remote village on the north Gower coast, has spectacular views over the estuary. It is the least populated part of the peninsula, and has become a haven for wildlife, including wild marsh ponies, which graze among the rare wildfowl on the sweet marsh grasses, marsh mallow, and sea lavender that grows around the saltmarshes. The north Gower marshes extend for 13 km (8 miles) from Llanrhidian to Carmarthen Bay, and are designated internationally important wetlands.

Main: The limestone cliffs of the Gower Peninsula.

Left: Bladder wrack seaweed.

Right (left to right): Worm's Head, Gower; burnet roses grow on the sand dunes at Nicholaston Burrows; a fulmar calling.

Right panel (top and bottom): Visit Worm's Head for seabirds, such as this shag; bluebells flower on Gower's clifftops.

such as Long Hole Cliff and Overton Cliff, are thick with heath, gorse, hawthorn, blackthorn, and juniper thickets. On the poorer soils and well-trodden areas you're more likely to find typical limestone plants such as early purple orchids, shocking-pink splashes of bloody cranesbill, and the yellow carline thistle. Bird's-foot trefoil and kidney vetch abound, and there are whorls of the rare, green, Portland spurge. Look out for salt-tolerant plants, such as sea campion, golden samphire, rock sea-lavender, scurvygrass, sea beet, spring squill, and thrift, and the only maritime fern – sea spleenwort. Rarities include hoary rockrose, goldilocks aster, and wild asparagus, which has been greatly reduced by collectors and, like any rarity, should be left alone.

Over the sea there's a good chance of seeing passing Manx shearwaters and gannets, and the clifftops have ravens, jackdaws, choughs, stonechats, linnets, and yellowhammers. Buzzards are common on Gower, while Oxwich Marsh has reed and sedge warblers, herons, and kingfishers.

With its estuary, saltmarshes, sand dunes, beaches, woods, moors, and reedbeds, Gower has everything.

WHERE ELSE TO SEE
LIMESTONE CLIFFS

Hard cliffs – made up of granite, sandstone, or limestone – occur mainly in the south of England; northwest and southwest Wales; west and north Scotland; and the north coast of Northern Ireland.

Limestone cliffs and their associated flora and insect life can be enjoyed on the Dorset coast at **Portland** (*see pp.90–91*). **Durlston Head** near Swanage, Dorset, has Adonis blue butterflies and the extremely localized Lulworth skipper, while the cliffs west of **Hope's Nose** in Devon are great for limestone grassland flowers. [SW]

North Wales has areas of limestone grassland above cliffs at the Great Orme, **Conwy** (*see pp.278–279*). On Anglesey, maritime heathland around **South Stack** and **Penrhosfeilw** has flowers and butterflies as well as choughs, ravens, and stonechats. [W]

The great cliffs of **Bempton** (*see pp.104–105*) and **Flamborough Head** (*see pp.252–253*) in Yorkshire are limestone; areas of grassland between fields and along the cliff remain good for wildlife. [N]

THROUGH THE YEAR
GOWER PENINSULA

In **summer**, watch for gannets, shearwaters, and fulmars offshore, and, from Worm's Head, large flocks of common scoters. Listen for the distinct, summery warble of the many species of grasshopper and cricket resident on Gower. Check the stony, grassy clearings on the slopes above Mumbles Head for grayling, common and small blue, brown argus, and dark green fritillary butterflies, among the showy plants of red valerian, yellow-wort, common centaury, and pyramidal orchids.

The majestic oak and ash woodland of Parkwood, west of Swansea, is a great place to enjoy the rich colours of **autumn**, along with buzzards, woodpeckers, horseshoe bats, and a wealth of archaeological treasures dating back 14,000 years.

The cliffs are bleak in **winter**, but look for ravens and peregrines, and purple sandpipers and turnstones on the shore below.

Below: Gower has 16 species of grasshopper and cricket.

JAN
FEB
MAR
APR
MAY
JUN
JUL
AUG
SEP
OCT
NOV
DEC

Above (left to right): Fallow deer; a long-eared owl; badger cubs foraging.
Main: Ancient woodland at Wakerley Great Wood, part of Rockingham Forest.

HISTORIC WOODLANDS

L IKE THE NEW FOREST, ROCKINGHAM WAS AN IMPORTANT ROYAL FOREST during medieval times, reserved by William the Conqueror during the 11th century for hunting deer and wild boar. It consists of a mosaic of wooded areas and more open country, with farmland and small villages, beautiful historic buildings of local stone, and two extremely rare Bronze Age cairns. Only about half the ancient woodland remains – of ash, field maple, and oak, interspersed with rarer trees such as the wild service tree and the small-leaved lime.

For centuries the woods were managed by coppicing. The many branches this produced had a myriad of uses, from fencing and house-building to providing firewood or producing charcoal. Today, this traditional management is still carried out to encourage wildlife, and one bird that benefits particularly is the nightingale. Hazel dormice, scarce in much of the country, thrive here in the coppiced woodland and overgrown hedgerows, which provide them with essential food and shelter. Other mammals include foxes, badgers, polecats, stoats, fallow deer, and muntjac deer. The forest has an understorey of hawthorn, blackthorn, and hazel, and the ground layer is exceptionally rich in plant life. Bluebells and wood anemones abound, but there are also rarer plants, including various species of orchids, toothwort, and stinking hellebore.

Birdlife includes tawny and long-eared owls, all three species of British woodpeckers, marsh and willow tits, and hawfinches – whose huge bills are capable of cracking cherry stones. Most famous are the magnificent red kites that were introduced here in the 1990s, and have since built up a thriving self-sustaining population. Over 20 butterfly species breed here; look for the rare black hairstreak butterfly among mature stands of blackthorn bushes, especially in the sunny glades and woodland margins sheltered from the wind. Its caterpillars feed mainly on the blackthorn leaves. This is a very localized species – just 30 colonies remain, all in the woods of the East Midlands forest belt. Seeing this elusive little butterfly will give you a great sense of privilege: its flight period is very brief, from mid-June to mid-July, and it spends much of its time feeding on aphid honeydew in the tops of the larger trees. Three other species of hairstreaks can also be seen in Rockingham; try the nature reserve at Bedford Purlieus for the rarest one, the brown hairstreak, whose caterpillars feed on blackthorn. Those of the commoner purple hairstreak eat oak leaves, while the caterpillars of the white-letter hairstreak prefer elm.

Below (left to right): Red kites build untidy nests in trees; the tawny owl – the largest of the UK's native owls – is another forest breeder.

WHERE ELSE TO SEE
ANCIENT WOODLANDS

The ancient woodlands of England and Wales are those in which the trees have grown continuously since 1600 or earlier, and in Scotland since at least 1750. Although over half the ancient broadleaved woodland has been cleared or planted with conifers since the 1930s, valuable areas remain.

The best known and richest in wildlife of all is the **New Forest** (see pp.174–175). It is home to five species of deer, and an extraordinarily rich variety of fungi, wildflowers, dragonflies, reptiles, and rare birds. [SE]

Over 20 per cent of England's ancient woodlands are in the southwest. Two superb examples are on Dartmoor: **Wistman's Wood** (see pp.160–161) is a strange world of wind-dwarfed oaks growing among granite boulders, while **Black Tor Copse** is an exceptional site for lichens and woodland birds. [SW]

There are patches of ancient woodland within Greater London. **Highgate Wood** and **Queen's Wood** in north London are examples, while nearby **Epping Forest** is renowned for fungi, woodland birds, and insects, including 1,400 species of beetles. [SE]

THROUGH THE YEAR
ROCKINGHAM FOREST

Autumn is the time to seek out toadstools, from the bracket fungi that protrude from tree trunks, such as dryad's saddle, to the spectacular poisonous devil's bolete, found under oaks. Bedford Purlieus nature reserve, near Peterborough, is a great place to see the golden lime trees contrasting with dark-green conifers and blue-black sloes on blackthorn bushes.

By **winter**, many of the juvenile red kites have left and the adults form large roosts. There may be a total of up to 400 kites throughout the forest. Other winter birds include crossbills, siskins, and redpolls.

The greatest diversity of wildlife is in spring and summer, when the birds are breeding, and reptiles and insects are most active. **Spring** brings a swelling chorus of songbirds: listen for the newly arrived male nightingales in areas with dense coppice and brambles. Speckled wood butterflies are among the earliest on the wing.

Below: Wildflowers carpet the floor of the woodland glades in spring.

JAN

FEB

MAR

APR

MAY

JUN

JUL

AUG

SEP

OCT

NOV

DEC

SHIFTING SANDS

FOR ITS SIZE, THE ISLAND OF ANGLESEY HAS A REMARKABLE DIVERSITY of landscapes, from mountain to marsh, and cliff to mudflat. The sand dunes of its southern coast are internationally renowned, and the greatest of these is Newborough Warren (Niwbwrch in Welsh). The area stretches over 15 sq km (6 sq miles), and almost half of this was planted with Corsican and Scots pine in the last century. As you walk through the forest on your way to the Warren, listen and watch out for goldcrests and coal tits, and even red squirrels – the greys have been eradicated here, and the native reds reintroduced with considerable success.

Out of the forest and on to the open dunes, you are enveloped by an undulating sea of sand, clothed in the stiff waxy leaves of marram grass. The size of the Warren is such that the area's natural dynamism is still taking place – the dunes are mobile, and occasionally blow out, right down to the water table, forming a pool, or dune

WHERE
Newborough Warren, Isle of Anglesey (Ynys Môn in the Welsh language), LL61, Wales.

CONTACT
Tel: 01248 672500 (Warden), or 0845 1306229 (Countryside Council for Wales enquiry line); info@wales.info

GETTING THERE
From the Menai Bridge on the A5, take the A4080 south to Newborough village (Niwbwrch). Follow the signs to Newborough Warren and Llanddwyn (this is a Forestry Commission road and subject to a toll/parking fee). Llanddwyn Island is accessible on foot at low tide.

ACCESS AND FACILITIES
There is disabled access just off the main car park in Newborough Forest; there are also toilets here. There is an accessible bird hide by Llyn Rhos-Ddu.

OPENING TIMES
Open all year round.

CHARGES
Parking fee at Llanddwyn car park.

Marram grass

As with dunes worldwide, Newborough Warren's are dominated by marram. Indeed, the dunes' existence is due to the presence of this grass: its unique, almost unlimited ability to grow upwards and sideways through bare sand creates a three-dimensional mesh that helps stabilize the sand; as more sand is blown onshore, so the marram skeleton extends to build the dune. It is stabilization by marram that then allows a whole range of other plants to colonize and thrive on the dunes.

Left (left to right): Sea holly – an important nectar source for the dune's butterflies; marsh helleborine.

Right (left to right): Grass-of-Parnassus; the grayling butterfly seeks out open areas in which to bask in the sun – it can only fly when warm.

Right panel (top and bottom): Ravens live in the cliffs behind the dunes; the disused lighthouse at Porth Twr Mawr is Newborough Warren's main landmark.

slack. These slacks harbour many of the Warren's botanical treasures. Often the dominant plant, creeping willow, is in fruit in June, the cotton-wool of its wind-dispersed seeds erupting from a silvery-leaved shrub barely knee-high. Growing through it are orchids: bee, northern marsh, and early marsh (in its distinctive red-flowered dune form), among marsh and dune helleborines. The latter is the least attractive – with greenish flowers on drooping spikes – but arguably the most important: it is only known to grow here and on the dunes of the Lancashire coast. Bog pimpernel, butterwort, yellow bird's-nest, and round-leaved wintergreen all add to the spectacle.

If you can drag yourself away from the microcosm of the slacks, visit Llanddwyn Island, an exposed section of the volcanic rocks that run under the Warren. The lichens are spectacular: look out for the rare and extremely beautiful golden hair-lichen which has recently been discovered here. And look up from the rocks: cormorants and shags can be seen nesting on the cliffs and rocky islets.

WHERE ELSE TO SEE
SAND DUNES

Most of our larger sand-dune systems show the development of dune slacks. One feature of many of these sites is that they support the dune-loving natterjack toad.

Just a few kilometres west of Newborough, **Abberffraw** dunes are a little more compact, though lacking in some of the structural diversity. [W]

Some of the best dune slacks, including around half of the creeping willow scrub in Britain, can be found at **Ainsdale** (*see pp.88–89*) and other sites on the Sefton Coast on Merseyside. [N]

The dune systems at **Saltfleetby-Theddlethorpe** in Lincolnshire have a good slack system. [M]

Magilligan, near Londonderry, comprises almost all of the dune slack habitat of Northern Ireland. [NI]

In the southwest of England, good examples include **Braunton Burrows** (*see pp.68–69*) and **Dawlish Warren** in Devon, and **Studland Bay**, Dorset. [SW]

> As dusk falls, a huge flock of around 800 ravens flies in to roost, in the largest gathering of ravens worldwide.

THROUGH THE YEAR
NEWBOROUGH WARREN

As the summer slips into **autumn**, flowers keep coming: the beautiful pearly-white single flowers of the grass of Parnassus spring up in the slacks, and autumn lady's-tresses emerge from the turf. This is a small orchid, with spiralling spikes of white flowers.

In **winter**, ravens and choughs move down from the mountains and cliff-nesting areas to find food. Pintails are a particular feature of the mudflats, along with wigeons, teals, and redshanks. Purple sandpipers and turnstones feed around seaweed-covered rocks.

Spring sees the return of the breeding birds, both noisy, piping oystercatchers and the cliff-nesting cormorants and shags. The maritime turf becomes bedecked with the flowers of thrift, and – especially where there is a little shelter – bluebells. In early spring, the open dunes are busy with botanists, hunting for one of our rarest plants: the extremely minuscule early sand-grass.

Below: the sandy beach is about 1.6km (1 mile) in length.

JAN
FEB
MAR
APR
MAY
JUN
JUL
AUG
SEP
OCT
NOV
DEC

REALM OF THE RAPTORS

PERCHED ON A RIDGE 260M (850FT) HIGH, Haldon Forest lies at the southeastern edge of the Great Haldon ridge in Devon. Stand at any of its viewpoints for a thrilling view down and over the Exe Estuary and beyond. The forest is a mosaic of coniferous and broadleaved trees, dotted with woodland rides and glades.

It is worth a visit at any season, but in summer it is one of the best sites in Britain for watching one of our rarest breeding raptors: the honey buzzard. And there's more – the skies here are home to common buzzards, sparrowhawks, and even peregrine falcons. The goshawk, so difficult to see in the UK, can be spotted here most frequently between April and June, when they rise high into the sky to display. Hobbies hawk overhead for insect prey or the occasional hapless swallow or house martin. In both spring and autumn migrating raptors are around the forest, and in early June you may still see an osprey, heading north to breed.

WHERE
Haldon Forest Park, Kennford, Exeter, EX6 7XR; www.forestry.gov.uk/haldonforestpark

CONTACT
Haldon Forest Park Ranger, tel: 01392 834251; haldon.rangers@forestry.gsi.gov.uk

GETTING THERE
By car, take the Exeter Racecourse turning off the A38. From the A380, follow the brown tourist signs for Haldon Belvedere. By bus, catch the no. 360 to Belvedere Tower and join the trails through the woods from the lay-by. By cycle, follow the A38 Cycle Way, (part of the National Cycle Network). Turn off at the racecourse and follow the signs for Haldon Forest Park.

ACCESS AND FACILITIES
There are two all-ability trails and a "secret path" to follow. There is a picnic area and food van, and plans to open a permanent restaurant. Cycles can be hired from "the hub" near the ranger's office, near Gateway car park. The main car park has full-access toilets, and disabled parking bays.

OPENING TIMES
Haldon Forest Park is open all year round. The car park is open from 8.30am–5pm.

CHARGES
There is a small car parking charge.

Honey buzzard

Few sites in Britain can match Haldon Forest for views of honey buzzards. Primarily insect eaters, they relish the larvae and pupae of social wasps and bees, and will dig out a nest using their strong legs and blunt claws. The best chance of seeing a honey buzzard is to spend time in June at the bird of prey viewpoint. A bright sunny day will produce plenty of thermals – currents of warm air that rise up from the forest – and it is these thermals that the buzzards will use to soar effortlessly into the sky.

If you can drag your eyes away from the excitement overhead, Haldon Forest has more to offer on the ground. An impressive 34 species of butterfly live in the forest, including the rare and very beautiful pearl-bordered and silver-washed fritillaries. Take the butterfly trail from the Haldon Gateway, which will give you stunning views across the Teign Valley as well as the chance to see butterflies. Halfway through the walk you'll come to a pond that's home to large numbers of dragonflies and damselflies, including the golden-ringed dragonfly and the beautiful demoiselle damselfly. A multitude of small mammals call the forest home, including dormice – which spend three-quarters of their time asleep and so readily use the nestboxes put up for them. At dusk in June, head for a clear-fell area and you may hear the distinctive churring song of a nightjar. Follow the sound, and you may be rewarded with seeing them display or feed on the wing around the clearings and along the woodland rides of this huge and exciting forest.

WHERE ELSE TO SEE
BIRDS OF PREY

Seeing birds of prey in a woodland setting can be a challenge; keep your eyes and ears open, and look along rides and in glades.

Thetford Forest in Norfolk shares many of Haldon's birds, including goshawks and nightjars, and also offers a chance of seeing the rare firecrest. Roe deer are abundant. [SE]

Kielder Forest in Northumberland is England's largest forest, and is home to some spectacular wildlife, including goshawks, kestrels, and buzzards – and the very rare red squirrel. [N]

The wildlife of the **New Forest** (*see pp.174–175*) has been protected since 1079, and includes many birds of prey, including the honey buzzard. [SE]

The Wood of Cree, an ancient forest in southern Scotland, has a large population of kestrels, sparrowhawks, and buzzards. Hen harriers, merlins, and golden eagles are occasionally seen. [SC]

THROUGH THE YEAR
HALDON FOREST

Watch for migrant birds of prey from the viewpoint in **autumn**. Look for discarded hazelnuts with a small neat round hole nibbled in one side, which is a sure sign of a dormouse.

Crossbills may be in the conifers in **winter**. Look for dippers along the streams, and keep an eye out for goshawks from the bird of prey viewpoint.

Haldon Forest comes alive in **spring** with the first butterflies of the year on the wing. Arriving migrants include nightjars. Honey buzzards and goshawks will be displaying.

Main: Honey buzzards breed in the UK in June.

Left (top to bottom): Haldon Forest; a goshawk landing; the peregrine falcon is always alert.

Above: A sparrowhawk perches on a post – these birds particularly like the larch trees of Haldon Forest.

Below: A pearl-bordered fritillary can feed only on violet-coloured plants.

Below: A view across the estuary of the River Exe.

JAN
FEB
MAR
APR
MAY
JUN
JUL
AUG
SEP
OCT
NOV
DEC

WHERE
Whitbarrow, Howe, near Kendal, Cumbria.

CONTACT
Natural England, tel: 0845 600 3078;
enquiries@naturalengland.org.uk
Cumbria Wildlife Trust, tel: 01539 816300;
mail@cumbriawildlifetrust.org.uk

GETTING THERE
Whitbarrow National Nature Reserve is 8km
(5 miles) southwest of Kendal. By car, follow
signs to the A590; take the road signposted
to Witherslack; drive through the village then
turn right at Witherslack Hall into the
reserve. By train, travel to Kendal on the
TransPennine Express, or Grange-over-Sands
with Northern Rail.

ACCESS AND FACILITIES
There are no facilities on site; the nearest
are in Grange-over-Sands. The nature reserve
is not suitable for wheelchair users. There is
no formal car park, but you can leave your
car by the side of the road on the western
side of the reserve.

OPENING TIMES
Open all year round.

CHARGES
None.

Remnants of the Ice Age

This weird landscape is unique to limestone
regions that were covered by moving ice some
14,000 years ago, and regularly deluged by heavy
rain ever since. The grinding glaciers scoured the
landscape clean, allowing rainwater – naturally
slightly acid – to seep gradually into cracks and
erode the rock, creating deep fissures. The glacier
that moved over Whitbarrow also deposited the
stray boulders now seen on the surface, which it
had picked up earlier in its course.

LIMESTONE LANDSCAPE

ALL LANDSCAPES ARE DEFINED BY THEIR GEOLOGY. The nature of the rock gives the
land its form and character, and is reflected in the wild plants that colonize it. This is
true of all types of rock, but few display their influence quite so dramatically as limestone.
For although every rock has its unique qualities, limestone is special. At Whitbarrow National
Nature Reserve in southern Cumbria you can see this even from a distance: as you approach
from the village of Witherslack, the hill looming above you is castellated with an imposing
rampart of pale, bare rock rising high above the trees on the lower slopes. Yet this is nothing
compared to the view that starts to open out as you climb through the trees to the top.

> The fissures of a limestone
> pavement act as portholes for
> rainwater. It trickles down to a
> network of caves and streams
> beneath the rock – festooned with
> calcite curtains, hanging stalactites,
> and rising stalagmites.

As the trees thin out, you emerge into a different world. In summer it is a place of dazzling
colour and fragrance, with the bright wings of common blue butterflies or bigger, more
spectacular dark green fritillaries flitting between the flowers of wild strawberry, wild
thyme, and common rock-rose. In many places, especially along the eastern side of the
reserve, these plants sprout from a complex network of fissures and crevices between
blocks of bare limestone – the weird, almost alien terrain of a limestone pavement.

Rainwater runs down through the fissures, or "grikes", in the limestone, leaving
the rock surface itself dry and largely barren. But over the years pockets of soil have formed
in the grikes, which soak up water draining off the limestone blocks, or "clints", to provide
a moist roothold for lime-loving plants such as limestone oak fern, hart's-tongue fern,
meadow cranesbill, and even trees – such as juniper, ash, and rowan. Every crevice contains
its own community of plants, which flourish in the sheltered, damp, but perfectly drained
microclimate. So making your way across the limestone pavement can be a slow process as
you are distracted by each floral delight. But don't forget to look up, because the view over
the fells of southern Lakeland from the summit is nothing short of stupendous.

Main: The clints and grikes of Whitbarrow's limestone pavement.
Below (left to right): Meadow cranesbill; a common blue butterfly; limestone reflects the sun, helping to ripen wild strawberries.
Inset: Golden-leaved *Sedum acre*, commonly known as wall pepper, likes the wet, alkaline conditions of the pavement.

Above: Ash is a tree associated with limestone habitats.

JAN

FEB

MAR

APR

MAY

JUN

JUL

AUG

SEP

OCT

NOV

DEC

WHERE ELSE TO SEE
LIMESTONE PAVEMENT

In mainland Britain, the best examples of limestone pavement lie in northern England and north Wales.

The most famous limestone pavements in England lie in the southern Yorkshire Dales around **Ingleton** and **Malham**. **Scales Moor** above Chapel-le-Dale is a magnificent expanse of bare limestone dotted with boulders – "glacial erratics" – dropped by the Ice-Age glaciers as they melted away some 13,000 years ago. [N]

Gait Barrows National Nature Reserve and nearby **Arnside Knott** near Carnforth, in Lancashire, have extensive areas of limestone pavement, with a wonderful variety of plant life, including several species of orchid. [N]

There is a superb stretch of limestone pavement on **Great Orme's Head** in North Wales, which offers the bonus of a dramatic coastal backdrop. [W]

THROUGH THE YEAR
WHITBARROW

In September and October the path that leads up through woodland to the top of Whitbarrow glows with **autumn** colour, and the scent of fungi hangs in the air. Watch for birds gathering berries from the trees and shrubs.

Ice, snow, and even rain in **winter** can make the limestone pavements especially hazardous, so it is probably best to avoid them at such times. If you do decide to risk it, the panorama of lakeland from the summit – Lord's Seat – can make the climb worthwhile on a clear frosty day.

In **spring** skylarks hover above the rocky summit, pouring out their silvery stream of song. Wheatears are often to be seen searching for insects, and if you watch carefully you may see one taking food to a brood of young in a nest among the rocks.

WHERE
Wye Downs National Nature Reserve,
Wye, Ashford, Kent TN25 5HE;
www.naturalengland.org.uk

CONTACT
Natural England, Kent, tel: 01233 812525
or 0845 600 3078 (local rate);
enquiries@naturalengland.org.uk

GETTING THERE
The nature reserve is 2km (3¼ miles)
southeast of Wye and 6km (9½ miles)
northeast of Ashford, Kent. By car, follow
minor roads from the A28, about 1.5km
(1 mile) southeast of Wye. The reserve's
eastern boundary is marked by a road from
Wye to Hastingleigh; here you'll find a car
park. The nearest train station is in Wye. The
reserve lies on the Sustrans National Cycle
Network, Route 18.

ACCESS AND FACILITIES
Parking is available at the reserve. There are
no toilets and the 4km (6½ miles) of nature
trails are unsuitable for wheelchairs. Picnic
tables are available.

OPENING TIMES
Open all year round.

CHARGES
None.

Mimicry in orchids

Bee orchids only flower in June and July, and
can be difficult to find – if you're not a male bee.
The flowers are a delicate pink and brown, with
a furry, bee-like "body" designed to attract male
bees. The flowers release counterfeit bee sex
pheromones to further encourage the bees, who
attempt to copulate with the flower, so convinced
are they by the flower's disguise. They depart
frustrated, but carrying the flower's pollen, which
they then deposit on another flower, so fertilizing
the orchids.

Above (left to right): Some of the orchids found in the Wye Downs – the burnt orchid; military orchid; and frog orchid.
Main: A bee orchid, with flowers that mimic the shape of a bee to achieve pollination.

CHALKLAND ORCHIDS

TAKE TO THE NORTH DOWNS NEAR ASHFORD IN KENT, and you'll come across the outstanding chalkland reserve of Wye Downs. You'll first be struck by the magnificent views – west over Romney Marsh and the Weald, and east over the Channel coast. Then you notice the unusual plants – chalk and limestone allow for many specialized wild flowers.

The Wye Downs tumble in steep, emerald-green, grassy slopes to scattered hawthorn and bramble brakes, sweeping down into quiet valleys with patches of broadleaved woodland. It is all irresistibly beautiful, but if you want to hunt out the area's special prize – its orchids – head to the chalk grassland. Here you'll find as many as 21 species of orchid, including lady orchid, burnt orchid, fly orchid, the rare late and early spider orchids, and man orchid. Be careful where you walk, as many of these plants are inconspicuous, and you need to develop a slow, systematic searching technique to see the best of them. Or you can let nature lead you, and just take a simple walk along the footpaths, which is a delight in summer when an abundance of colourful flowers and butterflies can be seen with ease. The grassland is grazed to prevent the encroachment of trees and bushes, and it's an outstanding mixture of elegant grasses and flowers in summer. Notice the pale yellow of horseshoe vetch and cowslips, and the rare, diminutive but vivid Kentish milkwort.

The grasslands of the Wye Downs contain up to 40 plant species in one square metre (10 sq ft). This reserve is home to around 4,000 different plant species in all.

Butterflies abound, and usually include a range of the more common ones, such as small coppers, meadow browns, gatekeepers, and common blues, plus a much rarer one: the brown-and-orange chequered Duke of Burgundy. Look for the butterflies on the flowering brambles, where they seek out nectar on sunny days. If you walk quietly, especially on a warm summer morning before it gets too hot, you might also find an adder or two, a grass snake, a slow-worm, or a common lizard winding across your path.

Inset: The common spotted orchid.
Below (left to right): The slopes of the Wye Downs; cattle grazing controls scrub.

WHERE ELSE TO SEE
CHALKLAND FLORA

Chalklands exist across the country, both on the coast and inland. Orchids can be found in many places across Britain, although some species can only grow in very specific conditions. Alkaline soils suit a wide variety of orchids, while acid soils can only support a few.

Chalk downs can be enjoyed at **Ivinghoe Beacon**, Buckinghamshire, and **Dunstable Downs**, Bedfordshire; orchids can be seen at reserves with grassland in the Chilterns, including **Aston Rowant** (see pp.222–223), Oxfordshire, and the excellent **Warburg** reserve near Henley-on-Thames. [SE].

Martin Down, Salisbury, is a magnificent stretch of grassland, rich in flowers and butterflies. [SE]

Orchids and butterflies can be found on sand dune habitats such as the Kenfig reserve near Bridgend in Wales. [W]

Folkestone Warren, at the end of the chalk downs on the Kent coast, has chalk plants and butterflies including the vivid Adonis blue. [SE]

THROUGH THE YEAR
WYE DOWNS

Flowers and butterflies appear in sequence from April to September, so these downs are well worth visiting through the **summer** and **autumn**. Look out especially for the subtle, purplish-blue flowers of autumn gentian. Various migrant birds, such as redwings, can be seen from October onwards.

In **winter**, there are stonechats, linnets, yellowhammers, and a few birds of prey. Farmers leave areas of stubble in the fields to provide a feeding place for the birds.

By **spring** the birds are looking for breeding grounds, so some fields are left fallow for birds such as skylarks, which like to nest in open fields. Brimstones and orange-tip butterflies, and early flowers including cowslips, lady's smock, primroses, violets, and celandines start to appear.

Below: Kestrels hunt over the Wye Downs.

JAN

FEB

MAR

APR

MAY

JUN

JUL

AUG

SEP

OCT

NOV

DEC

Left (left to right): Skomer Island is home to around 500,000 seabirds; the Skomer vole is larger and paler than mainland voles.

Right (left to right): A puffin takes off from the sea; puffins are also known as "sea clowns", for good reason!

Panel (below right): Puffins can carry around 10 sand eels in their beaks at any one time.

WHERE
Skomer Island, South West Wales, SA62 3BE; www.welshwildlife.org

CONTACT
The Wildlife Trust South and West Wales, tel: 01656 724100; info@welshwildlife.org

GETTING THERE
The island is reached by boat from Martin's Haven, a small cove 3.2km (2 miles) from the village of Marloes, which is off the B4327 from Haverfordwest towards Dale. Pass through the village and turn left for Martin's Haven. Boat trips, which take 20 minutes, depart between 10am–noon and return between 3pm–4pm. The boatman will advise on the day.

ACCESS AND FACILITIES
There's a National Trust car park at Martin's Haven. There are no refreshments, so take a picnic and plenty to drink. There are toilets situated in the centre of the island beside the old farmhouse. Wheelchair users should check with The Wildlife Trust (www.welshwildlife.org) before visiting.

OPENING TIMES
Boat trips run from Easter to the end of October, weather permitting.

CHARGES
Yes, for car parking and the boat trip.

Nesting burrows
There are around 6,000 breeding pairs of puffins on Skomer during the spring and summer. They build nests of grass, sea campion, and bluebell stems in burrows on the slopes or rocky cliffs, and the female puffin lays a single egg. After an incubation of 39–45 days, the fluffy grey "puffling" hatches out. At the end of July the young puffins begin to leave the island – at night – to escape predatory gulls. They stay at sea for two years, before returning to the colony.

Main: Skomer's puffin population returns faithfully to this tiny island to breed each year.

THE CLOWNS OF THE SEA

THE ISLANDS OFF THE WEST OF WALES – Bardsey in the north, Ramsey, Skokholm, Skomer, and Grassholm in the south – all have a special character and charm. Skomer, one of the largest and most appealing in spring and summer, is full of interest and excitement. The boat that takes you to the island drops off at "The Neck", a thin strip of land where the main island is almost severed from its smaller eastern extension by the sea. You can explore the main section on well-used footpaths, from which you soon see that thousands of handsome herring and lesser black-backed gulls populate the middle of the island.

You'll also notice that the island is riddled with holes. These are the homes of tens of thousands of rabbits and Manx shearwaters, but some of them – such as the burrows on the steep grassy slopes above the sea cliffs – contain puffins. Puffins are smaller than you probably think, barely as big as a town pigeon, but always comical

THROUGH THE YEAR
SKOMER ISLAND

Autumn is a great time to see migrant birds, including thousands of swallows; tree pipits, meadow pipits, and various warblers; occasional Lapland buntings; and black redstarts and ring ouzels. Islands are often good sites for finding rarities, and it is worth exploring the adjacent headlands in September and October. Ravens can sometimes be seen in scores. Watch the sea for dolphins and even sunfish.

The island's mallards are joined in **winter** by wigeons, teals, and a small flock of barnacle geese. Choughs fly around the mainland cliffs near St David's, and peregrines can be seen chasing pigeons.

The white flowers of scurvy grass announce **spring** on Skomer. The gulls look stunning standing in dense swathes of tall bluebells and red campion, while the puffin pairs can be seen busily courting and reinforcing their long-lasting pair bonds. Offshore, watch for gannets, dolphins, porpoises, and seals. Choughs cavort around the coastal cliffs.

WHERE ELSE TO SEE
PUFFINS

Very few puffins breed on the British mainland, but there are many colonies on the offshore islands dotted around the coast.

Puffins can be enjoyed in very small numbers at **South Stack**, Anglesey. [W]

There is a large puffin colony at **Farne Islands** (*see pp.126–127*), Northumberland, and a smaller one at **Bempton Cliffs** (*see pp.104–105*) in Yorkshire. [N]

Northerly seabird colonies in Scotland often include puffins, try **Fowlsheugh**, south of Aberdeen, **Troup Head** on the Moray Firth (*see pp.220–221*), and the great cliffs of Caithness including those near **Berriedale**, **Wick**, **Duncansby Head,** and **Dunnet Head**. A popular place to see them remarkably closely is Lunga, one of the **Treshnish Islands**, off Mull (*see pp.226–227*). [SC]

JAN
FEB
MAR
APR
MAY
JUN
JUL
AUG
SEP
OCT
NOV
DEC

Puffins use their wings not only to fly but also to propel themselves through water, in long dives chasing fish.

and fun to watch, even from a distance: their inky-black backs, sparkling white undersides, and orange legs often catch the eye before the famously colourful beak. When several get together they seem incurably nosy, poking their red, yellow, and blue beaks into other puffins' business and not infrequently getting fiercely pecked for their trouble. You can sometimes see puffins locked in fairly harmless combat, rolling down a slope until they fall off the cliff and take flight.

What is truly amazing about puffins is that they live all winter in the most savage conditions, far out in the Atlantic – certainly entirely out of sight of land – but, every spring, driven by mysterious instincts and helped by even more remarkable means of navigation, they fly back to their very own burrow, and probably meet up once again with their own familiar mate.

The puffins of Grassholm, farther out to sea, died out long ago when their burrowing simply eroded all the soil from that small island, and they scratched and scraped themselves out of house and home. There is no such problem here on Skomer, but southern puffin colonies are generally declining, possibly because rising sea temperatures are affecting the marine food chain.

Below: Skomer Island during winter.

WHERE
RSPB Strumpshaw Fen, Brundall, Norfolk
NR13 4HS; www.rspb.org.uk

CONTACT
RSPB Strumpshaw Fen, tel: 01603 715191;
strumpshaw@rspb.org.uk

GETTING THERE
The reserve is just beyond the village of
Brundall, which lies east of Norwich off
the A47. From the A47 roundabout, drive
through Brundall and continue on the same
road towards Strumpshaw. Turn right into
Stone Road, then follow RSPB signs. The
closest train station is Brundall, which is on
the Norwich–Lowestoft line. An hourly bus
service from Norwich stops 1.1km (¾ mile)
from the reserve on the Brundall to
Strumpshaw road at the junction of Long
Lane and Stone Road (except Sundays).

ACCESS AND FACILITIES
The information centre is wheelchair friendly.
Some trails are accessible by wheelchair and
there is an accessible viewing platform. The
two circular walks through fenland and
woodland are not advisable by wheelchair.

OPENING TIMES
Open from dawn until dusk every day.

CHARGES
For non-RSPB members.

Harriers gain ground

The marsh harrier used to nest in large numbers
in the UK, but egg theft and the drainage of
wetlands left only one breeding pair in 1971.
Protection of its favourite nesting sites – dense
reedbeds – has resulted in numbers of breeding
females rising to around 350. With luck, you'll
see fledgling harriers over the reedbeds at
Strumpshaw in summer, as around a dozen
birds breed there.

Above (left to right): A swallowtail caterpillar eating milk-parsley; reed warbler; barn owls can be seen during the day in summer.
Main: Strumpshaw Fen is part of the Mid Yare Reserve in the Norfolk Broads.

SUMMER ON THE BROADS

THE NORFOLK BROADS ARE A MAGNIFICENT AREA OF WILDERNESS in the heart of Norfolk, combining shallow freshwater lakes, rivers and canals, and low-lying pastureland, reedbeds, and swamp. The flat landscapes create a huge feeling of open space, and the area is as famous for its enormous, dramatic skies as for its teeming wildlife.

Strumpshaw Fen is a relatively small, accessible, and manageable area from which to begin exploring the Broads. It is loved by birdwatchers and butterfly fans, offering plenty to see all summer. Butterfly enthusiasts travel here in June to see the spectacular swallowtail butterfly – it is Britain's largest butterfly, and one of the rarest. Its caterpillars feed on milk-parsley, which used to grow in sedge fens in several places in eastern England, but now grows only on the Norfolk Broads. The adult butterfly flies strongly over the fens, seeking out milk-parsley on which to lay eggs, but feeding eagerly from pink or mauve flowers, such as ragged robin and creeping thistle.

> On warm sunny days, Strumpshaw Fen is alive with the flutter of wings, as butterflies, dragonflies, and damselflies take flight.

In June you'll also see marsh harriers, the males perhaps still performing their spectacular displays high overhead. The marsh is alive with the songs of sedge and reed warblers, cuckoos, grasshopper warblers, and whitethroats. Look for lesser spotted woodpeckers in surrounding woodland: this is not a bird you are often likely to come across, as it is declining almost everywhere.

Linger in the meadow, where you can enjoy a rich display of wild flowers, including six species of orchids. There are around 20 kinds of dragonfly here, including the rare Norfolk hawker. Dragonflies in turn attract hobbies, those small, agile falcons that specialize in catching large flying insects in summer, and small birds later in the autumn. Add this to the year-long treats that the fen has to offer – including kingfishers, Cetti's warblers, and even bitterns – and you begin to see why the Broads are one of Britain's favourite wildlife haunts.

Inset: Bitterns hide in the Strumpshaw Fen reedbeds.
Below (left to right): A tufted duck; the rare swallowtail butterfly.

WHERE ELSE TO SEE
REEDBED WILDLIFE

Britain's reedbeds are a relic of what existed before the drainage of our wetlands. They are evocative places, filled with the sounds of unseen birds and insects, and harbour the diversity of life you would expect at the boundary between water and land.

Ranworth Broad in Norfolk has swallowtail butterflies in June, a large variety of dragonflies, and wild flowers including marsh valerian, royal fern, and marsh fern. Look for Cetti's warblers in the low bushes and reeds, redpolls and siskins in the alders, and cormorants and great crested grebes on the open water. [SE]

The **London Wetlands Centre**, in Barnes (see pp.16–17) is a good urban reserve for seeing hobbies and peregrine falcons, and some of the more unusual butterflies and damselflies, such as the painted lady and the blue-tailed damselfly. [SE]

THROUGH THE YEAR
STRUMPSHAW FEN

In **autumn**, you'll see wading birds and water rails on muddy patches if the water level is low. Marsh harriers gather in groups to roost. In early autumn, ospreys are regularly seen fishing, as they linger on their southward migration.

Hundreds of ducks, including teals, gadwalls, and shovelers, feed in the reedbed pools during the **winter**. In some winters, thousands of starlings also roost in the reeds, attracting sparrowhawks, peregrines, and merlins. Shy Chinese water deer are often spotted early and late in the day.

In **spring**, listen out for booming bitterns and the drumming of woodpeckers. Swallows and swifts flit across the pools where great crested grebes build their nests.

Summer dawn choruses are great experiences, with the songs of woodland birds mingling with sedge and reed warblers. Marsh harriers nest and you may see bearded tits and kingfishers.

Below: In winter, the fen offers a welcome home to migrating birds.

JAN
FEB
MAR
APR
MAY
JUN
JUL
AUG
SEP
OCT
NOV
DEC

A WESTERLY HAVEN

LAKE VYRNWY, IN THE HEART OF WALES, IS A MAN-MADE WONDER. The long, fork-tipped reservoir that lies so serenely in the Berwyn Mountains was actually created by flooding a valley in the 1880s, to store water for the city of Liverpool. The beautiful wildlife reserve around the lake has many habitats, many favoured by birds of prey: cliffs with peregrines and ravens; conifer forest with goshawks, sparrowhawks, and buzzards; and moorland with merlins, hen harriers, and kestrels. But it also contains one of the wildlife glories of Wales – old, gnarled oak woods, filled with the sound and activity of delightful small woodland birds.

A narrow road runs around the reservoir, starting at the Victorian stone dam at the southern end; much of it runs through dense conifer plantations, but in hidden dips and valleys you suddenly come across patches of oakwood. Seek these out in early summer, before the foliage becomes too dense, and before the birds stop singing.

WHERE
Lake Vyrnwy, Bryn Awel, Llanwddyn, Powys, Wales SY10 0LZ; www.rspb.org.uk

CONTACT
RSPB Lake Vyrnwy Reserve, tel: 01691 870278; vyrnwy@rspb.org.uk

GETTING THERE
Lake Vyrnwy lies just west of the village of Llanfyllin. By car from Llanfyllin, take the B4393 to Llanwddyn and continue along this road until you reach the dam. Turn left here, then left again at the end of the dam. The RSPB visitor centre is on the right. The reserve is difficult to reach by public transport. By train, travel to Welshpool, 32km (20 miles) away. There is an infrequent bus service to the Vyrnwy dam.

ACCESS AND FACILITIES
The reserve has a visitor centre with information, refreshments, shop, toilets, baby-changing facilities, picnic area, and wheelchair/pushchair-friendly trails.

OPENING TIMES
Open daily from 1 April to 24 December, 10.30am–5.30pm (closing at 4.30pm in winter). Open weekends only from 1 January to 31 March.

CHARGES
None.

Food for life

It is difficult to know why the redstart, wood warbler, and pied flycatcher have such a westerly distribution in the UK. Perhaps it is because these long-distance migrants from Africa all like an open woodland floor, and a dense canopy full of foliage brimming with caterpillars – exactly the conditions supplied by these lush Welsh woodlands. The fortunes of all breeding birds are strongly linked to the variable numbers of moth caterpillars in the oak leaves in spring – which are reliably high at Lake Vyrnwy in most years.

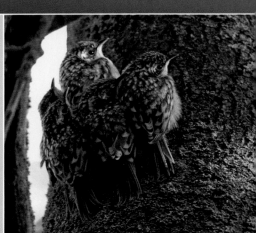

Main: Clear, still days provide magnificent views over the lake.

Left: A grey wagtail sings his right to territory and calls for a mate.

Right (left to right): A family of treecreepers huddles together on a tree trunk; a brightly coloured chaffinch flies down towards a woodland drinking pool; a pied flycatcher patiently waits for its insect prey.

Right panel (above and below): More than 30 streams splash down through the woods into the lake; a seedling oak.

Three new arrivals make this time of year really special in these western woods: redstarts, wood warblers, and pied flycatchers. All spend the winter in Africa; the males return as early as they dare to carve out a breeding territory, defending it against all comers with their song, while the females return a few days later. Males that fail to find a mate may sing for weeks; successful birds settle to a less punishing schedule of singing, but have more work to do rearing a family.

      See if you can find all three of these determined songsters. The male redstart is a dandy: blue-grey above, rich-orange below, with a striking white forehead and inky-black bib. Wood warblers are sleek birds, with a pale-green, white, and soft-yellow plumage. It is easiest to find a male by his song: a hesitant, thin, metallic ticking sound that accelerates into a silvery, shivery trill. Pied flycatchers do as they promise: they catch flies and the males, at least, are black and white, with an upright, short-legged, long-winged shape that helps them dart from a perch to a fly in a "snap"!

WHERE ELSE TO SEE
OAKWOOD BIRDS

Loss of woodland around the country has led to a decline in oakwood birds, and it's thought that lack of management of the remaining woodlands has exacerbated the problem – overcrowding of trees leads to canopy closure, loss of open space, and a shaded understorey.

The ancient oak woodland of **Strid Wood**, at Bolton Abbey in the Yorkshire Dales, has a similar range of bird species to those at Lake Vyrnwy, including dippers. [N]

Coombes Valley Nature Reserve in Staffordshire is a peaceful oak woodland where you're likely to see redstarts, pied flycatchers, woodcocks, and great spotted woodpeckers. [M]

The woodland of **Cwm Clydach** in South Wales grows on steep slopes down to the Clydach gorge. There are spectacular waterfalls and a great variety of butterfly, fungi, and woodland birds. **Ynys-hir** (see pp.106–107) on the Dyfi estuary near Machynlleth also has superb oakwood birds, including the westerly trio of redstarts, wood warblers, and pied flycatchers. [W]

THROUGH THE YEAR
LAKE VYRNWY

Spring is a good time to watch for birds of prey hunting across open land and water. Great crested grebes display on the lake, and you stand a good chance of seeing goosanders on the water too.

Autumn is a quiet time, but you may still find some butterflies, such as the pearl-bordered fritillaries, haunting the woodland glades. This is a good area for polecats and otters too, but both are quick to hide, and hard to find. The fairytale fly agaric fungi, bright red with white spots, grows in the woodlands.

Winter sees large flocks of redwings and fieldfares around the lake. Siskins join the tits and other finches at the bird feeders by the visitor centre. Look for treecreepers in the woods, and dippers by the streams. There are teals, goosanders, and little grebes to be found, and ravens begin their tumbling displays.

The pure air, spectacular mountain scenery, and large, languid lake here are reminiscent of the Alps.

Below: Goshawks fly down from the woodlands to catch prey.

JAN

FEB

MAR

APR

MAY

JUN

JUL

AUG

SEP

OCT

NOV

DEC

WHERE
Canvey Wick, Canvey Island, Essex SS8 0PT;
www.naturalengland.org.uk

CONTACT
Natural England, tel: 0845 6003078;
enquiries@naturalengland.org.uk

GETTING THERE
By car, take the A130 as far as the B1014.
The nearest train station is Benfleet. From
there you can take a bus to the Canvey
Island supermarket on Northwick Road,
next to the reserve's entrance.

ACCESS AND FACILITIES
As yet there are no facilities on site and
wheelchair access is problematic.

CHARGES
None.

A return to nature

"Brownfield" simply means land that has been developed in the past. There are numerous examples – like Canvey Wick – of areas where nature has reasserted itself after development, but arguably the most surprising are the Norfolk Broads (*pictured below*). Now an internationally important wetland site, the origins of the Broads lie in medieval peat diggings, which were left to fill with water. The resulting rivers, dykes, and cuts allowed wildlife to flourish undisturbed.

NEW LIFE AT CANVEY WICK

TAKE ONE TRACT OF ESSEX GRAZING MARSH, add hundreds of truckloads of sand and silt, build an oil refinery, knock it down, then apply a liberal dose of informal recreation. Let it stand for 30 years, and what do you get? A nationally important wildlife site.

This is the story of Canvey Wick, an area of some 80 hectares (200 acres) that forms the southwestern portion of Canvey Island, and is now recognized as a hotbed of biodiversity. As a result of its history, climate, and use, Canvey Wick is home to an incredible array of plants and animals. It supports hundreds of types of insects, many of which are locally or nationally rare, including some that have long been believed to be extinct in Britain, and

Canvey Wick was the first brownfield site to be protected specifically for its invertebrates – among them the shrill and brown-banded carder-bees, the five-banded weevil wasp, and the scarce emerald damselfly.

others that have never before been found in this country. Perhaps most significantly, it has a thriving population of the shrill carder-bee, once widespread across England, but now, with most of its flower-rich habitats destroyed, on the verge of extinction. At Canvey Wick it forages from a range of plants, both natives (like the narrow-leaved bird's-foot trefoil) and aliens, such as goat's-rue and the broad-leaved everlasting pea. In June it buzzes among the Wick's beautiful butterflies, including the marbled white, common blue, and Essex skipper.

Other protected species live here too, such as common lizards, adders, badgers, and water voles. There are thriving populations of the songbirds that are in decline throughout Britain's countryside, and swathes of attractive flowers, including four species of orchid and spectacular yellow splashes of biting stonecrop.

With more rare insects than any other English site of its size, Canvey Wick is unique. But then, so is every brownfield site such as this – each is the product of its singular geography, geology, and history, and each offers a uniquely developed habitat. Any such previously developed site has the potential to be a haven for wildlife. The message is clear – don't overlook the wildlife on your doorstep in your quest for the best spots to go wild.

Main: Canvey Wick is swathed in orchids, including the beautiful southern marsh orchid, which flowers in June.
Below (left to right): The marbled white butterfly; the everlasting pea, a favourite food plant of carder-bees; the bee orchid.
Inset: Canvey Wick has the most important population of the shrill carder-bee in the Thames region, and possibly the UK.

JAN

FEB

MAR

APR

MAY

JUN

JUL

AUG

SEP

OCT

NOV

DEC

Above: Adders can be seen around Canvey Wick in spring and summer.

THROUGH THE YEAR
CANVEY WICK

As the flowers and insects fade away at the end of **summer**, the fruits and berries of sea buckthorn and other bushes attract feeding birds, such as the resident blackbirds and immigrant redwings. Bullfinches, always present but hard to see, become more obvious among the bare trees of autumn.

All is quiet on Canvey Wick in the **winter**, except perhaps for a burst of song from a Cetti's warbler on a warm day, or a snipe rising from a winter-wet puddle. But take a look over the sea wall: at low tide, Holehaven Creek is home to internationally important numbers of black-tailed godwits, and you may see a peregrine hunting smaller waders like dunlin over the mudflats.

Spring brings a resumption of reptile activity, with common lizards, grass snakes, and adders basking in any early warmth, while great crested newts return to their breeding ponds and ditches. The blackthorn bursts into a profusion of white flowers, which, along with the pollen from goat willow, forms a vital source of energy and food for early emerging queen bumblebees.

WHERE ELSE TO SEE
BROWNFIELD RESERVES

Nature reserves are one of the more ingenious ways to reuse old brownfield sites, bringing animals and flora back into otherwise barren areas.

The **Old Moor and Fairburn Ings** nature reserves in Yorkshire were formed as a result of mining subsidence. The alkaline slag heaps of **Nob End**, near Bolton, Lancashire, have had a new lease of life and been colonized by thousands of orchids. [N]

The **Cotswold Water Park** in Gloucestershire is a huge collection of gravel pits that is now of immense value to wildlife and recreational interests alike. [M]

"Green roofs" are miniature, artificial brownfield sites that use the roofs of large industrial buildings as nature reserves, such as the **Creekside Nature Conservation Centre** in Deptford, London, which is dedicated to preserving the black redstart. [SE]

REEDBED WILDLIFE

BLACKTOFT SANDS LIES ON THE INNER HUMBER ESTUARY, out of sight of the main river, in an area of extraordinary calm. It is a vast expanse of tidal reedbeds – the largest in England – dotted with artificial lagoons and dykes. The reserve appeals to a huge range of breeding birds, including several of the classic, rare reedbed specialities that are more often associated with East Anglia. Even the elusive bitterns arrive; they are easiest to see in June, as they often fly over the reedbeds carrying fish to their chicks.

Marsh harriers, big birds that hunt on the wing, fly low over the reed tops and lagoon edges, or across neighbouring fields. You'll know them by their long, up-tilted wings. In June the male does the hunting, bringing food back for his mate and young. As he arrives he calls to the female, who flies from the nest to receive the food in a mid-air "food pass", rolling over beneath the male, mid-air, to take the prey from his outstretched feet.

WHERE
Blacktoft Sands RSPB reserve, near Goole, East Yorkshire; www.rspb.org.uk

CONTACT
RSPB Blacktoft Sands, tel: 01405 704665; blacktoftsands@rspb.org.uk

GETTING THERE
From Goole, take the A161 to Swinefleet, turn left at the mini-roundabout in Swinefleet, then right at the next T-junction and follow the minor road for the next 8km (5 miles) through Reedness, Whitgift, and Ousefleet. About 0.5km (⅓ mile) past Ousefleet, heading towards Adlingfleet, turn left into the reserve's car park.

ACCESS AND FACILITIES
The car park has disabled parking, an information centre, picnic area, and toilets. A 1.2km (¾ mile) trail links all six of the reserve's hides. There is firm, level path leading to five of the hides, and all have wheelchair access. The path to Ousefleet hide is rough in places.

OPENING TIMES
Open daily 9am–9pm, or dusk if earlier.

CHARGES
For non-RSPB members.

Hunting out treasure

It can be hard to believe that sweeping a bill through mud or silt can yield a nutritious meal for a bird. However, mud is packed with living organisms and organic material and different species have evolved their own ways to find these foods. Birds with long bills, such as curlews and godwits go deep to pull out worms, while shorter-beaked coots, dunlins, and sanderlings pick off insects from the surface, and avocets have upturned bills, which are ideal for filtering food from fine mud and silt.

Main: The vast expanses of tidal reedbeds at Blacktoft Sands.

Left: A greenshank in flight.

Right (left to right): A brown hare drinks at the water's edge; a bearded tit feeds on insects amongst the reeds.

Right panel (top and bottom): A male marsh harrier passes food to a female in flight; the black-tailed godwit.

Many visitors come to see the owls: short-eared owls hunt during the day, and barn owls – who prefer the dark – may join them when they have young to feed. Equally important are the bearded tits: listen out for their sharp, metallic "pinging" calls. With patience, a bit of luck, and some good weather, you should see them frollicking around in the reedbeds.

From the main central hide you can see avocets nesting, and in the ditches just in front of you, the furry water voles: rare little creatures, with appealing short, fat faces, stub noses, and dainty forefeet, which they use to manipulate their food. There's an abundance of butterflies, including painted ladies, red admirals, and peacocks. Walk one way into the reserve, pausing at the various hides, then return to the centre and go on in the other direction to repeat the process. The sun swings around behind you, so the light over the reserve is extraordinarily good – and in this wide coastal landscape, the cloudscapes add magnificently to the scene.

> Blacktoft is in the perfect place for coastal migrants. Over 200 bird species have been recorded here.

WHERE ELSE TO SEE
REEDBEDS AND LAGOONS

The reedbed and coastal lagoon combination is found at a number of sites, mainly in East Anglia – the classic home for reedbed birds.

Norfolk coastal sites, from **Holme** and **Cley-next-the-sea** to **Breydon Water**, are wonderful places to see reedbed birds, as are those further south, along the Suffolk coast, such as **Walberswick** and **Minsmere** (*see pp.100–101*). **Fingringhoe Wick** (*see pp.124–125*), in Essex, also sees an influx of wildfowl. [SE]

Many of the waders and wildfowl seen at Blacktoft can also be seen around Kent, at **Elmley Marshes** (*see pp.306–307*), **Dungeness** (*see pp.162–163*), and **Cliffe Pools**. [SE]

More westerly sites are home to some of the birds seen at Blacktoft, but not the full coastal lagoon and reedbed range. These include **Radipole Lake** (*see pp.60–61*) and **Lodmoor** in Dorset; and **Chew Valley Lake** and **Ham Wall** in Somerset. [SW]

THROUGH THE YEAR
BLACKTOFT SANDS

Autumn brings large numbers of greenshanks, ruffs, black-tailed godwits, spotted redshanks, and dunlins, as well as water rails, which like to run around the lagoon edges. Stay late to witness the roosting flocks of swallows and martins.

The best time for hen harriers and merlins roosting in the reeds at dusk is in **winter**; marsh harriers return from mid-February. Teals and wigeons are common, but check for shovelers, pintails, gadwalls, and other ducks from the Ousefleet Hide. Look out, too, for tree sparrows and barn owls.

In **spring** the reserve is alive with reed, sedge, and willow warblers, blackcaps, and whitethroats. The marsh harriers begin their stunning aerial courtship displays, while the eery sound of bitterns booming can be heard at dawn and dusk.

Below: The barn owl prefers hunting at night.

JAN
FEB
MAR
APR
MAY
JUN
JUL
AUG
SEP
OCT
NOV
DEC

Left (left to right): A view of Wistman's Wood, showing the low profile of its dwarf oaks; the migrant whinchat returns to the wood to breed in spring.

Right (left to right): Beard lichen, just one of the many varieties found in the wood; an emperor moth.

Panel (below right): The common polypody fern growing on an oak trunk.

WHERE
Wistman's Wood National Nature Reserve, Two Bridges, Devon PL20 6SW; www.naturalengland.org.uk

CONTACT
Natural England Devon, tel: 0300 0601110; devon@english-nature.org.uk; Wistman's Wood site manager, tel: 01626 832330.

GETTING THERE
Wistman's Wood is near the centre of the Dartmoor National Park. By car it's 2km (1¼ miles) north of Princetown at the junction of the B3357 and B3212 between Tavistock and Ashburton. The nearest train station is 25km (15½ miles) away at Newton Abbot.

ACCESS AND FACILITIES
There are no facilities on site and no car park nearby. There is no wheelchair access. The nearest car park is at the old quarry in Two Bridges. In Princetown you will find The High Moorland Visitor Centre, which is wheelchair friendly and has toilets. The site is approx. 2km (1¼ miles) north of Princetown – about 25 minutes on foot.

OPENING TIMES
Open all year round.

CHARGES
None.

Rare lichens and ferns

Despite its small size, Wistman's Wood has an astonishing diversity of life. It is home to 119 species of lichens and 47 species of mosses and liverworts, including one of the rarest lichens in Britain, *Bryoria smithii*. There are also two rare species of filmy ferns: Wilson's, and Tunbridge (*shown below*) – which have fronds just one cell thick. They can survive only in places with constantly damp conditions – like the dark, wet, and ancient rocks of Wistman's Wood.

Main: The oak trees of Wistman's Wood are likely to have grown here in prehistoric times.

IN THE WILD WOOD

FEW PLACES IN BRITAIN CAN EVOKE SUCH A SENSE OF WILDERNESS AS DARTMOOR. Even in June, beneath a blue sky, its vast, trackless expanses of heather and shattered granite have an air of savage mystery that is both hostile and exhilarating. For many people, the almost mystical power of the place is most intensely felt in a small area in the very heart of the moor, in the green shade of Wistman's Wood.

It is a tiny woodland, little more than a dab of green on a large-scale map, and as you approach it along the valley of the West Dart River it looks like barely more than a thicket clinging to the eastern slope of the valley. But when you walk into the wood you realize that this is no mere patch of scrub. The trees are pedunculate oaks, exactly like those that grace the parks and hedgerows of middle England, but here stunted by hardship into dwarf, elfin forms barely twice the height of a man, with gnarled and twisted limbs that are smothered with luxuriant

Above: Bilberry grows among the mosses and ferns within the wood.

Sunlight filters through the green canopy, creating a magical, almost luminous atmosphere.

THROUGH THE YEAR
WISTMAN'S WOOD

In **autumn** the dwarf oaks lose their leaves, letting more light through to the rocky ground below and revealing the contorted shapes of the trees. Meanwhile, heavy rain can turn the nearby West Dart River into a turbulent torrent.

As **winter** tightens its grip on the moor, the weather can be harsh, encouraging small birds to take refuge among the trees. A dusting of snow on the ground creates a completely different atmosphere within the wood, reflecting sunlight up into the branches.

Migrant whinchats and wheatears return to breed alongside resident stonechats on the surrounding moorland and within the wood itself during the **spring**. Wet patches of ground become flushed with colour as acid-loving plants burst into bloom.

WHERE ELSE TO SEE
ANCIENT WOODS

Few woodlands have such an atmosphere of antiquity as Wistman's Wood, because most have undergone centuries of management. Despite this, old woodlands have a distinct appeal, and boast a rich diversity of plant species.

One woodland with the same magical air as Wistman's Wood is **Kingley Vale** (see pp.310–311) in West Sussex: a grove of ancient yew trees that lies at the heart of one of Europe's finest yew forests. [SE]

Bradfield Woods, in Suffolk, has been under continuous management since the 13th century, and many of the trees there are still coppiced in the traditional way. [SE]

Birklands Wood, situated in Sherwood Forest, Nottinghamshire (see p.36–37), contains a great number of veteran oak trees that have been allowed to mature naturally. [M]

The **Black Wood of Rannoch** (see pp.66–67) is one of the last patches of the Caledonian pine forest that covered most of Scotland. [SC]

lichens. They sprout from a tumbled mass of granite boulders, themselves thickly felted with mosses, which combines with the pervading smell of earthy antiquity to create a supremely eerie, magical effect. Small wonder that the place is associated with legends of ghosts, fairies, and druids. Luckily the days are long in June, for you might not want to stay here after dusk has fallen.

Even in broad daylight the trees look as if they have been here for ever, and in a sense this may be true. Fossil pollen preserved in the moorland peat shows that until about 7,000 years ago much of Dartmoor was wooded, but then the pollen record shows a sudden increase in bracken and grasses, almost certainly because the woodland was being cleared by people, probably by burning. Remains of their settlements can be seen near Wistman's Wood, and indeed all over Dartmoor. Eventually nearly all the trees were destroyed, but for some reason – probably the boulders – Wistman's Wood seems to have been left uncleared. If so, this means that the trees are descended from the last surviving fragment of primeval wildwood on Dartmoor. If you visit it, you will not doubt this for a second.

JAN FEB MAR APR MAY JUN JUL AUG SEP OCT NOV DEC

SHINGLE WILDERNESS

NOTHING REALLY PREPARES YOU FOR THE MAGICAL DESOLATION OF DUNGENESS. The shark-fin-shaped promontory sticks out into the Straits of Dover, in a huge, wide-open, flat expanse that stretches for miles and miles, occasionally punctured with low patches of vegetation and artistically scattered flotsam and jetsam.

Natural England classes Dungeness as a desert, but in fact it is one of the largest shingle landscapes in the world. Although it may look deserted, there's a lot going on here. Not only are there two nuclear power stations (only one is active), but there are two lighthouses, a visitor centre, a bird observatory, a miniature railway, and an RSPB reserve. However large these man-made edifices may be, they are dwarfed by the vast landscape, which has a unique ecosystem. The shingle supports a specialized plant community, which in turn encourages rare insects and lichens. The brown-banded carder bee (almost extinct in the UK), is doing well here. Some of the shingle

WHERE
Dungeness, Dungeness Rd, Lydd, Kent TN29 9PN.

CONTACT
RSPB Dungeness Nature Reserve, tel: 01797 320588; dungeness@rspb.org.uk

GETTING THERE
By car take the Dungeness road out of Lydd and after 1.5km (1 mile) turn right. The RSPB visitor centre and car park are one mile along the entrance track. The nearest train station is Rye; take the no.711 bus to Lydd, then change to the no.12. A popular way to arrive is via the miniature railway that runs to Dungeness from Hythe; visit www.rhdr.org.uk for details. Dungeness lies on Route 2 on the Sustrans National Cycle Network.

ACCESS AND FACILITIES
The RSPB visitor centre has full-access toilets, and hot and cold drinks and snacks. The car park for the RSPB Hanson ARC site, with short, accessible trails to birdwatching hides, is opposite the reserve main entrance on the left of the Dungeness Road.

OPENING TIMES
Year-round. The visitor centre is open from 10am–5pm (or 4pm November–February).

CHARGES
Parking charges for non-RSPB members.

The medicinal leech

The shallow muddy pools at Dungeness are the perfect habitat for the medicinal leech. These blood-sucking, worm-like creatures grow to 20cm (8 in) long, and were nearly used to extinction by doctors in the 18th century. Leeches only have to feed every six months, and never take more than they need. They have strong suckers on both ends of their bodies – one for biting, and one for latching on to a host, which may be a bird, fish, or frog.

Main and far right: Boardwalks protect the shingle habitat; the black-and-white lighthouse is a landmark.

Left (left to right): The very rare great crested newt; the view across the lagoons managed by the RSPB.

Right (left to right): Wild carrot; viper's bugloss; the Nottingham catchfly, with insects caught by its sticky glands.

speicialities include the fragrant Nottingham catchfly. This nectar-rich plant flowers at night, attracting moths such as the rare Sussex emerald. Dense clusters of white-flowering sea kale hug the outer shingle ridges and dotted around the numerous pools of water you can see swathes of viper's bugloss, short-stemmed foxgloves, and wild carrot – perfect food for the Sussex emerald caterpillar. In the areas of undisturbed shingle you'll find lichen-rich communities supporting myriad species, including the very rare pygmy footman moth. Lichens are also useful in that they help build up the soil content in the shingle, encouraging other plants to grow.

Towards the interior of the promontory lies the RSPB reserve: a vast network of gravel pits, reedbeds, and shingle that attracts seabirds and wintering wildfowl. Look out too for the great crested newt and the enormous green medicinal leech. The promontory itself is one of the best places in the UK to watch the spring and autumn migration.

> The stark beauty of Dungeness belies its rich wildlife: over 60 bird species and 600 plant types thrive here.

THROUGH THE YEAR
DUNGENESS

In **autumn** there are always lots of migrating birds in passage, such as redstarts and wheatears. The goldeneyes arrive in October, but you'll need to wait until November to be in with a chance of seeing smews, goosanders, and hen harriers.

Although an amazing variety of duck species spend the **winter** on the lagoons at Dungeness, you can also see wild swans and white-fronted geese. There's a pretty good chance of seeing merlins and peregrines, and – spectacularly – flocks of up to 6,000 lapwings.

As the winter migrants leave in **spring**, a new wave of birds arrive, some passing through Dungeness, while others stay to breed. You'll see an increase in warblers; sedge warblers, reed warblers, and whitethroats all nest on the reserve. As the waters warm up in the lakes and ditches, great crested newts start returning to still water to breed. Listen out for the raucous chuckle of male marsh frogs as they start calling for mates in early spring.

WHERE ELSE TO SEE
SHINGLE HABITATS

There are three other major shingle habitats in Britain, although none as large as Dungeness.

On the Suffolk coast, **Orford Ness** is a 15km (9 mile) shingle spit. Like Dungeness it also has a variety of specialized flora, including sea pea and false oat-grass. [SE]

The long, wild, and windswept **Chesil Beach** (*see pp.180–181*) in Dorset is another fine example of shingle habitat. This storm beach has been colonized by a host of species, ranging from breeding birds to rare flora. [S]

The **Culbin Shingle Bar** on the coast of Scotland's Moray Firth (*see pp.220–221*) is the most northerly shingle habitat. The bar is roughly 7km (4 miles) long and is a pristine remnant of a much larger shingle habitat. [SC]

Below: Sea kale, dwarfed by the onshore winds, in flower.

JAN · FEB · MAR · APR · MAY · JUN · JUL · AUG · SEP · OCT · NOV · DEC

JULY

Where to Go: July

Summer continues unabated: but already we see the freshness of the green woods and hedges begin to fade a fraction, and the brightest greens turn just a touch darker. Butterflies, bees, and grasshoppers are at their peak, and dragonflies and damselflies are still increasing in number as the summer progresses. Common blue, chalkhill blue and, in rare places, Adonis blue butterflies can be seen on short, cropped grassland, while other splendid butterflies – purple emperors, white admirals, silver-washed fritillaries and purple hairstreaks – can be seen in some of our mature woods. The birds, those great indicators of the state of the world around us, are already signalling that the best of the summer might have gone. The woods are quieter: only on the

COAST

ABBOTTS HALL The marshes are covered in wildflowers in summer.

ABBOTTS HALL FARM
COLCHESTER, ESSEX [SE]

Conservationists here are experimenting with letting the sea reclaim the land, resulting in a botanical feast on the saltmarshes.
See pp.192–193

CHESIL BEACH
DORSET [SW]

An elemental place, with the world's largest tombolo, or shingle bank. Massive cliffs and coastal shingle allow only the hardiest of plants to grow.
See pp.180–181

ORFORD NESS
ORFORD, SUFFOLK [SE]

Europe's largest shingle spit is a truly wild and remote location, harbouring rare shingle flora. Winter flooding encourages large numbers of wildfowl and waders.
See pp.180–181

SOUTH STACK
ANGLESEY, NORTH WALES [W]

The cliffs contain some of Wales' oldest rocks, and are home to over 8,000 nesting birds in summer. Adders bask around the cliff tops.
See pp.182–183

ISLANDS

RAMSEY ISLAND Choughs perform aerial displays around the cliffs.

RAMSEY ISLAND
PEMBROKESHIRE, WALES [W]

Grey seals offshore, and whole families of choughs cavorting around the cliffs. Peregrines hunt in the air above them.
See pp.182–183

Look for groups of gannets plunge-diving: the huge white birds enter the ocean like darts, their wings closing just a second before entry.

RATHLIN ISLAND
COUNTY ANTRIM [NI]

The windswept rocks, cliffs, and grasslands of Rathlin Island are a haven for wildlife. In summer the island is vibrant with pinks and purples from the abundant flora.
See pp.182–183

AILSA CRAIG
FIRTH OF CLYDE [SC]

This isolated granite island has high, dramatic seacliffs, which make the perfect home for breeding seabirds in summer.
See pp.168–169

BASS ROCK
EAST LOTHIAN [SC]

This volcanic rock towers out of the ocean, covered in nesting seabirds – especially gannets – during the summer.
See pp.168–169

NOSS
SHETLAND [SC]

The rugged, uninhabited island of Noss might be one of the best places in the UK to watch seabirds, but in summer the ungrazed, high moors are awash with colourful wildflowers.
See pp.168–169

PARKS AND GRASSLAND

WIMBLEDON COMMON Rival male stag beetles show off their prowess.

WIMBLEDON COMMON
LONDON [SE]

The deadwood around the common provides the perfect arena for pitched battles between stag beetles; duck to avoid their clumsy flights.
See pp.188–189

FARTHING DOWNS AND HAPPY VALLEY
LONDON [SE]

These North Downs chalklands are a stretch of green within the M25. By day, look for wildflowers and butterflies; by night, watch for the light of the glow worm.
See pp.176–177

RODBOROUGH COMMON
GLOUCESTERSHIRE [M]

Some of our rarest grassland butterflies live on this Cotswold common in summer, including the beautiful Adonis blue, which can be seen among the grasses.
See pp.194–195

An area of rolling hills and broad views, the Cotswolds are blessed with a building stone the colour of honey that suffuses every one of the villages.

OLD WINCHESTER HILL
HAMPSHIRE [SE]

A reserve for lovers of wild flowers, with rare round-headed rampions, several types of unusual orchids, as well as some archaeological features.
See pp.176–177

Previous page: Summer on Ramsey Island.

heaths and commons does the yellowhammer keep going, singing all day, every day, all summer long. Swifts zoom around in screaming parties around the houses, already thinking of heading south. At reservoir edges and marshes, green sandpipers appear, having come back south from Scandinavia, and flocks of lapwings begin to decorate the shorelines. For them it is already autumn.

This is a wonderful time to visit an island, where the seabirds are still busy, and you might have the chance of a great day watching the aerial displays of peregrines or choughs. Stay overnight on Skomer or Skokholm to experience the magic of the Manx shearwaters, flying towards their nesting burrows with a great caterwauling chorus, under the cover of darkness.

UPLANDS

YORKSHIRE DALES One of the UK's last remaining hay meadows.

YORKSHIRE DALES
YORKSHIRE [N]

The valley meadows of The Dales are transformed into dazzling displays of floral diversity during the summer, as wildflowers grow among the grass before haymaking.
See pp.184–185

WEARDALE
COUNTY DURHAM [N]

One of the richest grassland habitats in Britain, this site overflows with wildflowers, and breeding waders can be seen foraging in the springy moist soil.
See pp.184–185

CHEDDAR GORGE
SOMERSET [SW]

The highest inland cliffs in the UK are spectacular; deep beneath, Cheddar's caves provide a refuge for bats, including the very rare lesser horseshoe bat.
See pp.186–187

Two of the largest caves in Cheddar are said to have inspired JRR Tolkien's trilogy, *The Lord of the Rings*, after his honeymoon visit to the gorge.

GORDALE SCAR
MALHAM, NORTH YORKSHIRE [N]

This awesome and dramatic gorge slices through the limestone cliffs of Malham, creating a unique wildlife habitat for rare flora. Peregrine falcons nest on the cliffs.
See pp.186–187

CORS CARON
CEREDIGION, MID WALES [W]

A glorious mosaic of colourful vegetation, the bog pools buzz with dragonflies, while red kites, merlins, and peregrines soar high in the skies above.
See pp.190–191

WOODLAND

NEW FOREST The perfect place for animal-oriented summer walks.

BOOKHAM COMMONS
LEATHERHEAD, SURREY [SE]

Two of our most magnificent butterflies – the silver-washed fritillary and rare purple emperor – can be found here.
See pp.170–171

THE NEW FOREST
HAMPSHIRE [SW]

This royal hunting ground is ablaze with yellow gorse and purple heather in summer. Ponies, deer, and squirrels roam in the ancient woodland.
See pp.174–175

KIELDER FOREST
NORTHUMBERLAND [N]

England's biggest forest also has the largest area of blanket bog. The many forest ponds teem with insect life, including the rare lesser Emperor dragonfly and the southern hawker.
See pp.170–171

BLEAN WOODS
FAVERSHAM, KENT [SE]

A huge, ancient broadleaved woodland that shelters nightingales and nightjars in summer. Look out, too, for the heath fritillary butterfly.
See pp.170–171

MOUNTAINS

SNOWDON Polecats hide among the mountains.

SNOWDON
GWYNEDD, NORTH WALES [W]

This enormous national park is full of wildlife and rare flowers, such as the Snowdon lily. Jackdaws, choughs, and ravens fly around the mountain.
See pp.172–173

The dramatic and varied landscapes of Snowdonia have all the grandeur of the Scottish Highlands, even though the scale is somewhat smaller.

INVERPOLLY
HIGHLAND [SC]

This vast and remote area of heather and grass moorland has divers and ducks on the lochs in summer; wheatears and ring ouzels breed on the slopes.
See pp.178–179

WINNATS PASS
CASTLETON, DERBYSHIRE [M]

The massive power of nature can be experienced at these towering, awesome crags. The fossilized coral reef limestone is rich with crinoids, ammonites, and brachiopods.
See pp.186–187

THE CAIRNGORMS
ABERDEENSHIRE [SC]

A true British wilderness hides our most sought-after wildlife, including reindeer, ptarmigans, snow buntings, and dotterel.
See pp.178–179

GLASLYN ESTUARY
PORTHMADOG, NORTH WALES [W]

This deep and dramatic ravine provides a harsh, rocky habitat for wildlife. Look to the skies for red kites, merlins, and peregrines.
See pp.172–173

WHERE
Bass Rock lies in the Firth of Forth, 1.6km (1 mile) off the coast of North Berwick, Scotland.

CONTACT
The Scottish Seabird Centre, The Harbour, North Berwick EH39 4SS, Scotland, tel: 01620 890202; www.seabird.org

GETTING THERE
The Scottish Seabird Centre at North Berwick runs wildlife-watching boat trips around the islands of Bass Rock and Craigleith, and to Fidra. The island of Fidra is an RSPB reserve (www.rspb.org.uk).

ACCESS AND FACILITIES
Access is by boat only; there are no facilities on the island. Visitors may need to use ladders to access the boat and the island.

OPENING TIMES
Boat trips generally run from April to October, from North Berwick, but only certain operators have landing rights for the island, so check before you book.

CHARGES
Boat trip charges vary.

Sky-pointing
The gannet is one of the most studied seabirds in the world. Ornithologists have noted that gannets exhibit ritualized behavior that communicates specific actions to their mate, possibly due to living in such a crowded colony. For example, when one of the pair is about to leave the nest, it will "sky-point" to indicate that it is about to fly off, by pointing its bill upwards and dropping its wings slightly. It holds this position for a few seconds before lifting off.

Above: Razorbills are found among the cliffs of Cable Gulley and around the inner landing.

Below (top to bottom): Seals can often be seen around the base of Bass Rock; a black-legged kittiwake.

Right panel (top and bottom): The birds nest in very close proximity to one another – just beyond pecking distance; the spectacular plunge-dive of the gannet.

Main: The gannet colony at Bass Rock was described by Sir David Attenborough as "one of the wildlife wonders of the world".

GANNETS ON BASS ROCK

RESEMBLING A WHITE ICED BUN FROM A DISTANCE, it is only when you approach Bass Rock by boat that you realize that the "icing" is a living mass of gannets. Deriving their species name *Morus bassana* from Bass Rock, the gannet reigns supreme here, with 75,000 pairs covering almost every square inch of ground and accessible cliff. As you reach the rock, you'll be struck by two more things: the overpowering smell of guano, and the sheer noise coming from this enormous colony of seabirds. This is truly an extravagance of birds.

Perched in the Firth of Forth and easily seen from the shore at North Berwick, the rock is a volcanic plug of phonolite standing over 100m (330ft) high, with a circumference of 1.6km (1 mile). Up close, "the Bass" towers out of the ocean; clouds of creamy-white gannets circle its cliffs and nearly every available space on land is taken by the nesting birds. These are the largest seabirds in the northern hemisphere, with a wingspan of

Above: Both the male and female gannets provide food for the chicks.

Gannets are made for high-speed diving: they have skulls as thick as crash helmets, and throat sacs that instantly swell with air.

WHERE ELSE TO SEE
GANNETS

Gannets nest in dense colonies on cliffs, rocks, grassy coastal slopes and flat-topped islands around the UK.

Ailsa Craig, a large rock off the west coast of Scotland in the Firth of Clyde, is home to a thriving gannet colony. [SC]

Bempton Cliffs RSPB Reserve in Yorkshire (*see pp.104–105*) is perhaps Britain's most accessible gannet colony. [N]

Hermaness and **Noss** in Shetland both have impressive colonies of gannets along with a suite of other seabirds. [SC]

St Kilda is home to one of our best known gannet colonies – tens of thousands nest on the sea stacks here – but access is tricky and only by boat from the Scottish west coast. [SC]

THROUGH THE YEAR
BASS ROCK

Gannets and other breeding seabirds will still be present on the rock in early **autumn**, as the gannet chicks prepare to leave for Africa, but weather dictates whether boat trips will run.

The first gannets start to return in February but the rock is inaccessible to humans at this time of year. The Scottish Seabird Centre at North Berwick has a live show of the birds, with images beamed from cameras around the rock; you can also watch the birds of nearby Fidra island. Look around just offshore from North Berwick too: a few sea ducks, divers, and grebes may be present in the Firth of Forth, and along the rocky shoreline look out for purple sandpipers.

Seabird breeding starts in the **spring**, and will be in full swing by May.

180cm (70in), and while they are ungainly on land, they glide low over the sea with extraordinary grace. Look out too, for groups plunge-diving: the birds enter the ocean like white darts, their wings closing just a second before entry, hitting the water at 100kph (60mph) in search of fish.

Other birds do breed here, too, where they can find space: guillemots, razorbills, eider ducks, gulls, and even a few comical puffins can be seen. A pair of peregrine falcons have taken up partial residence as they breed nearby – there is certainly no shortage of food for these fast raptors. Grey seals languish in the sun on the exposed rocks at the base of the rock, and if you're lucky, you might see porpoises and dolphins in the seas around the rock.

Looking at Bass Rock today, it is almost inconceivable to imagine that humans once inhabited it; even the lighthouse is now unmanned. But the Bass has a long and varied history stretching back more than a thousand years. Ruins of a pre-Reformation chapel, built around 1490, still stand halfway up the rock, and its isolated position has led to its use as both a fortress and a prison in the past – but the true owners have always been the hundreds of thousands of birds.

JAN
FEB
MAR
APR
MAY
JUN
JUL
AUG
SEP
OCT
NOV
DEC

WOODLAND BUTTERFLIES

WOODLAND IS NOT THE FIRST HABITAT YOU MIGHT ASSOCIATE with butterflies, yet woodlands have their sunny spots, at their edges and in clearings, and these often support a rich variety of flowering plants and shrubs that provide both nectar for adult butterflies and food for their caterpillars. Most of Britain's breeding species are regularly found in woodlands, and many rarely occur anywhere else. They include two of our most magnificent butterflies – the large silver-washed fritillary and the rare purple emperor – both among the most beautiful in Europe, and both of which can be found at Bookham Commons in Surrey. Donated to the National Trust in the 1920s, these three adjacent areas of common land on

WHERE
Bookham Commons, Leatherhead, North Downs, Surrey KT22.

CONTACT
The National Trust North Downs Countryside Office, tel: 01372 220641; bookham@nationaltrust.org.uk
Natural England Surrey, tel: 01483 568121.

GETTING THERE
The Commons are on the North Downs on the A246 between Leatherhead and Guildford. The nearest train station and bus stop is Bookham Station, from where you can walk to the Commons via a footbridge.

ACCESS AND FACILITIES
There are three parking areas, but no facilities of any sort on the Commons – the nearest are at Great Bookham. Wheelchair access is limited. The London Natural History Society (www.lnhs.org.uk) holds monthly meetings on the Commons as part of their ongoing ecological survey of the site, and will also host Field Study days for interested visitors, by prior arrangement.

OPENING TIMES
Open all year round.

CHARGES
None.

The comma butterfly is among more than 300 species of butterflies and moths that have been recorded at Bookham Commons – as well as 17 species of dragonfly, 611 different species of beetles, and 1,140 true flies.

the North Downs are dominated by oak woodland, one of the richest of all Britain's wildlife habitats. Visit them on a sunny day in July, and you are sure to see a good range of butterflies. The first you come across may be a speckled wood – a chocolate-brown, cream-spotted insect that enjoys basking in patches of sunlight. The males adopt these as territories, vigorously defending them against rival males but welcoming any visiting females.

The rarer, but far more spectacular silver-washed fritillary has a similar taste for sunny clearings with dense undergrowth (such as brambles), so if you see a suitable site, investigate it. The butterfly is unmistakable because of its size – it is by far the largest British species – and the striking silvery-green of its underwings. Another woodland specialist is the white admiral, a largely black butterfly with striking white wing-bands. But the real prize is the white admiral's close relative, the purple emperor, which spends its time high in the treetops sipping the sugary honeydew produced by aphids. The female looks like a larger version of the white admiral, but the wings of the male have an iridescent purple sheen, visible only at certain angles. Its treetop habits make it a rare sight, but occasionally the males fly down to the woodland floor to drink, and if you happen to be watching, you will not be disappointed.

Main: A pearl-bordered fritillary, feeding on foxglove.
Below (left to right): Speckled wood butterfly; a brimstone butterfly; the purple emperor.
Inset: The comma butterfly is easily identified by its ragged wings.

Strange tastes

The purple emperor is notoriously elusive, but the iridescent males do flutter to the ground for several minutes to sip at what we would consider disgusting sources – such as muddy puddles, the decaying remains of dead animals, and even fresh dung. They do this to obtain sodium and other minerals that are essential for the healthy function of their reproductive systems. Females do not need these mineral supplements, so they normally stay high in the treetops.

Above: A trail through Bookham Commons, crossing a wooden bridge.

THROUGH THE YEAR
BOOKHAM COMMONS

All woodlands are glorious places to visit in **autumn**, and those of Bookham Commons are no exception. A few butterflies may still be on the wing, especially species that hibernate as adults, such as the comma and the brimstone. There may also be some late dragonflies patrolling the paths and clearings.

In **winter** the bare branches allow light through to the woodland floor, and provide good views of woodland birds. This is a good place to look for the massive-billed hawfinch, a typically elusive bird that becomes more visible when feeding in flocks at this time of year.

Spring sees the return of migrant breeding birds, notably the nightingale, which sings among patches of scrub on the site. The first butterfly to appear is nearly always the yellow-winged brimstone.

WHERE ELSE TO SEE
WOODLAND BUTTERFLIES

The best butterfly woods are old, species-rich, broadleaved woodlands with plenty of open spaces, so low-growing plants – the perfect caterpillar food – can flourish. Coppicing creates ideal woodland butterfly habitat, so the best sites are ancient woodlands that are coppiced for nature conservation.

The rare heath fritillary can be found in **Blean Woods** near Faversham, Kent, and **Thrift Wood** and **Hockley Woods** in Essex. [SE]

Bernwood Forest, near Oxford, is a good site for the purple emperor and silver-washed fritillary, as well as the smaller black, brown, and purple hairstreaks, which are also woodland specialists. [SE]

Kielder Forest, Northumberland, is home to the small pearl-bordered fritillary, large heath fritillary, and dark green fritillary. [N]

JAN

FEB

MAR

APR

MAY

JUN

JUL

AUG

SEP

OCT

NOV

DEC

WHERE
Snowdon/Yr Wyddfa, Snowdonia National Park, Gwynedd, Wales; www.eryri-npa.gov.uk

CONTACT
Snowdonia National Park Authority, National Park Office, Penrhyndeudraeth, Gwynedd LL48 6LF, tel: 01766 770274; parc@snowdonia-npa.gov.uk

GETTING THERE
Llanberis is the nearest town to Snowdon. By car, leave the A55 at J11, and follow signs for the B4366 towards Bethesda until you see signs for Llanberis. By rail, travel to Bangor, then take a bus either to Llanberis, or go to Pen-y-pas, 359m (1,117ft) above sea level – getting a walk off to a good start.

ACCESS AND FACILITIES
The local council runs a Sherpa "hop on, hop off" bus service that stops at many places within Snowdonia, including Snowdon. You can also catch a train right to the top of Snowdon (www.snowdonrailway.co.uk) from Llanberis. The visitor centres at Llanberis and at the top of the mountain are wheelchair friendly, with refreshments and toilets.

OPENING TIMES
Open all year round (weather dependent).

CHARGES
For car parking.

An Ice-Age fish

Llyn Tegid lake, in the Snowdonia National Park, is home to the very rare gwyniad fish, which was trapped in the lake at the end of the last Ice Age – around 10,000 years ago – and does not exist anywhere else. A combination of deteriorating water quality and competition from an introduced fish, the ruffe, in the 1980s, means that the gwyniad could face extinction. Conservationists are moving its eggs to safer sites in the hope of starting a new population elsewhere.

Above (top and bottom): Rainbow leaf beetles mating; the rare Snowdon lily grows from crevices.

Below: There are around 1,000 goats in Snowdonia, which winter up in the mountains, but can be seen further down, among the lakes, in summer.

Right panel (top and bottom): A raven parent feeds its one-week-old chicks in their nest; Snowdonia is one of the main strongholds for polecats in the UK.

Main: Walking at an average rate, it takes a little over 3 hours to climb up one of the easier paths to the summit of Snowdon.

MOUNTAIN MAJESTY

SNOWDONIA'S RICH WILDLIFE IS PROTECTED within the Snowdonia National Park, which stretches for a breathtaking 2,131 sq km (823 sq miles). The dramatic and varied landscapes have all the grandeur of the Scottish Highlands, even though the scale is reduced – in fact, the smaller area seems to make the mountains look even more dramatic. The biggest of all is, at 1,085 m (3,560 ft), the highest British mountain outside Scotland. This is Snowdon, known in Welsh as *Yr Wyddfa*, meaning "The Burial Place" – legend has it that the cairn at the top of the mountain marks the grave of a local giant.

Situated almost at the centre of Snowdonia, Snowdon's pyramid-shaped peak is particularly imposing, as it stands apart from the many other surrounding mountains and can be seen from afar. Much of the mountain is a Site of Special Scientific Interest, and it is home to rare wildlife. Among the hardy alpine wildflowers that survive

JAN

FEB

MAR

APR

MAY

JUN

JUL

AUG

SEP

OCT

NOV

DEC

Above: Snowdon makes treacherous climbing in winter.

Snowdonia is especially significant for the polecat, as it spread from this refuge to recolonize most of Wales and the English Midlands.

THROUGH THE YEAR
SNOWDON

Fine weather in **autumn** can make a walk up Snowdon very enjoyable. Remember, though, that snow can fall any time from October. The colours of oaks, larches, and other trees, and of the bracken are spectacular. This is a good time to look for birds of prey, including merlins, hen harriers, and red kites, while winter-visiting wildfowl, such as goldeneyes and goosanders, arrive from September onwards.

Winter requires special care on the slopes. The weather is especially variable, and may change from sunshine to driving rain and back within an hour. Winter also brings extremely harsh weather, making it a challenging time even for the tough mountain sheep and feral goats. Ravens rely a great deal on sheep carrion for survival during this season.

Spring may come late and snow can linger until late May or even early June. Ring ouzels, which look like blackbirds but have a white crescent on the chest, return from the Mediterranean region to breed in remote gulleys. Smaller, black-and-white-tailed wheatears are more common. Purple saxifrage is one of the first wildflowers to appear as the snow melts.

WHERE ELSE TO SEE
MOUNTAIN WILDLIFE

There are well over 100 other fine mountains to explore in Snowdonia. The Welsh name for the region, *Eryri*, means "Land of the Eagle", and while there are no eagles, there are other birds of prey, such as kestrels, merlins, peregrines, and buzzards.

At **Glaslyn Estuary**, Porthmadog, on the north west corner of Snowdonia National Park, you can get great views of Wales's only pair of breeding ospreys. [W]

Other good areas for mountain wildlife, geology, and scenery include the **Lake District** and **Pennines** in northern England. [N]

The most extreme conditions in all Britain's mountain regions are to be found in the **Cairngorms** (*see pp.178–179*), where the high tops are the nearest thing we have to Arctic landscapes. This is the land of golden eagles and Britain's only herd of reindeer. [SC]

there, the Snowdon lily has pride of place, because in Britain it occurs at only a few sites, and these are all in Snowdonia. The lily grows here among inaccessible patches of poor soil on sheer north- and north east facing cliffs. Other alpines include several saxifrages, among them mossy saxifrage, which produces drifts of nodding white flowers in late spring and summer, and moss campion, whose pink summer flowers rise above cushions of tiny pointed leaves. There are also scarce species of clubmosses and many rare lichens.

Rare insects include the dwarf willow-feeding sawfly, which feed on the shrub whose name it bears, and two beetles very rare in Britain: the dull-coloured ground beetle *Nebria nivalis*, which lives among the frost-shattered boulders at the top of Snowdon; and the striped rainbow leaf beetle, which is found only on Snowdon and nearby Cwm Idwal, on the leaves of wild thyme. Jackdaws, carrion crows, and ravens can be seen, as well as their scarcer relative the chough, its black plumage contrasting with bright red legs and feet, and a bright-red, downcurved bill. There are lots of herring gulls, too, and if a group of them suddenly scatters, look for a peregrine.

WHERE
The New Forest, Hampshire, SO40 2LR;
www.thenewforest.co.uk

CONTACT
Lyndhurst Visitor Information Centre,
tel: 02380 282269;
Lymington Visitor Information Centre,
tel: 01590 689000;
Ringwood Visitor Information Centre,
tel: 01425 470896.

GETTING THERE
There are three main routes in to the
New Forest: from the M27 J1, the A35
from Southampton, and the A31 from
Bournemouth. Trains stop at Ashurst,
Beaulieu Road, Brockenhurst, and Sway.

ACCESS AND FACILITIES
The New Forest National Park is well
equipped for visitors; car parking, toilets, and
picnic areas are plentiful. Ranger-led walks
can all be booked via the website. There are
three access-friendly trails for wheelchairs
and pushchairs. The New Forest can be very
boggy in winter, so keep to the gravel tracks.

OPENING TIMES
Open all year round.

CHARGES
None.

Singing cicadas

One of the more unusual creatures to be found in
the New Forest is the New Forest cicada – the only
cicada that lives in Britain. At this time of year, in
open, sunny woodland rides and clearings
bordered by scrub, the males can be heard singing
with a high-pitched ringing buzz more reminiscent
of the Mediterranean than an English woodland.
The adults do not live long after breeding, but
their young live underground for up to 10 years,
feeding on the root sap of plants, before emerging
as adults to sing and breed in their turn.

Above (left to right): A sundew, one of the native carnivorous plants; a smooth snake, Britain's rarest reptile, basks in the sunshine.
Main: Wild ponies browse on New Forest heathland.

Above: Beechwood in autumn colour.

A ROYAL PRESERVE

D ESPITE ITS NAME, THE "NEW" FOREST is one of the most ancient landscapes in lowland Britain, where archaic forest laws have conserved an internationally important patchwork of unenclosed pasture, heathland, and ancient woodland. The New Forest was created by King William I in 1079 and the local people were given grazing rights for their animals but not permitted to fence their land; as a result cattle, pigs, and ponies still roam freely with the wild deer. In medieval times a "forest" was simply an area set aside for hunting – less than half of the New Forest Heritage Area is broadleaved woodland, while the remainder is open heath, rough grassland, and bog.

July is high season on the heathlands, which become the most dramatic features of the New Forest, with great tracts of heather and gorse extending to the horizon. The gorse, blazing with coconut-scented yellow flowers and with seedpods cracking audibly in the heat, offers a thorny refuge for the secretive Dartford warbler – a small, red-eyed songbird with a buzzy call.

Far more conspicuous are the stonechats that perch high on the bushes giving their loud "chack-chack" alarm calls, and the dragonflies that flash through the air on rattling wings. These beautiful insects breed in the dark, peaty water of the mires and valley bogs – such as the one at Wilverley between Brockenhurst and Burley – which also support unusual plants such as insectivorous sundews, bog asphodel, and the rare marsh gentian.

> The New Forest's ancient woodlands and wilderness heath have remained largely unchanged over the past 1,000 years.

The extensive beech and oak woodlands contain flourishing populations of fallow, roe, and red deer. These can be elusive, but at dawn – a magical time in the forest – they emerge onto the grassy, mossy clearings or "lawns" to feed. Deeper into the woods, squirrels and woodland birds provide prey for the magnificent goshawk, a powerful ambush hunter that has started to breed again in the wild, having been driven to extinction in Britain by 1900. Several pairs now nest high in the treetops of the New Forest.

Inset: The New Forest has the highest concentration of veteran trees in western Europe.
Below (left to right): Fallow deer; a Dartford warbler perches on gorse.

THROUGH THE YEAR
THE NEW FOREST

As summer turns to **autumn** the heather begins to glow with purple flowers, creating a rich tapestry of colour, and the deciduous trees in the woodlands turn shades of brown, yellow, and even red.

Bare trees in **winter** make woodland wildlife such as deer and foxes much easier to see, provided you stay downwind and keep very still.

In **spring** the woodlands erupt with song as breeding birds claim their territories, and heathland reptiles such as adders and lizards emerge from hibernation to warm themselves in the sun.

The Reptiliary near Lyndhurst, open all year round, is an ideal place for a guaranteed sighting of snakes, natterjack toads, sand lizards, and other reptiles.

WHERE ELSE TO SEE
HEATH AND WOODLAND

The variety of habitats that make up the New Forest make it an excellent destination for wildlife watchers, but similar habitats can be visited elsewhere in Britain.

Ashdown Forest in East Sussex and **Thursley Common** (*see pp.128–129*) in Surrey feature lowland heath similar to that of the New Forest, with many of the same species occupying boggy areas as well as large expanses of heather and gorse. The beechwoods of the **Chilterns** are also magnificent in autumn. [SE]

For long walks in large tracts of broadleaved woodland visit the **Forest of Dean**, Gloucestershire, or **Sherwood Forest**, Nottinghamshire. Like the New Forest, these woodlands have a long history of management, but this has only enhanced their value as wildlife habitats. [M]

Arne (*see pp.138–139*) in Dorset is a wonderful expanse of heathland and old oak woodland. Both the Dartford warbler and several native reptiles can be heard and seen on the open heath. [SW]

JAN
FEB
MAR
APR
MAY
JUN
JUL
AUG
SEP
OCT
NOV
DEC

WHERE
Farthing Downs and Happy Valley, Ditches Lane, Coulsdon, Surrey CR5 3EA; www.croydon.gov.uk

CONTACT
Merlewood Estate Office, tel: 020 8660 8533
Croydon Tourist Information Centre, tel: 020 8253 1000

GETTING THERE
The site is very close to Coulsdon South train station, 30 minutes from London Charing Cross and 26 minutes from London Victoria. By car, take the A23 east, turning off at the B276 junction (Marlpit Lane), then take the second right into Downs Road, and left into Ditches Lane where you will find a car park.

ACCESS AND FACILITIES
The only facilities are the car park and toilets in Ditches Lane.

CHARGES
There are no charges for entry to the downs, but car-parking fees may apply.

The Roman snail

Roman snails are very rare in the UK, where they are found only on the downlands of southern England. The snail's shell measures around 5cm (2 in) across, so is very distinctive, but no fossils of this animal have ever been found, leading experts to believe that the snail was introduced to Britain possibly by the Romans (hence its name). The snails mate on cool, damp nights, when you might see them "kissing" one another, by joining their tentacles.

Above: The purple blooms of round-headed rampion.

Right panel (top and bottom): The pretty chalkhill blue butterfly lives on the horseshoe vetch that grows on the chalk grasslands; the greater yellow-rattle, which weakens grass and opens up the grassland, allowing other plants to grow and creating a species-rich area.

Below: Dropwort in flower.

Main: The "unimproved" grasslands of Farthing Downs and Happy Valley provide the perfect habitat for hundreds of rare wild plants.

GLORIOUS GRASSLANDS

THANK GOODNESS FOR PLACES LIKE FARTHING DOWNS AND HAPPY VALLEY. The hill and valley are part of the North Downs, a chalkland that sits within the bounds of the M25 on the doorstep of millions of people, acting like a green lung for the metropolis. The City of London Corporation manages it precisely for this purpose, along with other major open spaces such as Hampstead Heath and Epping Forest.

But it is far from being a glorified country park. Its downland habitats are so rich in wildlife that they would merit an honourable mention in any setting. The chalk grassland supports a colourful range of plants: round-headed rampion, dropwort, several species of orchids including the man orchid, and the greater yellow-rattle, a nationally rare and protected species. You might also find the yellow-flowered horseshoe vetch, which acts as a foodplant for the caterpillars of one of the site's many butterflies, the chalkhill blue. Other insects

One of Britain's rarest plants, the greater yellow-rattle, thrives on these grasslands within the bounds of its largest city.

Above: Redwings rely on winter berries for food during the colder months.

THROUGH THE YEAR
FARTHING DOWNS

The fruits of **autumn** appear all over the downs: spindle and hawthorn berries brighten the scrub areas; yew and guelder-rose add colour in the woodland. As they ripen, the fruits are devoured by birds, particularly thrushes such as blackbirds and winter-visiting redwings; in some years you may even spot a flock of colourful waxwings.

The last berries to form and to ripen are those on ivy, which become an essential food resource for birds and field mice in **winter**, especially in severe weather. Wintering flocks of starlings roost in the denser scrub, and long-eared owls roost and nest in the older, taller thickets.

As **spring** progresses, look for butterflies emerging from hibernation, especially brimstones. Skylarks are in song, setting up territories, and in April the summer migrants arrive – willow warblers, chiffchaffs, and whitethroats adding their voices to the chorus. And take a walk into the woods: where the ground is not shaded by yew trees, bluebells and greater stitchwort are bursting into flower.

WHERE ELSE TO SEE
CHALK DOWNLANDS

Chalk downland habitats can be found in all major chalk regions, although they have become fragmented as a result of modern agriculture.

Elsewhere on the North Downs, **Box Hill**, Surrey, is characterized by the abundance of its eponymous shrub, and around **Down House**, near Bromley, Kent, you can experience the environment that inspired Charles Darwin's evolutionary theories. [SE]

On the South Downs in Sussex, **Kingley Vale** (see pp.310–311), **Seven Sisters**, and **Old Winchester Hill** are among the numerous nature reserves, while Chilterns chalklands can be visited at **Aston Rowant** (see pp.222–223). [SE]

Two chalkland reserves that have survived in the north are are **Red Hill** in Lincolnshire [M] and **Millington Pastures**, Pocklington, Yorkshire [N].

include the glow worm (*see pp.222–223*), despite the level of nocturnal light pollution, which can upset the breeding behaviour of this snail-eating beetle. And while rambling across the Downs, you are likely to come across the golfball-sized shells of the Roman snail, some, especially after rain, still with their equally impressive occupants. Over much of the site, there is a constant battle with invasive scrub; a combination of cutting and goat-browsing is used to tackle established areas, after which mowing and grazing – by sheep and cattle – continue the good work.

Areas of ancient ash and oak woodland, such as Devilsden Wood, which have an understorey of hazel and yew, have developed on the valley slopes. The yew casts such dense shade that few plants can survive under it, but where the canopy is more open, the white-flowered sweet woodruff and fast-spreading yellow archangel are typical late spring indicators of the antiquity of the woodland. You may come across two more orchids – white helleborine and bird's-nest orchid – around the scattered stands of beech. Both flower in summer despite the gloomy conditions under a mature beech tree.

JAN
FEB
MAR
APR
MAY
JUN
JUL
AUG
SEP
OCT
NOV
DEC

UP AMONG THE CLOUDS

THE CAIRNGORMS NATIONAL PARK IS HOME TO SOME OF OUR MOST SOUGHT-AFTER WILDLIFE. It is a huge area of real wilderness – its mountains, moorlands, forests, rivers, lochs, and glens cover 3,800 sq km (1,400 sq miles) – and endures some of Britain's toughest weather conditions. The mountains are the UK's highest and largest, with peaks rising above 1,000m (3,280ft). The highest – Ben Macdui – rises to 1,310m (4,300ft). The stunning scenery of this national park lures climbers and serious walkers even in winter, with its thick layer of tempting snow, but it is June and July when the mountains are at their easiest and safest to explore.

In summer the Arctic-alpine flora is at its best; in July the corries offer shelter to roseroot and mountain sorrell, while the rock walls are covered in purple saxifrage. There are a huge number of walks through the park, but whichever one you take, it will be brightened by moss campion, trailing azaleas, alpine lady's-mantle, and

WHERE
The Cairngorms National Park, Aviemore, Scottish Highlands.

CONTACT
Cairngorms National Park Authority, tel: 01479 873535; enquiries@cairngorms.co.uk Glenmore Visitor Centre, Glenmore Forest Park, Aviemore, Highland PH22 1QU, Scotland; tel: 01479 861220.
The Reindeer Centre: 01479 861228; www.reindeer-company.demon.co.uk

GETTING THERE
By road, take the A9 to Aviemore, then follow signs to the Cairngorms National Park. By train, travel to Aviemore. By bus, take the no. 501 Heather Hopper, which connects Ballater and Grantown-on-Spey, and travels right through the centre of the National Park.

ACCESS AND FACILITIES
Wheelchair access is limited; contact the Park Authority (see details above) before arriving, as some access can be arranged. The visitor centre has parking and a full range of facilities. There is a funicular railway to the Ptarmigan Restaurant, which is the UK's highest restaurant. There is also a viewing platform giving views for miles around.

CHARGES
Car-parking charges only.

Role reversal

Dotterels are rarely seen in Britain outside Scotland, where they start to arrive on the high tops in early May. Unusually, it is the male not the female that has the dowdier plumage. When the brighter-looking female displays over her territory, it is a further indication of the way in which gender roles are reversed in this member of the plover family, with the male being left to incubate the eggs and rear the chicks. Dotterels can be extremely tame and will, if disturbed, often not fly up, but run off quickly in short, fast bursts.

Left: Purple saxifrage growing on rocky ground in the summer; the long shoots of starry saxifrage.

Right (left to right): The snow bunting's summer plumage is monochrome – its white head sits above a black mantle and wing tips; ptarmigans can only be found in the Scottish highlands, where they live on the highest mountains.

starry saxifrage. This is also the best time to see the mountain birds that breed on the summits, such as the beautiful montane wader, the dotterel. Snow buntings and ptarmigans breed in this desolate landscape too, but they are harder to find. Ptarmigans are a very tame type of grouse; they spend all year at high altitudes, and are rarely seen, especially as their summer plumage of speckled grey camouflages them so remarkably well among the lichen-covered rocks.

The ptarmigan always keeps an eye directed towards the sky – as golden eagles patrol these mountains – and they breed in the more remote corners. Mountain hares are their favourite prey, and these animals have become particularly cautious, running away at the slightest sound. Red grouse and red deer live on the lower slopes in summer, the deer grazing on fresh, young shoots. A herd of around 150 Scandinavian reindeer roam around the foot of the Cairngorm Mountain, and guides are available to help you safely approach and even hand-feed these gentle creatures.

Main image: The granite walls of the Sticil, one of the most impressive cliffs in the Cairngorms, surround Loch Avon, sending streams tumbling down to the meadows and sands that sit close to the crystal blue water's edge.

Above and below: All reindeer – males and females alike – grow a new set of antlers every year; mountain hares are always alert to potential danger.

WHERE ELSE TO SEE
MOUNTAIN WILDLIFE

The wild northern tundra of the Cairngorms, coupled with its ancient Caledonian forests, makes the area unique. However, you can experience some of its wildlife and types of habitat elsewhere in Scotland.

The large reserve of **Inverpolly** on the northwest coast of Scotland is a mix of mountains, bogs, lochs, and rushing streams. The high tops are home to ptarmigans and golden eagles. [SC]

Pine forest and mountain tops support many Scottish Highland birds at **Beinn Eighe** (see pp.202–203), together with some beautiful montane flora. [SC]

Snowdonia (see pp.172–173) in North Wales has a similar mixture of mountains, forests, and rivers, but a very different climate. Its birds include peregrines and ring ouzels, and it has two unique species: the Snowdon lily and the rainbow leaf beetle. [W]

THROUGH THE YEAR
THE CAIRNGORMS

As summer turns to **autumn**, the dotterels leave the area, while the ptarmigans and mountain hares start to moult into their white winter plumage and coats. Flocks of snow buntings fly overhead, and otters can sometimes be seen swimming along the River Spey, hunting for food.

Winter is harsh on the Cairngorm plateaux. Ptarmigans and mountain hares favour the corries in winter but may be hard to see. Snow buntings take shelter around the ski car parks. The reindeer roam widely, still warm in their woollier winter coats.

As the snows melt in **spring**, life returns to the tops. Snow buntings start singing, while the ptarmigans get busy calling and displaying. Dotterels arrive in May. The rivers Dee, Don, and Spey are full of salmon and trout, while freshwater pearl mussels cling to the river floor, sadly in ever-declining numbers.

Below: The Cairngorm reindeer in their thick winter coats.

JAN
FEB
MAR
APR
MAY
JUN
JUL
AUG
SEP
OCT
NOV
DEC

CHESIL BEACH

MOST PEOPLE'S IDEA OF A BEACH IS A COMFORTABLE CRESCENT of golden sand within a sheltered bay that's perfect for a picnic. Chesil Beach is nothing like this. It is a stupendous, elemental place, which you visit because it is a wonder of nature – a colossal shingle bank or "tombolo" extending in a magnificent arc from the Dorset coast to the Isle of Portland. It is the largest tombolo in the world, running for 29km (18 miles); on a warm July day, the far end is often lost in the heat haze. For around half of its length it is separated from the mainland by a shallow, salty lagoon called the Fleet, which is the home of the Abbotsbury swannery and its flock of breeding mute swans.

WHERE
Chesil Bank and Fleet Nature Reserve, Portland Beach Road, Portland, Dorset DT4 9XE; www.chesilbeach.org

CONTACT
Chesil Bank and Fleet Nature Reserve, tel: 01305 760579; reserve@chesil.fsworld.co.uk

GETTING THERE
The visitor centre is located off the A354 between Weymouth and Portland. Follow signs to Portland. About 0.8km (½ mile) after crossing Ferrybridge at Wyke Regis, you will see the centre on the right-hand side of the road. By public transport, take a bus to Portland (1 or X1) and get off at Ferrybridge.

ACCESS AND FACILITIES
The visitor centre has a car park, toilets, and a café as well as information boards and telescopes. Access to the beach for disabled visitors is possible at West Bexington, Chiswell, and Abbotsbury.

OPENING TIMES
The beach and visitor centre are open all year round.

CHARGES
Yes, for car parking only.

Chesil Beach probably formed well south of its current position around 12,000 years ago, at the end of the last ice age. As the glaciers and ice sheets melted, the sea levels rose, and the waves pushed the beach north to where it is today.

For an excellent view of the offhore section of Chesil Beach, stop on the heights of White Hill, just west of Abbotsbury. Then go to either end of the bank: Burton Bradstock near Bridport, or Ferrybridge near Portland – site of the Chesil Beach visitor centre – for a dramatically close view. The Portland end is massive; its great ridge of shingle has been built up by winter storms to reach up to 14m (46ft) high. Curiously, the pebbles that form the beach are also bigger at this end, being roughly the size of hens' eggs, while those at Burton Bradstock are pea-sized. They are graded, becoming progressively larger as you head east.

Mobile coastal shingle is a hostile plant habitat, but where it has stabilized on the landward side of the bank it provides a roothold for plants such as sea campion, sea kale, yellow horned poppy, the rare sea pea, and, in places, the spectacular sea holly. There are also saltmarsh plants such as shrubby sea-blite and sea purslane on the fringes of the Fleet. Many are in bloom in July, and land birds such as linnets, skylarks, and meadow pipits nest among the vegetation. Chesil also provides a breeding site for the rare little tern, in a fenced-off area in Ferrybridge. You can still see the birds, however, and marvel at the way such fragile-looking creatures can flourish in such a windswept, dramatic place.

Main: The shingle ridge of Chesil Beach is unusual because it is no longer being actively formed.
Inset: The rocky outcrop of East Cliff, seen from West Bay harbour.
Below (left to right): Little tern chicks can be seen in summer; sea campion growing at the northwest end of the beach; sea holly.

Abbotsbury swannery

This famous swannery was established by Benedictine monks around 1040, who used to farm the swans for food. It is now home to a protected herd of around 800 wild mute swans that feed on the eel-grass that grows extensively around Chesil Beach. At the end of July, the birds are unable to fly due to moulting their flight feathers and are driven into the swannery using canoes. Here they can be recorded and have their health checked.

Above: A gannet in flight.

THROUGH THE YEAR
CHESIL BEACH

As summer fades into **autumn**, a lot of the beach flora dies back, and the breeding birds leave for warmer winter quarters. But the beach is still spectacular, and autumn is the best season for sea anglers looking to catch bass, cod, or plaice.

Winter can be a bleak season on Chesil Beach, which is notorious for its ferocious storm waves. Visit the beach during one of these storms and you will get a real idea of the power of the sea.

Chesil Beach is often the landfall for many migrant birds from southern Europe and Africa that stop off to feed and rest in **spring**, before flying north to their breeding grounds. This is also the best time to visit the swannery at Abbotsbury, when the swans are nesting and rearing their cygnets.

WHERE ELSE TO SEE
SHINGLE BEACHES

Shingle is nearly always formed of flints, which have been washed out of chalk cliffs and eroded into rounded shapes by the sea. This means that the shingle beaches of Britain are characteristic of the east and south coasts, rich in chalk and flint.

Dungeness in Kent (*see pp.162–163*) is a huge shingle beach, shaped into a triangular headland rather than a long bank. It is famous for its unusual migrant birds, huge variety of insects, and over 600 different plant species. [SE]

To see an elongated shingle bank that is still extending, through the process of longshore drift, visit **Orford Ness** in Suffolk. Some 15km (9 miles) long, it is the largest vegetated shingle spit in Europe. [SE]

Further north, a series of sand and shingle banks stretching across the Humber Estuary leads out to **Spurn Point** (*see pp.264–265*). The curving spit is only 50m (160ft) wide in places, but is held together by marram grass and sea buckthorn. [N]

JAN
FEB
MAR
APR
MAY
JUN
JUL
AUG
SEP
OCT
NOV
DEC

RETURN OF THE CHOUGHS

THE JOYFUL, EXCITED CALL OF A CHOUGH ECHOES AROUND THE SEA CLIFFS above a wave-washed bay. Go to Ramsey Island and you will see the chough in its element, exploiting the air currents around the cliffs, soaring on fingered wings, diving down in fast, controlled swerves to disappear into sea caves, or simply bouncing around the sky for fun. A single chough, or a whole family group, will suddenly fold its wings back towards its tail, the tips still slightly separated into fingers for expert control, and see-saw through the air, head up one moment, tail up the next. Few birds express such apparent joy in their everyday actions.

Like most crows, choughs are black, but with an intense sheen of blue and purple. They have a special bonus feature: both the bill and the thick legs are bright red. That curved, sharp-pointed bill is used to probe beneath patches of soil and grass against the edge of a rock, between loose stones and firm earth, into the base

WHERE
Ramsey Island, Pembrokeshire, West Wales; www.rspb.org.uk

CONTACT
RSPB Ramsey Island, tel: 07836 535733; ramsey.island@rspb.org.uk

GETTING THERE
The island is only accessible by boat from St Justinians harbour. By car, follow the A487 from Haverfordwest to St Davids for 25.6km (16 miles). From Cross Square in St Davids, follow signs for St Justinians, which is 2.5km (1½ miles) away. A regular bus service runs between Haverfordwest and St Davids and a shuttle bus runs to St Justinians, which is also on National Cycle Network Route 4.

ACCESS AND FACILITIES
There is parking at St Justinians, while on the island there is an information centre serving hot drinks and snacks, toilets, and a picnic area. The trails are unsuitable for wheelchairs. The main trail is 5.6km (3½ miles), but this can be divided into two loops.

OPENING TIMES
The reserve is open from April to October, 10am–4pm.

CHARGES
For the boat crossing. Landing fees also apply for non-RSPB members.

Nesting and rearing

Choughs' bulky, scrappy nests are made from twigs and roots held together by mud and lined with wool or other soft materials. Rocky crevices and cliff ledges are their favourite nest sites. Both parents are involved in rearing young. While the female broods, the male often brings her food; the female feeds the young for the first few days, then the male joins in with the feeding until the young fledge. Choughs live in small, tight-knit family groups, but come breeding time, each couple will fiercely defend its territory.

Main: Sea pinks (thrift) on the cliffs of Ramsey Island.

Left (top to bottom): A grey seal swimming into one of the island's caves; a bird's-eye view of Ramsey Island; golden hair lichen.

Right (left to right): Sociable adult choughs feeding on the beach; chough in flight; choughs pair for life and use the same nesting site every year.

of a grass tussock, or even underneath a cowpat: anywhere that it can find some scurrying insect or other creepy-crawly to snap up. In winter, the chough also forages on wave-washed sandy beaches, looking for sandhoppers in the tideline tangle of seaweed and detritus.

Choughs pair for life. They first breed at three years old and raise just one brood each year, using the same nest site year after year. It is often on a ledge far inside a dark sea cave, or in a deep crevice on a cliff face; quarries or mineshafts are used inland. The bulky nests are made of sticks, heather stems, and wool, ready for the three mottled cream eggs. The female sits for 17–18 days and then cares for the chicks for the first 10 days or so, when the male begins to do his share.

British and Irish choughs are restricted to small areas on the coast and islands, and they number around 1,200 breeding pairs today. They stopped breeding in England in 1948, but returned to Cornwall in 2001, and now nest at Lizard Point (*see pp.116–117*) and Land's End.

Above: A soaring flock of choughs.

WHERE ELSE TO SEE CHOUGHS

Following a long period of decline, chough populations in the UK have recently shown signs of recovery, though there are still only around 500 pairs of these birds in Britain.

Choughs can be seen on **Islay** (*see pp.12–13*) in the Inner Hebrides off western Scotland, especially at the south end of the island. [SC]

Rathlin Island, just off the coast of County Antrim, Northern Ireland, used to be a haven for choughs, but there are only a few pairs there today. [NI]

The beautiful cliffs of the **Isle of Man** (*see pp.300–301*) are home to seabirds and choughs, even quite close to Douglas. There are more on the **Calf of Man**, at the southern tip. [N]

You will see choughs easily at **South Stack** on Anglesey in Wales. Try cliffs along the **Lleyn Peninsula** in North Wales, and on the Cardiganshire and Pembrokeshire coastline as well. [W]

THROUGH THE YEAR RAMSEY ISLAND

In the **autumn**, you can watch a colony of breeding grey seals. Look and listen for the females and their white pups on the beaches, and the large, dark males patrolling just offshore.

Choughs gather in large groups in the **winter**, which clearly have significance for this sociable bird. Ramsey Island is closed to visitors over the winter, but you might come across choughs in around the adjacent coastline footpaths.

In **spring** Ramsey becomes awash with colour as bluebells, red campion, sea pink (thrift), and purple heather take turns to dominate the scene. The cliff-top has a wild rock garden of sea campion, spring squill, and yellow rockroses. From the summit of Carn Llundain, look for displaying lapwings below, and keep an eye out for stonechats and wheatears.

JAN
FEB
MAR
APR
MAY
JUN
JUL
AUG
SEP
OCT
NOV
DEC

Left: Hay meadows are actively farmed and often privately owned, so always keep to footpaths when visiting.

Right (left to right): Pignut in flower; melancholy thistle.

Right panel (top to bottom): The striking yellow globeflower; a marbled white butterfly feeding on a field scabious flower.

WHERE
The Yorkshire Dales, Yorkshire.

CONTACT
Yorkshire Dales National Park Authority, tel: 01756 751600; info@yorkshiredales.org.uk Dales Countryside Museum, Station Yard, Hawes, North Yorkshire DL8 3NT; tel: 01969 666220.

GETTING THERE
The Muker Meadows surround the Swaledale village of Muker, which lies on the B6270, just east of Thwaite. Upper Wensleydale is the area surrounding the town of Hawes, on the A684, where the Dales Countryside Museum (*see above*) is situated. The Yorkshire Dales National Park Authority is committed to encouraging the use of public transport to and within the area; visit its travel information site, www.traveldales.org.uk

ACCESS AND FACILITIES
The towns of Hawes, Aysgarth, and Leyburn offer full facilities, including parking and toilets. There are no facilities along walks within the Yorkshire Dales themselves. Always keep to the public rights of way.

OPENING TIMES
Open all year round.

CHARGES
None.

Reviving a tradition
Restoration projects are helping to recreate precious hay meadow habitat. The projects involve harvesting hay from ancient meadows and spreading it on selected sites so the seed falls naturally to the ground. The owners of the new sites then follow the traditional haymaking regime to encourage a variety of flowers. Grants cover any loss of income, but in any case the species-rich hay has a nutritive value for livestock that cannot be matched by grass alone.

Main: A buttercup meadow near Muker, Swaledale.

TRADITIONAL HAY MEADOWS

THE YORKSHIRE DALES ARE AMONG THE MOST ICONIC OF ENGLISH LANDSCAPES. Their long, grassy valleys, etched with stone walls and dotted with isolated field barns, are part of everyone's vision of England at its best. Much of their charm is perennial, but for a few weeks in high summer some of the valley meadows are transformed into dazzling displays of floral diversity, as they burst into a mass of short-lived flower.

Hay meadows in the Dales are traditionally cleared of grazing animals in May, allowing grasses and plants to grow until late July or August. These are cut and left to dry before being baled. The land is then grazed by farm animals until winter closes in. The haymaking calendar gives the plants a chance to flower and set seed, and since the land is not fertilized, flowering plants are able to flourish without being overwhelmed by dense grass. The result is a spectacular tapestry of colour as whole meadows flower at once. The dominant yellow of meadow

> Some hay meadows in the Yorkshire Dales can boast more than 80 wildflower species.

JAN

FEB

MAR

APR

MAY

JUN

JUL

AUG

SEP

OCT

NOV

DEC

WHERE ELSE TO SEE
UPLAND HAY MEADOWS

Traditional, flower-rich, upland hay meadow is one of the rarest types of grassland in Britain. It occurs mainly in the north of England – almost half the total occurs within the northern Pennines. In most areas the amount of hay meadow is shrinking rapidly.

The hay meadows of **Moor House** Nature Reserve in Upper Teesdale, Cumbria (*see pp.114–115*) lie at the highest altitude in Britain, and support several rare species of lady's-mantle and a flourishing population of globeflower. [N]

The hay meadows of **Weardale**, County Durham, provide excellent sightings of birds, such as lapwings and waders, which come for the moist soils that harbour plentiful worms. Common sandpipers, grey wagtails, redshanks, and curlews may all be seen in the area. [N]

To see fields of wild flowers, albeit in a different type of managed landscape, visit **West Pentire**, Cornwall (*see pp. 136–137*), where areas of land have been dedicated to traditional cornfield wild flowers.

THROUGH THE YEAR
THE YORKSHIRE DALES

By **autumn** the hay has been cut and cattle and sheep graze where the flowers once stood. But clear, crisp air and the rich colours of the season create some of the best views of the year from the hills flanking the meadow valleys.

Winter snowfall transforms the Dales, with the network of stone walls forming an intricate web of lines across a white landscape. Many waterfalls are at their most spectacular as the snow starts to melt.

In **spring**, wading birds such as curlews, golden plovers, and oystercatchers return to breed on the hills, filling the air with their calls, while the pastures and woodlands become bright with wild flowers.

buttercup is punctuated by the deep pink of red clover, the delicate white sprays of pignut – a relative of cow parsley – and the rich reddish-purple of a real hay-meadow specialist, the wood cranesbill. On the oldest meadows, managed in this way for centuries, there may be more than 30 different plant species for every square metre (10 sq ft). All these flowers attract a host of butterflies, bees, and other nectar-feeding insects.

One of the best places to witness this celebration of biodiversity is Muker Meadows in Swaledale, where you can find specialist plants such as globeflower, lady's-mantle, eyebright, and melancholy thistle, and well as the more widespread species. And in Upper Wensleydale, beside the River Ure, below Askrigg or beyond Appersett, you can stroll past meadows full of blue cranesbill accompanied by the constant song of common sandpipers. There are also some superb hay meadows further south in Yorkshire alongside the River Wharfe in Upper Wharfedale, and in neighbouring Littondale. Like all these meadows, they also support the sweet vernal grass that imparts such a delicious fragrance to the hay when it is cut.

Below: The Yorkshire Dales in winter.

CLIFFS AND CAVES

S LICED THROUGH THE HEART OF THE BEAUTIFUL MENDIP HILLS lies the truly magnificent Cheddar Gorge, whose towering limestone walls are the highest inland cliffs in the UK. The gorge itself was formed over a million years ago by melting glaciers, and around 40,000 years ago our ancestors lived in these caves. Two of the largest caves here are called Gough's and Cox's, after their discoverers, and they are said to have inspired JRR Tolkien's trilogy, *The Lord of the Rings*, after his honeymoon visit to the gorge.

These days the caves are an important refuge for some of our rarest species of bats. The lesser horseshoe and the even rarer greater horseshoe bat regularly use these caves as roost sites. The bats hang upside-down in the caves during the day, leaving them by night to hunt for insects in the woodlands. They're easy to miss, but you'll almost certainly see one of the gentle giants of the spider world, *Meta menardi*, the photophobic cave spider.

WHERE
Cheddar Gorge, Cheddar, Somerset
BS27 3QF; www.cheddarcaves.co.uk

CONTACT
Cheddar Caves, tel: 01934 742343;
caves@cheddarcaves.co.uk

GETTING THERE
Cheddar Gorge is southwest of Bristol, off the M4 motorway. Take the A38 out of Bristol to Axbridge, and follow the A371 for a short distance to the B3135, which is the actual road through the gorge itself.

ACCESS AND FACILITIES
The visitor centre features shops, cafes, and toilets, and is wheelchair friendly. The cliff-top walk is unsuitable for wheelchairs but there is good access to Gough's cave, and open-top bus rides offer a good overview of the gorge. Dormouse tours are available through the Mammal Society (tel: 01458 210345).

OPENING TIMES
The caves are open all year round (except Christmas Day), 10am–5.30pm in July and August, and 10.30am–5pm from September to June.

CHARGES
There are no charges for the walks, but entry to the caves is subject to charges. Parking is pay-and-display.

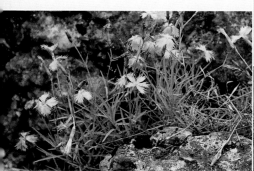

Unique Cheddar plants

The Cheddar pink (*pictured above*) and Cheddar bedstraw are both examples of Britain's rarest plants. They are unique to Cheddar Gorge, where they thrive due to their fully protected status. Both flower around late spring and early summer, making this an ideal time to visit the gorge. The low-growing, bluish-grey leaves of the Cheddar pink, related to garden pinks, stay green all year round. Other nationally rare plant species growing around the gorge include little robin, slender tare, and rock stonecrop.

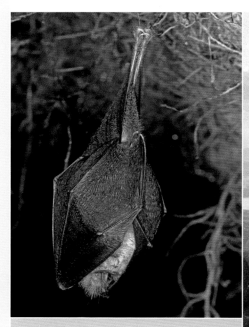

Above and below: Lesser horseshoe bats hang from roots in the caves; the caves of the gorge all feature both stalactites and stalagmites.

Main: Cheddar Gorge is 113m (371ft) at its deepest point, and has a near-vertical cliff face to the south.

Right panel (top and bottom): Feral goats around the gorge help keep the scrub in check; the limestone cliffs seen from Landslip Quarry.

The crags and ledges throughout the gorge support numerous rare and specialized plant species, including the Cheddar pink and Cheddar bedstraw, both species unique to Cheddar. At the top of the gorge you'll find limestone plateaus covered in calciferous grasslands packed full of sweet-scented flowers. Summer is a great time to visit: not only is the air full of heady aromas from plants such as wild marjoram and thyme, but wild orchids will also be flowering.

On the lower slopes you can see areas of ancient woodland, thick with oak, hazel, whitebeam, and holly. Dormice live in the thick cover of hazel and oak coppice, and peregrine falcons fly overhead. A good way to get a feel for the area is to walk up the 274 steps of Jacob's Ladder. This route takes you up to Pavey's lookout tower, where you can take in the views across the Mendips and towards Exmoor. From there you can pick up the cliff-top gorge walk, a 5km (3 mile) circular route, where you just might be accompanied by feral goats and ravens.

Harebell, rockrose, and marjoram grow in the thin soil overlaying much of the rock, while lizards, adders, and grass snakes bask on warm, bare rock.

WHERE ELSE TO SEE
GORGES

Most of the gorges in the UK are found in limestone country, and although Cheddar is the largest, there are many others dotted around the UK.

Britain's second-largest gorge, **Winnats Pass**, is in Derbyshire. Its magnificent, towering limestone sides are home to a variety of wild flowers, including Jacob's ladder and bird's-foot trefoil. [M]

Near to the vast limestone cliff face of Malham Cove in North Yorkshire is the mighty **Gordale Scar**. This impressive gorge is 1km (½ mile) long with sides raising up to 80m (260ft) at its highest points. [N]

The **Avon Gorge** on the River Avon in Bristol is home to some spectacular wildlife, including breeding peregrine falcons and the rare Bristol rock-cress. [SW]

One of the most atmospheric gorges must be Wales's **Fairy Glen** in Snowdonia, which has been the inspiration for many artists and writers. Swallow Falls and Conwy Falls are not far away. [W]

THROUGH THE YEAR
CHEDDAR GORGE

From **autumn** onwards, Cheddar's dormice feast on nuts, seeds, and insects – they also enjoy blackberries – fattening themselves up to almost double their normal body weight to see them through their long winter nap.

The bats regularly use the caves as their **winter** roost sites, and although they spend periods of time between October to April hibernating, they can occasionally be quite active.

By late **spring**, the Cheddar pink will begin to flower. Look out for purple gromwell and starved wood-sedge in the woodlands around the gorge, and many species of mosses and lichens on the limestone rock itself. Peregrine falcons nest around the gorge in spring, and may be seen hunting or displaying.

Below: Hazel dormice sleeping.

JAN FEB MAR APR MAY JUN JUL AUG SEP OCT NOV DEC

WHERE
Wimbledon Common, London SW19 5NR;
www.wpcc.org.uk

CONTACT
The Ranger's Office, Manor Cottage,
Windmill Road, Wimbledon Common, tel:
020 8788 7655; rangersoffice@wpcc.org.uk

GETTING THERE
By car, the A3 is the main route to
Wimbledon from the M25 Motorway. The
A219 runs through Wimbledon Hill Road.
The nearest train station is Wimbledon, with
regular trains from central London. The
nearest London Underground stations are
South Wimbledon on the Northern Line, and
Wimbledon on the District Line. Bus nos.
493, 93, 156, and 200 go through the area.

ACCESS AND FACILITIES
There's a car park and Information Centre at
the windmill – now a museum – on the
common, and both are wheelchair friendly.

OPENING TIMES
Open all year round.

CHARGES
None.

Long-lived larvae

Having suffered a sharp decline over recent
decades, the stag beetle is a protected species. It
breeds in old, rotting timber, but modern forestry
practice and tidy gardening have made breeding
sites harder to find. The larvae need to feed on
rotting wood for up to six years before crawling
out to burrow into the soil. Here they pupate,
while their bodies are rebuilt into adult form. The
beetles emerge from early summer, and spend
the last few weeks of their lives breeding.

Left (left to right):
Wimbledon Common has
many accessible paths;
fierce little shrews are
among the few small
predators that will take
on a male stag beetle.

Right (left to right): The
shorter jaws of the female
stag beetle can still deliver
a sharp nip; a stag beetle
spreads its wing-cases to
unfurl its wings.

Main and far right: Stag beetles fight for females – the "winner" is the beetle that turns the other one on its back.

BATTLING BEETLES

NOTHING CAN QUITE PREPARE YOU FOR YOUR FIRST ENCOUNTER with a flying male stag beetle on a
summer evening. Heralded by a gentle buzzing, a bizarre vision looms out of the twilight, with six
outstretched legs, flared wing-cases, and a pair of alarmingly long, spiked, antler-like jaws, hanging half upright
on apparently inadequate wings as it blunders towards you through the warm air.

Instinctively you duck, and possibly scream, because the whole experience feels like something out of a
science-fiction film. It is certainly not what you expect when you're out for an evening stroll in July, especially
somewhere such as Wimbledon Common. Yet this suburban parkland is a key site for these magnificent, if
disconcerting, insects. The females lay their eggs in decaying timber, preferably oak, and there is plenty of this
lying on the ground along the western side of the common. The woodland in this part of the common is very

The male stag beetle is the biggest British beetle, but despite its appearance it is quite harmless.

JAN

FEB

MAR

APR

MAY

JUN

JUL

AUG

SEP

OCT

NOV

DEC

WHERE ELSE TO SEE
STAG BEETLES

In Britain, stag beetles are confined to the southern counties of England, extending north to Norfolk and South Wales. Within this region they are associated with old woodlands, but they often turn up in suburban streets, where beetles flying by night are attracted to street lamps.

Several London parks besides Wimbledon Common have flourishing populations of stag beetles. They include **Richmond Park** (*see pp.276–277*), where their presence was one reason for the Park's designation as a National Nature Reserve. [SE]

Stag beetles are common in the **New Forest** (*see pp.174–175*) where they breed in decaying timber in the large areas of oak woodland. [SE]

Epping Forest is also a good place to find stag beetles. Since regular cutting of the larger forest trees stopped in 1878, a large quantity of dead wood has piled up on the forest floor, creating ideal conditions for stag beetles and a host of other insects. [SE]

THROUGH THE YEAR
WIMBLEDON COMMON

In early **autumn**, watch for bats fluttering through the dusk in pursuit of moths and flies. Six species are regularly seen over the common, including the biggest British bat, the noctule. Among the trees, look for the long-eared bat, which is able to pluck insects from their perches on leaves.

The shallow pools on the common attract a variety of ducks and geese in **winter**, including the spectacular mandarin duck. The male ducks are in their finest plumage at this time of year as they court the females before the spring breeding season.

Spring sees the emergence of innumerable caterpillars in the trees, which attract breeding songbirds that rely on the caterpillars as a food for their nestlings. You may also see sparrowhawks hunting to feed their own families.

carefully managed to help encourage wildlife, which includes leaving the dead timber where it falls. The big male beetles that waver through the dusk towards you across the common are, of course, in search of females, who are much smaller, far less inclined to fly, and do not have the enormous reddish jaws that make the males look so intimidating.

This is, in fact, their function, for the long mandibles are too weak to inflict anything more than a determined nip. Rival males flaunt them at each other and may use them to fight over females, gripping their opponents around the body and trying to toss them aside like miniature sumo wrestlers. The winner then mates with the female, enabling her to go off and lay clusters of large yellow eggs, which will take six years to grow into adults.

Having achieved this, the adults' job is done, and since they eat only a little sugary tree sap, they soon die. Most of a stag beetle's life is spent as a burrowing larva, slowly building up the resources that will fuel its meteoric career as a flying adult. If it thinks at all, it must be baffled by its astonishing, if short-lived, transformation.

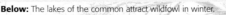

Below: The lakes of the common attract wildfowl in winter.

WHERE
Cors Caron National Nature Reserve,
Tregaron, Ceredigion, SY25 6AN Wales.

CONTACT
Tel: 0845 1306229; info@wales.info

GETTING THERE
The reserve is 3.2km (2 miles) to the
north of the village of Tregaron, which
lies on the A485 between Lampeter and
Aberystwyth. The main access to the reserve
is from the new car park on the B4343.
Cyclists and walkers can use the Ystwyth
Trail. There is a very limited bus service,
contact Traveline Cymru on 0870 6082608
or www.traveline-cymru.org.uk

ACCESS AND FACILITIES
The boardwalk to the viewing hide to the
south of the car park is wheelchair friendly,
although the hide 2km (1¼ miles) to the
north of the car park is not. There are toilets
in the car park. Just north of the reserve, in
the nearby town of Pontrhydfendigaid, there
are public toilets and two pubs.

OPENING TIMES
Open all year round.

CHARGES
None.

Preserving the peat

For centuries locals cut peat from the Welsh
boglands to burn on their hearths. Over the
years, the horticultural demand for peat grew,
so much so that by 1955 Cors Caron was
designated a National Nature Reserve in order to
save this precious habitat. Peat extraction has
become a major environmental issue. Most
multi-purpose composts for garden use will
contain between 70 and 100 per cent peat.
Many alternative products are widely available,
so look for products labelled as "peat-free".

Above (left to right): Sphagnum moss acidifies the water; bogbean grows around the pools; redshanks breed at Cors Caron in summer.
Main: The reserve at Cors Caron stretches over an area of 816 acres (330 hectares).

PEATLAND PARADISE

THERE CAN BE FEW LANDSCAPES MORE TREACHEROUS THAN RAISED BOGS. These vast, quaking sponges of water-saturated peat and moss have a reputation as quagmires into which people disappear without trace, and while the reality is rarely quite so dramatic, they are still places to treat with respect. On the other hand, where people dare not go, wildlife can flourish – so they are exciting places to visit, provided you do not stray from the marked paths.

Cors Caron in mid Wales is one of the finest examples of a raised bog system in Britain, and one of the most accessible. In July it is a glorious mosaic of colourful vegetation, buzzing with dragonflies that breed in the bog pools. The bogs formed on the site of an ancient shallow lake that became gradually choked with aquatic plants until it turned into a marshy, wooded fen. Dead vegetation cannot decay properly in such waterlogged conditions, so the area began to build up thick layers of peat. These were colonized by sphagnum mosses – plants that can absorb many times their own weight of water and grow well above the groundwater level – forming great domes of moss and peat that overwhelm even the trees.

There are three of these domes at Cors Caron, interlocking to form a complex that demonstrates every stage of the bog's development over the last 12,000 years. The sphagnum moss creates an acidic environment that suits specialized plants such as cottongrass, bog asphodel, and insect-eating sundews. You can see these at close quarters from the boardwalk that runs for some 3.5km (2 miles) over the southeast bog, together with 16 different species of dragonfly and, occasionally, the beautiful large heath butterfly, which lays its eggs on the white-beaked sedge that lines the edges of the pools. Watch out for red kites, merlins, and peregrines soaring overhead, and be sure to visit the lake hide for a chance of seeing curlews, redshanks, otters, and polecats.

Cors Caron was the last stronghold for the magnificent red kite when it was hunted to near-extinction in Britain during the 16th–19th centuries.

Inset: A red kite in flight above the bogs.
Below (left to right): Fluffy cottongrass; an insectivorous sundew plant.

JAN
FEB
MAR
APR
MAY
JUN
JUL
AUG
SEP
OCT
NOV
DEC

WHERE ELSE TO SEE
RAISED BOGS

Raised bogs develop in high-rainfall areas, often with hard, impermeable bedrock that impedes drainage. They are characteristic of northwest England, Wales, Scotland, and Ireland.

Whixall Moss is one of a complex of three raised bogs near the Llangollen Canal in Shropshire (*see pp.94–95*). They are among the most southerly raised bogs in Britain, which suffered acute damage from peat-cutting in the past, but have been restored to encourage a rich diversity of wildlife. [M]

Peatlands Park near Dungannon in Northern Ireland is a large raised bog that supports insectivorous plants, many species of dragonfly and a wide variety of birds. There is also a boggy woodland growing on drumlins – rounded heaps of debris created by moving ice during the last Ice Age. [NI]

Braehead Moss in south Lanarkshire, Scotland, consists of two linked, raised bogs with large areas of undisturbed bog vegetation that is home to breeding populations of red grouse and curlews. [SC]

THROUGH THE YEAR
CORS CARON

In **autumn** the bog attracts passage migrants, such as the green sandpiper, that stop off on their way south to their winter refuges. Waterfowl arrive to stay over winter. This includes whooper swans – the most southerly large wintering flock in Britain.

Winter is an excellent time to watch for raptors such as hen harriers, buzzards, and peregrines. In winter the local red kites are fed every day at Pont Einon overlooking the bog.

Highlights of **spring** include the return of many small migrant songbirds such as the sedge warbler and willow warbler, shadowed by the cuckoos that parasitize them by laying eggs in their nests. Check the bog pools for early dragonflies such as the four-spotted chaser and large red damselfly.

Below: Cors Caron provides excellent cover for migrant birds in autumn.

WHERE
Abbotts Hall Farm, Great Wigborough,
Colchester, Essex CO5 7RZ;
www.essexwt.org.uk

CONTACT
Essex Wildlife Trust, tel: 01621 862960;
admin@essexwt.org.uk

GETTING THERE
Take the B1026 from Colchester towards
Peldon; about 3km (1¾ miles) south of the
causeway across Abberton Reservoir, turn
east. The entrance to Abbotts Hall Farm is
about 1km (²/₃ mile) on the right.

ACCESS AND FACILITIES
Abbotts Hall Farm has not long been open
to the public, so facilities are basic, but being
developed all the time – the Essex Wildlife
Trust has opened a new headquarters on
the site. There is currently a car park and
full-access toilets, but no refreshment
facilities – the nearest are at Abberton
Reservoir, 10 minutes away by car.

OPENING TIMES
Tuesday to Friday 9am–5pm.

CHARGES
None.

Working with nature

Managed realignment – allowing nature to
reclaim areas that humans previously claimed
from the sea – began in Essex in the 1980s, as
an initiative to restore saltmarshes and create
natural sea defences. Initial small-scale
experiments were successful and led to much
larger schemes. This principle, of working with
nature rather than against it, is now accepted
as a fundamental part of our efforts to manage
the risks from both tidal and river flooding.

Above: The little tern hovers with flickering wings
forming a characteristic "V" shape.

Right panel (top and bottom): Spotted redshanks
are often early-returning migrants; painted lady
butterflies enjoy the nectar of saltmarsh flowers.

Below (top and bottom): Around seven pairs of
shelducks breed at Abbotts Hall Farm; sea aster, looking
much like its garden relatives, flowers in summer.

Main: Abbotts Hall Farm marshes are covered by the delicate flowers of sea pinks and sea lavender in summer.

THE SALTMARSHES OF ESSEX

ESSEX SALTMARSHES ARE UNDER THREAT: THEY ARE SUFFERING EROSION as sea levels rise, which has
been happening ever since the retreat of the last Ice Age but is now speeding up due to global warming.
One possible response runs contrary to instinct: rather than shore up sea walls, why not breach them ourselves?
Letting in the sea, and allowing the tides do some good by bringing in silt and seeds from saltmarshes beyond
the old sea walls, recreates valuable saltmarsh without any further intervention. At Abbotts Hall Farm on the
Blackwater Estuary, the Essex Wildlife Trust has done just this, returning, in 2002, 50 hectares (25 acres) of land
to the influence of the tides. At the time, this was the largest example of managed realignment of the coastline in
Britain. And with every year that passes, the new saltmarshes get bigger and better, increasingly coming to
resemble the remaining marshes in the estuary as more plants colonize, creating a summertime wash of colour.

Above: Glassworts create a warm-toned carpet with their autumn colours.

Marine life around
the saltmarshes
includes shore crabs,
jellyfish, lugworms,
and shrimp, and fish
such as sand smelt,
herring, and goby.

THROUGH THE YEAR
ABBOTTS HALL FARM

As summer gives way to **autumn**, more waders and other water birds arrive, some of which will remain for the winter, while others continue their migration as far south as Africa. The marshes adopt a range of hues from the glassworts, a group of succulent plant species differentiated by their autumn colours, which range from yellow to brown and purple.

During **winter**, the marshes are frequented by large flocks of dark-bellied brent geese from Siberia that add their soft, liquid cackle to the general sounds of an Essex winter. Short-eared owls and hen harriers hunt over the marshes, and flocks of buntings and finches, often including a few twites, feed on the seeds of saltmarsh plants such as sea-purslane.

The first sign of **spring** is the increase in territorial behaviour of those birds that remain to breed. Redshanks hover over the marshes, pairs of oystercatchers and ringed plovers set up territories on any sandy patch, and the songs of skylarks and meadow pipits fill the air in the spring sunshine.

WHERE ELSE TO SEE
SALTMARSHES

Saltmarshes are found on the coastline wherever there is a degree of shelter – allowing muddy sediments to be deposited. They also lie in the heart of estuaries such as the Thames, Medway, and Solent, and in the lee of barrier beaches.

Elsewhere in Essex, **Hamford Water** is a complex series of backwaters within a natural bay; further south on the remote **Dengie Marshes**, saltings extend out from the sea wall on the open coast. [SE]

On the north Norfolk coast, the best saltmarshes have developed behind the shelter of **Scolt Head Island** and **Blakeney Point** (see pp.214–215). [SE]

In the southwest, saltmarshes can be found at **Poole Harbour** in Dorset (see pp.48–49). [SW]

JAN
FEB
MAR
APR
MAY
JUN
JUL
AUG
SEP
OCT
NOV
DEC

One of the first flowers to come to prominence in early summer is thrift, or sea pink, which has delicate shell-pink flowerheads. In July, swathes of flowers erupt: sea-lavender creates a serene purple haze, followed and topped by sea aster, whose Michaelmas daisy-like flowerheads are a magnet for nectar-feeding insects. Migrating butterflies such as red admirals and painted ladies take advantage of the refuelling stop as they arrive on our shores, before moving inland.

Amid this botanical palette there are, of course, birds, who find the habitat irresistible. Redshanks, incessantly piping alarm calls in their role as "warden of the marshes", breed on the upper saltmarsh, out of reach of all but the highest tides. They mingle with the first returning migrants from the north, perhaps a greenshank or a spotted redshank, often showing traces of its blackish breeding dress. Little terns from nearby beach colonies hover with rapidly beating wings over the shallow pools, plunge-diving to catch small fish. Little egrets stalk through the shallows after the same food, but by their own hunting method. Graceful, sweeping avocets and parties of shelducks, accompanied by their piebald chicks, feed on the innumerable tiny snails in the mud.

WHERE
Rodborough Common, Stroud,
Gloucestershire GL5 5DE;
www.nationaltrust.org.uk

CONTACT
The National Trust, tel: 0844 8001895;
enquiries@thenationaltrust.org.uk or
Gloucester Wildlife Trust, tel: 01452 383333;
info@gloucestershirewildlifetrust.co.uk

GETTING THERE
Exit the M5 at junction 13 for Stroud.
Rodborough Common lies between the A46
and the A419 south of Stroud. By train, travel
to Stroud railway station, then catch the
Cotswold Green bus, no. 28 (Stroud–
Cirencester). By bicycle, National Cycle
Network Route no. 45 runs within 1.5km
(1 mile) of the common.

ACCESS AND FACILITIES
There are two free car parks: The Fort and
The Sunken, which both display information
about the common. The nearest toilets are in
Minchinhampton or Stroud, and the nearest
refreshments can be found in the various
pubs that border the common.

OPENING TIMES
Open all year round.

CHARGES
None.

The Adonis blue returns

During the 1950s, many of the Cotswold
grasslands became overgrown and the Adonis
blue butterfly disappeared. But conservation
work has led to it recolonizing many of its former
sites, including Rodborough Common, where the
Jurassic limestone grasslands provide the perfect
habitat. Interestingly, the larvae are often cared
for by ants. This symbiotic relationship is good
for both species: the larvae are protected from
predators, and the ants feed on the secretions
provided by the obliging larvae.

Above (left to right): A burnet moth; cinnabar moth caterpillars on ragwort; a meadow brown butterfly.
Main: The enchanting chalkhill blue butterfly (this is a female) can be found at Rodborough from mid-July to mid-September.

GRASSLAND BUTTERFLIES

THE COTSWOLDS ARE THE QUINTESSENTIAL ENGLISH LANDSCAPE – a region of rolling hills and broad views, blessed with a local building stone the colour of pale honey that suffuses every village with a glorious golden glow. This Jurassic limestone forms a plateau that slopes towards the northwest, ending abruptly in a series of steep "edges" that overlook the Severn Vale. Around Stroud, five streams converge, to create a network of valleys with south-facing grassy slopes that support a wide variety of delicate, lime-loving plants. The combination of sunny conditions and floral diversity provides ideal conditions for some of our rarest grassland butterflies.

One of the best places to look for them is Rodborough Common, just to the south of Stroud, which is managed by the National Trust. On a sunny day in early July, the most conspicuous species is likely to be the marbled white, a striking butterfly with black-and-white wings that is easy to spot as it sips nectar from a scabious or knapweed flower. It will often share a perch with the far less showy meadow brown, which exists in large numbers around the grassland.

Both these butterflies lay their eggs on grasses, but the much smaller common blue relies on small vetches like bird's-foot trefoil, which flourish on these sunny slopes. The warmth is particularly important for the horseshoe vetch, a spreading, yellow-flowered plant that is essential to the rarer chalkhill blue and the very scarce Adonis blue (*see box, below left*), since it is the only plant that is eaten by their caterpillars. A male chalkhill blue butterfly has distinctive milky-blue wings bordered with dark brown, but it literally pales into insignificance if seen beside the brilliant sky blue of a male Adonis. The male will mate with a number of females on the first day of emerging, before bedding down in a communal roost, closing its wings to sleep in a rough pocket of grass.

The distinctive marbled white butterfly is widespread throughout the south of the UK, and has started to expand its range to the north and east in recent years.

Inset: The marbled white can be seen from mid-June to mid-August.
Below (left to right): The male chalkhill blue; a dark green fritillary butterfly.

WHERE ELSE TO SEE
GRASSLAND BUTTERFLIES

Some grassland butterflies, such as the meadow brown, are widespread, but others are very selective about where they live, because their caterpillars rely on certain foodplants. Grassland species were always uncommon, but now that so many wild grasslands have been ploughed up or "improved" by spreading fertilizers – which eliminate the natural flora – many species are now rare. The best places to look are warm, south-facing slopes with ancient grassland.

Prehistoric earthworks are ideal sites, since they have natural turf that is thousands of years old. Look in the sunny areas of places like **Old Winchester Hill** in Hampshire, or **Cissbury Ring** in West Sussex. [SE]

In the west of England, investigate the magnificent ramparts of **Maiden Castle**, near Dorchester in Dorset, where you might see some butterflies. [SW]

The **Aston Rowant** nature reserve (*see pp.222–223*) on the Chilterns in Oxfordshire is a prime site for the very rare silver-spotted skipper butterfly. [SE]

THROUGH THE YEAR
RODBOROUGH COMMON

In **autumn**, look for grassland fungi like the field mushroom, the imposing parasol mushroom, and the shaggy ink cap. Most of the butterflies will have gone, but you may see a few common blues and big species like the red admiral, peacock, and comma.

Cold days in **winter** can provide the most beautiful views over the Severn Vale, since all the moisture is frozen out of the air.

Spring is a glorious time to visit Rodborough Common, as it offers the chance to see the Duke of Burgundy, a very rare butterfly that flourishes here and flies in April and May. The site is also famous for its beautiful spring flowers, including the pasque flower, which blooms around Easter. At least 13 species of orchid flower on the grasslands in spring and summer.

Below: Riders enjoy a morning trek around Rodborough Common.

JAN
FEB
MAR
APR
MAY
JUN
JUL
AUG
SEP
OCT
NOV
DEC

Where to Go: **August**

In Scotland you must contend with the midge: the one part of British wildlife that most of us would prefer to avoid. But you can be saved by even a moderate breeze, which will keep them off as you peer across moors and lochs for otters, deer, eagles, hen harriers, ospreys, and red and black grouse. Heading south, you'll find a different kind of wildlife, enjoying the all-too-rare heat; this is a good month on far southern heaths for searching out our scarcer smooth snakes and sand lizards, and watching dragonflies and the smaller damselflies. The trees are full of birds – such as Dartford warblers, families of woodlarks, and young buzzards – all calling to be fed. On the coast, look out to sea for Manx shearwaters, fulmars, gannets, and those seafaring

UPLANDS

BEINN EIGHE A cluster of rocky peaks in the northwest Highlands.

COAST

BLAKENEY POINT Seals love to bask on the shingle.

WETLANDS

FORSINARD One of our few remaining peatlands sparkles in summer.

BEINN EIGHE
HIGHLAND [SC]

Britain's first National Nature Reserve is a wild and forbidding landscape.
See pp.202–203

The Highlands are the British stronghold for a group of plants that evolved to cope with life on the freezing Arctic tundra.

BLAKENEY POINT
NORTH NORFOLK [SE]

Around 500 seals – both common and grey – haul themselves on to Blakeney Point in the summer. There should be lots of pups at this time of year.
See pp.214–215

GIANT'S CAUSEWAY
COUNTY ANTRIM [NI]

Europe's largest lava plateau makes huge and wondrous shapes on this beach – walk out to sea on the stacks and try sitting on a "giant's boot".
See pp.208–209

ROSS LOUGH
COUNTY FERMANAGH [NI]

The open water, fen, and wet meadow here are home to many wetland plants, such as purple loosestrife, and an abundance of insects.
See pp.204–205

FORSINARD FLOWS
HIGHLAND [SC]

The immense peatland of the Flow Country is dotted with black pools and an army of carnivorous plants.
See pp.216–217

MIGNEINT MOORS
NORTH WALES [W]

The river Conwy (Afon Conwy) rises on the great upland plateau of Migneint, where wild and open moorland abounds with wildlife.
See pp.216–217

FOWLSHEUGH
ABERDEENSHIRE [SC]

This coastal nature has high cliffs teeming with nesting seabirds. Seals, porpoises, and occasionally even minke whales visit its waters.
See pp.208–209

WICKEN FEN
ELY, CAMBRIDGESHIRE [SE]

Our most famous fenland has an astonishing wealth of wildlife – the shimmering wings of dragonflies seem to be absolutely everywhere.
See pp.204–205

ASTON ROWANT
THE CHILTERNS, OXFORDSHIRE [SE]

This downland turf has remained uncultivated for centuries, and its wildflowers conceal, until dusk, large numbers of the astonishing glow worm.
See pp.222–223

LYME BAY
DEVON/DORSET [SW]

As well as its Jurassic rocks, the bay is home to some of the best underwater wildlife in the UK, with reefs and rare sealife.
See pp.226–227

BAY OF BISCAY
NORTH ATLANTIC OCEAN

Take a sea voyage to the Bay to see marine mammals, such as whales and dolphins.
See pp.200–201

CORNHILL MEADOWS
WALTHAM ABBEY, ESSEX [SE]

This dragonfly sanctuary within the Lee Valley Park shelters 21 species of damselflies and dragonflies, really challenging your identification skills.
See pp.210–211

BEN NEVIS
FORT WILLIAM [SC]

The highest mountain in the UK; its specialities include the mountain ringlet butterfly and the magnificent golden eagle.
See pp.208–209

HAM WALL
SOMERSET LEVELS [SW]

This newly created wetland provides a safe home for many rare species, including water voles and otters.
See pp.204–205

Previous page: A female otter surfaces from a wetland pool.

thieves, the skuas. Watch the waves for the rolling backs of cetaceans, large and small: porpoises and dolphins for sure, but also minke whales and killer whales if you have a real slice of luck. The tall, lazy fin of a gigantic basking shark is a possibility, too. Island life is full and busy in August: Mull is the place for otters and eagles, both golden and white-tailed, as well as familiar but beautiful birds such as oystercatchers and eiders, which stalk around the rocky shores. Wherever you are, you will notice little signs that summer is coming to an end: a dryness in the grass, a dullness in the leaves, the absence of some familiar birds, even berries appearing on the rowans and hedgerow shrubs. Autumn is coming.

INLETS AND ESTUARIES

MORAY FIRTH The best and easiest place to see bottlenose dolphins.

MORAY FIRTH
ROSS-SHIRE [SC]

Salmon return to the Firth in summer, pursued by over 130 bottlenose dolphins. Harbour porpoises are common, and a few minke whales coast around the outer bay.
See pp.220–221

DORNOCH FIRTH
ROSS-SHIRE [SC]

This is the northernmost firth on the east coast of Scotland. It has significant numbers of osprey, bar-tailed godwits, and curlew. Common seals give birth to pups here in August.
See pp.214–215

ARDTORNISH
OBAN, ARGYLL [SC]

You can see families of otters around the shores of Loch Aline on this estate, where they hunt in daylight, catching fish and crabs at low tide.
See pp.206–207

On the Moray Firth, with luck, dolphins will appear in front of you, surfacing and leaping clear of the water, just a little way from the shore.

CROMARTY FIRTH
ROSS-SHIRE [SC]

An inlet of the Moray Firth, the Cromarty Firth is a great place to see dolphins, seals, otters, and osprey.
See pp.220–221

LAKES AND WATERWAYS

FRIARS CRAG The still waters reflect the glorious landscape.

FRIARS CRAG
KESWICK, CUMBRIA [N]

This promontory juts out into Derwentwater, long considered one of the most beautiful scenes in Europe. Watch ospreys snatch fish straight from the lake.
See pp.212–213

TRENTHAM ESTATE
STOKE ON TRENT, STAFFORDSHIRE [N]

This is a great place to enjoy walks along the lakeside and in the woodlands. Good for ducks and grebes, it is also home to a large heronry.
See pp.212–213

BLASHFORD LAKES
NEW FOREST, HAMPSHIRE [SW]

Wetland birds, badgers, and deer make their homes around this series of tranquil man-made lakes surrounded by woodland, reeds, and grassland.
See pp.212–213

On the River Test on a still, summer evening, it's magical to watch flies tempting the trout to rise and take their prey with a noisy splash.

THE RIVER TEST
HAMPSHIRE [SW]

Our most famous trout stream travels through some of England's finest countryside. Brown trout, sea trout, chub, graylings, dace, and roach swim below the kingfishers.
See pp.218–219

ISLANDS

ISLE OF MULL Eagles swoop along the island's mountain slopes.

ISLE OF MULL
INNER HEBRIDES [SC]

Renowned for its otters, dolphins, and whales, Mull is also home to golden eagles and the very rare – and elegant – white-tailed sea eagles.
See pp.226–227

Sea eagles can be seen hunting over the lochs and rocky shores of Mull, or around their nesting site near Loch Frisa in early summer.

ISLE OF WIGHT
ENGLISH CHANNEL [SE]

Clouds of butterflies and moths, including the rare hummingbird moth, spill across the Channel to feed on the island's flowers.
See pp.224–225

ISLE OF SKYE
INNER HEBRIDES [SC]

Visit the otter centre on the Isle of Skye and watch otters hunt and play on the length of the shoreline.
See pp.206–207

ISLE OF MAY
FIRTH OF FORTH [SC]

This small island is owned by Scottish Natural Heritage, which protects its breeding birds including puffins, guillemots, and razorbills. Watch out for seals that swim offshore.
See pp.214–215

ISLE OF LEWIS
WESTERN ISLES [SC]

Seabirds live all around the coast; dolphins, porpoises, and sharks swim in its seas. Ancient stone circles add to the attractions inland, along with otters, eagles, and peregrine falcons.
See pp.216–217

GIANTS OF THE DEEP

KAIKOURA IN NEW ZEALAND, MONTEREY BAY IN CALIFORNIA, HERMANUS IN SOUTH AFRICA – these are names to conjure with on the trail of great whales. But there are places in the northeast Atlantic to rival any of these, and a ferry trip from Portsmouth or Plymouth to northern Spain will take you through some of the richest waters for cetaceans – whales, dolphins, and porpoises – anywhere in the world: the Bay of Biscay.

An evening sailing means you wake up rounding Finisterre, already into exciting waters. Relatively shallow and cool, these waters are likely to be harbouring minke whale, harbour porpoises, and bottlenose dolphins. A few hours later the real treats begin, as the ferry crosses the edge of the continental shelf and the water depth plunges rapidly from 200 to 4,000m (650–13,000ft). If sea conditions allow, the tall blows of large whales, mostly fin whales, should now start to appear, singly, or in small groups, sometimes more than a hundred on a single

WHERE
Sailing from the south coast of England to the Bay of Biscay, North Atlantic Ocean, off the coasts of France and Spain.

CONTACT
P&O Ferries, tel: 08716 645645; www.poferries.com; help@poferries.com or companies specialising in whale-watching cruises around the bay lasting several days.

GETTING THERE
Car ferries sail from Portsmouth to Bilbao and from Plymouth, Portsmouth, and Poole to Santander. Most of the specialist whale-watching cruise companies tend to depart from Plymouth or Portsmouth.

ACCESS AND FACILITIES
Ferries and sight-seeing boats generally have good wheelchair facilities and access.

CHARGES
These vary depending on the length of trip and time of year: check for prices with individual ferry and boat companies.

Whale-watching tips

Identifying whales and dolphins is quite an art. Although the larger boats and ferries are stable, they don't stop or steer nearer to the cetaceans, and some of the animals only surface for a few seconds at a time. Move between decks if you can: a lower deck will bring you a closer view, but upper decks allow you to see further. Take a good pair of binoculars, and a polarized lens for your camera if possible, as this will allow you to see the whale's body under the water. Start by scanning the sea for the misty blow of a whale.

Main: The deep-diving sperm whale surfaces for air for 8–10 minutes before diving again.

Left (left to right): A Cory's shearwater skims the waves of the bay; the ocean sunfish is the heaviest bony fish in the world.

Right: The distinctive dorsal fin of a fin whale, which may measure up to 24m (80ft) long.

Right panel (top and bottom): Great skuas; a minke whale.

voyage, and they often approach the ships very closely. The helicopter deck of the ferries provides an admirably stable and elevated viewing platform, and on many services expert guidance is on hand to point things out. Fin whales may predominate, but there are likely to be other species too: sperm whales, with their forward-directed, low, bushy spouts, and habit of raising their tail flukes out of the water as they dive deep in search of squid; schools of common and striped dolphins, sometimes riding the bow wave of the vessel; and – especially over the deep water canyons nearer the Spanish coast – small parties of the little-known Cuvier's beaked whale. You might also see ocean sunfish and basking sharks, along with numerous seabirds, especially just after stormy weather. Shearwater species – including great, Cory's, and the globally threatened Balearic – skim the waves. Gannets fly by in battalions, while storm petrels flitter over the surface of the water and skuas cause mayhem as they steal food from other seabirds.

THROUGH THE YEAR
BAY OF BISCAY

Whale-watching in Biscay is best in the summer and early **autumn**, though it's not clear whether this is because there are more whales then, or because the calmer seas make them easier to see. Sightings of female cetaceans with their young are frequent during June and July. Be sure to take a look around the boat itself: boats often provide a refuge for small birds migrating across the bay, and anything could turn up, from warblers and swallows to turtle doves and merlins. Likewise, migrating moths and butterflies often take advantage of the unexpected availability of "dry ground".

Numbers of fin whales in particular drop in **winter** and sightings become sporadic. The area is a regular wintering area for flocks of Sabine's gulls, little gulls, and kittiwakes, together with great skuas, fulmars, and possibly Leach's petrels.

In **spring**, whale sightings pick up from around April. By May, ferry passengers begin to see mother whales, dolphins, and harbour porpoises with their young, which tend to be about half the size of the adult cetaceans.

Over 30 species of whale and dolphin have been recorded in the Bay of Biscay.

WHERE ELSE TO SEE
WHALES

Although you're likely to get the best view of cetaceans from boats, it is also possible to do some whale- or dolphin-watching from land.

The Inner and Outer **Hebrides** provide many opportunities to see larger cetaceans, particularly minke whales and sometimes killer whales during the summer. A trip from **Tobermory** on the **Isle of Mull** (see pp.226–227) should reveal whales, bottlenose dolphins, and basking sharks. Large whales are not a regular sight in the North Sea, although a few minkes turn up in the **Moray Firth** (see pp.220–221) from time to time. [SC]

For land-based observers, headlands in southwest England and Wales give the best chance of spotting whales. Try **Lands End** and **The Lizard** (see pp.116–117) in Cornwall. [SW]

Below: The white-headed Cuvier's beaked whale.

JAN
FEB
MAR
APR
MAY
JUN
JUL
AUG
SEP
OCT
NOV
DEC

WHERE
Beinn Eighe National Nature Reserve, Torridon Mountains, Kinlochewe, Highland, Scotland.

CONTACT
Scottish National Heritage, Kinlochewe Office, IV22 2PD; tel: 01445 760254; Beinn Eighe Visitor Centre, tel: 01445 760254.

GETTING THERE
Beinn Eighe lies at the southeast end of Loch Maree, near the village of Kinlochewe. It can be reached from two roads: the A832 and the A896. The nearest train station is 30km (19 miles) away at Achnasheen. There is a limited bus service from Inverness.

ACCESS AND FACILITIES
The visitor centre is wheelchair friendly, and offers parking, toilets, a picnic area, cycle rack, and interpretive displays. There is also a basic camp site. Short wheelchair-friendly trails lead out from the visitor centre. For a more strenuous walk, with slopes and steps, take the mountain trail.

OPENING TIMES
The visitor centre is open April–October.

CHARGES
None.

Ancient forests
When you visit Beinn Eighe, make sure you have time to include the Scots pine woodland beside Loch Maree. Some of these trees are more than 350 years old, and they are part of a wood that has been growing here for over 8,000 years. The wood is one of the few surviving fragments of the original Caledonian pine forest, which spread north after the Ice-Age glaciers retreated and the climate gradually warmed up. Such pine trees once covered most of Scotland.

Above: A thin carpet of vegetation covers all but the highest peaks of this seemingly barren landscape.

Right panel (top and bottom): Unusual clubmosses cling to life in this harsh environment for plants; cowberry fruits.

Below (top and bottom): Heathers and other wiry shrubs bind the thin, rocky soil with their roots; the insect-eating butterwort grows in patches of wet soil lower down the slopes.

Main: The Beinn Eighe National Nature Reserve includes all of the Torridon Mountains.

LIFE AT THE TOP

THE SCOTTISH HIGHLANDS ARE THE MOST RUGGED, WILD, AND FORBIDDING landscapes in Britain. Even in August their climate can be bracing, to say the least, so it's no surprise that they are the British stronghold for a group of plants that evolved to cope with life on the Arctic tundra. These Arctic-alpines were widespread in southern Britain 20,000 years ago, during the last Ice Age, but as the climate warmed, they retreated to the highest, most northerly peaks, where the harsh growing conditions remain very like those at sea level on the polar fringes.

You can see this for yourself if you climb the slopes of Beinn Eighe, a great cluster of rocky peaks and ridges in the northwest Highlands, which was declared a National Nature Reserve as long ago as 1951. The peaks are capped with pale, glittering quartzite, which is all but barren, but many of the higher slopes are covered with a low-growing scrub of tough woody plants, such as dwarf willow and prostrate juniper, interspersed with blaeberry,

JAN

FEB

MAR

APR

MAY

JUN

JUL

AUG

SEP

OCT

NOV

DEC

Beinn Eighe was
Britain's first
National Nature
Reserve – reflecting
its value to botanists,
naturalists, and
geologists.

WHERE ELSE TO SEE
MOUNTAIN PLANTS

By their nature, Arctic-alpines and other mountain plants are normally restricted to high mountains in Britain, although they grow at sea level in the Arctic. Many are commonly cultivated, but to see them growing wild, you need to visit the uplands – and especially the Scottish Highlands – in summer.

One of the best sites is **Ben Lawers**, near Loch Tay in the Breadalbane Hills of the southern Highlands. Its mica schist rocks have created lime-rich soils that support more than 60 per cent of the mountain plant species native to Britain. [SC]

The Cairngorms in the eastern Highlands (see pp.178–179) form a high plateau with large areas that rise above 1,100m (3,600ft). Although the rock is acid granite, the region can boast a wide variety of mountain plants. [SC]

In England, the sugar limestone habitat of **Upper Teesdale** (see pp.114–115) in the Pennines, Cumbria, supports rare mountain plants that have survived here since just after the last Ice Age. [N]

THROUGH THE YEAR
BEINN EIGHE

In **autumn** the mountain plants start to shut down for the winter, but there is still plenty to see on the lower slopes. Watch out for red squirrels and deer, and scan the ancient pine forest for Scottish crossbills using their modified beaks to extract seeds from pine cones.

The climate on Beinn Eighe in **winter** can be truly glacial, so you are unlikely to venture far up the mountain trail. But look out for mountain hares in their white winter coats on lower slopes and around Loch Maree, and if it has snowed, check the ground for footprints. Both pine martens and wildcats live on the reserve, and this offers the best chance of detecting them.

Spring sees a burst of plant growth on the mountain as the winter snows melt. Watch for ravens tumbling through the sky as they perform their aerial courtship displays. Black-throated divers start arriving to breed, and the white-tailed eagles begin nest building.

Below: Wildcats live and breed in the Caledonian forest.

cowberry, heather, clubmosses, and sedges. Aptly known to botanists as "dwarf shrub heath", this is almost exactly like the vegetation that covers vast areas of Arctic tundra. Standing here, you could be on the rocky, windswept fringes of Greenland.

The quartzite and sandstone of Beinn Eighe are hard, acid rocks that break down only reluctantly, so the soil here is poor in minerals and consists largely of acid peat. In some parts of the Highlands, however, outcrops of lime-rich rock provide nutrients that allow a wider diversity of plants to grow. An intriguing variety of microhabitats such as loose scree, wet flushes, and rock ledges are colonized by a range of Arctic-alpines such as alpine forget-me-not, moss campion, alpine saxifrage, mountain avens, and alpine gentian – many of which will be in flower in August.

The best places to find botanical rarities are the ungrazed crags and cliffs, so look up as well as down, and take a pair of binoculars. They can save a lot of fruitless and possibly dangerous exploration – and you will be very glad of them if a golden eagle or a white-tailed eagle soars into view around the flank of the mountain, or a cautious pine marten shows its heart-shaped face.

WHERE
Wicken Fen, Lode Lane, Wicken, Ely,
Cambridgeshire, CB7 5XP;
www.wicken.org.uk

CONTACT
The National Trust, tel: 01353 720274;
wickenfen@nationaltrust.org.uk

GETTING THERE
Wicken Fen lies just south of the A1123 and
4.8km (3 miles) west of Soham, near the
town of Ely. The nearest train station is in Ely,
from where you can catch a bus to Soham or
Stretham. By cycle, the reserve is on Route
11 of the National Cycle Network.

ACCESS AND FACILITIES
Of the three trails, the boardwalk trail is the
easiest; it is ideal for wheelchairs and buggies
and has a specially adapted hide. The visitor
centre has a shop, toilets, and refreshments.
The café – next door to the visitor centre –
provides a wide range of hot and cold food.

OPENING TIMES
The visitor centre is open daily, 10am–5pm,
(Tuesdays–Sundays) all year except for
Christmas Day.

CHARGES
Small entry charge for non-National Trust
members.

Wind-pump drainage

The wind pump on Sedge Fen is now the only
working woodpump in the whole of the Fens,
though at one time there were around 700. In
the 17th century, landowners tried to reclaim
fenland by draining it, but the drying out of the
fens caused them to sink below river levels
– when it rained, excess rain could no longer
reach the river, so the fens flooded. Wind pumps
were then introduced to control the water levels.
The pump at Sedge Fen was last used to drain
the land for food production during World War II.

Above (left to right): The very rare great crested newt; marsh harriers specialize in hunting at low level over the wetlands; a water rail.
Main: Wicken Fen is a surviving fragment of the once huge fenland that stretched from Cambridge to The Wash.

A PATCH OF TRUE FENLAND

FOUR HUNDRED YEARS AGO A VAST AREA OF EASTERN ENGLAND to the south of The Wash was fenland – a waterlogged, peaty landscape of reeds, willow, and alder, dotted with meres of open water and teeming with animal life. From the 1620s onwards, the land was progressively drained to turn the fen peat into extremely fertile farmland, and today nearly all the wild fenland has disappeared. Just a few patches remain, and of these the most famous is certainly Wicken Fen.

One of the first nature reserves to be created in Britain, Wicken Fen was saved thanks to the foresight of Victorian naturalists who bought sections of the fen and presented them to the National Trust. Even then they could see that the site had an astonishing wealth of wildlife, considering its relatively small area. It is particularly rich in insects, something that becomes very clear if you visit the reserve in August. The shimmering wings of dragonflies are everywhere – 19 species breed in the ditches and ponds on the reserve – and every flower is alive with nectar-feeding butterflies, hoverflies, and beetles. And if you look down into the clear water you will see roach, rudd, and perch, and maybe a water vole or even a swimming grass snake. The nearby mere is a magnet for ducks, geese, and herons, and there is a good chance of seeing the magnificent marsh harrier.

Apart from the wonderful wildlife, the most intriguing thing about Wicken Fen is its relationship to the surrounding landscape. When the fenland peat was drained for agriculture it dried out, shrank, and started wasting away, to the point where some areas now lie more than 2.4m (8ft) below sea level. But Wicken Fen has never been drained, and it now stands high above the surrounding fields like a slice of rich, moist cake on a dry, almost empty, plate. Despite this, when you are in the middle of the fen itself, all that you see is the watery wilderness of a lost world. Wicken Fen is not just a nature reserve – it is a window into the past.

An amazing total of more than 8,000 species of plants, fungi, and animals have been recorded at Wicken Fen – including over 20 types of dragonfly and damselfly.

Inset: Look for the emperor dragonfly around the fen's lodes, or waterways.
Below (left to right): Grass snakes swim the ditches looking for frogs; a water vole.

WHERE ELSE TO SEE FENS

Nearly all – 99.9 per cent – of the once vast fens of eastern England is now arable farmland. Wicken Fen is one of just four surviving patches of wild fenland in the region. Other areas of fenland do exist elsewhere in Britain, but most fenland has been drained because, unlike the acid peat of upland bogs, the alkaline peat of fenland makes very fertile soil.

In the Fens proper, **Woodwalton Fen** near Huntingdon in north Cambridgeshire is a superb example of a near-natural wetland, rivalling Wicken Fen in biodiversity. The "Great Fen Project" aims to link Woodwalton with nearby **Holme Fen**, another good site. [SE]

Further east, there is plenty of fenland surviving in the Norfolk Broads. One of the best sites is **Strumpshaw Fen** (*see pp.152–153*), one of the last strongholds of the swallowtail butterfly. [SE]

Ham Wall nature reserve on the Somerset Levels is an extensive area of reedbed and fen recreated by wetland restoration. [SW]

Ross Lough nature reserve in County Fermanagh, Northern Ireland, is a mosaic of habitats including open water, swamp, and fen, supporting a rich variety of wildlife. [NI]

THROUGH THE YEAR WICKEN FEN

In **autumn**, winter migrants such as hen harriers and short-eared owls come here from the uplands to join the resident marsh harriers. The reserve also attracts large numbers of overwintering waterfowl.

Winter is a good time to look for resident mammals such as foxes, stoats, and weasels. Brown hares are regularly seen on Adventurer's Fen, and the site has started to attract visiting otters.

The reserve bursts into flower in **spring**, as colourful plants such as the yellow flag iris bloom along the waterways. Migrant songbirds such as blackcaps and reed warblers return to breed, and male bitterns can be heard booming in the reedbeds.

Below: Reed grows in the tall fen, which is flooded during the winter.

JAN
FEB
MAR
APR
MAY
JUN
JUL
AUG
SEP
OCT
NOV
DEC

WHERE
Ardtornish Estate, Morvern, near Oban, Argyll, Scotland, PA34 5UZ; www.ardtornish.co.uk

CONTACT
Ardtornish Estate Office, tel: 01967 421288; tourism@ardtornish.co.uk

GETTING THERE
Fort William is the nearest transport hub; the onward journey via the Corran Ferry to Ardtornish, at the southern end of the peninsula, is only practicable for the visitor by car. There is also a ferry between Lochaline to the Isle of Mull; a Caledonian MacBrayne ferry connects Mull with Oban on the Scottish mainland.

ACCESS AND FACILITIES
Although Ardtornish is a private estate there is open access for walkers to the sea lochs. The estate also includes and co-manages part of the Scottish Wildlife Trust's Rahoy Hills Reserve, most easily accessed from Acharn; you must contact the Ardtornish Estate office or the Trust (01463 714746) if you intend to enter the higher areas of the reserve.

OPENING TIMES
Open all year round.

CHARGES
For ferries, and to visit Ardtornish Gardens.

Breeding time

Otters are generally solitary, but when females are ready to breed – usually in spring – they attract males and indulge in an energetic courtship before mating. Two or three cubs are born two months later – between May and August – in an underground den, or holt. Their mother raises them alone, feeding them on her milk inside the den. At 10 weeks they venture outside to play, but do not enter the water until they are three months old, and it may be another six months before they can hunt and fend for themselves.

Main: A young otter dries off amidst the seaweed on the lochside.

LAND OF THE OTTER

LYING ON THE WEST COAST OF SCOTLAND, the Morvern Peninsula – separated from the Isle of Mull by only a narrow strip of water – is one of the most remote regions of Scotland. Few people live here, and its rugged landscape, with spectacular views and tranquil shores, has changed little over the centuries. But while it may not be among the most accessible of places, this is a magical destination for wildlife watchers. Its perfectly preserved habitats host a tremendous diversity of flowers, birds, and animals, and perhaps most excitingly, it is the home of one of the UK's most charismatic creatures: the otter.

Loch Aline, a quiet and sheltered sea loch on the Ardtornish Estate, is a wonderful otter-spotting area, and August is a great time to visit, when the climate is generally at its mildest, and when you are most likely to see families of otter cubs (*see box, left*). Otters are usually thought of as river animals, but the shores of western

Left (left to right): Loch Sunart separates the Morvern Peninsula from the Isle of Mull; a golden eagle soars overhead.

Right (top and bottom): A female otter catches a crab to take back to her cubs; their sleek, streamlined form makes otters the perfect swimming machines.

Above: The cubs stay together on their first open-air expeditions.

> This remote peninsula is one of the very rare places in Britain where otters may regularly be seen during daylight.

WHERE ELSE TO SEE OTTERS

After decades of decline, the otter population is recovering and is beginning to recolonize former haunts around Britain. River otters are more elusive than those that live on the coast, and are rarely seen; years of disturbance have made them wary and they nearly always hunt at night. Otters can usually be detected by the signs they leave – dark, oily, fish-scented droppings, their five-toed footprints in muddy river banks, and the chutes and slides they use to slip into the water.

The RSPB reserve at **Leighton Moss** in Lancashire (*see pp.78–79*) is home to several otters that can often be seen from the birdwatching hides. [N]

The **Somerset Levels** is ideal otter country, but good vantage points are scarce. Try the Mere Hide at **Shapwick Heath** reserve (*see pp.120–121*). [SW]

The Camel Valley, in Cornwall, has a healthy otter population. Bicycles can be hired at several points along the peaceful 27.3km (17 miles) Camel cycle trail. [SW]

The west coast of Scotland and the islands of the **Hebrides**, **Shetland**, and **Orkney** are among the best places to spot coastal otters, on quiet rocky shores and in sea lochs. There is an otter haven and hide on the **Isle of Skye**. [SC]

THROUGH THE YEAR ARDTORNISH ESTATE

During the **summer**, the ferry trip from the Isle of Mull to the Morvern Peninsula may well offer sightings of minke whales and basking sharks.

Long-legged, spiny shore crabs may be seen at the margins of Loch Aline in **autumn**, just as young otters are learning to catch their own food. Lengthy chases often ensue.

In **winter** sea eagles and golden eagles may be seen ranging across the clear, cold skies. Pine martens become less cautious, venturing out from cover to forage for food. These creatures exist in very small numbers outside Scotland, and the Morvern Peninsula is one of the best places to spot them.

Scotland host one of the largest otter populations in Europe, and on the Ardtornish Estate the otters have been left to their own devices. Otters are much easier to see here than on inland rivers, partly because of their numbers but also because, unlike river otters, these coastal-dwelling animals routinely hunt in daylight. The summer nights are very short in this part of Scotland, so they have little option, but since they suffer so little disturbance, they also have no reason to hide away. Instead, the lives of coastal otters are governed by the tides, for they find it much easier to catch fish and crabs at low tide when the rich seaweed beds that lie just offshore are within easy reach of the surface.

Otters can often be seen eating small prey in the water, or hauling large fish such as eels or lumpsuckers ashore to devour at leisure among the weed-strewn rocks. Look out for the distinctive V-shaped wake of an otter swimming low in the water when they are out fishing for food. Otters spend a lot of time grooming their dense brown fur, which tends to become matted by the salty seawater, and if you move quietly, you may glimpse one resting in the seaweed on the lochside.

JAN
FEB
MAR
APR
MAY
JUN
JUL
AUG
SEP
OCT
NOV
DEC

GIANT STEPPING STONES

MYTH AND LEGEND SURROUND THE BEAUTIFUL CAUSEWAY COAST. The star attraction – The Giant's Causeway – is a UNESCO World Heritage site consisting of 40,000 basalt columns along the coastline, which were formed at various stages from 60 million to 15,000 years ago, when lava from volcanic eruptions met the sea. The Causeway itself is a promontory made of columns, but there are many other interesting formations: follow the Finn MacCool Trail to visit them all, including The Wishing Chair and The Giant's Boot. The immense columns of The Giant's Organ and The Giant's Gate will tempt you to believe that these were the work of a giant's hand.

This part of the North Antrim coast has Ireland's most spectacular scenery: enormous cliffs, haunting basalt columns, secluded bays, and eerie, isolated ruins. While you're following the trail around the Causeway, keep an eye out for some interesting plants and birds, too. Black guillemots nest close by, and you might see

WHERE
The Giant's Causeway, Bushmills, County Antrim, BT57 8SU Northern Ireland; www.northantrim.com/giantscauseway.htm

CONTACT
National Trust (Co. Antrim), tel: 028 20731582; giantscauseway@nationaltrust.org.uk

GETTING THERE
The Causeway is 3.2km (2 miles) east of Bushmills. Take the B17 from Coleraine to Bushmills, then the A2 until you see the Causeway Road signposted left. By rail, catch a train to Coleraine (16km/10 miles) or Portrush (13km/8 miles). Ulsterbus routes 172 and 177 run to the Causeway; in summer you can also catch the Causeway Rambler Bus (Ulsterbus no. 376).

ACCESS AND FACILITIES
The visitor centre has parking (including disabled-reserved), a cafe, and full-access toilets. There is a wheelchair- and pushchair-friendly bus that runs from the visitor centre to the Causeway. The site is partly accessible, but much of the area has uneven terrain that is difficult to negotiate.

OPENING TIMES
Open all year round.

CHARGES
None, but donations are welcome.

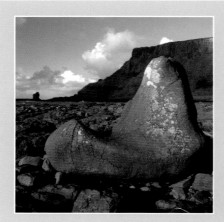

The Giant's Causeway is the largest lava plateau in Europe, covered with intriguing rock formations like the famous Giant's Boot.

Colour contrasts

As you walk along the Causeway, be sure to look closely at the rocks themselves, which are extremely colourful in places. Look out especially for places where the oldest, lowest layer of rock, known as "lower basalt" shows through – this has weathered to a deep red colour. Red rock pools may have a base of this ancient red basalt, or – on closer inspection – turn out to have a covering of rare red algae. A surrounding of green algae and black tar lichen (*as shown above*) usually suggests the "red" is living algae.

them just offshore: look out for their striking black-and-white breeding plumage. Buzzards, peregrines, and ravens nest on the cliffs, while rock pipits live among the rocks along the shore. Stonechats fly above the path that leads down from the visitor centre to the shore.

More than 200 species of plant occur around the Causeway, including some rarities such as Scots lovage and the waxy-leaved oyster plant, whose leaves actually taste like oysters. Devil's-bit scabious, thrift, and sea and bladder campion grow wherever they can, as do some beautiful orchids, including the heath spotted, early purple, and the very rare frog orchid. Down on the rocks, scrambled over by hundreds of people each day, there are some plants that are so inconspicuous they probably go unnoticed by most visitors, but take a closer look: the black stripes on the rocks are tar lichens. The rock pools hide winkles, limpets, and the aptly-strange sea anemones, which look like plants growing underwater, but are in fact meat-eating animals.

WHERE ELSE TO SEE
VOLCANIC LANDSCAPES

Volcanic activity during the Palaeozoic era, 425 million years ago, led to the creation of Scotland's Caledonian mountains. Volcanoes were still erupting in western Scotland, around Mull, Skye, and St Kilda, during the Tertiary period, 2.5–65 million years ago, when The Giant's Causeway was formed.

Fingal's Cave, on the Hebridean island of **Staffa**, is made of basalt columns like the Giant's Causeway, and was formed in the same way, at the same time. **St Abb's Head**, Berwickshire, is another complex coastline of cliffs and offshore stacks formed by volcanoes that has outstanding wildlife. [SC]

The sandstone cliffs of **Fowlsheugh**, Aberdeenshire, have green volcanic extrusions, and the cliffs themselves include sections of volcanic stone. The area is home to over 150,000 birds in summer. [SC]

The area around **Ben Nevis** in Scotland is a huge volcanic complex. Ben Nevis – itself a volcanic outcrop – rises from Loch Linnhe like a huge granite whale-back, to a height of 1,344m (4,406ft). The Nevis gorge, to its south, contains remnants of the ancient Caledonian pine forest. [SC]

THROUGH THE YEAR
GIANT'S CAUSEWAY

In **autumn**, look for the bobbing heads of grey seals offshore. Ravens, buzzards, and peregrines will be out looking for prey, while smaller birds will be trying to avoid them as they forage for food among the cliffs, seashore, and grasslands.

In many ways, the stones can be enjoyed at their best in **winter**, when the summer crowds have gone and huge waves crash over the stepped stones. If you're feeling brave, you might want to visit the Carrick-a-rede rope bridge, near Ballintoy, where you can cross from the mainland to the island of Carrick some 30m (100ft) above the crashing waves, amid steep and scary cliffs.

Seabirds return to the cliffs in **spring**, including black guillemots and fulmars. A pair of choughs – rarely seen in Northern Ireland – breeds at the site. Look for early spring flowers along the cliff paths, and emerging animals – Irish hares, foxes, badgers, rabbits, and stoats all live along this coast.

Main: Spectacular scenery combines with myth and legend to make The Giant's Causeway awe-inspring.

Above and below: Oyster plants grows on the shingle near the sea; Scots lovage grows only in Scotland and here, in Northern Ireland.

Left panel (inset and below): The Giant's Boot, in legend cast off by the mythical Finn MacCool; the Chimney Stacks are a number of columns separated from the cliffs by erosion.

Below: Little rock pipits flit among the giant rocks of the Causeway.

JAN
FEB
MAR
APR
MAY
JUN
JUL
AUG
SEP
OCT
NOV
DEC

WHERE
Cornmill Meadows Dragonfly Sanctuary,
Abbey Gardens, Waltham Abbey,
Essex EN9 1XQ;
www.leevalleypark.org.uk

CONTACT
Lee Valley Park rangers, tel: 01992 717711;
info@leevalleypark.org.uk

GETTING THERE
By car, exit the M25 at junction 26 and join
the A121; go straight through several sets
of traffic lights, then turn left at the next
roundabout into the car park for Abbey
Gardens. By rail, travel to Waltham Cross,
Cheshunt, or Broxbourne. Bus numbers 211,
212, 213, 240, 250, 251, and 505 all stop
at Cornmill Meadows.

ACCESS AND FACILITIES
The sanctuary has full wheelchair and
pushchair access, and full-access toilets.
There is a picnic site, and guided tours
can be arranged. Dogs are welcome.

OPENING TIMES
Open all year round.

CHARGES
None.

Below the surface

Dragonflies and damselflies lay their eggs on
aquatic plants; these hatch into nymphs (*above*)
that live underwater for 1–3 years, feeding on
minnows, tadpoles, and aquatic insects. They are
ambush predators, hiding by underwater rocks
or leaves until prey swims close enough for the
nymph to grab it with its extendable jaws. When
it is ready to emerge, the nymph climbs up a leaf
from the water to the air, and waits until its outer
case dries and splits. The adult then emerges, and
gradually stretches out its glorious wings.

Above (left to right): Cornmill Meadows; brilliant emerald dragonfly.
Main: An emperor dragonfly laying its eggs.

DAZZLING DRAGONFLIES

█NSECTS ARE EXTRAORDINARY CREATURES. For many people they are just pests, but once you start to look at them carefully, it's hard not to become fascinated by their sculptured bodies, iridescent colours, and weirdly mechanical movements. Some of the most dazzling are the dragonflies and their smaller relatives, the damselflies; and one of the best places to see them is the Cornmill Meadows Dragonfly Sanctuary in the River Lee Country Park in Essex. This mosaic of wetland habitats provides a home for 21 of the 38 species that regularly breed in Britain, and if you visit on a sunny day in August you stand a good chance of seeing most of them.

Seeing dragonflies is one thing, but identifying them is not always so easy. The bigger, more powerful "hawkers" move very fast, displaying amazing agility as they loop and swerve through the air in pursuit of small airborne insects. There is little chance of noting their more subtle distinguishing features unless they land in front of you, but luckily some are unmistakable,

Damselflies and dragonflies are expert fliers, able to swerve, dive, and change direction instantly in order to catch other, slower, flying insects.

like the magnificent male emperor dragonfly with its kingfisher-blue body, and the brown hawker with its glowing amber wings. The difference between dragonflies and the closely related damselflies is subtle. Dragonflies are fast and aggressive; they perch with their wings held wide open, and have extremely big eyes that meet in the middle to create a helmet-like effect (*see emerald dragonfly, top right*). Damselflies, on the other hand, are smaller and more delicate; they perch with their wings folded back, and their smaller, spherical eyes are widely separated (*see blue-tailed damselfly, left*). Several of the smaller dragonflies spend a lot of time perched – as do the less frenetic damselflies – and this permits more leisurely inspection, especially if you have equipped yourself with a pair of close-range binoculars. Even without them, the paths through the Dragonfly Sanctuary will give you plenty of close views.

Inset: The fairy-like blue-tailed damselfly.
Below (left to right): Golden-ringed dragonfly; a pair of migrant hawker dragonflies.

THROUGH THE YEAR
CORNMILL MEADOWS

In **autumn** the Lee Valley Park, in which Cornmill Meadows is situated, attracts bitterns. The water birds come to avoid icy conditions further north, and stay over the winter. They are very elusive, but are regularly seen from the bittern watchpoint near the Fisher's Green visitor centre (*see pp.26–27*).

Throughout the **winter** the lakes provide a home for large numbers of waterfowl, which are in splendid breeding plumage at this time of year. In late winter, herons start breeding in the trees overlooking Hooks Marsh, near the Dragonfly Sanctuary.

Spring is when dragonflies start hatching. Look for drab brown nymphs climbing the stems of emergent plants, and check for their empty skins. The emergence takes some time, but you may see different insects at different stages of the process.

WHERE ELSE TO SEE
DRAGONFLIES AND DAMSELFLIES

Dragonflies and damselflies breed in still or slow-flowing fresh water, so they are usually associated with ponds, lakes, and wetlands. Damselflies stay close to water, but dragonflies range much more widely. Some species have a restricted distribution, but many are widespread throughout Britain.

One of the best sites for these insects is **Thursley Common** in Surrey (*see pp.128–129*), a heathland and acid bog that supports 26 breeding species. [SE]

Another good place to look is Crockford Bridge in the **New Forest** (*see pp.174–175*) in Hampshire, where a wide variety of species can be seen on a relatively short stretch of stream. [SE]

Upton Fen in Norfolk is an excellent site, with a waymarked trail taking you through habitats including ditches and pools, open fen, and woodland. [SE]

Plantain Loch in **Dalbeattie Forest**, Scotland, is a good place to look for northern species. The Bridge of Grudie by **Loch Maree** is also a fine example of a bog habitat. [SC]

Below: The broad-bodied chaser is found around ponds and lakes.

JAN

FEB

MAR

APR

MAY

JUN

JUL

AUG

SEP

OCT

NOV

DEC

THE BEAUTY OF THE LAKES

FRIARS CRAG IS THE PERFECT PLACE FOR FANS OF LITERATURE AND NATURE. This promontory jutting out into the wide-open space of Derwentwater in the Lake District has breathtaking views. The writer John Ruskin claimed it was "one of the three most beautiful scenes in Europe", while another literary giant, Arthur Ransome, immortalized the crag as "Darien" in his most famous book: *Swallows and Amazons*.

Friars Crag is also brilliantly accessible: the short path from Keswick town centre is suitable for everyone, whether walking or in buggies or wheelchairs. If you wish, you can then continue along the nature trail for another 5.6 km (3½ miles). The area is wonderful in the summer – you can see right across the water towards the dramatic "Jaws of Borrowdale" and to Cat Bells, or watch the incredible skies reflected in Derwent's mirror-glass waters. On closer inspection of the crystal-clear water, you'll soon realize that it contains some interesting wildlife.

WHERE
Friars Crag, Derwentwater, Keswick, Cumbria, CA12 5DJ; www.lake-district.gov.uk

CONTACT
Lake District National Park Authority; tel: 01539 724555; hq@lake-district.gov.uk

GETTING THERE
To reach Keswick by car, take junction 40 off the M6, and then take the A66 to Keswick. By train, travel to Penrith, and then take a bus (nos. X4, X5, or X50) to Keswick. You can walk to Friars Crag from the centre of Keswick, or park at Derwentwater's lakeside car park and walk from there. Walk past the theatre by the Lake to the shore, then take the wide path, keeping the lake to your right.

ACCESS AND FACILITIES
There are toilets in the lake-side car park; the key is held at the National Trust shop and information centre (this is closed in winter). The path to Friars Crag is partially paved in places and is suitable for wheelchairs and pushchairs; there are no steep slopes. Plenty of facilities of all types can be found in the town of Keswick.

OPENING TIMES
Open all year round.

CHARGES
For car parking.

Crayfish wars

Cumbria remains one of the last strongholds for the native white-clawed crayfish, which has been decimated by the North American signal crayfish (*shown above*). These escaped from captivity into British waters in the late 1970s, carrying spores of a fungal disease that is harmless to itself, but deadly to the white-clawed crayfish. As a last resort, conservationists are transferring native white-clawed crayfish to extremely remote bodies of water around the UK in the hope of protecting the species.

Main: The still surface of Derwentwater acts as a mirror.

Left (left to right): Otters are shy, but can sometimes be seen at the water's edge; signs of otter activity: prints in the soft mud.

Right (left to right): An osprey "catch" from the water is fast and dramatic; a migrant hawker dragonfly.

JAN

FEB

MAR

APR

MAY

JUN

JUL

AUG

SEP

OCT

NOV

DEC

Watch out for the native white-clawed crayfish that scuttle across the tea-coloured pebbles, and study the depths for a glimpse of the small and incredibly rare vendace fish, with its bluish-green back, white belly, and silvery flanks. Derwentwater and the adjacent Bassenthwaite Lake are the only two places in the UK where this fish occurs naturally. Otters are seen around the water's edge, although they quickly vanish on sensing human presence. In late summer, particularly August, you will be treated to a fantastic display of hawker dragonflies. Migrant and southern hawkers hover around the water, and if you're lucky, you might see a stunning golden-ringed dragonfly zoom by.

One of the most impressive birds you might spy over the water is the osprey. This rare, fish-eating bird of prey breeds nearby, and it hunts over the lake for fish below, snatching them from the water with its razor-sharp talons. From a distance ospreys are frequently mistaken for big seagulls, so it's worth taking a closer look at every large "gull" that flies close to the water.

WHERE ELSE TO SEE
LAKESIDE WALKS

There are lots of stunning places for gentle wildlife walks around water in Britain, both within nature reserves and around the countryside generally. Some are especially beautiful, tranquil, and teeming with wildlife.

The many other lakes of the **Lake District** offer wonderful views and a wide range of wildlife, often in very accessible settings. The gentle walk along the shores of Brotherswater from the Cow Bridge car park offers stunning views and hopefully a good collection of water birds, including a variety of duck species, grebes, and goosanders. [N]

Blashford Lakes Wildlife Reserve, in the New Forest (*see pp. 174–175*), has paths and a hide centred around flooded gravel pits. [SE]

The **Trentham Estate**, near Stoke on Trent, has a huge and beautiful lake, enlarged by Capability Brown in the 18th century, that is home to a large colony of herons. There are five walks around the park and woodlands. [M]

THROUGH THE YEAR
FRIARS CRAG

Although it's only a short walk to Friars Crag, it's surprising just how much wildlife you can see. In **autumn**, don't forget to look up into the trees by the shoreline, where tits form large feeding groups. Often, the first sign that they're around is their high-pitched call. Look out for Europe's smallest bird flying in with the flock; goldcrests are common here but are often hard to see.

During **winter**, you may see large flotillas of coots gathered on Derwentwater.

In **spring**, if you visit on a still, sunny spring day, you might be lucky enough to see the first emerging dragonflies and damselflies flying alongside the lake. The exquisite downy emerald dragonfly emerges in early May, but it is scarce. You're more likely to see the small, red common darter.

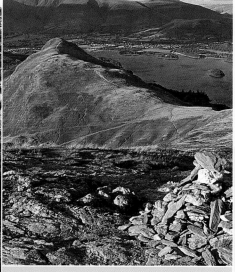

Above: Derwentwater viewed from Cat Bells, which derives its name from the Middle English *cat bield* – the lair of the wildcat.

Below: Friars Crag provides spectacular views over Derwentwater and, in the distance, the hill country of the Lake District.

Below: Enjoying the Friars Crag walk in autumn.

SEAL-SPOTTING PARADISE

TWO SPECIES OF SEAL BREED IN BRITAIN: THE GREY AND THE COMMON SEAL. The common seal is not the commonest species in the UK, and its alternative name of harbour seal is certainly more appropriate in Scotland, where it is found along the west coast; but in eastern England it is more often found on estuaries and sand flats. Pupping takes place ashore. Common seals, which breed in summer, can use sand flats as the pups can swim almost as soon as they are born. Grey seals are born in winter and cannot swim until they shed their first white coat after two or three weeks, before which they must remain out of the water.

Both species spend much of their time when not feeding hauled out on beaches, often in mixed species groups. Blakeney Point on the north Norfolk Coast is one such haul-out spot, and some 500 seals of the two species can be found here during the summer. You can see them from seal-watching boat trips from Morston and

WHERE
Blakeney Point, Blakeney, North Norfolk, NR25 7NW; www.nationaltrust.org.uk

CONTACT
Norfolk Coast Office, tel: 01263 740241; blakeneypoint@nationaltrust.org.uk

GETTING THERE
Blakeney Point is 8km (5 miles) from Wells-next-the-sea on the North Norfolk coast. Park at Cley-next-the-sea and walk to the Point from Cley beach car park (5km/3 miles), or at Morston Quay and take a boat (times depending on tides). The nearest train station is Sheringham; from there take the Coasthopper bus to Cley or Morston. Both are on National Cycle Network Route 30.

ACCESS AND FACILITIES
Boat trips either make a round trip without disembarking, or allow for an hour or two exploring on the Point. The sand and shingle terrain is inaccessible by wheelchair. There are refreshments and toilets at Morston car park and at the Old Lifeboat Station on the Point (closed September–April). Some areas of the Point are out of bounds during the bird breeding season (April–August).

CHARGES
Car parking charges apply (NT members park free at Morston); the seal trip firms all charge the same or very similar rates.

Above: A common tern fiercely guards her chick.

Main: Both seal species bask sociably together on Blakeney Point.

Right panel (top to bottom): Low tide reveals wider stretches of sand and shallow pools inhabited by small marine creatures including the common starfish; a grey seal, with its long muzzle giving it an often mournful expression; a common or harbour seal looks perkier than a grey, with its rounder head and more cat-like, tip-tilted nose.

Below: Sea campion grows on the shingle bank.

Seeing seals up close

Seal-watching boat trips run from Morston and Blakeney quays from February until the end of October. This can be a wonderful way of seeing seals up close, and in their natural habitat – especially for children. You are likely to see seals basking on the sandbanks at the end of the Point, as well as some swimming through the sea – often up to the boat itself. You can identify the grey seals by their longer, more pointed heads, and their parallel nostrils; common seals have a more rounded face, and V-shaped nostrils.

Blakeney, or by making the energetic 5km- (3 mile-) trek west from Cley-next-the-sea. In the past, common seals predominated on the Point, but things are changing: it has now been more or less abandoned for pupping, and grey seals are on the increase. These two facts may not be unrelated, as grey seals tend to pack very tightly and could eventually displace the smaller common seals.

The Point also hosts important breeding colonies of water birds, especially terns. Sandwich, common, little, and a few Arctic terns wheel screechily around, plunge-diving and feeding their raucous chicks. Locally breeding ringed plovers and oystercatchers congregate at high tide, mingling with the returning Arctic waders, whose numbers increase daily at this time of year. If you go ashore, look out for the fading flowers of the shingle plants: yellow horned poppy, sea campion, and biting stonecrop. On the adjacent saltmarshes, look for the dense thickets of shrubby sea-blite, and several species of sea-lavender, including the rare matted sea-lavender.

WHERE ELSE TO SEE
SEAL COLONIES

Hauled-out grey seals can be seen in several parts of Britain, especially on northern and western coasts. Common seals, in contrast, tend to be more dispersed, especially around the Scottish west coast. Many of their locations are served by boat trips, and this can be a great way to see the seals at close range.

Boat trips also run from **Hunstanton** in Norfolk to Seal Island, in The Wash, to see a large common seal colony – around 7 per cent of the UK total. [SE]

Grey seals predominate in western Scotland on the **Isle of May** (the largest British pupping site), the **Monach Isles** (*see pp.268–269*), and **Treshnish Islands**. Scottish colonies of common seals live on **Dornoch Firth**, **Firth of Tay**, and **Skye**. [SC]

The **Farne Islands** (*see pp.126–127*) have one of Europe's largest grey seal populations. [N]

Donna Nook in Lincolnshire is one of the most accessible sites for seeing breeding seals. [M]

The seals live here all year round, so close-up views from the seal boats are guaranteed.

THROUGH THE YEAR
BLAKENEY POINT

Autumn brings seabirds close in to Blakeney Point. Skuas and shearwaters pass in numbers, together with a few Sabine's gulls and other scarce species. After easterly winds, the shrubby sea-blite can be teeming with smaller migrants, including Siberian rarities such as Richard's and olive-backed pipits.

In **midwinter**, the marshes behind the Point play host to hordes of wildfowl, including dark-bellied brent geese and wigeons, often in large flocks. Along the drift-line of the shingle bank, look out for flocks of snow buntings and smaller parties of shore larks, feeding unobtrusively among the debris.

The noisy arrival of the breeding terns is a sure sign that **spring** has sprung. When the winds come from the southeast, it can be a migrant hotspot, with wheatears and whinchats, and perhaps a gem of a bluethroat around the cover of the sea-blite scrub.

Below: The male sandwich tern offers fish to the female during courtship.

JAN

FEB

MAR

APR

MAY

JUN

JUL

AUG

SEP

OCT

NOV

DEC

Left (left to right): Harriers hunt over the moorland; brown trout live in the peatland lochs and rivers.

Right (left to right): The peak of Morven dominates the peatlands; common butterwort flowers in August.

Below right: Golden plovers nest in large numbers around the peatlands of Forsinard.

WHERE
RSPB Forsinard Flows, Forsinard, nr Thurso, Highland, KW13 6YT; www.rspb.co.uk

CONTACT
Tel: 01641 571225; forsinard@rspb.org.uk.

GETTING THERE
Forsinard lies on the A897, 38km (24 miles) north of Helmsdale. From Melvich on the north coast, turn south 3.2km (2 miles) east of Melvich on to the A897 for 22.5km (14 miles). There is no bus to Forsinard but Highland Council subsidize a taxi service from Thurso, Bettyhill, and Melvich; book in advance on 01641 541297.

ACCESS AND FACILITIES
The visitor centre at Forsinard railway station has car parking and cycle racks, and good access, with ramps. Toilet facilities accommodate all users' needs. The public road allows for observing the nearby countryside. The Dubh Lochan Trail is a 1.6km (1 mile) circular route on to the bog, with a stepping-stone-style flagstone surface, unsuitable for pushchairs and wheelchairs.

OPENING TIMES
The reserve is open at all times; the visitor centre is open daily from Easter to October, 9am–5.30pm.

Caught in a trap
One of the most interesting plants on British peat bogs is the insect-eating sundew plant. Its Latin name, *Drosera*, means "dewy", referring to the sticky droplets of mucilage that cling to its leaf hairs and never dry out. The plants rely on insects to supply vital nutrients that are not available from the ground. The sundew catches an unlucky insect with its sticky hairs, enfolds around it, then secretes enzymes to digest the insect and release the essential nutrients.

Main: The lochs and lochans are an important feature of blanket bogs and esssential to their flora and fauna.

ANCIENT BOG LAND

WHEN THE PURPLE HEATHER BLOOMS IN AUGUST, and the sun glints on the small, still peatland pools, the vast prehistoric landscape of the Flow Country is a magnificent sight. This immense peatland blanket, lying between Caithness and Sutherland, is the largest area of blanket bog in the UK, and perhaps the world. If you love wild and remote places, this is undeniably the place for you.

The area came to ecological prominence in the 1980s when it became clear that government tax incentives had encouraged commercial conifer plantations on the irreplaceable peat bogs. This was stopped, and the challenging task of removing conifers and restoring the peatlands began. Thousands of ditches that had drained the life from these wet bogs were dammed, and thousands of alien trees uprooted. Gradually the sphagnum moss and the heather are reclaiming the land, and returning it to wildlife-rich peatland flows.

Waxcap fungi are named for the waxy surface of their caps, or fruiting bodies, although many are more sticky, greasy, or slimy to the touch. Some have an aroma of honey, while others are more acrid. Some waxcaps are dull-coloured, but most are bright red, orange, or yellow, or delicate shades of pink or violet. Their common names are almost as exotic as their colours, which they reflect: snowy waxcap, citrine waxcap, vermilion waxcap, and scarlet waxcap. The parrot waxcap gets its name from its feathered green and yellow coloration; the date waxcap is brown; while the ballerina (or pink) waxcap is a delicate pink, just like a classical ballerina's tutu.

There are over 40 different waxcap species in Britain, although many have become rare as the old, unspoilt grasslands that they need are left ungrazed – allowing tall vegetation to invade – or ploughed up, "improved" with artificial fertilizers, or built upon. But still the waxcaps persist, in small numbers, making an exciting find for those willing to search for their rainbow colours.

WHERE ELSE TO SEE
WAXCAP FUNGI

Look for waxcaps where the grass is kept short and contains plenty of moss. As well as areas of ancient grassland like Blaenavon, some of the best sites for waxcaps are old, unspoiled lawns, such as those surrounding ancient monuments and stately homes. Many old churchyards and cemeteries have good populations of waxcaps too.

Downe House, Kent, where Charles Darwin spent most of his life, has large numbers of ballerina waxcaps. [SE]

Windsor Great Park (*see pp.258–259*) is home to waxcaps and other scarce fungi, ancient trees, rare beetles, deer, and a wide variety of birds. [SE]

Waxcaps are generally more abundant in the wetter western parts of Britain. Good waxcap grasslands in southwest England include **Stonehenge**, Wiltshire, and **Knightshayes Court**, Devon. [SW]

Farther north, try the grasslands of **Blencathra**, Cumbria, an area rich in fungi. [N]

THROUGH THE YEAR
BLAENAVON

Sometimes the above-ground fruiting bodies of the waxcaps appear outside the traditional mushroom-hunting period of autumn. They may be seen as early as June, especially after an extensive period of rainfall, and can also linger for longer, even well into **winter**, in milder years. It is increasingly possible to find a display in late December.

In **spring**, look out for linnets, Dartford warblers, and red grouse on the heathland; lapwings, grey partridges, and yellowhammers in the grassland; and reed buntings in the blanket bog.

From late May to early August, a very local insect, the scarce blue-tailed damselfly, flies around the pools on the bogland. You should also look out for the rare great crested newts that breed in the ponds in spring and **summer**, and the otters that hide there.

Below: The scarlet waxcap only grows in "unimproved" short grassland.

JAN
FEB
MAR
APR
MAY
JUN
JUL
AUG
SEP
OCT
NOV
DEC

WHERE
Ariundle Nature Reserve, Strontian, Argyll, Scotland PH36; www.snh.org.uk

CONTACT
Reserve Manager, Scottish National Heritage, tel: 01397 704716; enquiries@snh.gov.uk

GETTING THERE
Heading north from Glasgow, take the A82 from Stirling to the Corran Ferry; turn left off the ferry on to the A861 towards the small village of Strontian. Follow the Forestry Commission signs to Airigh Fhionndail car park, 3.2km (2 miles) north of Strontian. Access the reserve via a track, which also forms part of the Strontian River Trail, leading to the reserve's nature trail.

ACCESS AND FACILITIES
There are no facilities other than information boards. The forest trail is 3km (5 miles) long and takes around two-and-a-half hours to walk. There is a teashop nearby, or you can find facilities in Strontian, the nearest town.

OPENING TIMES
Open all year round.

CHARGES
None.

The chequered skipper

The jewel in the crown of Ariundle is a small chocolate-brown butterfly called the chequered skipper. It used to occur throughout the British Isles, but now only survives in a few places in Scotland. Its favourite habitat is broad-leaved woodland next to grasslands rich with purple moor-grass, which is essential to successful breeding. The caterpillar pulls a tube of the moor-grass around itself, before hibernating in a tent of the grass's leaf blades. Look out for the butterfly's fast, darting flight.

Above (left to right): Small bonnet fungi grow through mosses on oak trunks; fruticose lichen; ferns grow from tree trunks and branches.
Main: The green carpeting over boulders and wood in Ariundle is made up of rare mosses and liverworts.

PREHISTORIC ADVENTURE

S TEPPING INTO THE ARIUNDLE FOREST is like taking a step back in time. This damp, moss-covered oak forest is reminiscent of a time when dinosaurs hunted and pterosaurs soared in the skies. Ariundle Nature Reserve is part of the larger Sunart woods, one of Britain's finest examples of ancient Atlantic oakwoods, and the last remnant of the native forest that once covered most of the west coast of Scotland. The prehistoric feel comes in part from the thick carpet of mosses, lichens, and liverworts that cling to almost every surface. As these plants don't have roots – they take in water and minerals through their leaves and stems instead – the clean sea air and damp climate present ideal conditions for them to thrive. Collectively they are called the "Lower Plants" and a staggering 500 species of moss, liverwort, and lichen have been recorded here. As you walk through you'll see ferns hanging, like epiphytes in tropical rainforests, from the mossy branches. And in the dwindling light, gnarled tree trunks take on magical shapes; you can

The cool, clean, clear, and wet environment of the Scottish Atlantic woodlands has led them to be described as "temperate rainforests".

almost convince yourself that you have, in fact, spotted a prehistoric creature.

The predominant trees in Ariundle are sessile oaks, but there are many other native trees scattered throughout the forest. Hazel, birch, and rowan are typical examples, whereas larch and beech have been introduced. It's not surprising that, with the impressive list of deciduous trees here, autumn is a good time to visit. As well as the myriad autumn colours throughout the forest, many trees are fruiting. Rowans are laden with berries, while hazels attract squirrels with their crop of nuts.

The best time to try to find Ariundle's shyest creatures is dawn and dusk. Listen out for the squeak of a shrew or pipistrelle bat. If you're very, very lucky you might chance upon a pine marten or a wildcat; but you're more likely to see the white rump of a roe deer as it vanishes like magic into the forest.

Inset: The distinctive leaves of the sessile oak in their autumn colours.
Below (left to right): Roe deer with fawn; wildcats live here but are rarely seen.

WHERE ELSE TO SEE
NATIVE FOREST

Scotland is thought to have lost 99 per cent of its native forests, but those that remain are testimony to the vital ecosystems they supported.

Knapdale Forest, Lochgilphead, is an ancient Caledonian forest situated in a National Scenic Area. It has an interesting mix of animals, including red squirrels, wildcats, pine martens, and otters. Its birds include black grouse, ospreys, peregrines, and golden eagles. [SC]

Glen Nant National Nature Reserve is a small remant of the extensive native forests that once dominated the Scottish Highlands. The mixed woodlands are mainly oak and birch, with ash, elm, and hazel in the more fertile, sheltered areas. [SC]

The sessile oaks of the **Wood of Cree** are intermixed with hazel, rowan, birch, ash, and willow. This RPSB reserve has many breeding songbirds, including redstarts and pied flycatchers; butterflies include purple hairstreak and Scotch argus, and there are otters along the river. [SC]

THROUGH THE YEAR
ARIUNDLE NATURE RESERVE

In **winter** you can clearly see the epiphytes and bryophytes (liverworts, lichens, mosses, and more) that grow on the ancient trees. The bare trees also give you a better chance of spotting some of Ariundle's mammals, especially badgers.

A walk around the looping forest track in early **spring** gives you a very different experience. Lesser celandine, wood anenome, and primrose are among some of the early flowerers. Overhead, many species of birds call out their territorial songs, especially the woodland specialists, such as wood and willow warblers.

Butterflies and moths abound in the forest in **summer** – there are over 200 species of moth here. Watch out especially for the chequered skipper butterfly (*see box, far left*) and the small pearl-bordered fritillary. The northern emerald dragonfly can be found around Sunart Loch.

Below: Willow warblers visit Ariundle in spring.

JAN
FEB
MAR
APR
MAY
JUN
JUL
AUG
SEP
OCT
NOV
DEC

BADGERS IN THE VALLEY

WITH LUSH, GENTLY UNDULATING PASTURES, STEEP HILLSIDES and stunning panoramic scenery, it's not surprising that many call the Cotswolds the most beautiful place in England. The whole of the Cotswolds is classed as an Area of Outstanding Natural Beauty (AONB), but there's one area in particular that stands out, especially for nature: the sumptuous Slad Valley, immortalized in Laurie Lee's *Cider with Rosie*. Of the five beautiful valleys that surround Stroud, the Slad Valley – a treasure trove of wildlife habitats – is probably the least spoilt, and as a consequence it is one of the best places in the UK to watch badgers.

Badger-watching trips run throughout the year in the Slad Valley, and they are certainly the best way to guarantee seeing these shy and elusive animals. Expect some strange requests from the trip organizers: you'll be asked to avoid wearing perfume or deodorant. Badgers live in family groups of around 14 animals, called clans,

WHERE
The Slad Valley is centred around Slad, near Stroud, Gloucestershire, GL6 7QA; www.visitthecotswolds.org.uk
www.gloucestershirewildlifetrust.co.uk

CONTACT
To find out how you can see the Slad Valley badgers, contact The Gloucestershire Badger Group: www.badgerland.co.uk
For everywhere else, contact The Badger Trust: www.badger.org.uk
Snows Farm nature reserve is run by the Gloucestershire Wildlife Trust.

GETTING THERE
By car, take the Stroud to Slad road (B4070). Stroud has a rail and bus station.

ACCESS AND FACILITIES
Trip organizers will supply details of meeting points, parking etc. For general visits to the area, the Slad Valley Wildlife Way is a five-hour walk that takes you right through the valley. The walk begins at the Bulls Cross layby on the B4070, near Frith Wood, where there is car parking. There are no facilities on the walk or in the valley outside of villages.

OPENING TIMES
Open all year round.

CHARGES
None.

Looking for badgers

Badger watching can be fantastically frustrating, but there are a few easy things you can do to increase your chances. Look for holes into the ground with D-shaped entrances that are at least 20cm (7½in) wide. Ignore any with bones nearby, as these are likely to be fox holes. Look for fresh muddy tracks from the sett entrances. Badger tracks are wider than dog or fox tracks, and have five small pads (with claw marks) on top of a larger, kidney-shaped pad, while fox tracks have four pads on top of a smaller pad.

Main: An adult badger foraging in the Slad Valley in autumn.

Left: The rolling landscape of the Cotswolds.

Right (left to right): Badgers playing; young badgers looking for worms, their favourite food.

Right panel (top and bottom): The badger sett hole is D-shaped, with the flat edge at the bottom; a badger drinking from a river.

that do a lot of rubbing and scratching. This is to cover each other and their territory in their own special clan scent or musk. For an animal whose primary sense is smell, these scents are vital. Any unusual smells will send the badgers into hiding. In September you'll see the badgers preparing for winter, dragging fresh bedding down into their tunnels. These animals are quite particular about where they make their underground homes – they need fairly soft soils for excavating setts, ample forest for cover, and rich feeding areas nearby – just the kind of habitat found around the Slad Valley. You'll notice that these opportunistic feeders seem to eat almost anything, from other mammals to insects, frogs, and fruit, although their favourite food is worms. Sometimes you can spot badgers feeding on more open areas with short grass, such as the nearby Snows Farm nature reserve, where the worms are easier to find. This reserve is well worth visiting for its 300 species of plants, especially in September, when you'll be able to see the late-flowering autumn gentian.

WHERE ELSE TO SEE
BADGERS

Badgers can be found in all of Britain's counties, although they are less common in East Anglia and most common around the southwest. The locations of badger setts are not publicized, to protect them from persecution.

The best way to see badgers is to join one of the 100 or so badger groups around the country, that are interested in studying and protecting badgers. They will know the places and times that are most likely to result in seeing badgers. Contact The Badger Trust, based in East Grinstead: www.badger.org.uk or your local wildlife trust via www.wildlifetrusts.org

The **Falls of Clyde** Scottish Wildlife Trust reserve in New Lanark [SC] organizes badger-watching evening expeditions, as does **Dalby Forest** visitor centre near Thornton-le-Vale in Yorkshire [N]. Visitors to **Clumber Park** in Cheshire [N] in search of nightjars at dusk (*see pp.118–119*) may also spot badgers.

THROUGH THE YEAR
THE SLAD VALLEY

Early **winter** is a great time to look for fungi. Frith Wood has over 100 species, including a variety of waxcaps. It's also a good time to go on night walks – the valley is home to one of the country's rarest bats: the greater horseshoe bat.

Spring is the best time of year to visit the valley if you want to see wild flowers. Badger cubs are born in January or February, but they don't leave the sett until around April. Watching cubs emerge nervously from the sett, then quickly losing themselves in the important business of play, is utterly enchanting.

Summer is the time to see the Slad Valley's orchid species. Visit Swifts Hill, also known as Elliott Reserve, in early June, and you're likely to see up to 11 species of orchid, including the bee orchid and the last orchid to appear in late August: the beautiful ladies tresses. The nationally scarce musk orchid flowers on Painswick Hill in July. Butterflies and grasshoppers abound; look out for the rare stripe-winged and rufous grasshoppers at Swifts Hill or the even rarer Adonis blue butterfly at Rodborough Common.

A walk in the woods at dusk is made magical by the sight of these charming creatures.

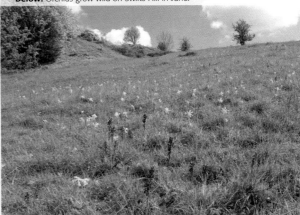

Below: Orchids grow wild on Swifts Hill in June.

JAN

FEB

MAR

APR

MAY

JUN

JUL

AUG

SEP

OCT

NOV

DEC

WHERE
RSPB Birsay Moors, Orkney Islands, Scotland;
www.rspb.org.uk

CONTACT
RSPB Birsay Moors, tel: 01856 850176;
orkney@rspb.org.uk

GETTING THERE
By road the reserve is west of Evie on the
A966. The B9057 (Hillside Road), between
Evie and Dounby, cuts right through the
reserve. Buses stop at Evie, 3.2km (2 miles)
to the east of the reserve, and also in Dounby,
4.8km (3 miles) to the west. Durkadale is to
the west of Birsay Moors and extends to the
southern shore of the Loch of Hundland.

ACCESS AND FACILITIES
The reserve has car parks and a picnic area,
but no toilets or refreshments. The hide on
Burgar Hill is accessible to the disabled and
wheelchair users. Much of the reserve's best
bird life can be easily viewed from a car on
the hillside road (B9057) that runs between
Evie and Dounby.

OPENING TIMES
Open all year round.

CHARGES
None.

Harrier displays

When they move to their nesting grounds in
March, hen harriers perform a spectacular aerial
display, known as skydancing. The male bird
climbs steeply before somersaulting and diving
straight down. Females also display, but less
often. Another acrobatic behaviour is the food
pass, in which the male approaches with food
and the female flies beneath him, turning on to
her back or side and catching the prey with a
foot as he drops it.

Above (top to bottom): The remains of the
Norse settlement on the Brough of Birsay; Ring
of Brodgar – Orkney's neolithic standing stones.

Below: A group of feeding twite.

Right (top to bottom): A short-eared owl hunting;
the view over moorland habitat at Birsay Moors; the
Orkney vole was thought to have been introduced
to the island by Neolithic man.

Main: Cliffs on the Brough of Birsay, Orkney Islands.

ORKNEY ODYSSEY

ORKNEY IS AN ARCHIPELAGO OF 70 ISLANDS just 16 km (10 miles) north of mainland Scotland, where the
Atlantic Ocean swirls into the North Sea. A visit to this rugged wilderness, lashed by angry seas, always
leaves a lasting impression, not only because of the archipelago's remarkable Neolithic and Viking ruins, which
helped make Orkney a UNESCO World Heritage Site, but because of its outstanding landscape and wildlife.

There are few places in the UK that can boast such a mixture of bird habitats within such a small area as
the Orkneys. The area is a stronghold for divers, waterfowl, seabirds, raptors, and owls. A staggering 385 species
have been counted among the cliffs, moors, marshes, and heath, and even more remarkably, 116 are known to
breed here. In the heart of the largest island, known as Mainland, lies one of the UK's most northerly moors,
Birsay, which is a fabulous example of rough moorland teeming with wildlife.

Above: The flooded marshes of Orkney.

THROUGH THE YEAR
BIRSAY MOORS

Winter is a good time to see the communal roost of hen harriers at Durkadale, as well as visiting birds, such as great northern divers, long-tailed ducks, and Slavonian grebes.

Moorland nesting birds jostle and sing for territory in **spring**. Skylarks and meadow pipits perform their enthralling skyward display flights, while the eerie call of the curlews is never far away. Both Arctic and great skuas arrive back on territories and the red-throated divers return to the hill-top lochans to breed.

You need to take extra care if you're walking in **summer**. Great skuas – huge, dark birds that look like giant muddy seagulls – will dive bomb anything that gets too close. Also, from the Burgar Hill hide, you may be lucky enough to see red-throated diver chicks, which are present until the end of August.

WHERE ELSE TO SEE
NORTHERN MOORS

Northern moors are wondrous places of wild and windswept beauty.

Moine Mhor National Nature Reserve, Argyll, is one of the last wild, raised bogs left in Britain, where hen harriers and curlews can be seen hunting over the ancient hill fort of Dunadd. [SC]

Hatfield Moor, Yorkshire, is a remanant of the once-extensive Humberhead Levels; you're likely to see both hen and marsh harriers, and occasionally long-eared owls. [N]

Bleaklow, Derbyshire, is an eerie expanse of peat-covered moorland sitting about 600m (2,000ft) above sea level. Large eroded rocks sit among vast plateaus, divided by deep river valleys. Golden plovers, dunlins, and curlews live here, surrounded by cloudberry, hell heath, and the rare bog rosemary. [M]

Run by the RSPB, Birsay Moors reserve glitters with wildlife gems. Summer is a wonderful time to visit; the whole area is awash with wild flowers, including thrift and grass of Parnassus. If you're lucky, you may see the rare Scottish primrose still in flower in September, when male hen harriers are in their striking, pale-grey breeding plumage and the moor hums with insects, including the rare great yellow bumblebee. Towards the end of September, moorland berries, such as crowberry and bearberry, start to appear alongside the cheery purple flowers of devil's bit scabious.

In autumn, Orkney becomes a staging post for birds moving south from the Arctic; almost anything can turn up. Around 50,000 birds arrive on the shoreline, while whooper swans and greylag geese feed on open fields. This is a good time to see visitors such as the great northern diver, long-tailed duck, and Slavonian grebe. Durkadale in Birsay Moors – a sumptuous habitat of sedge meadows, reedbeds, willow scrub, and bog – is great place to watch raptors, especially hen harriers. By November you can see up to 25 harriers coming in to roost. Stand by the road at dawn or dusk, and be mesmerized as their dark silhouettes glide in silently.

JAN
FEB
MAR
APR
MAY
JUN
JUL
AUG
SEP
OCT
NOV
DEC

THE DARK HEART OF DARTMOOR

NESTLED IN THE MOUNTAIN PASS BETWEEN HOOKNEY and Hambledown Tor, amidst the rolling, windswept uplands of Dartmoor, Grimspound is one of the finest examples of a Bronze-Age settlement in the UK. At 450m (1,476ft) above sea level, it's easy to feel like you're part of the enormous skies; in fact, you're never far from the weather here. Mist, rain, fog, and snow can be upon you in minutes, sometimes all in the same day; the fickle weather and random areas of bog reinforce the exhilarating experience this lonely landscape offers.

Climb up Hookney Tor, from where you can look down on to the Grimspound remains: an enormous circular perimeter wall, at points 4.5m (15ft) thick, enclosing almost 1.6 hectares (4 acres) of land and the ruins of 24 dwellings. The ruins are so well preserved, it's possible to tell how the homes were constructed, and the outside wall – built either to keep predators out, or livestock in – seems to have used drystone-walling techniques.

WHERE
Grimspound, Dartmoor National Park, Newton Abbot, Devon TQ13 9JQ.

CONTACT
Dartmoor National Park Authority: 01626 832093; hq@dartmoor-npa.gov.uk

GETTING THERE
Grimspound hut circles and settlement are 9.6km (6 miles) southwest of Moretonhampstead; they are not signposted. By car, follow the B3212 for about 6km (4 miles) from Postbridge towards Moretonhampstead. When you reach Challacombe Cross, turn right into a road signposted "Widecombe In The Moor". Travel about 2km (1 mile) down this narrow road until you see a car-parking area to your right. By bus, take the Countybus no. 82. By rail, travel to Exeter, and take the no.82 Transmoor bus (this only runs on Sundays). If you are walking, follow the Two Moors Way.

ACCESS AND FACILITIES
There are no facilities on site. The path from the car park to the site is clear and well-worn, but not suitable for wheelchairs. There are facilities and an information centre at Postbridge, 6.4km (4 miles) away, including full-access toilets.

CHARGES
None.

Keeping the balance

Moorland can be deceptively fragile. Hazards such as overgrazing or irresponsible hiking can drastically upset the natural balance of the habitat. Dartmoor is an important breeding area for many birds, some of which are rare. Although fewer than 20 dunlin nest here, it is still the most southerly site in the whole world. Nationally important numbers of wheatears (*above*) also breed here, along with golden plovers and the rare ring ouzel. During the breeding season (March–July) it is essential to keep to the paths.

Main image: Granite rock outcrops at Grimspound.

Left: Dartmoor ponies were once used to haul tin mined on the moor.

Right (left to right): Red grouse amongst heather; acidic pools form within the ruins of the prehistoric hutments.

Right panel (top to bottom): Skylark; curlew; golden plover.

Most of the ruins of huts lie in the southern sector of the enclosure, and archaeologists believe that the outer huts were probably used for livestock and storage. Where once the Bronze Age farmers eked out a living on the moor, now a wonderful wildlife habitat abounds. Skylarks battle the winds, and low-flying red grouse skim the heather, calling – "go back, go back" – while our smallest raptor, the merlin, darts close to the ground to hunt for prey. In September many birds are "moulting" and hide themselves away, although you will see family groups of stonechats; some males develop sooty-black faces that cover their white cheeks. There are still some butterflies to be seen, such as speckled woods, large whites, brimstones, and the occasional small copper.

But still, it is the landscape that commands your attention. If you are on the moor as the swirling mists start to gather, as they often do, and the curlew utters its eerie call, it's all too easy to remember that the site inspired Sir Arthur Conan Doyle's terrifying *Hound of the Baskervilles.*

WHERE ELSE TO SEE
UPLAND HEATH

Dartmoor is one of the largest areas of upland heath in southwest England, and it is a unique combination of craggy tors, vast bogs, wild ponies, and massive tracts of colourful heathers. Other moors tend to offer a similarly interesting combination of habitat and history.

Exmoor (see pp.44–45), an old royal hunting forest, is home to threatened fritillary butterflies (including the heath, high brown, and marsh species), the rare whitebeam tree, and birds such as ring ouzels, curlews, stonechats, Dartford warblers, grasshopper warblers, and reed buntings. [SW]

If you're looking for a moorland walk with historical interest, **Bodmin Moor**, Cornwall is covered with interesting stone buildings, tombs, and memorials dating back 5,000 years. [SW]

For interesting ruins in wild spaces, visit King Arthur's Quoit – also known as **Trethevy Quoit** – near St Cleer, Cornwall. These huge, intriguing stones also date back to the Bronze Age. [SW]

THROUGH THE YEAR
GRIMSPOUND

In **winter**, the moors become difficult for animals – and walkers. Mist, rain, and even snow can come and go in minutes. The red grouse become increasingly territorial during winter. Lapwings and fieldfares brave the moors, under the watchful eyes of sparrowhawks, buzzards, and brown owls.

Heather and ling start to flower in **spring,** dominating the upland heath of the moor. You'll also notice bilberry, cross-leaved heath, and western gorse in the drier areas. The eggs of any breeding red grouse hatch in May and June, and the young fly after 12–13 days.

The Two Moors Way walking path becomes very busy in **summer**. Meadow pipits, stonechats, and skylarks chatter around the moor, while lizards bask in the sun. Foals of the Dartmoor ponies frolic on the grassland. Look out for the rare high brown fritillary butterfly, which lives in the bracken stands, and the green hairstreak butterly.

The curlew's haunting cry over Conan Doyle's "Grimspound Mire" sends a shiver down the spine.

Below: Dartmoor ponies enjoy the grassland just below the heath.

JAN
FEB
MAR
APR
MAY
JUN
JUL
AUG
SEP
OCT
NOV
DEC

Left: The brown, peaty Water of Tanar flows through the heathery moorland.

Right (left to right): Wild blaeberries are vital food for the capercaillie; funnel-tooth fungus; Glen Tanar supports the UK's largest population of Scottish crossbills.

Right below: The Scots pine was the main tree of the first wildwood to grow after the last Ice Age.

WHERE
Glen Tanar, Aboyne, Aberdeenshire AB34 5EU, Scotland; www.glentanar.co.uk

CONTACT
Glen Tanar Ranger Service, tel: 01339 886072; ranger@glentanar.co.uk

GETTING THERE
The reserve is 4.8km (3miles) southwest of Aboyne, across the River Dee; it is signposted off the B976 from Aboyne. There are buses between the reserve and Aboyne, and the nearest rail stations are Stonehaven and Aberdeen. The reserve is around one hour's drive from Aberdeen airport.

ACCESS AND FACILITIES
The Glen Tanar Visitor Centre at Braeloine has full-access toilets, parking, and information displays. There are no refreshment facilities but there are picnic areas. All-ability trails radiate out from the visitor centre: the red trail takes visitors on a circular loop along the waterway, through the pine forest, and across farmland.

OPENING TIMES
The reserve is open all year round. The visitor centre is open from 10am to 5pm daily except Tuesdays. Times vary in winter.

CHARGES
Car-parking charges only.

Capercaillie watching
This is one of the best places in the Highlands to see capercaillie, but make sure you don't disturb them while they display or feed, as their numbers are now so low in the UK that they are in danger of extinction. Follow the capercaillie Code of Conduct (see pp.66–67). You may also see black grouse among the scattered pines or where the forest abuts the moorland; if you want to watch them safely, follow the black grouse Code of Conduct (see pp.102–103).

Main: Glen Tanar is a Caledonian forest with areas of dry and wet heath, blanket bogs, and lochans, where otters can sometimes be seen.

CALEDONIAN DELIGHT

GLEN TANAR NATIONAL NATURE RESERVE EXTENDS UPWARDS into the mountains from the wooded valley of the Dee, on the southeastern flanks of the vast brooding massif of the Cairngorm Mountains. The reserve contains one of the largest and finest remaining stands of ancient native Caledonian Scots pine forest, and careful management has helped to create the best possible environment for its special animals, including the capercaillie.

The area's royal connections date back to 1852, when Queen Victoria and Prince Albert bought nearby Balmoral castle. Much of the heather moorland is managed for red grouse: bracken and heather are thinned or cleared to encourage the growth of blaeberry, which the grouse relies upon for food, both as an adult and as a chick, when it eats the caterpillars and other insects associated with the plants. The estate staff at Glen Tanar have also created thickets and brushwood shelters where the grouse can find shelter from harsh weather and predators.

Above: The bare trees of winter open up the skies for birdwatching.

This is one of the best places to explore the wonders of an ancient Caledonian Scots pine forest: the huge capercaillie, the Scottish crossbill, red squirrels, and Highland plants.

THROUGH THE YEAR
GLEN TANAR

Winter brings harsh conditions to Glen Tanar, and you'll need to take extra care if you are venturing on to the moor and mountains. Wildlife is sparse, apart from ptarmigan – now in their all-white winter plumage – and the occasional golden eagle.

Goshawks perform soaring and diving display flights above the trees in **spring**. Migrant birds include wheatears and ring ouzels on the moorland and redstarts in the woods. Woodcocks perform their slow-flying "roding" displays – males fly over the treetops at dusk and dawn, patrolling their territories, uttering strange croaking and sneezing sounds.

In **summer** the many rare wildflowers include the delicate pink, drooping, bell-shaped blooms of twinflower, and the spirals of white flowers of an endangered wild orchid: creeping lady's tresses.

WHERE ELSE TO SEE
HIGHLAND BIRDS

The whole of the Upper Deeside region is a superb place to see the special birds of the Highlands.

The high tops of the mountains around **Lochnagar**, overlooking the royal forest of Balmoral, have the greatest breeding density of one of the Highland's most special birds, the dotterel, and a few pairs of nesting snow buntings. Be careful to avoid undue disturbance. The 21km (13 mile) walk to the summit and back is for experienced hill-walkers only. [SC]

Just north of the A93, the **Davan** and **Kinnord** lochs are worth a visit in late autumn or winter for the whooper swans and thousands of greylag and pink-footed geese that winter there. [SC]

On the other side of the Cairngorms National Park, **Rannoch** (see pp.66–67) has all the birds of Glen Tanar, plus crested tits. Visit in spring or autumn, when it is less crowded than in summer. [SC]

This part of Scotland is also salmon-fishing country, and Glen Tanar – which flanks the upper reaches of the Tanar river and the Dee – is one of the best places to see salmon spawn in late autumn. The river also draws birds into the area, and you'll often see dippers and grey wagtails on the water, while siskins and Scottish crossbills feed in the pines. This is one of the best of all sites for crossbills, which may even be seen from the car park of the visitor centre. Red deer remain for much of the year on the higher ground, while roe deer roam the valley woodlands. The forest is rich in rare fungi, such as the scaly-tooth and goblet-scented spine fungi, which favour pine forests.

At the head of the glen, the Mount Keen area is a good place to look for ptarmigan, those high-altitude relatives of the red grouse. Up on the open mountains above the forest, look out for buzzards; there is also a good chance of seeing a merlin or a peregrine flashing past, or perching, perfectly still, on a rock. Scan the skies for hen harriers quartering the heather moorland, their wings forming a perfect "V". This region is also home to majestic golden eagles; watching them glide alongside a ridge or soar high into the skies is one of nature's finest sights.

JAN
FEB
MAR
APR
MAY
JUN
JUL
AUG
SEP
OCT
NOV
DEC

OCTOBER

Where to Go: **October**

A month of storms, lashing rain, and days of the most beautiful peace and stillness, coupled with splendid autumn colours. October has everything: it is arguably one of the finest times of the year for anyone who enjoys wildlife and rural landscapes. While most summer birds have gone – except perhaps for a few lingering swallows and chiffchaffs – vast numbers of new arrivals make up for their departure; we begin to see fieldfares, redwings, and the various geese and ducks of the coast. At Loch of Strathbeg, north of Aberdeen, more than 50,000 geese assemble, creating an awesome spectacle for people in the area, before moving further south, to Norfolk, just a few weeks later. This is a great month, too, for birds that simply pass through our islands, not

COAST

FLAMBOROUGH HEAD A classic east-coast seawatching point.

MOUNTAINS

CADER IDRIS A sublime and exhilarating landscape.

INLETS AND ESTUARIES

LOUGH FOYLE The vast mudflats provide rich pickings for birds.

FLAMBOROUGH HEAD
BRIDLINGTON, YORKSHIRE [N]

This is one of the best places in the UK to see small, perching birds in huge numbers on their migration. Exciting rarities may blow in, such as Pallas's warbler.
See pp.252–253

CADER IDRIS
GWYNEDD, NORTH WALES [W]

This majestic mountain rises abruptly from the land to give incredible views over the surrounding uplands. High glacial lakes are flanked by dizzying precipices.
See pp.254–255

LOUGH FOYLE
LONDONDERRY [NI]

Over 20,000 wildfowl visit this shallow sea inlet in October to take advantage of Ireland's milder weather. Threatened fish species such as allis shad swim in the lough's waters.
See pp.266–267

SHERINGHAM CLIFFS
NORTH NORFOLK [SE]

Soft, sandy material deposited during the last Ice Age makes up Sheringham's crumbly cliffs. This is an ideal place to watch for passing seabirds, and occasionally harbour porpoises.
See pp.252–253

Far below, you can see the U-shaped valleys of Snowdonia, carved by the massive weight of ice as the glaciers ground their way towards the sea.

SNOWDON
GWYNEDD, NORTH WALES [W]

Wales's highest mountain has everything, from dramatic views and a wide range of habitats and animals, to rare flowers, insects, and abandoned mines.
See pp.254–255

BANN ESTUARY
NORTH ANTRIM [NI]

This is a wonderful estuary for birds, especially wintering waders and wildfowl, with around 4,000 birds feeding on the mudflats in October.
See pp.266–267

SPURN POINT
KILNSEA, HUMBERSIDE [N]

There is a bird observatory at the Point to record the exceptional number of passage birds – but everyone can join in the fun, while sheltering in the dunes.
See pp.264–265

LOCH SPYNIE
ELGIN, MORAY [SC]

The special habitat surrounding this loch gives rise to rare aquatic flora. Its large roost of Icelandic greylag geese is astonishing to watch in October.
See pp.260–261

GLENCANISP FOREST
ASSYNT, SUTHERLAND [SC]

Canisp is an isolated mountain that rises out of the Glencanisp forest, close to the magnificent "pillar mountain" of Suilven, a renowned climbing challenge.
See pp.254–255

THAMES ESTUARY
KENT/ESSEX [SE]

This vast estuary is an important refuelling point for hungry migrating birds. Brent geese can be seen here in huge numbers.
See pp.252–253

The estuary is at its best at high tide, when waders roost on the saltmarsh close to shore, their outlines ghostly as the dusk deepens.

FILEY BAY
FILEY, EAST YORKSHIRE [N]

Walk along the seemingly endless sands of Filey Bay to the sheer cliffs of Filey Brigg, where you can join the bird observatory in watching large numbers of migrating birds.
See pp.264–265

THE LAKE DISTRICT
CUMBRIA [N]

The mountains and lakes of the Lake District are rich in wildlife in autumn, including red deer, golden eagles, red squirrels, and natterjack toads.
See pp.254–255

SLIMBRIDGE
GLOUCESTERSHIRE [SE]

Slimbridge is located on the edge of the Severn estuary, and it is a good place to see returning waders in autumn. Large flocks of starlings swirl in displays overhead.
See pp.256–257

Previous page: Autumn colour in Thetford Forest.

settling for the winter but hurrying on south; on the coast, especially, who knows what you might find in this annual rush – October is a time to see rarities from Siberia and even North America. It sees the real beginning, too, of the season for fungi enthusiasts: so many and so varied – mushrooms, toadstools, brackets, and puffballs appear everywhere, especially after rain.

They are a treat, but a challenge to your identification skills; find a good guide, and never eat any that you are unsure about. On the coast, the grey seals are giving birth to their white-coated pups. In Pembrokeshire, they give birth on secluded stony beaches, but in Lincolnshire, they can be seen on more accessible sandy shores. Be sure to give them respectful peace and quiet.

WOODLANDS

THE BIRKS OF ABERFELDY Red and orange leaves carpet the forest.

THE BIRKS OF ABERFELDY
PERTH AND KINROSS [SC]

Warm autumn colours are seen at their finest in this birch wood, which hugs the sides of the Moness Burn. Dippers dive for prey and fungi hide among fallen leaves.
See pp.262–263

DENDLES WOOD
DARTMOOR, DEVON [SW]

A wonderful stretch of upland, this oak-beech woodland lies to the south of Dartmoor National Park. It is rich in ferns, mosses, and lichens, and home to the UK's rarest bat, the barbastelle.
See pp.262–263

WINDSOR GREAT PARK
BERKSHIRE [SE]

Cranbourne Chase is Windsor's oldest wood, dating back some 400 years. In October, the woodland floor is covered in fungi, including the delicate purple amethyst deceiver.
See pp.258–259

EPPING FOREST
LONDON [SE]

Epping Forest is an ancient deciduous woodland that is designated a Site of Special Scientific Interest for its varied habitats and wildlife.
See pp.258–259

THE HERMITAGE
DUNKELD, PERTHSHIRE [SC]

The trail here leads you along the River Braan, through an ancient woodland rich in autumnal colour to a waterfall, gorge, and folly.
See pp.262–263

ISLANDS

MONACH ISLES Home to over 30,000 breeding grey seals.

THE MONACH ISLES
WESTERN ISLES [SC]

Grey seals can breed here without being disturbed by humans, and Monach's colony produces around 9,000 pups every year here in October.
See pp.268–269

STRANGFORD LOUGH
DOWNPATRICK, CO.DOWN [NI]

There are over 120 islands within the lough, including some that are important homes for wildlife. Bird island has 400 pairs of cormorants living on it in winter.
See pp.266–267

THE FARNE ISLANDS
NORTHUMBERLAND [N]

These rugged islands have a famous sea bird sanctuary and an internationally important colony of grey seals, with pups born every day in October.
See pp.268–269

As you approach the sandy beaches and dunes of the remote islands in October, a mass of bobbing seal heads rise to greet you.

PORTLAND BILL
DORSET [SW]

This is one of the best places in the UK to see the Balearic shearwater, a threatened bird, during the autumn migration.
See pp.252–253

WETLANDS

MARTIN MERE Huge flocks of pink-footed geese spend winter here.

MARTIN MERE
BURSCOUGH, LANCASHIRE [N]

This Wildfowl & Wetlands Trust site is famed for its overwintering wildfowl – by October it plays host to 1,000 whooper swans and 17,000 pink-footed geese.
See pp.256–257

During October thousands of geese, ducks, and swans converge on the low-lying marshes and lagoons of Martin Mere.

LOCH LEVEN
PERTH AND KINROSS [SC]

Lying just below the Lomond hills, the islands, lagoons, and reedbeds of this reserve fill with wild geese in October; the birds swoop in huge flocks as if choreographed.
See pp.260–261

MARSHSIDE
SOUTHPORT, LANCASHIRE [N]

The RSPB reserve here lies on the edge of the famous Ribble estuary, and has large roosts of pink-footed geese at dusk and dawn. Migrant hawker dragonflies patrol the ditches.
See pp.256–257

COTSWOLD WATER PARK
GLOUCESTERSHIRE [SE]

Britain's largest water park is great in autumn; head for Coke's Pit Nature Reserve, where you can see water voles and Daubenton's bats.
See pp.261–262

WHERE
Flamborough Head, Bridlington, Yorkshire
YO15 1AR; www.flamboroughuk.net

CONTACT
Bridlington Tourist Information, tel: 01262
673474; bridlington.tic@eastriding.gov.uk

GETTING THERE
By car, drive through Flamborough on the
B1255 and head out on the B1259. The
Head lies 3km (2 miles) east of the village.
By bus, catch the Bridlington–Speeton bus,
alighting at Flamborough. The nearest rail
stations are Bridlington and Bempton.

ACCESS AND FACILITIES
There are several car parks; the main
lighthouse car park has toilets, and a shop
and café with wheelchair access. The
headland terrain is difficult for wheelchair
users and pushchairs, but the Lighthouse,
North Landing, and South Landing car parks
all offer good viewpoints. Warning: stay well
clear of the crumbling cliff edges and under
no circumstances attempt to climb the cliffs
from the beaches below.

OPENING TIMES
Open all year round.

CHARGES
Yes, for the lighthouse car park. The
lighthouse is closed in the winter.

Getting your bearings
Seawatching needs patience, a comfortable
sitting position, shelter from the elements, and
a good deal of optimism. When you arrive, take
note of the main direction of bird movement,
then start scanning the sea with binoculars,
using a telescope if necessary when you spot
something. Be aware of the position of buoys,
ships, or other seamarks – these are essential to
point something out to fellow observers in the
vastness of the vista.

Above: The sooty shearwater's plumage is completely
dark, except for the pale flashes in its underwings.

Below: A pair of fulmars squabble on the cliffs.

Right panel (top to bottom): The cliffs of
Flamborough Head; little auks seem to have almost
no neck or beak, and endure the nickname of "flying
cotton bobbins".

Main: Flocks of sooty shearwaters and kittiwakes feeding off the coast of Flamborough Head.

SEAWATCHING OFF THE HEAD

SEAWATCHING IS AN ACQUIRED TASTE: IT MEANS AN AWFUL LOT of time doing just that – watching the
sea. But if birds are moving they can be in huge numbers, and the thrill lies in never quite knowing what will
come in with the wind. To give yourself the best chance of witnessing seabird movements, get out to sea on a boat
or visit one of our great coastal headlands, with an eye to the weather – onshore gales should blow birds towards
the land. Or wait until the wind has subsided and then watch as the displaced birds reorient themselves.

Flamborough Head is a classic east-coast seawatching point. Sightings of guillemots, kittiwakes, fulmars,
and gannets are guaranteed; with luck, there could be divers heading to their wintering grounds, and manx or
sooty shearwaters, not to mention a variety of other, rarer species sailing past or skimming the waves. Skuas
could be coasting south, especially in October, when storms often bring the rarest species, the long-tailed skua,

Above: Puffins breed on Flamborough Head in the spring.

THROUGH THE YEAR
FLAMBOROUGH HEAD

Seabirds are still moving through Flamborough in the **winter**. Divers are ever-present, often including a few great northern, and after an Arctic blast, the stream of little auks can number tens of thousands. The cliff-top stubble fields may hold a few snow and Lapland buntings among the skylarks.

Breeding seabirds return to the cliffs in **spring**, with guillemots and kittiwakes on the faces, and puffins in holes in the grassy slopes. Gannets are always offshore, moving to and from their nesting colony a few kilometres up the coast at Bempton Cliffs (*see pp.104–105*), in Yorkshire.

In high **summer**, with noisy nesting under way, the first shearwaters can appear as early as July. The cliff slopes are a riot of colour, with flowering red campion, kidney vetch, lady's bedstraw, and wild carrot, colourfully setting off the deep purple spikes of northern marsh orchid.

Flamborough Head is brilliantly placed for seabird watching – it juts out 10km (6 miles) into the North Sea, into the path of passing birds.

WHERE ELSE TO SEE
PASSING SEABIRDS

Go to any headland, and you have a good chance of seeing seabird movements. You will need binoculars or a telescope to see seabirds well; try to avoid looking into the light if you want to pick up any details of colour.

Classic sites include the numerous Cornish headlands, among them **Pendeen**, **Porthgwarra**, and **Lizard Point** (*see pp.116–117*). **Portland Bill** (*see pp.90–91*) in Dorset is one of the premier mainland sites to see the Balearic shearwater, a threatened bird. [SW]

Although lacking peninsulas, the north Norfolk coast can be productive for sightings of seabirds, especially the cliffs at **Sheringham**. [SE]

Southend Pier in Essex stretches 1.6km (1 mile) into the Thames Estuary and is well known for its terns and skuas. Seabirds also collect offshore around the cooling water outflows of the power stations at **Dungeness** (*see pp.162–163*) in Kent and **Sizewell** in Suffolk. [SE]

within sight. Watch out for the great skuas, too, who deploy their hit-and-run food-stealing tactics on victims as large as gannets. The first couple of hours of daylight often provide the most birds when you're seawatching, but the views are extraordinarily atmospheric in the evening, when the sunlight falls on the passing birds. Just beware of fog – the most convenient watchpoint is the cliff slopes below the foghorn, which can suddenly produce a deafening blast.

Scan the sea for groups of diving gannets – they gather when they have found a shoal of fish. This is a dramatic spectacle in its own right, but those same fish might also attract other predators, especially harbour porpoises, often in surprising numbers: 10, 20, or more.

In October Flamborough also welcomes migrating songbirds. The hedges and bushes in an otherwise windswept landscape become a magnet for birds that have just made landfall after crossing the North Sea. Hawthorn berries are greedily devoured by redwings and fieldfares, and perhaps a ring ouzel or two, while the more skulking warblers, deep in the gorse, could include anything from a barred warbler to that diminutive jewel of Siberia: the Pallas's warbler.

JAN
FEB
MAR
APR
MAY
JUN
JUL
AUG
SEP
OCT
NOV
DEC

THE GIANT'S THRONE

I T MAY NOT BE THE HIGHEST MOUNTAIN IN WALES, but Cader Idris is certainly one of the most impressive. Towering 893m (2930ft) above the Mawddach estuary on the mid-Wales coast, its long, rocky ridge is all the more spectacular for rising virtually from sea level. The majesty of its skyline is more than matched by the magnificence of the view from its summit, which on a clear day takes in the sea off Barmouth, the mountains of Snowdonia, and, nearer to hand, some of the most dramatic upland terrain in Britain.

This is a landscape carved by ice. During the last Ice Age, glaciers scooped away the slopes of the mountain to form crater-like corries or cwms, now occupied by high glacial lakes such as Llyn Cau and Llyn y Gadair. The cwms are divided by the narrow ridge that forms the long spine of Cader Idris, flanked by dizzying precipices. Far below can be seen the deep U-shaped valleys carved by the massive weight of ice as the glaciers ground their way

WHERE
Cader Idris National Nature Reserve, Dolgellau, Gwynedd, LL40 2HZ, Wales; www.snowdonia-npa.gov.uk

CONTACT
Snowdonia National Park Authority, tel: 01766 770274.

GETTING THERE
Cader Idris lies at the southern end of the Snowdonia National Park. Dolgellau is the nearest town. Travel out of Corris and Corris Uchaf on the A487 and take a left on to B4405 signposted Tywyn.

ACCESS AND FACILITIES
There is free parking, but no facilities, other than toilets and a visitor centre. Cader Idris is most easily climbed by the Pony Path, which starts 3.2km (2 miles) southwest of Dolgellau, from the car park at Ty-nant, near Llyn Gwernan. It leads to the highest point, Penygadair. There is a steeper route from Minffordd in the Tal-y-llyn valley, from the Dôl Idris car park near the junction of the A487 and the B4405 Dolgellau to Tywyn road.

OPENING TIMES
Open all year round. The visitor centre has a reduced service during winter.

CHARGES
None.

Mountain flora

The sheer cliffs and crags of Cader Idris provide refuges for specialized plants that flourish in the harsh conditions. They include purple saxifrage (*above*) and dwarf willow, both more commonly seen in the Arctic, as well as the dense green cushions of moss campion, with its small pink flowers. These "Arctic-alpines" are relics of the late Ice Age, when the ice sheets had retreated but the region was still half-frozen tundra. They are on the edge of their range in mid Wales and their survival may be threatened by climate change.

Above: The mountain slopes are said to form the *cader* (chair) from which the mythological giant Idris surveyed the land.

Left: Waterfall in Cwm Amarch on Cader Idris.

Right (left to right): Looking across the Llyn Cau lake; a hovering hen harrier.

Right panel (top to bottom): Meadow pipit; purple heather.

towards the sea some 20,000 years ago, now occupied by bright-green pastures, sinuous rivers, and the glittering Tal-y-llyn lake. Everywhere there are relics of the glaciation, with ice-scoured rocks and piles of rocky debris left by the ice when it finally melted away.

Above the valley floors, vivid-green farmland gives way to the darker hues of heather, moor grass, and bare rock, enriched in October by glowing autumn colour. Meadow pipits flushed from the grass flutter erratically into the air with thin, sharp cries of alarm, while overhead a deep croaking call may betray the dark, ragged form of a raven. If you are lucky you may see a merlin darting low in pursuit of a smaller bird – meadow pipits are among its favourite prey – or a hen harrier floating buoyantly over the rough grass as it searches for small animals. Many of these birds will move to more sheltered lower ground as autumn hardens into winter, but while the weather holds they stay on, as if reluctant to abandon this sublime and exhilarating landscape.

As summer's vegetation fades, the bare bones of a 20,000-year-old landscape are revealed.

WHERE ELSE TO SEE
GLACIATED LANDSCAPES

There are many other regions of Britain that offer a similar experience and equally graphic evidence of our Ice-Age past.

Elsewhere in the Snowdonia National Park in North Wales, the landscape around **Snowdon** (*see pp.172–173*) is equally spectacular, with similar mountain flora that includes the Snowdon lily, found nowhere else in Britain. [W]

The valleys of the Lake District, formed by glaciers that radiated from a central dome of ancient rock like the spokes of a wheel, now contain lakes of limpid beauty. [N]

The Scottish Highlands were so deeply buried by ice that only the highest peaks remained exposed. The rest was stripped of all soft rock, creating the largely barren terrain of regions like **Glencanisp Forest** in Wester Ross. [SC]

Strangford Lough in Northern Ireland (*see pp.288–289*) is dotted with low, rounded drumlins – islands shaped by the moving ice sheets. [NI]

THROUGH THE YEAR
CADER IDRIS

While the autumn often provides the clear skies essential to the most rewarding ascent of Cader Idris, this dramatic landscape retains its breathtaking beauty year-round.

Winter can be a dangerous time to climb any mountain, owing to the hazards of ice and exposure, but for the experienced it can provide a memorable insight into the elemental forces that shaped this landscape.

Spring is superb for both flowers and birds, with ravens frequently seen tumbling through the sky in their aerobatic courtship displays. Watch too for the ring ouzel, a summer visitor that resembles a blackbird with a white chest.

In **summer** the mountain can be surprisingly popular, but heading east away from the summit towards Mynydd Moel soon leaves the crowds behind.

Below: The summit of Cader Idris in winter.

JAN

FEB

MAR

APR

MAY

JUN

JUL

AUG

SEP

OCT

NOV

DEC

WHERE
Martin Mere Wetland Centre, Fish Lane, Burscough, Lancashire L40 0TA; www.wwt.org.uk

CONTACT
Martin Mere Wetland Centre, tel: 01704 895181; info.martinmere@wwt.org.uk

GETTING THERE
The Wetland Centre lies 9.5km (6 miles) from Ormskirk. It is signposted from junction 8 of the M61, junction 3 of the M58, and junction 27 of the M6. The nearest train stations are New Lane and Burscough Bridge; both are within walking distance, around 3km (2 miles) away along signposted paths. A bus service runs from Ormskirk bus station.

ACCESS AND FACILITIES
The visitor centre has a large viewing area, with a range of facilities. The reserve is very wheelchair-friendly: all trails and hides are accessible. There are 10 hides, four of which are multi-storey. The visitor centre has a restaurant, shop, and full-access toilets.

OPENING TIMES
Open all year round (except Christmas Day) from 9.30am–5.30pm (5pm in winter).

CHARGES
Yes, for non-WWT members. Essential helpers for disabled visitors are free.

The beaver returns

The Eurasian beaver used to live in Britain in large numbers, but it became extinct by the 1500s, and by the end of the 1800s there were only a few hundred left in Europe. It is now on the European Species Action List, which recommends reintroducing the animal into its former habitats, and in 2007, Martin Mere did just this, releasing four Eurasian beavers into a "natural-habitat" enclosure. The beavers are monogamous, family-oriented herbivores, who love to sink their teeth into woody, broadleaved plants.

Above (left to right): A male ruff; a brambling flock above the lagoon; look for redwings along the hedgerows.
Main: Whooper swans roosting at Martin Mere call to each other through the autumn dusk.

LANCASHIRE HOTSPOT

SITUATED NORTH OF ORMSKIRK, THIS WILDFOWL & WETLANDS TRUST reserve is famed for its overwintering wildfowl. During October thousands of geese, ducks, and swans converge on the low-lying marshes and lagoons, and spectacular roosts of thousands of geese take place at dusk. Pink-footed geese migrate from Greenland and Iceland, whooper swans come from Iceland, while a handful of Bewicks's swans migrate from Russia. Dabbling ducks are attracted to the shallow lagoons and marshy fields, where the wigeons, pintails, teals, mallards, and a few shovelers can be seen tipping upside down in the water to feed on the aquatic plants.

Visit one of the various hides around the reserve to enjoy some wonderful views of the wildfowl. By late October there may be more than 1,000 whooper swans, and 17,000 pink-footed geese, often harbouring small numbers of other species, such as white-fronted, barnacle, and bean geese. The geese spend much of their day grazing on the fields, but you'll see these large birds take to the air as they commute between favourable feeding sites. Martin Mere is one of the country's most important wintering sites for ruffs, with more than 100 overwintering here. Look towards the wet fields to see these waders, together with huge flocks of lapwings and golden plovers – perhaps 1,000 or more of each. Snipe feed along the muddy margins, keeping a watchful eye on the sky for birds of prey such as merlins and peregrines. Marsh and hen harriers hunt over the area too.

Martin Mere's other big attractions are a large captive collection of waterfowl – representing more than 100 species from around the world – and two pairs of the world's second-largest rodents, the European beavers. These animals are nature's engineers – they love excavating canals and building dams using branches and earth, so the reserve has installed a "beaver deceiver" to provide them with a water flow that constantly needs damming.

Martin Mere Wetland Centre is home to a splendid range of endangered wildfowl, including more than 100 rare species of geese, swans, and ducks.

Inset: A pintail in flight at last light.
Below (left to right): A flock of bramblings tree-roosting; pink-footed geese.

WHERE ELSE TO SEE
WETLANDS

Wetland centres provide a mosaic of habitats and so attract a very diverse range of species. They are often particularly good for children, providing information, hides, observatories, and suggestions for exploration.

RSPB **Marshside** nature reserve is situated nearby, not far from Southport. Grazing marsh and lagoons attract plenty of wildfowl and waders. [N]

Holkham (see pp.18–19) in North Norfolk is a dramatic wetland reserve on the coast that hosts the largest concentration of wintering pink-footed geese in Britain. Go to Lady Ann's Drive an hour before dusk to see spectacular numbers. [SE]

The **London Wetland Centre** (see pp.16–17), Barnes, is a great urban reserve for watching wildlife, including bitterns, kingfishers, and water voles. [SE]

The Wildfowl & Wetlands Trust has a number of centres around the country that combine a captive collection with great birdwatching in winter. Try **Slimbridge** in Gloucestershire (see pp.34–35), their flagship reserve, for plenty of wildfowl. [M]

THROUGH THE YEAR
MARTIN MERE

Wildfowl swarm across the lagoons and marshes in **winter**. Pink-footed geese and whooper swans are joined by various dabbling ducks and wintering waders and raptors – a sighting of the lightning-fast peregrine falcon is almost guaranteed.

The winter visitors depart in **spring**. Migrants passing through Martin Mere may include spotted redshanks and whimbrels. Birds arriving to breed here include garganeys and yellow wagtails.

Breeding shelducks and avocets are among the highlights at the centre in **summer**. Returning autumn waders may include black-tailed godwits, green sandpipers, ruffs, and others. The centre runs a programme of interesting activities for children right through the summer, including pond dipping and interactive workshops on topics such as the mysteries of the food chain and how birds move.

Below: Shelduck family feeding in shallow water in summer.

JAN
FEB
MAR
APR
MAY
JUN
JUL
AUG
SEP
OCT
NOV
DEC

WHERE
Windsor Great Park, Windsor, Berkshire
SL4 2HT; www.thecrownestate.co.uk

CONTACT
The Crown Estate Office, tel: 01753 860222.

GETTING THERE
The A332 runs directly through the centre of Windsor Great Park. By train, travel to Windsor Central or Windsor Riverside. By bus, take White Bus Services no.1 bus to Windsor Great Park Post Office. National Cycle Network route no. 4 runs through the park.

ACCESS AND FACILITIES
Car parks are located along the A332, which runs through the park. Roads and paths through the park are suitable for pushchairs and wheelchairs, and wheelchairs are available at Savill Garden.

OPENING TIMES
Open all year, from 7am to 5pm. Savill Garden is open from 10am until around dusk (4pm November–February, 6pm March–October).

CHARGES
Entry to the park is free, but there is a charge to enter Savill Garden.

Common earth-star

This extraordinary soil fungus is part of the Gasteromycetes ("stomach fungi") group, members of which all feature a stomach-shaped sac filled with spores. It is called an "earth-star" because when it rains, the outer walls split open into sections, widening flat out into the shape of a star, pushing the spore-filled inner sac up above any surrounding leaves. As raindrops hit the thin-walled spore sac, the spores puff out of the pore at the top of the sac.

Left: The rich colours of the woodland in autumn.

Right (left to right): Poisonous fly agaric toadstools; common stinkhorns have a vile-smelling sticky spore mass when fresh; the stems of amethyst deceiver are covered in tiny white hairs; the highly-prized *Boletus edulis* – the cep or porcini mushroom.

Main: The fruiting bodies of honey fungus. **Far right:** Sulphur polypore on bark.

WOODLAND FUNGI AT WINDSOR

THE REMNANT OF AN ANCIENT FOREST AT THE EASTERN EDGE of Cranbourne Chase was incorporated into Windsor Great Park in the 1790s. It is celebrated for its ancient trees, many of them oaks over 400 years old. Dotted among them on October mornings you can find organisms that are here one day and gone the next – fungi.

Fungi are famous for the way they spring up overnight and vanish almost as fast. Some are culinary delicacies, while others are notoriously deadly. Many have a slightly sinister beauty. They seem like alien life forms, which is not far from the truth, because although most people think of them as plants, they comprise a separate kingdom of life that has a lot in common with animals. Instead of making food, as plants do, they consume it, usually in the form of dead wood and other plant material. In the process they break down dead organic matter and release nutrients that are vital to living plants. Without them, many plants could not grow at all.

Scientists believe there may be over a million species of fungi, only 10 per cent of which have been officially described.

JAN
FEB
MAR
APR
MAY
JUN
JUL
AUG
SEP
OCT
NOV
DEC

WHERE ELSE TO SEE
WOODLAND FUNGI

Almost any wood in Britain will sprout a variety of fungi in the damp, yet still quite warm, weeks of autumn. Most species have associations with certain trees, such as the well-known partnership of fly agaric with birch. This means that different types of woodland support different types of fungi, and the more diverse the habitat, the greater the variety.

One of the best places to look is the **New Forest** in Hampshire (*see pp.174–175*). It has a wide range of woodland habitats, from ancient oakwoods to conifer plantations, as well as grasslands and heaths that support distinctive fungi of their own. [SE]

Epping Forest in London is a well-known hunting ground for fungi enthusiasts, with large areas of oak, beech, hornbeam, and birch, and plenty of dead wood left to rot on the forest floor. [SE]

Some of the older parts of **Sherwood Forest** in Nottinghamshire (*see pp.36–37*) are also excellent places to search for fungi. Check inside old hollow trees as well as on the ground around them. [M]

THROUGH THE YEAR
WINDSOR GREAT PARK

The woodlands have their own stark beauty in **winter** when the dark tracery of branches is revealed by the fallen leaves. Look for woodpeckers, nuthatches, and treecreepers searching for food on the tree bark; if you search hard you may spot a tawny owl roosting on a branch close to a tree trunk.

Spring sees the trees burst into leaf, an event that triggers a mass hatching of leaf-eating insects. These in turn are gathered in their thousands by the breeding woodland birds whose songs fill the air.

In **summer**, look for woodland butterflies such as the purple emperor and white admiral, as well as visitors like the painted lady. Look up to check for hobbies – fast-flying falcons that pluck dragonflies out of the air and eat them on the wing.

As you walk among the old trees near Forest Gate, you will find all kinds of fungi pushing up through the autumn leaf litter at your feet. Some are conspicuous, like the bright red russulas and white-spotted fly agaric. Others are easy to overlook, like the delicate purple amethyst deceiver. But the more you look, the more you see, both on the ground and sprouting from trees and old stumps. You might even find the rare bearded tooth fungus, a species that is only found here and a few other places in Britain. You can smell the fungi too – the delicious mushroomy fragrance of ceps and the disgusting smell of the stinkhorn that attracts flies to carry away its spores.

Spore dispersal is the function of all these fungi. They are the seasonal "fruiting bodies" of much larger organisms that form complex networks in the soil and dead timber. These networks enmesh tree roots, supplying them with nutrients while absorbing sugars from the trees' root sap. They occupy hollow trees and convert the dead heartwood into substances that help nourish the living parts of the tree. As old parts of the network die off, new stems grow, so the organism is effectively immortal. The trees of the forest are old, but many of its fungi may be even older.

Below: Rhododendrons bloom in late spring in the Park's Savill Garden.

AUTUMN BY THE LOCH

LOCH LEVEN NATIONAL NATURE RESERVE LIES BELOW THE LOMOND HILLS, where its vast, tranquil loch spreads over 16 sq km (6 sq miles). The loch encompasses islands, lagoons, reedbeds, and grazing marshes, which provide food and shelter for thousands of birds in the autumn and winter. The best place to appreciate the wildlife, especially close up, is the RSPB reserve at Vane Farm, which has excellent views across the main loch, specially created shallow lagoons, and nature trails on nearby wooded hillsides.

In October, it is one of the best places in the UK to see vast numbers of wild geese. These iconic birds are closely associated with the romance and mystery of migration and the changing of the seasons. In England, the increase of semi-wild Canada and greylag geese has devalued them somewhat, but the real thing – the truly wild birds that annually cross the seas from the north to spend the winter with us – are magnificent.

WHERE
Loch Leven, Perth and Kinross KY13 7LX, Scotland.

CONTACT
RSPB Vane Farm Nature Reserve, tel: 01577 862355; vanefarm@rspb.org.uk

GETTING THERE
By car, take the M90 to Junction 5, then follow signs to the reserve. The nearest train station is Cowdenbeath, 11km (7 miles) away, but there is no onward public transport. A bus runs from Kinross on Wednesdays and Saturdays. Vane Farm lies 7km (4 miles) off Route 1 of the National Cycle Network.

ACCESS AND FACILITIES
There are three hides at Vane Farm, all with good access. The visitor centre has a café, trail and bird information, car park, full-access toilets, and good facilities for wheelchair users. Some of the trails are difficult for wheelchairs.

OPENING TIMES
Loch Leven is accessible at all times. Vane Farm visitor centre is open 10am–5pm daily, but the trails and hides are open 24 hours a day all year, except for Christmas Day, Boxing Day, New Year's Day and 2 January.

CHARGES
A small charge applies, except for RSPB and Wildlife Explorer members.

Above: The first sight of pink-footed geese in flight is symbolic of the changing seasons.

Below (top and bottom): Vane Farm Nature Reserve from above; the reserve lies along the south shore of Loch Leven, and includes a trail up to the top of Vane Hill, from where you can gain spectacular views.

Bilberry lover

The bilberry bumblebee, which is found at Loch Leven, is particularly fond of bilberry – a wild, wiry shrub that grows best on the heathlands and high grounds of northern Britain – hence the bee's other name, the mountain bumblebee, or "humble-bee". This heart-shaped, red-tailed bee emerges in early spring as the bilberry flowers. Deer grazing, dense forest canopies, and an inability to compete successfully against the fiercier heathers has led to a decrease in plants, and a serious decline in numbers of the bee.

They are at their best in large, flying flocks, when they make the familiar V-shapes, chevrons, and wavy lines and the air fills with their ringing, clanging, and clattering calls. You can distinguish the greylag geese by their harsher, more rattling notes; the pink-footed geese form a more musical chorus – deep calls interspersed with high, sharp "win-wink" notes. On the ground, the geese march steadily along in tightly packed groups, often squabbling and calling, making them always interesting to watch.

With the geese, or nearby, will be hordes of ducks: the wigeons like to patrol the grass, while pintails, teals, and mallards stay close to the water. Look for lapwings and golden plovers; these are the signalling birds, who will suddenly take flight, and noisily sound the alarm if birds of prey appear in the skies overhead. Groups of whooper swans may be hiding a few rarer Bewick's; smaller wading birds can be found at the edges of the water.

WHERE ELSE TO SEE
FRESHWATER WILDFOWL

Loch Leven is Scotland's largest lowland freshwater loch. This kind of natural standing water habitat is imitated by man-made waters such as reservoirs, and provides a perfect habitat for wintering birds.

Lochs Oire, **na Bo**, and **Spynie**, in Moray, Scotland, are all freshwater lochs with winter wildfowl. Loch Spynie is a large loch with reedbeds, fen, and woodlands, famous for the huge numbers of greylag and pink-footed geese that roost there in winter. [SC]

Pink-footed geese can be seen at **Marshside** and **Martin Mere** (*see pp.256–257*) in Lancashire, where they come to feed on crop waste. [N]

At **Holkham**, Norfolk (*see pp.18–19*), and the **Sevenoaks Wildlife Reserve**, Kent, you can see geese aplenty. [SE]

The Cotswold Water Park, near Cirencester in Gloucestershire, has 147 lakes that were formerly gravel pits and now provide a winter home for thousands of wintering waterbirds and gulls. [M]

THROUGH THE YEAR
LOCH LEVEN

In **winter**, look for birds of prey over the hill, and roe deer, which seek shelter in the woods. Finches and tits visit bird feeders, while geese live around the loch.

Spring sees toads emerging from the loch, just as the last geese leave for Iceland. The birchwoods come back to life, and begin to fill with visiting summer birds. Look out especially for great spotted woodpeckers and lesser redpolls.

In **summer** it's worth staying until dusk, when you can see Daubenton's and pipistrelle bats emerging. Ospreys hover over the loch in the early morning and late afternoon, while damselflies enjoy the water during the heat of the day. A beautiful flowery meadow has recently been created as a bumblebee sanctuary (*see box, facing page*), and it is a great place to see a wide variety of insects, including bees and butterflies.

Main: Loch Leven was formed by retreating glaciers.

Above: Greylag geese are the largest of the UK's geese; whooper swans' bills have long triangles of yellow.

Below: A redshank preens itself.

Below: The common toad emerges from the loch during spring.

JAN

FEB

MAR

APR

MAY

JUN

JUL

AUG

SEP

OCT

NOV

DEC

WHERE
The Birks of Aberfeldy, Aberfeldy, Perthshire, Scotland; www.perthshire.co.uk

CONTACT
Aberfeldy Tourist Information Centre, The Square, Aberfeldy, PH15 2DD, tel: 01887 820276 or Visit Scotland, tel: 01738 627958; info@visitscotland.com

GETTING THERE
From Perth, take the A9 north towards Pitlochry, then turn left onto the A827 at Ballinluig towards Aberfeldy.

ACCESS AND FACILITIES
The nearest facilities are in Aberfeldy town. The 4km (2½ mile) circular walk is accessible from the centre of Aberfeldy or from the Birks car park, reached by following the A826 south and following the signs. There are seats and viewpoints along the walk. For those not so mobile, there is a picnic area at the car park that gives a good flavour of the walk. There is also a short tree trail identifying a large number of tree species for people unable to climb the main path.

OPENING HOURS
Open all year round.

CHARGES
None.

Map lichen

Lichens are ancient, slow-growing plants that can survive in harsh environments, including extreme temperatures or seemingly nutrient-free areas. They do not have roots and do not need water, so they can live on bare rock or sand. They also grow at a uniform rate, and are now often used to reveal the age of the exposed rock surface on which they live. Map lichen (*below*) is particularly useful for this, as it grows less than 1mm (¹⁄₃₂ inch) each year, allowing for finely tuned dating.

Left: Yellow chanterelle thrives among moss in the beech woodland of the Birks.

Right (left to right): Common yellow russula loves the cool dampness of the gorge; ferns thrive in the Birks; the Birks of Aberfeldy Walking Trail.

Right panel: The walking trail leads you past many small waterfalls, up to the bridge overlooking the Upper Falls.

Main: The woodland path through the Birks of Aberfeldy is most atmospheric in autumn.

AUTUMN FIRE IN THE FOREST

TUCKED AWAY IN THE FOLDS OF THE PERTHSHIRE HILLS LIES an enchanting, steep-sided wooded glen, with magical mosses, stunning waterfalls, and breathtaking views. The wild, ancient woodlands that once covered the entire landscape have all but disappeared, and while there are a few remnants of the Caledonian forest tucked away in the most inaccessible parts of this glen, the predominant trees now are the "birks" – the Scottish gaelic word for "birch trees". These elegant, silver-barked species hug the upper slopes either side of the rushing, tumbling white waters of the Moness Burn, a tributary of the Tay – itself the longest river in Britain. The looping 3.2km (2 mile) nature trail takes you up to the wooden bridge that runs right over the top of the impressive waterfall, called the Falls of Moness. Once at the top, the views are incredible. The Falls tumble some 150m (492ft) down the ancient gorge, where bright red and orange leaves carpet the dark-green, mossy forest; some fall

Above: Ramsons, or wild garlic, grows in the damper woodland in spring.

The myriad colours of this wildwood of birch, oak, and ash trees make autumn the perfect time to visit.

THROUGH THE YEAR
THE BIRKS OF ABERFELDY

Winter is a great time to study the multitude of mosses around the gorge, after the trees have died back. Take an identification guide with you, and don't miss the very fine hair moss, fork moss, and tamarisk-leaved feather moss.

In **spring**, forest buds and blossom attract early-flying insects, which is encouraging for one of the Birks' most important breeding birds, the attractive pied flycatcher. Woodland plants light up the forest floor, as wild flowers like the yellow pimpernel, bugle, and sweet woodruff give way to creamy white carpets of wild garlic, also known as ramsons.

Red campion and wood crane's bill grow around the gorge in **summer**. You may see yellow and grey wagtails flit up and down the streams with bills crammed full of insects. The forest acts as a crèche for the many woodland birds that breed here, and young birds, such as woodpeckers and warblers, can be seen learning life skills from their parents. The pinkish-white bell-like flowers of wintergreen and the white flowers of wood vetch, finely lined with blue or purple, flourish between **June** and **August**.

WHERE ELSE TO SEE
AUTUMN COLOUR

Oak, ash, beech, birch, and maple woodland produces spectacular colours in autumn. For more suggestions of colourful displays near you, visit the Woodland Trust website (www.woodland-trust.org.uk).

The Hermitage, at Dunkeld in Perthshire, is a grove of giant oak, rowan, and Douglas and Scot's pine growing beside the dramatic waterfalls, rapids, and swirling pools of the river Braan. [SC]

Dendles Wood in Devon has barely been managed during its long history and is home to the rare barbastelle bat. [SW]

Dunkery and Horner Wood, in Somerset is an ancient sessile oakwood where you can see tawny owls, green woodpeckers, stoats, slow-worms, weasels, and squirrels. Heath fritillary butterflies breed there. Look out for red deer in October. [SW]

onto the dark, water-washed rocks, while others get carried away downstream by the frothing white water. Birch might be the predominant species here, but other trees cloak the steep edges, including ashes, oaks, and willows. As the path winds its way through the overhanging trees, the sheer power of the roaring falls can be felt, especially if you visit after heavy rain. In sheltered pools beside the cascading waters, dippers bob up and down on rocks; their white bibs are usually the first thing to catch your eye. Remarkably, these water-loving birds not only dive for their underwater prey – they also run along the bottom of the riverbed to catch it. Look for interesting fungi among the fallen leaves; russulas are probably the most common, but you should also see the unusual shapes of helvellas, otherwise known as "elfin saddles".

An amazing collection of ferns, liverworts, and mosses – feather, fork, and hair – prosper in the constant water spray of the gorge's cool depths. Almost the whole gorge has been designated a Site of Special Scientific Interest – but you might be happy just sitting on the same stone seat on which the poet Robert Burns sat in 1787, soaking up the magical atmosphere of the Birks.

JAN

FEB

MAR

APR

MAY

JUN

JUL

AUG

SEP

OCT

NOV

DEC

OCTOBER

WHERE
Spurn Point, Spurn, near Kilnsea, Humberside
HU12 0UB; www.ywt.org.uk

CONTACT
Tel: 01964 650533 or 01904 659570;
info@yorkshirewt.cix.co.uk

GETTING THERE
The reserve is located at the extreme
southeastern tip of the Yorkshire coast, 32km
(20 miles) from Hull. By car, take the A1033
east towards Withernsea; then the B1445
from Patrington towards Easington village.
From Easington follow the brown tourist signs
to Spurn Point. The nearest train station is
Hull. By bus, take "The Spurn Ranger" (nos.
71 and 73) which runs from Withernsea
through Patrington to Spurn Point.

ACCESS AND FACILITIES
Wheelchair access is limited due to the
terrain, however there is disabled parking in
the car park at the end of the Point, with
toilets and a café. The are good viewpoints
from paths around the Point car park, plus
two viewing hides.

CHARGES
There is a charge to drive to the Point, but
once there, parking is free.

Beware buckthorn!

Spurn's dunes are dominated by sea buckthorn.
This invasive plant is native to the UK, and it
produces nutritious berries in winter that are a
vital food source for migrating birds. But be
careful around these bushes – brown-tail moth
has become established in them, and in autumn
you can see their silken tents in the branches.
The caterpillars (*above*) are covered in irritant
hairs that can trigger a severe reaction if you
touch them or breathe them in. Cuckoos have a
very tolerant digestion and feed on the caterpillars.

Above (left to right): Sea-buckthorn (*see feature box, below left*); the UK's smallest songbird, the goldcrest; fieldfare feeding on berries.
Main: A landmark lighthouse sits above the dunes at Spurn Point.

MIGRATION IN ACTION

BIRD MIGRATION CAN PRODUCE SIGHTS AND SURPRISES throughout the country, especially in autumn. For the greatest chance of catching up with autumn migrants, it's best to head to a place with a good track record at a time when the winds are in the right direction. Spurn Point is one of Britain's classic birdwatching locations – especially in October. This fragile finger of sand stretches 5km (3 miles) south from Yorkshire into the Humber estuary, and it is best visited after easterlies. However, some migrants are likely to appear whatever the wind, which is why it is home to one of the UK's Bird Observatories. These are located around the coastline at strategic locations to record bird movements through ringing and observation.

Some birds typically migrate under the cover of night, such as warblers, flycatchers, and most of the chats. For a chance of seeing these, you'll need to be up at first light, examining all the available bushes and perches for anything that might have dropped in overnight. But for most people, the excitement lies in actually seeing the birds fly by – a phenomenon known as "visible migration". Spurn is spectacularly good for this, because its funnel shape helps to concentrate the birds as they fly southwards.

In a landscape dominated by sea and sky, Spurn's narrow strip of sand and shrubs is a beacon for birds looking for food and rest on their long journey.

All you need to do is to find some shelter on the dunes, and then wait. The visible migration of swifts, swallows, and martins happens in July and August; as autumn sets in, they are replaced by pipits, larks, finches, thrushes, and pigeons – often as many as tens of thousands of birds per day. Identify them through a combination of flight action, silhouette, and particularly their call. If in doubt, remember that most of the birds you see will be common birds, rather than the hoped-for rarities. But stay a while, and be patient; you might just hear a chirping Richard's pipit among the "teezing" tree pipits, or a late honey buzzard – giving a tantalizing glimpse of the raptor migration within Europe.

Inset: Spurn Point's sea buckthorn bushes provide food for a hungry blackcap.
Below (left to right): Northern wheatear; snow buntings.

WHERE ELSE TO SEE
VISIBLE MIGRATION

Migration is something you can witness anywhere, from your office window or your garden, or indeed wherever you can see the sky. Even inland can be excellent – the heights of Parliament Hill on **Hampstead Heath** (*see pp110–111*) in London are renowned for it and anywhere within the great cross-country flyways, such as the Humber–Trent–Severn, or the Wash–Great Ouse–Lee Valley–Thames has a great chance of producing migrants.

For migrant birds, try any of the British Bird Observatories (www.birdobscouncil.org.uk), but note that many of them are not open all the time – always call to arrange a visit with the warden.

Landguard is an exposed sand and shingle peninsula in Suffolk that sees a breathtaking number of migrating birds, as does **Sandwich Bay** in Kent. Both locations also have bird observatories. [SE]

Further north, **Filey** in Yorkshire is good for watching birds moving south from the near continent and our own birds departing. [N]

THROUGH THE YEAR
SPURN POINT

Water birds flock to the sheltered mudflats of the Humber estuary, visible from the Point, during **winter**. You should see good numbers of shelducks and dark-bellied brent geese; when the tide is out, they will be joined by curlews, lapwings, dunlins, bar-tailed godwits, and a host of others.

In **spring**, the migrants start to reappear, usually in smaller numbers but some in much brighter plumage than during the autumn. Wheatears and black redstarts may well be the first, arriving usually from mid-March. Surprisingly, visible migration of birds such as swallows is often in a southerly direction.

The dunes are covered in flowers in **summer**: sea-holly, sea bindweed, and viper's-bugloss nestle among the sea-buckthorn bushes and clumps of marram grass. Little terns nest on the beach, hopefully within the protected fenced area. Keep an eye open for basking common lizards.

Below: Sea bindweed grows on the dunes during the summer.

What lies beneath

Look out across the mud around Lough Foyle, and you may wonder why it is so attractive to so many birds. The answer is food. The light-bellied Brent geese like grazing on the extensive beds of eelgrass that grows on the mud in the autumn. There are also plenty of lugworms (*below*) and ragworms, shrimps, periwinkles, and vast mussel beds concealed in the mud – all foods that the clever waders can find by probing in the mud with their different-shaped bills.

Above: Whooper swans arrive in large groups on the mud banks of Lough Foyle.

Below (top and bottom): Dunlins probe for molluscs, worms, and crustaceans along the lough; wigeons enjoy the lough's shallow waters.

Right (top and bottom): A flock of oystercatchers; the light-bellied Brent goose has a smudgy-white half collar.

Main: The mudflats and mussel beds of Lough Foyle, looking towards Donegal.

FLOCKING TO THE LOUGH

LOUGH FOYLE IS A LARGE SHALLOW SEA LOUGH OR INLET that combines with the river estuaries of the Roe, Foyle, and Faughan to support an internationally important number of birds. The lough separates County Londonderry from County Donegal, and it is the Londonderry side of the lough that is richest for birds.

A late-October visit should provide some wonderful birdwatching. Over 20,000 waterfowl arrive here in autumn from Iceland, Greenland, and the Canadian Arctic to take advantage of Ireland's milder weather. Huge flocks of of whooper swans and light-bellied Brent geese arrive, along with smaller flocks of Bewick's swans. The later-arriving wigeons make the most of the lough's abundance of food, spending a few days – or sometimes a few weeks – before dispersing to sites around Ireland. At low tide the mud and sand flats throng with waders: bar-tailed godwits, oystercatchers, grey plovers, and curlews are easy to see, but look around too, at the river estuaries

Across this vast intertidal lough, seagrass and mussel beds provide a feasting ground for waterfowl.

Above: Summer wild flowers on the banks of Lough Foyle.

THROUGH THE YEAR
LOUGH FOYLE

Look out for divers and grebes at high tide in **winter**, especially the great northern diver. Wildfowl and waders dominate the lough, especially whooper swans and light-bellied Brent geese. Winter stubble provides food for flocks of finches, larks, and buntings – and so, in turn, attracts raptors, including buzzards, kestrels, merlins, peregrines, and sparrowhawks.

In **spring**, there are still a few lingering winter visitors, while whimbrels visit on passage. The damp coastal pastures are home to breeding waders, especially lapwings. You'll hear the hedgerows begin to fill with birds, and may see linnets, song thrushes, reed buntings, bullfinches, yellowhammers, spotted flycatchers, and skylarks.

Terns and skuas can be seen off Magilligan Point in **summer**, and waders return from their breeding grounds by July. Check the sand dunes – they support interesting plants at this time of year, including the pyramidal orchid and creeping thyme. Inside the railway bridge is an area of saltmarsh vegetation, where you can watch the lapwings' aerobatic displays in early summer.

WHERE ELSE TO SEE
ESTUARY WILDLIFE

The intermingling of ocean salt water and river freshwater gives rise to a very productive ecosystem in estuaries and coastal loughs, providing vital plant material on the marshes for visiting birds. These areas are always great places to see winter wildlife.

The **Bann Estuary** on the North Antrim coast is good for wader watching in autumn. [NI]

Strangford Lough, County Down (*see pp.288–289*) is joined to the sea by a narrow strait, and has a number of small "islands" along its western shores. Huge numbers of Brent geese and grey seals spend the winter here. [NI]

Belfast Lough, Belfast (*see pp.38–39*), is an intertidal lough known for its flourishing mussel beds. It is home to an RSPB reserve, where the mudflats welcome significant numbers of winter waders. [NI]

where plentiful mud provides good feeding for dunlins, redshanks, and small numbers of wintering greenshanks. At high tide the lough attracts wintering divers and grebes, and the deeper water off Magilligan Point is a good place to look for them, especially the rarer Slavonian grebe. Magilligan Point is one of the largest sand-dune systems in the British Isles, and groups of sanderlings really make the most of it, scurrying to and fro on the shore as the waves wash in and out.

South of the point lies the Roe Estuary, the legendary roaming grounds of the very last Irish wolf. The Roe is at its best at high tide, when waders roost on the saltmarsh close to shore, their outlines ghostly as the dusk deepens. Peregrines and other raptors hunt overhead.

The lough has a rich and varied fish population including Atlantic salmon – which pass through the lough as they head for, or leave, their spawning grounds. Several species found here are listed as Red Data Book, or threatened, species, including allis shad, twaite shad, European smelt, and sea lamprey. The saltmarsh area inside the railway bridge is home to Lough Foyle's otters, which feed on the fish and crabs of the shallow pools, but are quick to hide.

JAN
FEB
MAR
APR
MAY
JUN
JUL
AUG
SEP
OCT
NOV
DEC

Left (left to right): The lighthouse on Sillay, or *Siolaigh*, westernmost of the Monachs; the beaches consist of calcium-rich shell-sand.

Right (left to right): Bulls and immature males gather on "bachelor beaches" during pupping; a seal pup shortly after losing its birth coat of white fur; the bulls return within weeks to mate.

WHERE
The Monach Isles, Western Isles, Scotland.

CONTACT
Scottish Natural Heritage, Stilligarry, Isle of South Uist, tel: 01870 620238.
The Uist Outdoor Centre, Loch Maddy, North Uist HS6 5AE is the main organizer of local trips to the islands, tel: 01876 500480 or visit www.uistoutdoorcentre.co.uk

GETTING THERE
The islands lie about 8km (5 miles) west of North Uist, and are visible from both North Uist and Benbecula. To see the seals, you need to take a local charter trip by boat from North Uist. Some wildlife-watching sea trips from Oban on the Scottish mainland include the Monach Isles.

ACCESS AND FACILITIES
Trips from North Uist outside the summer tourist season usually need to be chartered in advance and are weather-dependent; the Uist Outdoor Centre is a good source of information. This remote location is not easily accessible for wheelchair users, but boat trips are manageable by prior arrangement. The islands have no facilities of any sort, and trips do not normally include landing.

CHARGES
Charges vary for the boat trips.

Fattening up the pups

During the first few weeks, seal pups rely on their mother's milk, which is 60 per cent fat – during early life a pup can double its weight in one week. It is building a layer of blubber that will protect it from the cold, and sustain it while it refines its hunting skills. The mother fasts during the lactating period, but is finally forced to return to the sea to feed. The pup remains at the breeding ground for around two more weeks, before heading out to sea to fend for itself.

Main and far right: A pup cuddles up to its mother; male grey seals sparring in the surf around the island.

PUPPING GREY SEALS

AS YOU APPROACH THE SANDY BEACHES AND DUNES OF THE remote Monach Isles in October, a mass of bobbing heads rise to greet you. There are no people living here, the islands were abandoned in 1948 – these nodding heads belong to the largest colony of grey seals in Europe. The five low-lying isles are part of the Outer Hebrides; they lie 8km (5 miles) off the west coast of North Uist, and three of them are linked by shell-sand tombolos, or sandbars. Rocky reefs line the shores, and the shell content of the sandy beaches is reflected in the machair habitat (*see pp.108–109*) around the sand dunes, stabilized by the interweaving roots of marram grass.

The remoteness of these islands means the seals are rarely disturbed by humans during the breeding season. Estimates put the number of pups born in autumn at a staggering 9,000, and the total number of seals on the islands in the breeding season at around 30,000 animals – more than 25 per cent of the UK's entire grey seal

Above: A grey seal pup in the soft white coat in which it is born.

THROUGH THE YEAR
THE MONACH ISLANDS

The five Monach Islands – Ceann Ear, Shivinish, Ceann Iar, Sillay, and Stogay – are difficult to reach in **winter**, a time when the seals are joined by a wintering flock of around 500 barnacle geese.

The machair dune system starts to bloom in **spring**. This calcium-rich soil supports around 200 flowers, including stone-crop, kidney-vetch, thyme, heartsease, and bird's-foot trefoil. Oyster plant, a rare sub-Arctic plant of shingle beaches, can be seen growing on the shoreline of Stockay island.

The lack of cliff shelter on the islands means there are few seabirds in **summer**, but those that do come to the islands to breed include common, Arctic, and little terns (which make their nests in scoops in the sand); and a scattering of black guillemots, fulmars, shags, eiders, and dunlins.

In October, while the pups bask and learn to swim with their mothers, the males fight for their territory and harems.

WHERE ELSE TO SEE
SEALS PUPS

Seals produce their pups in the colder months of the year. In the UK, the pupping season runs between September and the end of December.

One of Britain's most accessible grey seal colonies can be found at **Donna Nook** in Lincolnshire. Visit from early November through to Christmas to see pups up close from special viewing areas. [M]

Blakeney Point in Norfolk (*see pp.214–215*) is home to a large colony of common seals, which produces hundreds of pups. Boats run regularly from Morston. [SE]

The **Farne Islands** (*see pp.126–127*) has a large grey seal colony that can be reached on boat trips from Seahouses in Northumberland. [N]

population. Seals eat a wide range of fish species, crustaceans, and even the odd seabird. The kelp forests of the shallow seas, the submerged sandbanks, and the reefs around the islands all provide a rich feeding ground for the seals, ensuring they don't have to travel far to feed; seals live here all year round, although many more arrive during the breeding season.

The grey seal's gestation period is just over 11 months, so the mating season follows close behind the pupping: the females give birth to the pups in October, and when they have finished suckling the pups, some three or four weeks later, they mate once more with the dominant males – known as "beach masters". These big male seals herd the females into harems of up to 10, which they defend aggressively from the amorous advances of rival males. After mating, the female seals can at last return to the sea to feed – they have been fasting during lactation.

If you can drag your eyes away from the seals, check offshore for divers and black guillemots, which can be seen around the islands throughout the year. Barnacle geese arrive during the autumn to graze; some using the islands for a short stop, others staying for the whole of the long winter.

JAN
FEB
MAR
APR
MAY
JUN
JUL
AUG
SEP
OCT
NOV
DEC

NOVEMBER

Where to Go: **November**

The clocks have changed: wrap up warm, and head for November, a month of stormy weather, but blessed with a wealth of colour and clarity that enduces a marvellous sense of tranquillity in those of us lucky enough to be outside. Birds are around in thrilling numbers; the marshes and grasslands on the coast welcome geese, ducks, and waders by the thousand. These birds are fresh from the Arctic, and have survived challenging journeys. The flocks of brent geese arriving at the southern estuaries have flown from far-off Siberia, while avocets are pausing before heading to their final winter refuges. This is a peak time for seeing estuary birds, which have come from all around the northern hemisphere. Even the towns feel the effect of the seasonal change;

ISLANDS

LINDISFARNE The wide-open shores of Holy Island.

PARKLAND AND GRASSLAND

RICHMOND PARK Around 350 fallow deer roam within the park.

WOODLANDS

CHURCH WOOD Flocks of bramblings forage and roost here.

LINDISFARNE
NORTHUMBERLAND [N]

This island, with its amazing lava rock shapes and complexity of habitats, is always worth visiting, but especially so in November, when the rockpools are fun and the birdwatching is outstanding.
See pp.274–275

RICHMOND PARK
RICHMOND, SURREY [SE]

The huge grounds of Richmond Park, so close to central London, are a great place to watch the rituals of the red deer rut, as the stags fight for supremacy.
See pp.276–277

SALTWELLS RESERVE
DUDLEY, WEST MIDLANDS [M]

Saltwells Wood lies at the heart of this reserve, its oak and beech trees sheltering many woodland birds. The incredible cliffs of Douton Claypit are well worth a visit.
See pp.282–283

CHURCH WOOD
HEDGERLEY, BUCKS [SE]

The beech mast attracts lots of birds in late autumn, including the hawfinch. An abundance of fungi grows among the fallen leaves.
See pp.280–281

HAVERGATE ISLAND
ALDEBURGH, SUFFOLK [SE]

This island is a winter haven for large numbers of ducks and wading birds. Birds of prey such as short-eared owls and marsh harriers hunt over the island.
See pp.286–287

> The grass is crisp with frost, and all is quiet, until the silence is suddenly shattered by a fearsome, drawn-out roar – the rutting season has begun.

BEDGEBURY ARBORETUM
GCUDHURST, KENT [SE]

Part of Bedgebury forest, the arboretum has one of the world's best collections of rare conifers. Goldcrests and migrant firecrests shelter here in winter.
See pp.280–281

ISLE OF RUM
WEST HIGHLANDS [SC]

The Isle of Rum on the west coast of Scotland is a National Nature Reserve, with red deer, feral goats, and spectacular birds, incuding sea eagles and golden eagles.
See pp.276–277

ASHTON COURT
LONG ASHTON, BRISTOL [SW]

This country house has vast grasslands and woods, and a 600-year-old deer park, where you can see red and fallow deer.
See pp.276–277

FOREST OF DEAN
GLOUCESTERSHIRE [SE]

Stunning countryside and woodland coincide here. Deer and wild boar wander within the forest, and you can watch peregrines and goshawks diving for fun and for prey.
See pp.280–281

ISLE OF MULL
ARGYLL AND BUTE [SC]

One of Scotland's most stunning islands on the west coast, here you can see a staggering array of wildlife from otters and puffins to basking sharks and whales.
See pp.288–289

> The Isle of Mull off the west coast of Scotland is a year-round destination for wildlife watching, both on land and at sea.

THETFORD FOREST
THETFORD, NORFOLK [SE]

The largest lowland forest in Britain never disappoints. Visit the arboretum for wonderful autumn colour.
See pp.276–277

Previous page: Strangford Lough estuary, Northern Ireland, at low tide.